From the libraey of
R C Couture

A Compendium of Christian Theology

A COMPENDIUM

OF

CHRISTIAN THEOLOGY.

A

COMPENDIUM

OF

CHRISTIAN THEOLOGY:

BEING

ANALYTICAL OUTLINES OF A COURSE OF
THEOLOGICAL STUDY,

BIBLICAL, DOGMATIC, HISTORICAL.

BY

WILLIAM BURT POPE, D.D.,

THEOLOGICAL TUTOR, DIDSBURY COLLEGE, MANCHESTER.

.

VOL. II.

SECOND EDITION, REVISED AND ENLARGED.

LONDON:
PUBLISHED FOR THE AUTHOR AT THE
WESLEYAN CONFERENCE OFFICE,
2, CASTLE STREET, CITY ROAD;
SOLD AT 66, PATERNOSTER ROW.
1877.

LONDON
PRINTED BY BEVERIDGE AND CO.
(SUCCESSORS TO R NEEDHAM),
HOLBORN PRINTING WORKS, FULLWOOD'S RENTS, W C

CONTENTS OF VOLUME TWO

SIN.

THE MEDIATORIAL MINISTRY.

CONTENTS.

THE ADMINISTRATION OF REDEMPTION.

SIN.

—

ORIGIN OF SIN.

THEORIES OF EVIL AND SIN.

NATURE OF SIN.

SIN AND REDEMPTION.

ORIGINAL SIN.

SIN.

THE discussion of Providence has exhibited Sin, the destruction of which was the object of the redeeming counsel, as contemplated from eternity in connection with the origin, development, and destiny of mankind. It is therefore as a doctrine interwoven with all the subsequent stages of theology, being in fact one centre from which the whole may be viewed. But it has its own range of independent topics, making it a distinct study. We ascend first to the mystery of its Origin, in the universe and on earth, this leading of necessity to the consideration of its Nature in itself and of the Theories devised to account for it, then follows the relation between Sin and Redemption, or rather the mitigating effect that the coming redemption throws back upon the evolution of evil; thus introducing, finally, its universality in mankind, or Original Sin, the sin adhering to the race as such and to every member of it naturally born into the world.

From ἁμαρτία, the general New-Testament denomination of sin as subjective or in the soul, has been derived the term HAMARTIOLOGY, occasionally used for this entire department It appears in some systems as PONEROLOGY, from πονηρόν or πονηρία, which indicates rather the objective character of sin or evil in its manifold relations and consequences. It is useful to note these terms, though they are not much used in English theology.

Terminology.

THE ORIGIN OF SIN.

Origin By a necessity of thought we commence with the origin of sin. The sacred record declares that it began in the universe with the fall of free intelligences, failing in their probation and that it began on earth with the disobedience of our first parents, which brought them the knowledge of evil as guilt and as punishment uniting in death. The history of the first transgression, whether of angels or of men, is so presented in Scripture as to show that the origination of evil is with the creature itself. Whatever differences there are in the two Falls, and however much of mystery remains in both, they unite in one thing. they preclude every theory that seeks the principle of sin in any other source than the freedom of the spirit created in the Divine image.

IN THE UNIVERSE

Fall of Angels The Scriptural account of the origin of sin in the external universe is very brief, but very distinct , and what it lacks is supplied by the fuller history of the fall of mankind One Original sinner is indicated, who was the cause of sin to his fellows, and the instrument of its introduction into this world

The Original Sinner 1 The absolute beginning of evil, and of sin as the cause of evil, is directly traced to the fall of the Devil and those who are called his angels Satan is the representative of evil as it had its beginning in him There are passages of Scripture which in a marked manner make him the father of all iniquity It is true that many of these refer to his connection with sin in this world ·

John viii. 44 for instance, the testimony that *he was a murderer from the beginning,* which sends us to the history of the human Fall. He was the

1 Tim ii 14. instrumental cause of death to the first man ; and therefore in one sense first *in the transgression,* behind Eve who was first in

another sense. But there are some which intimate darkly that the first spirit separated from God was his. ' Our Lord, who came into the world as the Antagonist of the evil one, gave His disciples on a memorable occasion a single hint of large meaning *I beheld* Luke x *Satan, as lightning, fall from heaven* While we must understand these words as condensing into.one flash of revelation the whole history of the conflict with the powers of darkness, so far as it concerns this earth, we must also regard them as giving testimony to the fact of the primal fall of one intelligence, so essentially the first and most prominent that he stands for the whole company who followed him. He was the head of those angels who *kept* Jude 6. *not their first estate*, of those *angels that sinned*. Of him our Lord, 2 Peter ii. who knew what was in devils as well as what is in man, said: 4 he *abode not in the truth, because there is no truth in him* This John viii. absolute negation of any element of truth in Satan is made more 44. emphatically positive · *when he speaketh a lie, he speaketh of his own · for he is a liar, and the father of it.* The lie is here essential evil, the denial of the truth of a creature's relation to God . he is the father of the universal lie, the father of evil and sin. And this is made more probable by the allusions to the *Devil and his angels*, Matt.xxv. as comprising all the beings for whom final and irreversible judg- 41. ment waits, having been *prepared* for them alone Always there Jude 6. is assigned to one Power a pre-eminence over a multitude of others who owed their sin to him · not, however, through the inheritance of a propagated bias to evil, but by each one independently yielding to his temptation or following his example. On this subject we can say but little , suffice, that the Devil is both directly and indirectly regarded as the Prince or ἀρχηγός of iniquity in the universe as well as in this world His was the original sin ; it was the misuse of freedom ; it was the mysterious birth in his nature of an ambition to rival God, or the Son of God, an ambition which was transferred to this world after his exclusion from heaven ; it was imitated by many others , it was irreparable, at least we hear of no redemption or hope ; and, lastly, it was the fountain of temptation to our race

2 Of Satan's relation to other worlds we know nothing. But The the introduction of evil into the world of mankind, and its history Original through all our generations, are in a special manner bound up with Sin.

his first apostasy, the Original Sin. The link between the pride
which caused his ruin and the transgression of our first parents,
Gen iii.5. was this : *ye shall be as gods!* Our sin is, so to speak, a reflection
or continuation of his   Hence he retains his empire and headship,
as the lord and representative of the principle of evil   He has
set up a kingdom of which he and not Adam is the head. Of
this more hereafter , for the present it will be enough to enume-
rate the names of the original sinner, whose relation to the lapse
of mankind is his aggravated condemnation, but not the excuse
of human depravity.   (1) As the representative of evil or sin in
1 John iii. itself he is called *That Wicked One,* absolutely; and of the pro-
12.
Matt.xiii. pagation of all the innumerable seeds of sin it is said : *the enemy*
30   *that sowed them is the Devil.* (2) As the representative and lord of
2 Cor iv the empire of sin, he is *the God of this world, the Prince of*
4.
John xiv. *this world, the Prince of the power of the air, the Spirit that now*
30   *worketh in the children of disobedience ,* a collocation which places
Eph. ii. 2. him in solemn antithesis to the Persons of the Holy Trinity
respectively, the first with the Father, the second with the Son,
Matt. xii and the third with the Holy Ghost , especially when *his kingdom*
26   is taken into the account.   (3) As the representative of the
Job i. 6, spirit of enmity to goodness he is *Satan,* or *the Adversary, the*
passim. Devil, and *the Tempter.* (4) The tenour of the New Testament
makes him generally the embodiment of sin · its origin, lord,
promoter, witness, and executioner. Always and everywhere
he and his angels are real persons   the personality of no agents is
more expressly revealed or spoken of in terms less liable to mis-
apprehension. But this question enters here indirectly.

Fall of   THE FALL OF MANKIND.
Man.

The Mosaic account of the Probation and Fall of the
First Pair is an inspired narrative of the origin of sin in
the human race; it is not a collection of early traditions
or myths; nor an allegorical method of teaching the moral
history of sin in man; nor a combination of history,
allegory, and legend , but an historical narrative of facts,
which, however, are bound up with symbols that must

have their interpretation as such. In that interpretation the utmost caution is necessary. But no exposition can pretend to solve every difficulty, or obviate every objection; because in our estate of sin we have no experience of the original condition of our first parents, and therefore have not the key to the solution of the mystery of their temptation and subjection to evil. The brief account records that man was placed in a state of trial, with the consciousness of the possibility of sin or separation of his will from the Divine will; it describes the circumstances and the nature, external and internal, of the temptation from without, and it sets before us the preliminaries, the act, and the immediate consequences of the first transgression or what in our human annals is the Fall of Man.

THE NARRATIVE.

The Record gives its account of the ruin of mankind as history: that of a beginning which flows on without break into the subsequent course of redemption. As a narrative of simple facts it is seldom alluded to in either Testament; but such allusions as we find assume its historical reality. Our Lord gives His sanction to the account of the creation, quoting its very words, and indirectly including the Fall itself. St. Paul again and again refers to the incidents as recorded in Genesis. The history is tacitly recognised as history—primitive, fragmentary, Oriental, it may be, and deeply symbolical, but Divine—throughout the sacred oracles.

The Record.

I. The few references in Scripture are very explicit. The more carefully they are observed, in their context, the more obvious will it be that the account of the first transgression must be received in its simplicity, with its commingled facts and symbols, by all who hold sacred the authority of our Lord and His Apostles.

Scripture.

Old Testament
Job xxxi. 33.

1. In the Old Testament there are few undeniable allusions to the circumstances of the Fall. We read in Job: *if I covered my transgressions as Adam, by hiding mine iniquity in my bosom.* To conceal iniquity is after the manner of men, but there appears to be a marked reference to the colloquy between Adam and his Maker. A passage in Hosea has been often quoted in favour of the Paradisiacal covenant of works *but they, like Adam, have transgressed the covenant.* This however may be, and is, translated, *like men.* Throughout the older economy Adam is merged in his posterity, and the fall of mankind, like the sin which caused it, is everywhere assumed as a postulate. The Old Testament is not constantly *laying again the foundation,* rather it is always *leaving the principles of the doctrine of Christ.* Hence, as in the two passages quoted above, man is Adam, and Adam is man.

Hos. vi. 7.

Heb. vi. 1

Gospels

2. In the Gospels there is literally not one express allusion to the narrative of the first catastrophe. It needed not our Lord's corroboration and therefore did not receive it. But if we weigh well His words, on the question of divorce, we must conclude that the whole record has His supreme sanction as historical. *Have ye not read that He which made them at the beginning made them male and female, and said, For this cause shall a man leave father and mother, and shall cleave to his wife: and they twain shall be one flesh?* They who read this as history read as history what immediately follows, and the Redeemer's declarations, already quoted, concerning the *murderer from the beginning,* refer obviously to the very narrative of Genesis.

Matt. xix. 4, 5.

John viii 44.

St. Paul

3. St. Paul, who inherited the later Jewish doctrine, and gave much of it Christian sanction, more than once confirms the literal texture of our narrative. So must we interpret his words, *as the serpent beguiled Eve through his subtilty,* where he means Satan, who was and is *transformed into an angel of light* instead of creeping on the earth. So also his prophecy and prayer, *the God of peace shall bruise Satan under your feet,* which is an echo of the first promise given to man through the condemnation of the Devil. Here it may be observed, in passing, that the Apostle by the use of the term *transformed* gives us the only solution we need of the difficulty of temptation through the voice of a serpent. St.

2 Cor xi. 3.

2 Cor xi 14.

Rom. xvi. 20.

Paul, moreover, as we shall see, founds his argument of Original Sin on the literal narrative of the Fall

4. The comparative reserve of the rest of Scripture as to the facts and symbols of the narrative is broken through in the last book. The Apocalypse returns back to Genesis, and quotes almost every particular in such a manner as at once to sanction the literalness of the account and to relieve it of some of its difficulties. The final promise to the first Church of the Seven is· *to him that overcometh will I give to eat of the tree of life, which is in the midst of the paradise of God*   Here the literal Eden of man, and the literal tree from which he was excluded, reappear in their heavenly significance , but the spiritual, which is afterward, implies the reality of the natural which was first   The doom upon Satan has also its spiritual and eternal meaning . *and the great Dragon was cast out, that old serpent, called the Devil and Satan, which deceiveth the whole world.*   His seduction of our first parents is merged in his universal temptation from the Fall downwards; but the tremendous reality of the conflict between him and the Seed of the Woman through all the ages of redemption is based upon, it flows from, the first literal triumph permitted of God. The light of the apocalyptic glory shines through all intervening ages up to the darkened paradise of the Fall, not relieving it of its impenetrable mystery, but confirming its literal truth.   It bids us study the narrative in the spirit of simple faith : leaving to God Himself the vindication of His righteous judgments and unsearchable ways, and rejoicing only that the *leaves of the Tree* of Life are *for the healing of the nations,* and that *there shall be no more curse* to those who enter the heavenly Paradise

II. The two theories of interpretation termed Mythical and Allegorical are really one ; with this important difference, however, that the former denies the Divine authority which the latter admits or does not exclude.

1 The Mythical theory appeals to the universal traditions of Paradise and the Golden Age, the unhistorical character of the Serpent, the trees, the walking of God in the evening, and other features of the detail, as all indicating a legendary origin.   It is said that the Hebrew narrative is only one tribal version of an idea common among the early nations   We accept the truth that

[marginal notes:]
Apocalypse.

Rev. ii. 7.

Rev xii. 9.

Rev xxii. 2, 3.

Theories.

Mythical.

underlies this false theory   The traditions of many nations contain
mythical accounts which have been woven out of the threads of a
primitive tradition , but they declare their legendary character
on the surface.   There is no Myth in the Bible, as has been
already shown ; and the traditions of the early history of the
world recorded in Genesis are in no way connected with any
particular people.   They profess to have been revealed to the first
writer of the Biblical documents ; and are incorporated into Scripture as such   They belong to the archives of the race, and not of
any one family in it   Divine Tradition before all human traditions.

**Allego-
rical.**
2. The Allegorical method of explaining this first chapter
of human history has been adopted by the mystical school,
from Philo, Clemens Alexandrinus, and Origen downwards,
through Maimonides, to modern times   It admits the Divine
origin of the Mosaic account of the introduction of sin , and
supposes that the whole scene is figurative, representing by a
continuous allegory the facts of the Fall, but having no more connection with those facts than the allegory of the Vine brought out
of Egypt had with the redemption of Israel.   Now it is undeniable that the essential meaning of the whole narrative may be
extracted from it on this principle, as may be seen in some of the
best expositions of the Alexandrian school   But this canon of
interpretation is repudiated, as will be seen, by the clear and un-
clouded testimony of later Scripture, as well as by the strict
literality of the style of the opening chapter of Genesis in
general.   Fact and Parable are Divinely interwoven.

**Symbo-
lism.**
3. The purely historical character of the narrative may be
maintained in perfect consistency with a full acknowledgment of
the large element of symbolism in it   It must be remembered
that the scene of Paradise, though introduced into human history,
belongs to an order of events very different from anything that
human experience knows or can rightly appreciate.

**Narrative
written
in Sacra-
mental
terms.**
(1) While the narrative is true, and every circumstance in it
real, there is not a feature of the Paradisaical history of man that
is purely natural, as we now understand the term.   The process
of human probation, whether longer or shorter, was supernaturally
conducted by symbols, the deep meaning of which we know now
only in part, though our first parents perhaps understood them by

express teaching. The garden enclosed ; the sacramental Tree of Life, the nourishment of conditional immortality ; the mystical Tree of Knowledge, the fruit of which would reveal the profound secret of freedom , the one positive precept, representing the whole law ; the symbolical serpent-form of the Tempter , the character of the threatenings and their fulfilment · on all the parties , the exclusion from the garden, and the flaming defences of the forfeited Eden ; all were emblems as well as facts, which almost without exception recur at the close of revelation in their new and higher symbolic meaning Both in Genesis and in Revelation they are symbols or signs with a deep spiritual significance. The remembrance of this serves two purposes. It suggests that our first parents were bound to their Creator by a religion which made all things around them sacramental, and some things more especially such. And it protects the simple details of the Garden from the contempt of unbelievers, who see in them nothing but what appears on the surface of the narrative. The water of baptism and the eucharistic bread and wine are slight and common things in relation to the amazing realities they signify. But the infidel spirit finds nothing in these symbols to object against as such. Then why should it be thought a thing incredible that the two trees of Paradise should have borne sacramental fruit?

(2.) This leads to the consideration that the history of the Fall is described to us with constant reference to the coming redemption · it is the first chapter in the history of man, but of man as redeemed. The whole requires to be read in the light of the great salvation even then ready to be revealed. The penalty of death not at once executed ; the expulsion from Eden with a prophecy of future deliverance , the Providential conditions under which the transgressors are sent forth into the world, all indicate that the narrative of the Fall and the end of the first probation is really the narrative of the beginning of the Gospel and the second probation of mankind. *In terms of coming Redemption.*

(3.) Once more, this record describes the Fall in terms taken, so to speak, from man's later history What form commandment would assume to the mind of an unfallen creature, what the idea of the alternative in good and evil would be, how temptation would *In terms of later knowledge.*

address itself to the will which had never yet been in a state of rebellion or vacillation, we cannot understand; for these things are not revealed The posture of the pure spirit in a state of probation and on the verge of falling, but hitherto unconscious of sin, is a secret lost to us: no mortal has since the Fall been in such a posture, nor will ever be, since temptation will not belong to our future heaven. The same inability to apprehend and state the truth applies to the history of the scene in our Lord's temptation. With regard to the temptation of both the first and the second Adam the record adopts the language known to man as a sinner. In the case of the sinless and impeccable Redeemer, His indwelling Divinity, or rather His essential and not merely indwelling Divinity, was an infinite safeguard against His undergoing what is of the essence of probationary temptation But the language used concerning His more than fiery trial adopts the terms with which our sin has made us familiar He was tested, and *declared to be the Son of God with power by the Spirit of holiness,* if we may thus apply St Paul's words. It was manifested through this ordeal that He was sinless and incapable of sin, just as it was proved in Gethsemane that no pressure upon His spirit could make it waver in the will of God. The hour of His highest honour on the Mount of Transfiguration was His temptation also, in the sense of trial. He was searched through and through by the glory of the Father and declared to be the Beloved Son, in whom, though He was that night anew consecrated to the cross, God was well pleased. But the temptation of our Lord is always spoken of in the same terms which would be used concerning a holy one among ourselves Unless we bear the same thing in mind in reading the account of the first human trial all will be most perplexing There was no evil concupiscence in man's nature; but the woman is addressed as if it were latent in her and might be excited. The meaning of God's words in the threatening is discussed by the Tempter before Eve as if she had been accustomed to compare truth and falsehood, and deduce the inferences of suspicion. The process of first admitting the possibility of the Divine word being untrue and His commandment not good, and then of consulting the appetite and its decision as to the desirableness of the tree, and then of actually

The temptation of the two Adams.

Rom. 1. 4.

taking the fruit, are all described after the manner of ordinary human temptation. So also is the immediate sense of guilt and shame. So also is the suggestion to Adam, and his yielding to the seduction of his temptress The whole process could not be described as it actually took place in the minds of our sinless first parents the phraseology is derived from our later guilty experience. We are taught in the only way in which we could be made to understand what it concerns us to know ; and must submit to the limitations of our fallen faculties.

THE ORIGINAL PROBATION.

The Original Probation

Nothing is said concerning the degree of knowledge imparted to Adam and Eve as to the nature, terms, and limits of their probationary estate. The record is very simple: containing only such a bare outline as it pleased God to communicate to the infancy of the world. But the fact of PROBATION is as plain as words can make it. Placed in the garden to dress it and to keep it as the centre of cultivation that might overspread the world, Adam, and the human race in him, was on his trial. He represented his posterity ; but not as a mediator between God and them ; and therefore the ordinance of probation had not the nature of a covenant. The so-called COVENANT OF WORKS has no place in the history of Paradise. It cannot be thought that moral creatures introduced into existence are dealt with as parties to a covenant. the covenant idea belongs to a different order of things, and requires a mediator. Our first parents were simply placed under the law of their Creator, and the penalty of disobedience made known to them. The counterpart of this, the establishment in a fixed and consummate eternal life, may be regarded as reserved in the Divine counsel.

The circumstances of the Probation were a positive commandment with its sanction, and temptation from without · both

Positive Law

appealing to a will consciously free or unrestrained, and as yet under the direction of a reason on which the law or obligation of obedience was supernaturally written.

The Trees.   1. The one absolute law had a negative and a positive form, as connected with the two symbolical trees of the garden . the Tree of Life and the Tree of Knowledge.   The eating of the one was a positive condition of continued life and every benefit of creation , abstinence from the other was the negative condition. It must not be supposed that the trees had any inherent virtue : the one to sustain life for ever ; the other to poison and corrupt the nature of man   The solemn eating of the fruit of the tree of life was only a sacrament of immortality; it was to the

Gen.ii 16. eating of *every tree of the garden* what the Christian Supper is to all other food.   The fatal eating of the tree of knowledge was only the outward and visible sign of a sin which, by the Divine law inwrought in human nature, would have been followed by shame and guilt and fear had no such tree existed.   Through eating its fruit man came to the actual knowledge of good and evil, to the knowledge of his misery a knowledge which made him acquainted with his own power over his destiny—as if he were his own god—and at the same time taught him that this power, independent of God, was his ruin.

The Serpent.   2. Temptation from without was more than symbolised by the instrument—fallen now like the real tempter himself from its

Rev xii. 9. first estate—of *that old serpent, called the Devil, and Satan, which deceiveth the whole world.*   The distinctness of this record is of great importance.   It establishes a difference between the original sin of earth and the original sin of the universe   We need not, indeed, assume that the angels who fell were only tempted from within   there is every reason to think that, as

Wisd ii 24. *through envy of the Devil came death into the world,* so through the same envy, excited by another Object in heaven, death entered among the angels   It cannot be that sin should have its origin within the spirit of a creature of God independently of solicitation from without   But, in the case of man, the agency of Satan is made prominent from the beginning of Scripture to the end not as reducing the guilt of the first transgression, but as mitigating its punishment, and suggesting at least a difference put between sinful angels and the human race.

3. As to the conduct of the first assault we have a very clear account, so far as it was external · the internal element of the temptation is not referred to, nor is the mysterious beginning of sin, the point where temptation finds, because it creates, something to lay hold on. In other words, the origin of sin in the as yet uncorrupt nature of man, like the origin of evil in the as yet uncorrupt universe, finds no solution in the revelation of God. How the pure desire of knowledge became the lust of independent forbidden knowledge, how the natural sensibility of the soul to the enjoyment of the Tree could become evil concupiscence, is not told. We are shut up to the solemn fact. *(Temptation from without)*

THE FALL.

The Fall.

The Fall into sin was internal and external; the sin first of the human spirit and then of the human flesh. Hence it may be further viewed as a voluntary or active, and as a passive or judicial, degradation from the high estate in which man was created.

I. The original lapse was at once both internal and external. *(Internal and External.)*

1. Separation from the Supreme Will was consummated within before it was exhibited in act. The inmost principle of sin is the severance of the self from God : the entertainment, therefore, of the question *Yea, hath God said ?* was the beginning of human evil This was the first Formal Sin, though not alluded to in Scripture as such. The outward act was the look of concupiscence towards the tree, which had in itself the guilt of partaking, and was followed by the partaking itself. Hence in all New-Testament references to the original sin its principle of disobedience is made prominent. *The woman being deceived was in the transgression: ἐν παραβάσει.* And when Adam yielded to the enticement of Eve, he only proved that he had already consented to her act; he also was *in the transgression.* His sin was *disobedience, παράπτωμα* and *παρακοή*: for, *Adam was not deceived.* *(Gen iii. 1.)* *(1 Tim. ii. 14)* *(Rom v. 15, 19)*

2. Hence the first offence was spiritual and sensuous : these being united inseparably, but, according to the Scriptural account, *(Spiritual and sensuous.)*

the sensuous temptation taking the lead in the transgression, though the more spiritual took the lead in the enticement. The Tempter's suggestion appealed to what was highest and to what was lowest in the elements of human nature · to its unbounded capacity of

Gen iii. 6. knowledge and to its sensibility of the pleasures of sense. *When the woman saw that the tree was good for food, and that it was pleasant to the eyes, and a tree to be desired to make one wise, she took of the fruit thereof* It must not, however, be inferred from this that the Fall of man was simply a decline into the slavery of sense There is no sin that does not begin in the spirit, though it may be made perfect in the flesh. The first sinners rejected the restraint of God's Holy Spirit, and made themselves independent in thought and will, before the fruit of the forbidden tree could become a real temptation This hidden mystery of iniquity, behind the act of transgression, was only brought to light in the recorded Fall.

Effects.   3. The immediate consequences of the lapse into sin are plainly disclosed, though still in a style partly symbolical and figurative The first effect is described in language with which the inmost experience of men makes them familiar. It was the immediate

Gen iii. 5. knowledge of *good and evil*. the birth of evil conscience, the moral consciousness disturbed by a sense of guilt; the beginning of shame, or the sense of degradation and vileness This double consciousness was, as it were, a new birth unto unrighteousness. the first realisation in experience of the distinction between good and evil, a distinction, however, which had been theoretically made known by revelation to our parents while yet untransgressing. Thus we see the external relations and the internal at once depicted : guilt before their Judge and pollution in His sight These drove the transgressors from the presence of their Maker, which was the converse of the sentiment of one of their descendants : *depart*

Luke v. 8 *from me, for I am a sinful man, O Lord !* They fled from God,

Gen. iii. 8. because God had departed from them They *hid themselves from the presence of the Lord God* not as if they had sunk so low as to think it possible that the trees should hide them, but from the sentiment of spiritual fear. They felt at once that they were, unless the Creator Himself should interfere, for ever separated from Him. Hence we have in the simple record of the effects of the first transgression all the elements of the doctrine of sin. It was the

internal deviation of the will from the will of the Supreme ; it was
objective guilt, the Divine vindication of eternal law in the conscience, it was guilt subjectively, as the consciousness of personal
fault and obligation to punishment, and it was the expression of
a sense of separation, for the time of hopeless separation, from the
presence of God : the supreme penalty of sin.

II. The term FALL is probably derived from the sublime descrip- The Fall
Active
and
Passive.
tion of Wisdom and her works in an apocryphal book which
contains some other references to the beginning of sin, showing
how much the later Jewish theology was occupied with the
subject. *She preserved the first formed father of the world, that was* Wisd x 1.
created alone, and brought him out of his Fall. Here, indeed, the
fall is that of the individual first father, but the true instinct of
interpretation has always made Adam and mankind one, and therefore adopted the expression FALL OF MAN. It was the voluntary
descent of the human will from its unity with the will of God, it
was the consequent degradation of mankind from the high prerogatives belonging to the Divine image in which man was
created. Both the active and the passive meaning of the word,
as introduced into theological language, must be retained.

1. As to the former, a superficial glance at the scene that The Fall
Active
begins human history in the garden has led many to the conclusion that our first parents were the victims of circumstance,
that they were deceived, and unwittingly stumbled ; that mighty
temptation from without co-operated with the simplicity of their
own unformed and undisciplined conscience to ruin them unawares.
But it must be remembered that the beings whose free personality
the Righteous God tested were created upright. Their liberty
was perfect that is, not merely they possessed the faculty of
willing or choosing indeterminately, as unconstrained by necessary law from without ; but their formal will was filled by its
real object, fixed upon God Himself. The very nature and the
terms of the test show that they understood the alternative of good
and evil · they were taught that good was perfect obedience to the
Divine will, and that evil—which they knew and yet knew
not—was disobedience to that will Though it was the Enemy
who said, *Ye shall be as gods, knowing good and evil*, it was not he Gen. iii. 5
who first introduced to the human mind the most tremendous of

Gen. ii 17.   all alternatives.   For God's warning was, *in the day that thou eatest thereof thou shalt surely die.*   What other teaching they had we are not informed , but certainly we may conclude that they were not left in ignorance of the relation between the solitary positive precept and the more general unspoken law of their duty as creatures of God.   Nor do we know what education they had received, nor how long they had received it, from communion with their Maker and the teaching of the Holy Ghost.   We only know that on the part both of Eve and of Adam there was a wilful revolt against the Almighty , that the act of their will was not simply the abuse of the liberty of indifference—which in their case could not exist—but the actual wresting of it from its determined and rightful Object , that never has human will been more absolute in its working than theirs ; that it was, so to speak, the concentrated will of humanity turned from good to evil

The Fall Passive Lu. ii 34   2 The passive Fall was commensurate with so great an evil.   Viewed apart from the *Rising Again* in Christ, it was a total descent of mankind from its high destination ; involving the very earth in its consequences , and deepening the doom of the chief agent of temptation, not omitting the degradation of the subordinate agent which he had employed.   Man was no longer the *image*

1 Cor xi. 7   *and glory of God ,* for, though he retained his human nature inviolate as created in the Divine *image,* the *glory* of that image was lost   His nature—using that term in its secondary sense as the moral quality of its disposition invariably appearing in every reproduction of the original type—became entirely perverted.

1 Cor. xi. 7.   Nor was woman any longer *the glory of the man,* in the best sense of that word : the relation of woman to man was deprived thenceforward of its highest perfection.   Man fell from his destination : that of an eternal progress from glory to glory in sinless fellowship with his Creator.   He declined into a lower sphere : out of communion with heaven, into a life of external discord and internal misery.   He lost his intuitive vision of God, no longer held discourse with his Maker through the symbols of nature, and had to begin, he and all that should be his, the very first principles of a spiritual world.   But we know not how great was the Fall . after the first words of the Divine displeasure, not another comment is made on the subject   Its further influence on the race, and its mitigation through

the universal Atonement is before us, but not immediately. If that Fall was not total, it was because the Redeemer's unseen Hand arrested it. The Child Jesus, already the new Father and Head of mankind, was even then *set for the Fall and* RISING AGAIN Lu. ii. 34. of the human race. More, however, on this brighter aspect of the subject must be reserved for the doctrine of Original Sin

3. In this fact—the coming redemption, or rather that redemption which was revealed before Paradise was shut on our first parents—we have the only answer that can be given to the protests which have been honestly or dishonestly urged against the narrative of the Fall We are not indeed at a loss to vindicate the justice of the Holy God in His deep displeasure at the first offence. But we have not to do with the holiness of God apart from His love. From the beginning *mercy rejoiceth against judgment* The James ii. Mediator is already between the Judge and the sinner. And if   13. God's justice turned the first transgressors *to destruction* when *He* Ps xc. 3. *drove out the man* from the Paradise of His presence forfeited Gen iii. by his sin, His mercy is still heard, following hard upon His   24. wrath, *Return, ye children of men.*

THEORIES OF THE ORIGIN OF SIN

Theories of sin   Philosophical speculation propounds various theories to account for the derivation of sin, which, as one of the most universal facts in experience, must have some common cause. These theories combine its origin and its nature in one, it being impossible perfectly to separate the two ideas. The most desperate of all expedients boldly assumes an eternal principle of evil, which in its creaturely workings becomes sin. The most specious solution makes what seems to be evil merely the creaturely limitation on its way to perfection. Between these and combining them is the less philosophical theory that makes sin the effect of the residence of the spirit in the flesh of concupiscence. A consideration of these hypotheses will lead to the true cause of sin as given by Scripture, and confirmed by man's common sense, the abuse of the gift of liberty.

ETERNAL PRINCIPLE OF EVIL

Original Principle of Evil   The first and most ancient speculations accounted for the existence of sin by assuming a necessary PRINCIPLE OF EVIL in the universe.

Parsism.   1. Inherited from the remote east, this notion was held in the Gnostic sects of early Christianity, in Manichæism, and in certain systems which sprang up in the mediæval Western Church. Zoroaster (Zarathustra), the real or imaginary founder of the religion of Parsism, about the time of the later Jewish prophets, represented Ormuzd (Ahura-Mazda) as the author of all good and Ahriman (Anra-Mainyus) as the author of all evil in the nature of things. These were independent personal spirits, ruling absolutely each in his own dominion; yet not so absolutely as to be unrelated to each other, since they were in perpetual conflict, and all created beings are called to make choice between them This

ancient speculation struck deep roots in human thought, and
reappeared in the Gnostic systems of early Christian times.   But
in these it was modified   The evil principle became the active agent
in the creation of the material universe, he was the Demiurgus
of a matter eternally existing as ὕλη, Hyle, the substance of all
evil, man was a product of the two kingdoms of light and of
darkness · having affinity with the former in his spirit, with the
latter in his soul and body   Human sin was the necessary defilement contracted by the spirit from its alliance with matter; and
redemption was the deliverance from this bondage.   Manes in
the third century revived this dogma of Gnosticism, and from
him it derived the name of Manichæism   he laid stress however
upon this, that these were not two eternal gods, but two eternal
principles.   In the twelfth century it appeared in the Paulician
heresy, and in all ages has had its supporters among those
who have rejected Pantheism, and yet have refused to accept
the personal God of the Scriptures.

2   Whatever form this old theory has assumed, it has paid its **Tribute to**
unconscious tribute to the truth   If that principle of evil is a   **Truth.**
Person, as in Persian Dualism, there can be no infinite and eternal
God   If it is Hyle or Matter, then its eternity as the material of
evil involves a denial of every Divine attribute   The human
mind has never found rest in this conception   Parsism itself
betrayed a tendency to struggle upward to the thought of an
eternal essence beyond and above Ormuzd and Ahriman, in which
they had their unity and in the process of ages would find their
reconciliation.   Nor are there wanting traces of the teaching that
Ahriman fell like Satan by an act of will.   Though these latent
protests did not affect the essential Dualism of the whole system,
they were silent expressions of the deep conviction of reason, that
there is and must be One absolute Being, and that evil, whatever
its source may be, is essentially wrong and in conflict with what
man surely knows to be right, or, in other words, that sin is the
worse eternally opposed to the better.   Hence, finally, it may be
said that there was a certain nobility in this ancient error contrasting favourably with that to which we shall next turn   It
admitted that there is an awful reality in sin; it represented man
as passing through a tremendous probation; it had a dim and

shadowy presentiment of guilt, thus making a great step towards the perfect doctrine of Scripture; and it aspired towards the still grander idea of a full and eternal redemption.

LIMITATION OF FINITE NATURE.

Finite
Limita-
tion.

The necessary LIMITATION OF FINITE NATURE is a popular philosophical expedient for the solution of the mystery. However stated and however limited, this theory must needs make the Author of finite nature the author of sin: either absolutely or as the necessary process of creaturely development towards the supreme good in Himself.

Sin
Abolished

1. As held by the various modifications of Pantheism this speculation abolishes sin altogether, and merges it in the general notion of the necessary development of the nature of things. But the nature of things is God Himself, who is at once the one eternal substance and an eternal development in two modes, thought and matter. There is no creature, for all things are the evolution of one substantial Being. What therefore seems to be the finite is only the infinite in phenomenal exhibition. During its transitory appearance it is subject to the metaphysical evil of limitation: the more of being is in the thing undergoing development the nearer it is to perfection; the less of being it has the more it is infected with evil, or what men call sin. But all things are only manifestations of the One; and what seems to us contrary to the will of God is only the process through which the end of return to the infinite essence is reached. Pantheism knows no sin, no moral obligation; it recognises only an eternal necessity of accomplishing through phases of metaphysical evil the transitory destiny of what man calls the creature.

Necessary
Process.

2. But something like this theory has been held by deep thinkers who are not Pantheists. These fall into two classes: such as make evil a necessary accident of the creature as limited, retaining its character as sin; and such as make it a necessary accident, but at the same time the Divinely appointed process through which by antagonism good is evolved.

Limita-
tion of
Being.

(1.) The radical principle of the former class is that sin is merely a negation of being, a quantitative less of the strength of existence. The creature cannot be perfect · its knowledge is liable to error, its will is liable to deviation   And this very liability is metaphysical evil · it cannot be conceived to be protected from the possibility of sin, and the possibility in the severe logic of facts is the sin itself   But that sin is only a negative thing; it has no positive existence, and needs no EFFICIENT cause for its origination.   If any cause is needed, a DEFICIENT cause may be invented for the purpose.   This philosophical expedient, it may be observed, was much in favour with St. Augustine and others of the earlier Fathers ; it is the strength of the Theodicy of Leibnitz ; and both in ancient and modern times has been resorted to for the vindication of the Divine character in the permission of evil.

(2) Many modern writers have dwelt much on a theory which accounts for sin on the principle of a necessary antagonism, or the operation of a universal law of action and reaction.   As life and death, light and darkness, attraction and repulsion, the centripetal and centrifugal energies of the universe, are opposites which in their interaction make the perfection of things, so virtue and vice, evil and goodness are opposites which cannot be separated in our estimate of probation   The Eternal purposed that there should be a knowledge of good and evil: of good as the survival in the contest with evil.   There is no virtue but as the victory over vice , no goodness but as the victory over evil.   The pilgrim to this Jerusalem must needs go through Samaria · it is the order of Providence that all creatures shall find their way thus to Himself   This is a theory which simply adopts into the moral domain the physical principle of evolution.   It is one which has much fascination for superficial speculatists who do not examine the eternal principles of religion in their own nature, and who are content to renounce the plain teaching of the Word of God.   The sentimental notion that human development cannot be conceived save as a process through evil to perfection, is disproved outside of our race by the angels who fell not, and within it by the Sinless Redeemer of mankind.   *Antagonism.*

(3) Whatever form these theories assume they either abolish sin altogether as such, or they make God its Author.   From this dilemma they cannot escape.   It is true that many who have maintained these views have found in them a refuge for minds   *Dilemma*

weary of the desperate struggle with the anomaly of evil in the
universe of a holy and almighty Creator But they have only given
additional evidence that such a struggle was not appointed for
the finite faculties of man. God does not sanction, nor does He
bless, the attempt to pry into this mystery It is true also that
these theories—apart from their pretension to solve the mystery
of evil—contain many elements of truth. The possibility of sin
and error is most assuredly an attribute of the creature as such, and
human freedom is the secret of human error , but metaphysical
imperfection is not necessarily moral evil, and the negative evil of
being imperfect is not the germ of sin. Undoubtedly, since the
Fall, and presupposing that the antagonism of good and evil works
out through the discipline of grace the highest perfection of the
creature, it may be that the conflict with sin will issue in a
kind of holiness and knowledge of God unknown to the unfallen
But the Father of spirits can never, by the Christian thinker,
be supposed to have created intelligent creatures under the law
of a necessary imperfection in which evil is bound up

SENSUOUS NATURE.

Sensuous   Another theory combines the two former, at least in some
Nature.   of their elements ; it derives human evil from the SENSUOUS
NATURE of man, and makes it the antagonism between the flesh
and the spirit, the ascendency of the former over the latter explaining both the origin and the nature of all sin

Christian   1. This hypothesis has assumed many forms, and reigned very
Specula-   extensively in Christian speculation. It suggests a Gnostic origin,
tion   so far as it seems to regard matter as the seat and source of sin ;
but differs from Gnosticism in making the ascendency of the flesh
question of personal and free choice. It enters into all the
theories which regard evil as a necessary stage of the development of a free intelligence ; but differs from those already spoken
of in this, that it makes the flesh only the accidental instrument
through which the inherent weakness of the higher powers is
shown   In the mediæval doctrine, which took its final form in
the Tridentine dogmas, the lower nature was regarded as being
restrained by the supernatural gift of righteousness, the with-

drawal of which released and set in operation the concupiscence of the flesh The most elaborate exposition of this theory is that of Schleiermacher, who sets the God-consciousness in man over against the self-consciousness as related to the world. In the Divine purpose the flesh, or the consciousness of self in the world, was by development to be brought into perfect submission to the God-consciousness. This development was hindered by the Fall , and the knowledge of failure in it is the sense of guilt or sin. In Christ, the Ideal Man, Who presents the reality of what human nature never reached apart from Him, the God-consciousness is perfectly ascendant ; and becomes so in us through communion with Him. It is obvious that in this nebulous system we may trace, beneath a cloud of words, the elements of all the errors already mentioned The general theory takes a more rational form in those writers who speak of sin as simply the result of a surrender of the will at the first dawn of conscious responsibility to the dominion of the objects of sense which solicit it at the very threshold of life and thus have the advantage of the first appeal. All these modifications, however, agree in the fundamental principle that in some way or other the sensuous or fleshly nature of man is the source and occasion of evil.

2 The refutation of this superficial solution involves the doctrine of Original Sin. Postponing, therefore, any more full examination of it—which indeed that doctrine will render needless—we may make a few remarks, especially on its appeal to the sanction of Scripture An examination of the various forms which the contrast of flesh and spirit assumes will show that nowhere is sin, even by implication, assigned to the flesh as its seat, much less as the secret of its origin.

Meaning of the Flesh.

(1.) The flesh is opposed to the spirit in man—the σάρξ to the πνεῦμα—just as we distinguish the body as the organ of the soul connected with the outer world, and the spirit which holds communion with invisible realities. In our present estate, *the spirit indeed is willing, but the flesh is weak,* but both the weakness of the flesh and the inability of the spirit to overcome its weakness are alike the result of sin. St. Paul speaks of that same weak spirit as itself in bondage *to the law of sin which is in my members.* It is true that he lays emphasis on the sin that *dwelleth in me, that is,*

Flesh and spirit

Matt. xxvi. 41.

Rom. vii 23

Rom vii. 17, 18

in my flesh; but the indwelling evil cannot be the same as the
tabernacle in which it dwells   So *the* BODY *of sin* is *the body of*
SIN ; not that the fleshly body is the sin, but its instrument only.
There is no support in this class of passages for the notion that
the flesh is only the prisonhouse of a spirit, holy in itself, though
fettered to a body of sin and death.

Rom vi 6

(2.) But the flesh and the Spirit are also contrasted; and in
this case the flesh signifies the nature of man, his entire nature,
as fallen from God.   Though the sins of the lower part of his
constitution give the name, spiritual sins are included · *the works
of the flesh* include vices which are wholly independent of the body ,
and ally the human transgressor with the unclean spirits who can
have no fleshly lusts.   When therefore St. Paul distinguishes
between the *carnal* man, as σαρκικός, and the *spiritual* man, as
πνευματικός, he is referring respectively to him whose whole
nature is under the sway of sin and to him whose whole nature
is under the sway of the Holy Ghost.   The Divine Spirit pos-
sesses the whole man, but inhabits his spirit especially ; and
through His sanctifying grace the *whole spirit and soul and body* of
the believer is made sinless, and preserved blameless.   The
superficial view of sin, therefore, which makes it the triumph of
the lower portion of man over the higher, the sense over the
reason, has no support in these passages   It is directly dis-
countenanced and condemned by them.

Flesh and
the Spirit

Gal v 19

1 Cor. iii.
1.

1 Thess. v.
23.

(3.) Lastly, the flesh is the designation of mankind as subjected
to vanity, weakness, and decay and death.   *He also is flesh* is the
first testimony to this, and throughout the Scriptures the infirmity
of man's whole estate is thus marked . *all flesh is as grass.*   But
this is the effect and not the cause of human sin.   The Lord who
received *power over all flesh,* was first *made flesh* Himself.   And
this very fact for ever disproves the theory that in this is the necessary seat and source of sin.   *Jesus Christ is come in the flesh* was
St. John's witness against Gnosticism in every form ; *and in Him
is no sin.*   After this we need no further witnesses.   It may be
said, indeed, that the flesh, as assumed by our Lord, was preserved
by His indwelling Deity from the uprising of its evil ; emphasis
being laid on His coming only *in the likeness of sinful flesh.*   But
we must remember that He *condemned sin in the flesh,* and restored

Vanity

Gen vi. 3

1 Pet. 1
24.

John xvii.
2
John i 14.
1 John iv
2
1 John iii.
5.

Rom. viii.
3.

it to its original freedom from evil as our first father possessed it He *was manifested* in the flesh *to take away our sins*, and to vindicate, for Himself and for us, the sanctity of the flesh as it was made the tabernacle of the human spirit.

1 John iii 5.

ABUSE OF FREEDOM.

The only theory that remains—if it may be called a theory— is that which seeks the cause of evil in the abuse of the freedom of the will. Of every phenomenon we ask the cause; and it is impossible to avoid asking the cause of this the worst of all phenomena. But causes are variously defined as originating, efficient, formal, instrumental and final Of evil we dare not ask the originating cause, save as it passes into the efficient; and that is the will of the created spirit The formal cause, which makes evil to be evil, is the abuse of the freedom of that will separating itself from God. An instrumental cause there could not be, in the case of the original sin of the universe As to the final cause we must not speak save to quote tremblingly our Saviour's words, spoken on the only occasion when the permission of evil was proposed to Him as a problem, *that the works of God should be made manifest.*

Abuse of Freedom.

John ix 3

1. The ORIGIN OF EVIL in its ultimate and final cause—its absolute beginning and its purposed end—can never be matter of theory, or even conjecture. It is a secret which is not revealed, nor probably ever to be revealed. It has excited human speculation from age to age only to baffle it. The genesis or birth of evil, whether physical or moral, is a MYSTERY OF INIQUITY : of that there can be no question to any sound mind. But how the first little cloud in the holy universe arose which has covered the heavens and overspread the earth, and why evil was permitted to enter and go no more out for ever, we may ask, but there is none to answer. It is the dignity of our created nature that we may struggle with the problem ; it is equally the necessary limitation of our created nature that we are overpowered by it.

Origin of Evil.

2 But when we study sin in ourselves as the subject of it we may at least arrange the elements of our ignorance, and analyse the mystery which we cannot solve. In our human par-

Causes of Sin.

ticipation of the great calamity we have an instrumental cause, the temptation introduced from without. But that temptation found no element of sin, though it found the possibility of it. in human nature. As yet Satan came and had nothing in man. The insoluble mystery remains among the secret things of the Divine counsel; like the general fact of probation itself, a mystery which underlies all the rest The origin of all sin, and therefore of all evil, which in one sense includes sin and Freedom. in another springs from it, is to be sought in the FREEDOM of the created will Conscious freedom in the origination of action, and the choice of the end of action, whether ultimate or subordinate, belongs to the PERSONALITY of our spirit stamped with the image of God. The Divine law in the creation of intelligent moral beings seems to be that they must voluntarily make the supreme end of life their own by a free self-determination; that, after a longer or shorter test, this freedom should become a necessity of nature, and perfection be found—whether by the operation of some spiritual law within, or by the vision of God without—in the relative bondage to good which is perfect freedom the highest idea we can form of resemblance to our Creator. Thus that likeness of God which is the note of our highest dignity involved the possibility of our deepest degradation. But when we are finally created anew in the image of the Son to which we are predestinated to be conformed, probation will have ceased, and our freedom will be the necessity of goodness, like that of God Himself.

THE NATURE OF SIN.

Sin, having been considered in its origin as matter of Nature of Sin. revelation and faith, may now be viewed as matter of experience in its nature and development. Here we are shut up to the definitions of Scripture, which are given in a variety of names by which sin is characterised. These names, which are few but distinct and clear, describe it in two ways. First, with reference to God, it is the voluntary separation of the human will from the Divine, expressed in disobedience to His law. Secondly, in relation to man, it is guilt, as the consciousness of personal wrong and personal liability to punishment. It will be found that all the revelations of the Word of God concerning sin as such, and apart from its peculiar aspect as original sin, or the sin of the race, may be reduced to these simple elements.

SELF-SEPARATION FROM GOD.

The essence of that mystery in the created spirit which Severance from God. we call sin is its voluntary separation from God: that is and must be the root and reality of all evil in the creature.

1. It may be questioned whether any Scriptural term expressly Scriptural terminology indicates this ultimate secret, behind the act of disobedience to law imposed. But more than one of them seem to point towards it. Thus חַטָּאת and עָוֹן, sin and iniquity, united in *the iniquity* Ps. xxxii. 5. *of my sin,* both signify deflection from the true aim · the former rather denoting the missing of the mark, the latter the perverseness in aiming wrong So the leading Greek term ἁμαρτία means also the missing of the mark, with the idea of deviation from it, as is seen in ἁμαρτεῖν, intransitively to become separate, and thus

to fail of its object. Still, the primary and fundamental quality of sin, that it is voluntary separation from God, is not absolutely expressed; it is everywhere implied as the hidden fountain of all the rivers that make sad the life of man.

Transgression.

2. Almost every definition of sin in the Scripture marks it as transgression of law. It is enough to refer to St. John's first epistle, which contains the profoundest doctrine of sin and redemption : ἡ ἁμαρτία ἐστὶν ἡ ἀνομία, *sin is the transgression of the law.* How fearful sin is, as the darkness which is not in God, the Apostle has shown at the outset ; but here at the end we have his only express definition, and with it the Scripture closes. A great variety both of Hebrew and of Greek terms unite in this central idea, that sin is departing from the prescribed way of duty, the disobedience to express commandment: as Cicero says, Peccare est tanquam lineas transilire. St. John's definition is important, as showing the difference between the act of transgression and the state of transgression. The words mean that the act is the result of the state, and the state also the result of the act. Sin is only the act of a primitive transgressing will, but that will forms the character behind the future will, and shapes its ends. This final statement of St. John may be divided into its two branches, each of which will shed light upon the general terminology of Scripture. Sin is the voluntary separation of the soul from God: this implies the setting up of the law of self actively, and passively the surrender to internal confusion.

1 John iii. 4.

Self.

(1.) Though the essence of sin is not selfishness, that is its first manifestation. Self is set up in the place of God ; it is ἀνομία, lawlessness in principle, having thrown off the Divine restraint ; παράβασις, transgression in act ; ἀδικία, iniquity ; ἁμαρτία, deviation from the way or end appointed of God, regarded both as an act and as a state ; ἀσέβεια, godlessness. While some of these terms are negative, expressing the deflection of the will from its harmony with that of the Supreme, whose nature and will are one, either or both being the ground of eternal moral obligation to the creature, they still describe sin as the positive condition of the soul : not indeed as any real entity within it, but as the active direction of the will. In the Old Testament this positive element is very prominent. In פֶּשַׁע sin is active lawlessness or wilful

transgression, as in the words of Job : *for he addeth rebellion unto* Job
his sin. It is revolt against rightful authority : *they have . . . tres-* xxxiv. 37.
passed against My law. ·In רָעָה or רַע, which is one of the earliest   Hos. viii.
terms, we have the ideas both of perverseness and of universal   1.
evil : *and God saw that the wickedness of man was great in the earth.* Gen. vi. 5.
There are some other words which include the thought of a violent
revolt against Divine authority. By שָׁגַג this is connected with
wandering from God ; probably it occurs in one of the earliest
and most solemn accounts of the effect of sin : *in their wandering* Gen. vi. 3.
they are flesh. It may be said that the great mass of the definitions in both the Old and the New Testaments stamp it as the
active uprising of the human will against the ordinances of Divine
law written either on the heart or in positive statutes.

(2.) It may be doubted, however, whether in the Old or in the Disorder.
New Testament there is any one term for sin which expresses its
activity as a principle, without a side reference to its privative
character and the ruin which it involves. Such terms as ἐπιθυμία,
lust in concupiscence, ἔχθρα εἰς θεόν, enmity against God, and
τὰ ἑαυτοῦ ζητεῖν, seeking one's own, seem only positive and active ;
but they regard sin under special aspects, and certainly include
its internal perversion. Though its energy as the root of
human evil is all but unbounded, it is an energy in evil which
is also the misuse of faculties created for good alone. Hence, sin
is in Scripture inward confusion, discord, disease, wretchedness,
vanity : especially, as will hereafter be seen, in the habitual use
of σάρξ or flesh to express both the vanity and the sinfulness of
human nature. The term πονηρία, evil, itself testifies to the labour
and wearisomeness and vanity of sin, as it is related to πόνος,
labour. In the Old Testament a considerable number of words
express the same characteristic of conscious turbulence, disorder,
and unrest. Such are עָמָל : *they conceive* MISCHIEF (or *vexation*) Job xv.
and bring forth vanity ; עָוֶל, evil or depravity, as the result of   35.
wrongdoing ; רָשָׁע, wickedness, pointing to its restless activity
whether as internal or as affecting others : *the wicked are like* Isa. lvii.
the troubled sea when it cannot rest, whose waters cast up mire and   20, 21.
dirt ; there is no peace, saith my God, to the WICKED ; אָוֶן indicating
the nothingness or vanity of sin : *he that soweth iniquity shall reap* Prov. xxii.
  8.

Job ɪv. 8.　VANITY ; and *they that plow iniquity and sow wickedness reap the same.*
These words do not exhaust the catalogue of terms which define
the quality of sin as substituting for the obedience of the Divine
law a state of internal anarchy, as throwing the whole soul into
confusion, as creating disturbance around, and ending in vanity
and wretchedness both physical and spiritual.

CONSCIOUSNESS OF GUILT.

Guilt　　　Viewed more particularly with regard to its effect upon
man's relation to God's law sin is guilt, or the human
consciousness of a Divine imputation · first, the consciousness of PERSONAL responsibility for the sin as committed
by self; and, secondly, the consciousness of personal
RESPONSIBILITY for the sin, as an obligation to punishment on account of it. These two inseparable attendants
on the act of transgression are in reality one; but may
be conveniently distinguished.

Unity of　　I How truly the idea of Guilt is distinct and unique may be
Guilt.　　seen in the language by which it is expressed in Scripture, first,
with reference to the Divine imputation of sin, and, secondly, in
the human echo of that imputation in conscience.

Guilt in　　1 The universal testimony of the Bible, from the first revela-
Scripture　tion of sin down to the last revelation of redemption from it,
declares that the Holy Lawgiver imputes man's evil to man as
its author ; and will reckon to him the violation of the law and the
dishonour done to the majesty of His own holiness. The evil that
is in the natural world—that is, what evil has-been brought into
it by the Fall—He reckons only indirectly to the human transgressor, but his sin He reckons directly to him　There is no
THOU more direct than that which guilt hears and which im-
Gen ɪii　prints the sentiment of guilt : Adam, *where art thou ?　Because* THOU
9, 14　*hast done this, thou art cursed !*　Because thou hast done it . here is
guilt in the sense of CULPA or fault.　Thou art cursed : here is
guilt in the sense of REATUS or penalty. That sin is guilt in both
these senses, and that guilt in both these senses is sin, the Old

Testament teaches in its entire doctrine of expiation   Offence against God passes not away with the act, it clings still to the transgressor, and can never be put away from him save by his rendering satisfaction   That satisfaction he can render only by the endurance of the penalty : either in his own person or through the intermediation of other satisfaction counted as his own   He must carry the burden of his sin with him, or *bear his* Lev v. 1 *iniquity.*   There is one word, אָשָׁם which, as connected with חַטָאת, expresses constantly the idea of guilt attaching to every sin. Although in many passages it has a limited sense, designating the trespass-offering appointed to be brought for offences committed through error, negligence or ignorance, yet that very limitation serves to impress all the more significantly the deep meaning of guilt as such   The trespass-offering, or, as it should be rendered, the guilt-offering, was itself guilt as the representative of guilt   it was ASHAM , and so in the supreme Offering our Lord was made *sin for us.*   It is enough to refer to one text, which may stand 2 Cor v for a large number.   *If a soul sin, and commit any of these things* 21.
Lev v. *which are forbidden to be done by the commandments of the Lord ,* 17—19. *though he wist it not, yet is he* GUILTY (PECCATI REUS), *and shall bear his iniquity ; and he shall bring a ram without blemish out of the flock, with thy estimation, for a trespass-offering, unto the priest · and the priest shall make an atonement for him concerning his ignorance wherein he erred and wist it not, and it shall be forgiven him.   It is a trespass-offering . he hath certainly trespassed against the Lord*   Here we discern distinction in guilt—as the Vulgate translates, *juxta mensuram æstimationemque peccati,*—in relation to the theocratic laws of the old covenant.   But the underlying trespass, the heart and root of all offences, is the same.   Hence when we pass into the New Testament, which makes sin *exceeding sinful* in the Rom. vii light of the finished Atonement, the distinction is done away   The 13. sin-offering and the trespass-offering are united in the *one sacrifice* Heb x 12 *for sins.*   The highest conception of guilt is that of man's ὑπόδικον Rom iii γενέσθαι τῷ Θεῷ—that *all the world may become guilty before God* 19 Though there is a sense in which the Gospel still marks the sin of *him that knoweth to do good and doeth it not,* and makes a differ- Jas. iv 17
Luke xii. ence between *that servant which knew his Lord's will* and him that 47, 48. *knew not,* between the debtor who *owed five hundred pence* and the Luke vii.
41.

debtor who owed *fifty*, yet all sin is debt, for which satisfaction must be made. The new covenant has introduced this new term, and teaches the exaction of *the utter most farthing* · teaching it all the more rigorously because the secret of a full satisfaction and a frank forgiveness is at hand *The wrath of God is revealed from heaven*, and the guilty are *children of wrath* The law accompanies the Gospel, and makes the offender in one point *guilty of all*, πάντων ἔνοχος, or, in our Lord's language, *guilty* or *in danger of eternal sin*. Hence this phrase, which expresses the New-Testament idea of guilt most emphatically, includes the two meanings with which we set out . personal guilt as breaking the law, and personal obligation to endure its punishment πάντων ἔνοχος and ἔνοχος θανάτου. These last words suggest the most affecting illustration of the distinction. We are guilty in both senses : our Holy Saviour was only *guilty of death*. And all is expressed in our word SIN , according to its most probable derivation from the Latin SONS, nocens, that which is the guilty cause of death to the soul.

Matt. v 26

Rom i. 18.
Eph. ii 3.

Mark iii. 29

Matt. xxvi. 66.

Con-scienco

2. The Conscience in man bears its own clear testimony. This faculty of our nature, or representative of the Judge in our personality, is simply in relation to sin the registrar of its guilt. It is the moral consciousness, rather of instinct than of reflection, though also of both, faithfully assuming the personal responsibility of the sin and anticipating its consequences Such is the Scriptural meaning of the word. It is not the standard of right and wrong set up in the moral nature. St Paul speaks of that as written in the heart of universal man the Gentiles *show the work of the law written in their hearts.* He goes on to speak of *their conscience also bearing witness*, by its *accusing or else excusing*, undoubtedly looking upward to a Judge and forward to a judgment. What St. Paul calls συνείδησις, St John calls καρδία, meaning, however, not the heart, in which St. Paul seats the law, but the consciousness of the inner man. The conscience is the self of the personality, in universal humanity never excusing, but always accusing, and is the *conscience of sins*. But of this we need not speak further now. It is enough to establish the distinction between the standard of right and wrong which may be defective and is not conscience proper, and that moral consciousness which

Rom. ii. 15.

Heb. x 2.

infallibly unites the fault and its consequences in the consciousness of the sinner.

GUILT AS FAULT AND PUNISHMENT.

We may now look more particularly at the idea of guilt under its two aspects: observing, however, preliminarily that what is here said has reference only to sin generally, without including those modifications of its phenomena and degrees of its guiltiness which are concerned rather with the doctrine of Original Sin.

THE PERSONAL FAULT.

Guilt is the personal consciousness of being responsible for the wrong: the transgressor violating the commands of the law acknowledges the law and its rights against himself.

Guilt.

1. This is the sense of the forensic term αἰτία: the sinner is and knows himself to be the agent and the cause of his own sin. Hence it is defined as reatus culpæ, or guilt in respect to its fault. The eternal alliance of sin and guilt in human consciousness cannot be too deeply pondered. This consciousness refutes all those theories of the origination of sin to which reference has been made: it exonerates God, it honours the law, while it does not excuse the Tempter, it lays not upon him as the instrument the guilt of which it assumes the responsibility In this conscience of sin the devils tremble. This is the deepest secret in the heart of every human transgressor: the mouth may deny it, not knowing what it says; but the inner man is true to its moral instinct. The first evasion of guilt was only an evasion; and it was Adam's guilt that said, *The woman whom Thou gavest to be with me, she gave me of the tree, and I did eat.* This was the knowledge of evil which had been threatened, and the very attempt to transfer the guilt of self to secondary agents was proof that evil was known Job represents all men when he speaks of the self-deception of covering sin with a covering not of

Reatus culpæ.

Gen. iii. 12.

D 2

Job xxxi. 33. Gen. iii. 13. the sanctuary : *If I covered my transgressions, as Adam, by hiding mine iniquity in my bosom.* When Eve said, *The serpent beguiled me, and I did eat,* it was her guilt that spoke. The English term Guilt has affinity with the term Beguiled, but with a far deeper meaning

2. This sure and unerring consciousness of wrong speaks in conscience; but conscience may be suppressed, may speak inarticulately, or may be perverted in its decisions. The whole economy of law is designed to revive it, to restore it to its sobriety, and constrain it to give its clear witness against self The sinner takes his first step towards return to God when he acknowledges himself inseparably Rom. vii 9 identified with his past transgression, and owns that himself and his sin are one St. Paul's words, making out of his own ex- Rom. vii. 17, 24 perience an example, are very clear : *I was alive without the law once, but when the commandment came, sin revived, and I died ·* I DIED. When afterwards he might seem to cover his sin like Adam, *Now then it is no more I that do it, but sin that dwelleth in me,* he does not impute to sin as another agent the guilt due to himself He only speaks as one who was *no longer* under the absolute bondage of sin, no longer insensible to its enormity, but struggling to get free. *No more I* only means that his better self, still guilty—*O wretched man that I am !*—was striving, though as yet in vain, to be free *the evil which I would not* THAT I DO But at present we are only considering the conscience of sin awakened by the conviction of the Spirit · the results of that awakening are in the future.

Guilt as Punishment.

THE PUNISHMENT.

Guilt has another meaning. It is the sure obligation to punishment; or what is sometimes called the reatus pœnæ. We must remember that it is here regarded as absolute, without reference to any atoning provision; that it is the penalty of a living soul, and not annihilation : and that it is the penalty of the human spirit informing Death. a human body. The soul that sinneth is GUILTY OF DEATH, or of being sundered from the Holy Spirit of life : the death of the spirit separated from God, involving the separation of soul and body, and in its issue eternal. This is a hard saying, taken alone; but its mitigation will come in due time.

I SPIRITUAL DEATH is the departure of the Holy Spirit as the bond of union between God and every living soul   Through His withdrawal the spirits, whether of angels or of men, are separated from fellowship with God, retaining the natural elements of His image, but no longer reflecting His holiness. This penalty we are now considering in the abstract, and without reference to its character as affected by redemption.   It is enough to say that in itself it is the departure of the life of the soul as the soul was created to exist in God.   This is not only the penalty of sin, but also gives it a specific nature, and leads to those manifestations of it which are the best and only definitions of spiritual death.   As *by the law is the knowledge of sin* positively, so also the absence of the Holy Ghost negatively makes its evil known in all its forms and characters

1. Instead of the Divine Spirit, SELF becomes the ascendant and ruling principle of the life: the mystery of sin in its origin was the severance of the free spirit from God and the aspiring to become its own god   Now the mystery is revealed . the spirit of man, without the Spirit of God, is surrendered to Self.   The life and activity of the self, or selfishness in all its forms, is, whether among angels or among men, the death of the soul.   Hence, as will be hereafter seen, the process of recovery from that death is the return of the Spirit of life in Christ Jesus, when the I no longer lives   *If any man will come after Me let him deny himself. He that loveth his life shall lose it, and he that hateth his life in this world shall keep it unto life eternal*   Such sayings point to the principle that true and essential death is the living to self

2. According to the original constitution of man the flesh was, in its innocent alliance with the things of sense, subject to his spirit governed by the Divine Spirit   the penalty of sin is the forfeiture of that dominion, as over the outer world generally, so over his own physical nature.   Hence the FLESH gives one of its prevalent denominations to sin as manifested in man and in this world.   The restoration of the Holy Ghost to human nature

Margin notes:

Spiritual

Rom iii 20.

Self.

Matt. xvi. 24.
John xii. 25

Flesh

Rom. viii. 6. restores it to spirituality again : *to be carnally minded is death, but to be spiritually minded is life.*

Idolatry. 3. The absence of the Spirit, making the heart of man an interior temple and all nature a temple external, surrenders man to IDOLATRY. He is a being formed for worship ; and his instinct, even in its perversion, is that of a creature bowing down to something above himself We can hardly imagine the lost spirits without this : there may be something corresponding to human idolatry among the fallen intelligences who followed the revolt of the archangel. But, as to man, while self becomes his interior god, the outer world becomes a vast Pantheon Hence this positive idolatry is also UNGODLINESS, the meaning of which, as the word tells us, is being without the worship of God, and therefore estranged from His holy nature.

Developing principle. 4. Sin also becomes a governing PRINCIPLE, capable of endless development This springs from the great fact that the elements of human nature were constructed for unlimited progress · if not from glory to glory, then from shame to shame

2 Tim. ii 16 There is a fearful self-generating power in evil, which grows *unto more ungodliness* It may not be lawful to say that sin is punished by sin , but most surely spiritual death to good has in it all the fulness of spiritual life to evil This accounts for the infinite varieties of transgression, from the secret fault known only to God, up to the sin against the Holy Ghost.

Only an accident 5. Lastly, it must be remembered that, whatever sin is, it is the accident of a nature that is not in itself changed It is only the separation from God ; but the soul going out of His presence still bears in its wanderings His image, the natural characteristics of which are not marred by the introduction of any new faculty created for evil alone. There is nothing new introduced into the fibres of our being as human In other words, sin must be left altogether to the region of tendency and bias of the WILL, as formed by the character and as forming it in return.

Physical II. PHYSICAL DEATH is the penalty of human sin : not however in itself, but as connected with death spiritual : connected with it in some sense as resulting from the same deprivation of

Rom. viii. 11. the Holy Ghost, Whose *indwelling* in regenerate man is the pledge of the physical resurrection, even as it is the principle of the

spirit's resurrection to life. But it is declared to be expressly
the penalty of sin in man; who was on its account subjected
to the vanity that was the lot of the lower creatures, denied
access to the Tree of Life, and surrendered to the dissolution that
had already been the natural termination of the existence of the
inferior orders of the inhabitants of earth From the moment of
the entrance of sin death reigned, as afterwards in Adam's
descendants, so in himself for death means mortality, and includes all the innumerable evils that introduce it It must be remembered that we have no experience of this doom as absolutely
unrelieved by the Gospel , but here we have only to do with the
punishment itself. As the penalty of spiritual death gives new
characteristics to sin, so also does the penalty of physical death.
It stamps upon it the attributes of impotence and misery; especially, as we have seen, in Old-Testament definitions. To this we
must refer again Meanwhile, it is enough to say that, whatever
our first parents may have understood, the sentence pronounced
upon their sin could not have been primarily even, certainly not
alone, the separation of soul and body Moreover, physical death
in the sense of the annihilation of man's whole physical nature,
as he is soul and spirit, is never once alluded to throughout the
Scriptures. To die never in the Bible means extinction.

III. DEATH as the doom of sin is of itself necessarily ETERNAL. Eternal.
1. This penalty is now regarded in the abstract, pronounced   Eternal
upon sin as such. It is the separation of the soul from God,   Death.
looked at apart from redemption, and therefore a sentence in
itself unrelieved and unqualified. This awful truth may be viewed
negatively and positively. The withdrawal of the Holy Spirit is
a penalty which leaves the sinner without the possibility of
self-restoration; and in that is everlasting death. But it is
also the positive decree of the Righteous Judge who separates
evil for ever from Himself In harmony with this distinction are
certain well-marked definitions of sin in the New Testament It
is *enmity against God,* and that implies in itself an eternal sever- Rom. viii.
ance, as in the case of the unredeemed spirits It is BONDAGE to   7.
evil : that is, the free spirit, never losing its power of self-determination, is determined by the presence of the sinful principle to
only evil continually And in the combination of these again lies Gen. vi. 5

the element of eternal death As the favour of God is life, so
death is His displeasure, the sense of guilt, uniting the personal
responsibility and the apprehension of punishment, is capable of
unlimited continuance. And when it is said that *the wrath of God
abideth on* the unbeliever, we need no other account of the penalty
of eternal death.

John iii.
36

2 As a sentence pronounced upon sin, death was not declared
to be eternal in the beginning, nor ever announced as such until
the Redeemer *brought life and immortality to light* It was a
suspended decree, as indeed every part of the sentence was
suspended Physical death immediately took effect, but only in
its preliminaries the deceiver spoke half the truth when he said
that, in the day they ate of the fruit, the Protoplasts should *not
surely die* Spiritual death took effect at once, but that also, as
we shall see, not without alleviation. That the severance of the
soul from God should endure for ever was not pronounced, because
the provisions of mercy might reverse that part of the decree.
But with those provisions of mercy we have not yet to do However, when the grace of God bringing salvation to man was fully
revealed, it most solemnly supplemented what had been lacking
in the primitive denunciation, and unfolded its deep hidden
meaning. It is the Scriptural characteristic of this *second death*
that it is never foreannounced as a threatening sanction, but always
predicted as a consequence of impenitent sin it is not so
much declared to be the penalty of guilt as the penalty of redemption rejected. The Gospel to *them that perish* is *the savour of death
unto death*, of death spiritual deepening into death eternal.

Rather a
Result
than a
Sanction
2 Tim. i.
10.

Gen. iii. 4.

Rev. ii. 11

2 Cor ii.
15, 16.

3 But though the sentence of eternal death is bound up with
the scheme of recovery, as the sanction of a rejected Gospel, it
must be remembered that it is everywhere declared to be the necessary issue of sin as the opposite of all that is called life. Life is
nowhere in the Word of God made equivalent to continuance in
being : were it so eternal death would be eternal annihilation.
Life is communion with God, and its consummation is eternal ;
death is the end of unrighteousness, and its consummation eternal
*For the wages of sin is death, but the gift of God is eternal life
through Jesus Christ our Lord* Doubtless there are great varieties
in the application of the term death, as there are also of the term

Death the
full
opposite
of Life.

Rom vi.
23.

life; but the applications of the two terms run parallel. Our Lord's words are emphatic: *Verily, verily, I say unto you, he that heareth My word, and believeth on Him that sent Me, hath everlasting life, and shall not come into condemnation* John v. 24. Here the contrast of life and death eternal is exhibited *Verily, verily, I say unto you, The hour is coming and now is, when the dead shall hear the voice of the Son of God; and they that hear shall live.* John v. 25. Here it is the contrast of spiritual life and death *Marvel not at this for the hour is coming in the which all that are in the graves shall hear His voice, and shall come forth they that have done good, unto the resurrection of life, and they that have done evil, unto the resurrection of damnation* John v 28, 29. Here the physical life is made eternal, and the spiritual is between them   It is in the light of these sovereign words that the contested passage of St Paul must be read . *as by one man sin entered into the world, and death by sin* Rom v. 12 Here physical death is the penalty of sin , but spiritual and eternal death cannot be excluded, as is evident from the context which surrounds this text in the Apostle's great chapter of Sin.   It closes with the sentence *that as sin hath reigned unto death, even so might grace reign through righteousness unto eternal life by Jesus Christ our Lord* Rom v. 21. In the earlier part of the chapter which deals with sin generally, before coming to Original Sin, we have four terms that express its whole nature, both in itself and in that penalty of death in its spiritual and its eternal sense from which the Atonement rescues us   Referring expressly to the state in which we were found by redemption, St. Paul calls men generally ἁμαρτωλοί, transgressors of the law in their very nature , ἀσεβεῖς, ungodly and cut off from the favour, presence, and service of God , ἀσθενεῖς, without strength, essentially impotent; and, finally, ἐχθροί, enemies, the objects of a positive displeasure or wrath of the Supreme which apart from the mediation of Christ will endure for ever.   This quaternion of terms must be carried on into the latter part of the chapter where it is shown how the first transgression paved the way for them   In their light sound exposition cannot limit death as the penalty of sin to the death of the body.

4. But this leads at once to the connection between moral evil and redemption , the consideration of which will pave the way for the doctrine of Original Sin.   In interposing the following Sin and Expiation united

section we follow the guidance of St. Paul himself, who passes, in
turning from his most complete description of sin generally to his
most complete account of its relation to our race, over that sacred
bridge · *we also joy in God through our Lord Jesus Christ, by whom*
Rom.v 11. *we have now received the Atonement.*   Not only he, but every writer
of Scripture, as well in the New Testament as in the Old,
constantly connects evil with the system of deliverance from it.
Sin is always discussed, defined, dwelt upon in all its development and issues, at the foot of the Altar in the old economy, and
at the foot of the Cross in the new   It is a fact which has
been alluded to already, and will recur hereafter, that many of
the Hebrew and Greek terms for sin itself are used also to express
the expiation of sin, while in some phrases the bearing of iniquity
and its forgiveness are actually one   It is sufficient to quote one
Lev xxiv instance   In Leviticus it is said : *Whosoever curseth his God shall*
15   *bear his sin,* נָשָׂא חֶטְאוֹ   Of the servant of God we read, *He*
Isa liii 12 *Himself bare the sins of many,* וְהוּא חֵטְא־רַבִּים נָשָׂא; this, if
Lev. xvi compared with the words concerning the scapegoat, *to bear upon*
22   *him all their iniquities to a land not inhabited,* shows that the
bearing sin was also the bearing it away by atonement   Then
Ps xxxii we hear the pardoned penitent crying, *Thou forgavest the iniquity*
5.   *of my sin,* נָשָׂאתָ עֲוֹן חַטָּאתִי·   Thus the guilt of the utmost sin,
the perfect propitiation provided for it, and the assured sense of
forgiveness, are all signified by the same profound phrase.   Passing by this, however, we must impress on our minds the blessed
truth that we at least, as sinners of mankind, never need study
sin save in the direct light of redemption.

SIN AND REDEMPTION.

Under whatever aspect viewed—whether as to the Being offended or the sinner who offends—there is no principle and no hope of redemption in sin itself. But, on the other hand, there is much both in the nature and in the development of human evil that suggests the possibility, probability, and certainty of a redemption from without. And the fact of this redemption gives a special character to the general doctrine of sin in all its branches.

Sin and Redemption

I. Sin has in itself no element of redemption, whether we think of the Divine character which makes sin what it is, or the human spirit in which the principle of evil resides

1 The Divine nature as holy must eternally abhor and can never be reconciled to it. God is *of purer eyes than to behold evil,* save to condemn and remove it from His presence. Man's fallen nature itself bears witness to this: its true instinct is *Depart from me, for I am a sinful man!* The God of love is a *consuming fire* to all that is contrary to His purity, and if that consuming fire becomes a saving destruction of evil, that belongs to the mystery of grace, which is not yet in question. But the Holy Being is also a righteous Lawgiver; His nature and His will are in the *revelation of the righteous judgment of God,* not only against the abominable thing itself, but against the soul that *doeth evil. O wicked man, thou shalt surely die!* is an Old-Testament word that finds its New-Testament confirmation *Cursed is every one that continueth not in all things which are written in the book of the law to do them* And here again the universal conscience of man finds that *book of the law* his own heart, where is written or engraven the sentence which, so far as it knows, is irrevocable. God *cannot deny Himself;* nor does the human spirit deny Him His eternal opposition to sin The justice of God Himself does not more faithfully guard His law than it is guarded by the conscience of man. Neither can conscience deny itself.

In the Divine Nature. Hab i.13.

Luke v 8.

Heb xii. 29.

Rom. ii 5, 9. Ezek xxxiii 8. Gal iii. 10

2 Tim. ii. 13

2. Nor has the sinner any power of redemption in himself.

In man himself.

He has indeed in every age wrestled with the sin that rests upon
him, but in vain: wrestled with it, knowing it to be wrong, and
under the unconscious influence of a grace of which he knows not
naturally the secret. He has striven to expiate its guilt by an
endless variety of sacrifices that have never availed to take
away the conscience of sin : he has never been satisfied with the
propitiation either of his substitutionary offerings or of his own
personal sufferings His experience has always denied that sin
could by its acts or sacrifices or sufferings put away its guilt. He
has striven also to redeem himself by the discipline of philosophy
and repentance. But equally in vain he has never even pro-
fessed to find holiness in philosophy, or to be capable of a true
repentance   The fact that he has always combined these two—
the offerings for expiation and the attempt to mend his own
nature—has attested the universal consciousness of our fallen race
that both are necessary ; the fact of universal failure has proved
that in himself the sinner has no help. The altars of expiation
in the temples of an unknown God, and the schools of philosophy
hard by, were heathen anticipations of the Gospel that unites
expiation and renewal, by one provision meeting both the guilt
and the defilement of transgression   They were most impressive
and affecting as such , but in themselves, and as evidences of the
inherent hopelessness of sin, supremely monitory.

Repent-
ance.

3. More modern theories, borrowing the light of the Atonement they reject, have argued that Repentance is both expiation
and recovery ; they have not only appealed to a human instinct
that accepts the penitence of an offender, but also to the language
of Scripture itself which describes God as always accepting the
penitent   Thus they contradict both the propositions which we
have been establishing . neither is the nature of God . eternally
opposed to sin, nor is man's nature incapable of putting it away.
As to the former argument, that of the analogy of human
tenderness towards repentance, it omits to consider the difference
not of degree only but of kind between our offences against each
other and our sin against God ; it forgets that there is no strict
relation of sin but as between the Supreme God and His creature;
no human analogy here suffices   As to the latter argument, that
Scripture represents our Heavenly Father as always ready to meet

His returning prodigal, it neglects to observe that wherever repentance is thus spoken of, an atonement either typical or real is always implied. The parable which brings the Father of spirits and the returning son to a midway place of reconciliation was spoken by Him whose name is the'Mediator, His cross is stamped upon it though as yet unseen, and it is recorded in the same Gospel in which the Redeemer says, *This cup is the new testament in My blood, which is shed for you* If, in St Luke's Gospel of free grace, the penitent *went down to his house justified*, after having only cried, *God be merciful to me the sinner '* we must remember that his very word ἱλάσθητι μοί savours of the propitiatory sacrifice, that he spoke his contrition in the presence of the altar of atonement, and that he is justified according to the gracious non-imputation of sin which rested upon a satisfaction for human guilt as yet unrevealed Both arguments fail to remember that man has no power to repent in the fulness of the meaning of the word; and that repentance is the gift of God, procured by the very Atonement that it is made to supersede the Atonement of Him who was exalted *to give repentance to Israel and forgiveness of sins*

Lu xxii. 20

Lu xviii. 13, 14.

Acts v. 31

II All this being true, it is obvious also that sin and redemption have been intimately bound up together in the history of man Sin exists in God's universe elsewhere; but, as it is found running its course upon earth, it gives tokens of a scheme of deliverance possible, probable, and certain.

Sin bound up with Redemption.

1. This may indeed be said of all evil, that, if a method of abolishing it can be found which shall be consistent with the Divine perfections, making objective atonement to His justice, and allowing His love subjectively to destroy the sin, it will be found by the Divine wisdom. The same instinct of our nature that assures us of the eternal hatefulness of sin to God teaches us that IF IT BE POSSIBLE it will be removed. It may be said that we are arguing here in a circle : that we are supposing the very redemption that we assume to be à priori contemplated as possible. The objection must be accepted, but it strengthens our position, that there is inwrought by some means or other in the human mind a daring trust that for man at least some infinite resource in God is available. The entire system of revelation tells us that in the internal mystery of the Trinity such a method

Εἰ δυνατόν ἐστι.

Matt. xxvi. 39.

The Trinity.

has been found.   And here lies the unutterable preciousness of the
doctrine of the Triune Essence   It is difficult to avoid anticipation
at this point   The glory of the future Cross already shines upon
the chaos of moral disorder   Christ Jesus, the representative of
man in the eternal counsel, if not in His eternal nature, has by
His oblation of Himself once offered absorbed the punishment of
sin and rendered its utter destruction certain in all those who
make His Atonement their own by faith

The lost   2 We need not complicate the question with the fact that
spirits   lost spirits are unredeemed : they tempted us to sin but must not
tempt our faith to doubt our recovery. Certainly there is nothing
in the condition of human nature that shuts out the possibility of
redemption   Its depravity, taken at the worst, is not a total
extinction of every element that grace might lay hold on. In fact,
the development of moral evil in the world has such a character as
to suggest that man's nature was not found unredeemable, that it
has been once the object of a mysterious intervention, and is ever
undergoing the discipline of a process of recovery   The universal
sentiment among men that God may be and in some sense is propitiated , the refusal of human guilt to give up its case as hopeless , the almost impossibility of persuading men generally that
their sin is unpardonable ; the voice of conscience speaking in
every language under heaven, in the accents both of fear and
of hope, the irrepressible yearnings after some great Deliverer and
some great Deliverance, all proclaim that there may be redemption
for man, and confirm the testimony of the Bible that for the race
Job   of human transgressors God has *found a ransom*
xxxiii 24   III Now the entire doctrine of Sin takes a new aspect from
New   this gracious intervention, from this mystery of atoning love   In
aspect of   how many ways it affects that doctrine as displayed in the scheme
sin.   of the Gospel we shall hereafter see   Meanwhile, it has this
preliminary effect, that it shows us moral evil as the penalty and
infection of a race continuing from generation to generation, and
counteracted and vanquished as such. But this leads us directly
to the doctrine of Original Sin, which marks the special peculiarity
of evil in the family of man : at once its universality as surely
propagated and the gracious alleviation it receives.

ORIGINAL SIN.

The effect of the Fall upon the posterity of Adam is described in Scripture as the universal diffusion of death as a condemnation, and of a bias of human nature towards evil. The Scriptural doctrine finds its expression in the theological term Original Sin: the hereditary sin and hereditary sinfulness of mankind derived from Adam its natural head and representative, but derived from him as he was under a constitution of redeeming grace and connected with the Second Adam, the spiritual Head of mankind.

Here we must first exhibit the testimony of inspiration, and then the historical development of the dogma. It may be observed at the outset that the doctrine of Original Sin is in an important respect the doctrine of sin itself, there is no aspect of the subject which is not more or less directly connected with the quality of evil as belonging to the race. Hence, many questions arising out of the subject generally will find their place here, having been indeed specially reserved for this section

THE NEW TESTAMENT DOCTRINE.

The relation of the universal hereditary sin of mankind to the original sin of Adam, its relation to the covenant of redemption in Christ, and its character as resulting from both, are the topics now before us.

ORIGINAL SIN IN RELATION TO THE FIRST ADAM.

St. Paul teaches that through one man sin entered into the world. It entered as bringing with it the condemnation of universal death: the guilt of the first transgression is reckoned in its consequences upon all the race represented by the first transgressor. But not apart from their own sin: all are not only regarded as sinners, but made sinners also through the inheritance of a nature of itself inclined only to evil. Thus the transmission of the penalty is both direct and indirect.

HEREDITARY GUILT.

Heredi-
tary
Guilt.

Hereditary guilt is not expressly stated in the form of a proposition : the phrase is of later than Scriptural origin. But where St. Paul establishes the connection between sin and death as its comprehensive penalty, he teaches that the condemnation of the first sin reigns over all mankind as in some sense one with Adam.

Rom. v 12.

1. After saying that *death passed upon all men, for that* (ἐφ' ᾧ, *on the ground or presupposition that*) *all have sinned* (or, *all sinned*), thus asserting that in Divine imputation all, in some sense, sinned originally in Adam, the Apostle goes on to show that the death

Rom. v 14

fell upon *them that had not sinned after the similitude of Adam's transgression.* It passed upon those who did not in Adam commit his offence, who did not, moreover, offend personally as he did. They sinned in Adam, though not guilty of the act of his sin : this then is hereditary condemnation, on those who were not

Physical
Death.

personal transgressors and on them all   Here, it is obvious, the penalty is primarily regarded as physical death. Every member of the race is involved in this consequence of the original sin of mankind.

Rom. v
15—19.

2. Then follows the parallel with the Second One, Jesus Christ, to the same effect . *If through the offence of one many be dead* (or *died*), *much more the grace of God, and the gift by grace, which is by One Man, Jesus Christ, hath abounded unto many.   And*

Death
Spiritual
and
Eternal.

not as it was by one that sinned (the many died), *so is the gift   for the judgment was by one to condemnation, but the free gift is of many offences unto justification.* In the three verses which follow the same deep truth is exhibited in three more forms, each increasing the strength of the preceding, and all culminating in the doctrine that *as by one man's disobedience many were made* (or *constituted,* both in fact and by imputation) *sinners, so by the obedience of One shall many be made righteous.* Five paraphrases of the same statement declare that, in whatever sense the Redemption was an act external to the race and for its benefit, the Fall was external to the successive generations of mankind and for their condemnation Here, it is obvious, or ought to be obvious, that the condemnation and the life are correlatives : the judgment is the opposite of the *reign in life* as the result of *abundance of grace* It is this which St Paul, the Christian expositor of original sin, stamps by a series of cumulative variations having no parallel in his writings

3 In the Epistle to the Corinthians the connection between the doom of death and the sin of Adam is stated in almost the same terms, but the reference seems more limited to physical death than in the Epistle to the Romans. A careful examination, however, will show that there also death has the same deep and wide meaning. The central text is : *for as in Adam all die, even so in Christ shall all be made alive* Here that process of death is going on which in the Romans passed forth as a decree once for all : it is πάντες ἀποθνήσκουσιν, but yet ἐν τῷ Ἀδάμ, in the one historical Man, and through their connection with him The bodily resurrection is the argument of the chapter. *The first man Adam was made a living soul, the last Adam was made a quickening Spirit* From the former we derive a corruptible body animated by a living soul, which through sin lost the provision for its continued immortality it is not taught that Adam received and transmitted only an animal or natural existence. From the Latter we receive the new gift of immortality, for soul and body, through the Spirit of life proceeding from Him But the direct argument is limited to the bodily resurrection. Indirectly, however, it asserts the great contrast between the sentence of eternal life and the sentence of eternal death. The chapter ends by saying that *the sting of death is sin :* it was the poison of that serpent which brought physical mortality into the race ; but Christ *died for our sins,* and not only for our resurrection from the grave as one penalty of offence. Death is abolished only AFTER the resurrection · *so when this corruptible shall have put on incorruption, and this mortal shall have put on immortality, then shall be*

Rom. v. 19.

Ver. 17

1 Cor. xv. 22

Ver 45

Ver 56

Ver 3.

brought to pass the saying that is written, Death is swallowed up in victory.

Ver 54. Universal death is, to the saints, lost in the victory of life.

Imputa-
tion 4 St Paul, to whom we owe the leading elements of this doctrine, does not carefully distinguish in what various senses the imputation of sin rests upon the race as death. The question will be raised in the historical controversies on the subject. Meanwhile, it may be observed that the strong word is ἁμαρτωλοὶ κατεστάθησαν οἱ πολλοί, which winds up his discussion, after the same idea had been several times left unexpressed, as the italics in our translation will show. Sinners all men were once for all accounted, or made, or constituted—they were placed in the category of transgressors. Sometimes this verb has the meaning of being made in the sense of being set or appointed by authority, but it never has that of being made through a process of

Rom. v
19 becoming. In the glorious parallel, *so by the obedience of One shall many be made righteous,* the term does not, strictly speaking, lose this meaning of establishment by imputation ; for, whatever may be the righteousness imparted to the justified in Christ, they will, both in this world and the next, be accounted righteous through the One meritorious obedience. But, neither this strong word nor any other used in Scripture precludes the thought that those who are constituted sinners by their unity in Adam make his act their own in another sense . all the individuals of the many are

Hos vi 7 accounted sinners, because they also, *like Adam, have transgressed the covenant* Still, the root of their offence is deeper than their individual life   Physical death precedes personal individual

John ix.
34.
John iii.
6, 3.
Rom viii
8 guilt All men are *altogether born in sins* in this the Jews spoke more truly than they intended. *That which is born of the flesh is flesh ,* and cannot as such *see the kingdom of God,* for *they that are in the flesh cannot please God.* But to be born of the flesh is now, to speak reverently, the ordinance of God Of the eternal penalty

Rom. v
18, 21. we speak not yet : *the free gift came upon all men unto justification of life,* of *eternal life ;* but justification presupposes a condemnation to be removed. And this must teach us not to soften down

Eph. ii 3 that strongest phrase of St Paul on this subject : *and were by nature the children of wrath, even as others,* τέκνα φύσει ὀργῆς.

Doctrine
of all
Scripture. 5 Though St. Paul has been spoken of as the teacher of original guilt, it must not be understood that he alone is responsible for this doctrine. He introduced nothing which he did not receive; and the Lord's words already quoted sanction his teaching It is not upon one isolated passage that the doctrine rests It pervades the Scripture It interprets the tone and spirit of the whole testimony of the Bible as to the fallen family of the first father who sinned, and especially it interprets the relation of the Redeemer to mankind, a relation which absolutely requires the condemnation of the race as its basis. But of this we shall speak more particularly.

HEREDITARY DEPRAVITY

The inheritance of a bias to evil is much more abundantly, though not more clearly, dwelt on in Scripture. The doctrine of a transmitted moral depravation or corruption pervades all the dispensations of revealed truth.

Hereditary Depravity.

1 In the Old Testament the proofs are ample and explicit

(1) Its historical narrative takes it for granted that the root of individual personal life is sinful, it abounds with testimonies both to the universality of the sinful taint and to the propagation of it in the race In the beginning of human history we find a *book of the generations of Adam* There it is stated that *in the day that God created man, in the likeness of God made He him,* that the two first parents of mankind were one Adam as the head of the race. *male and female created He them, and blessed them, and called then name Adam, in the day when they were created* The narrative then proceeds to say that *Adam lived an hundred and thirty years, and begat* (a son) *in his own likeness, after his image.* This kind of language is never repeated, and, regarded as the preface to the history of the human corruption that ended in the Flood, may be quoted as probably the earliest text of the hereditary sinful tendency of mankind The records of depravity which follow speak always of man as such, even when it excepts the godly. *My Spirit shall not always strive with man, for that he also is flesh* this verse is capable of another rendering, *My Spirit shall not always govern in man ; in their wandering they are flesh ;* which rather strengthens the denomination of mankind as flesh, resisting as

Old Testament.

Gen v. 1, 2.

Gen. v 3

Gen vi 3

Gen. vi 6   such the Spirit of grace. *It repented the Lord that He had made*
Gen vi 5.   *man on the earth ; for every imagination of the thoughts of his heart*
was only evil continually. At the Flood this was the case with the
ungodly, and the saved family of Noah were by nature no better
than the rest The history does not teach us that there were two
Gen. vi. 2.   races of men, one untainted by sin and the other corrupt. *The*
Gen. iv.   *sons of God* were those who *began to call themselves by the name of*
26   *the Lord.* Their father, as they were distinguished from the
Gen. v. 3   progeny of Cain, was Seth, whom *Adam begat in his own likeness.*
Their best descendant and representative was Noah, who was
saved to continue the race, not because he was without sin, but
Gen. vi 8   because he *found grace in the eyes of the Lord,* like Lot afterwards,
Gen. xix   who said, *Thy servant hath found grace in Thy sight, and Thou hast*
19.   *magnified Thy mercy* Noah, the new head of mankind, proved
that he continued the hereditary taint He was accepted after
Gen viii.   the Flood through sacrifice. *And the Lord said in His heart, I will*
21.   *not again curse the ground any more for man's sake , though the imagi-*
nation of man's heart is evil from his youth. Here the very words
which described the deep corruption of the race before it was
swept away are used to describe the germ of the same corruption
surviving the Flood.
Circum-   (2) There is no question that the course of sin is regarded as
cision.   running on from generation to generation among the nations of
the earth. That it continued among the chosen people to be the
law is proved by the institute of circumcision, which, whatever
other purpose it served, was the ordained memorial of the sin
connected with the propagation of the race, as well as by the
series of ceremonial purifications that attended the birth of
every child For the whole world—to anticipate—baptism
carries the same signification

(3) Individual testimonies are not wanting Job, the patri-
Job xiv. 4.   archal theologian, asks, *Who can bring a clean thing out of an*
unclean ? not one. This question is elsewhere answered by another:
Job xv.   *What is man, that he should be clean? and he which is born of a*
14   *woman, that he should be righteous?* *In sin did my mother conceive*
Ps. li 5.   *me,* is the confession of one for all; in which David responds to
Job xxv 4.   Job, and almost literally to Bildad, *how can he be clean that is born*
of a woman ? It is needless to quote other texts.

2. The New Testament throughout confirms this truth.

(1.) *Out of the heart*, the Redeemer declares, *proceed evil thoughts*, followed by the catalogue of sins in the life. The heart is the centre of the personality, of which the infallible Teacher says, *If ye, then,* BEING EVIL, and that in connection with the good still remaining through the secret of grace in human nature. Why man is thus fundamentally evil, our Lord tells us in one emphatic text, which is the key to the early testimony of Genesis and to many others, especially in St Paul · *that which is born of the flesh is flesh.* This word has stamped Christian phraseology . it takes the emblem of physical ruin, the flesh or mortal nature of man, to signify likewise his spiritual mortality, the flesh is the nature as tending not only to death but also to sin What dissolution of soul and body is, the dissolution of harmony between the flesh and spirit is But it more than hints at the derivation of the taint from natural descent . *that which is born* Thus also *we have borne the image of the earthy*, and not only in our corruptible bodies. This testimony of Jesus, who *knew what was in man*,—a most profound word,—is the supreme demonstration. It declares emphatically, what is nowhere else so plainly stated, that men are evil, because they are born evil, and pursue their way of life according to that evil beginning. The Master has Himself taken the responsibility of this deep utterance, to which, after He has spoken it, the guilty and sinful nature of man responds it reveals the thoughts of many hearts. It need not be said that He Himself is excepted who declares this fact of human generation When He testified, *Ye are from beneath, I am from above*, it may be thought that He was contrasting His spirit with that of His enemies; but when He added, *Ye are of this world, I am not of this world*, He proclaimed the universal difference between Himself and the children of men. The negative or apologetic appeal which follows, *Which of you convinceth me of sin?* is for His enemies; those who believe in Him know that it was uttered from the consciousness of the Holy One of God. the only Person in human history of whom it could be said, IN HIM IS NO SIN. And to them the highest confirmation of the doctrine of hereditary human depravity is the sinless conception of the Redeemer who *was manifested to take away our sins*

New Testament.
Matt. xv. 19
Our Lord. Matt. vii. 11

John iii. 6.

Gen v 3.
1 Cor. xv. 49.
John ii 25

John viii. 23

John viii. 46.

1 John iii. 5.

The
Apostles

(2.) St Paul, though he did not hear the Lord's words, faithfully draws out their meaning on this subject. He uses the expression Flesh in this connection more than any other writer, and in such a way as to establish the propagation of a corrupted nature. Lest this should be misunderstood, that flesh is said by

Rom. viii. 7 St. Paul to be *the carnal mind*, what in St. James is not the Jas i 14. φρόνημα, or thought, but, in a less dignified expression, the Rom. viii. 2 ἐπιθυμία, the *concupiscence* or *lust* of the flesh. He calls it *a law* Rom vii. 17, 23. *in my members*, and *the law of sin and death*, and *sin that dwelleth in me*, in the Me of the flesh. All these words, as following the Lord's, show that the bias to evil is congenital. It is in the heart, as the representative of man's being generally, and in his flesh, as the representative of his fallen estate, that sin dwelleth, not indeed as a revolution of the elements of human nature, but as a depravation of its tendency. The Apostle has given our theology its term, Indwelling Sin. The sin which reigns in the human race, transmitted from father to son, dwells in every Rom. vii 18 individual. It is an inmate in the soul, and an inmate only: *in me, that is in my flesh*, in me as under an alien dominion, in me who may be delivered from it wholly. But it belongs to every man that cometh into the world as a descendant of Adam, and it is bound up in his nature until the full deliverance is wrought: we may, therefore, with his full consent, invert the Apostle's words, and write them, *in my flesh, that is, in me*. St. Paul's exposition of original depravity, as illustrated by his own example, is closely connected with his struggles as a convinced sinner to find his way to the Redeemer. If we want the naked Rom. vii 7 strength of his doctrine, we find it in other words, *the carnal mind is enmity against God*, τὸ φρόνημα τῆς σαρκὸς ἔχθρα εἰς Θεόν, the terse epigrammatic force of which is matched by what precedes, τό γὰρ φρόνημα τῆς σαρκὸς θάνατος, *for that carnal mind is death*.

Guilt and Bias united.

3. It is to be observed that the Scripture never disjoins the condemnation from the depravity: the one is always implied in the other, while both are generally connected with the great salvation. It is impossible to conceive the two former apart from each other; though the precision of Scriptural language suggests rather that those who are born with a sinful bias are therefore

condemned than that being condemned they are necessarily
depraved. There is one passage that strikingly illustrates this.
The Apostle speaks of the Ephesian converts as having been under
the sway of the flesh, in the full sense as given above, and thus
showing that they were *by nature the children of wrath* The depra- Eph. ii 3
vity and condemnation of the natural estate are here once brought
together it is the solitary instance in which man's nature is said
to be under wrath , but the wrath is upon those who lived after
that nature rather than upon the nature itself; and both are
brought into close connection with Christ, the light of whose
coming redemption already shineth, though the darkness is not
yet wholly past

ORIGINAL SIN IN RELATION TO THE SECOND ADAM.

In Rela-
tion to
Second
Adam

The teaching of the later Scripture is summed up and
confirmed by St. Paul, to the effect that Jesus Christ, the
Second Adam, was given to the race of mankind, as the
Fountain of an Original Righteousness that avails to efface
and more than efface the effects of Original Sin in the
case of all those who should be His spiritual seed. Hence
this primitive Gift was an objective provision for all the
descendants of the first sinner, the benefits of which were
to be applied to those whose faith should embrace the
Saviour. But it is important to remember that it took
the form of an original Free Gift to the entire race, before
transgression began, and that it has in many respects
affected the character of Original Sin . suspending the full
strength of its condemnation, and in some degree counter-
acting its depravity.

I When St. Paul calls Adam the *figure of Him that was to come*, The Two
τύπος τοῦ μέλλοντος, the word has its full significance. The type Adams.
must precede the antitype in historical fact, but the antitype Rom v.
must precede the type in the Divine purpose : hence the Second 14
Adam might be called the First ; and the sin of Adam cannot

be disjoined from the righteous obedience of the Deliverer The
virtue of the Atonement began when the evil of sin began. The
Gospel was first preached when sin was first condemned preached
to the first offenders through the sentence passed upon Satan, the
instrumental cause of human sin, thus meeting sin in its very
origin While connecting it with Eve, its second original, the
Apostle omits the Serpent, omits Eve herself, and makes Adam
the fountain of sin to mankind, that he may draw the parallel
between the first and the Second heads of the human race. He
shows that, at all points and in all respects, the *grace* of God, and
the *gift by grace, which is by One Man, Jesus Christ*—the χάρις and
the δωρεά—are more abundant than the effects of the Fall The
provision of redemption from the disobedience meets it as sin
and in its consequence as death. All human life and destiny is
bound up with the relations of these two . the First and the Last
Adam.

Rom. v.
15.

II But the gift of righteousness to the race before the succession of its history began was of the nature of a provision to
counteract the effects of sin, when original sin should become
actual It did not at once abolish the effects of the Fall in the
first pair, whose original sin was also in their case actual transgression , it did not place them in a new probation, nor did it
preclude the possibility of a future race of sinners. The great
Atonement had now become necessary as necessary to these
parents of the race as it was after they had spread into countless
multitudes. The Redeemer was already the Gift of God to man ;
but He was still ὁ μέλλων, *the Coming One,* as St. Paul once only
calls Him in relation to this very fact: making the first sinner
the first type of the Saviour from sin The Atonement does not
put away sin in the sovereignty of arbitrary grace, but as the virtue
of grace pardoning and healing all who believe. It began at once
to build the house of a new humanity—a spiritual seed of the
Second Adam—the first Adam being himself the first living stone
of the new temple. And with reference to the life bestowed on
this new race St. Paul strains language to show how much it
superabounds, how much it surpasses the effect of the Fall. It
might have been replied by the objector that the virtue of the
gift fell short of the infliction of the first sentence , inasmuch as

The Free
Gift

Rom. v
14.

Heb ix.
26.

the sin sent forth death with absolute and unconditional effect upon all, while the grace reigns only in those who seek it and find it. But St Paul, always quick to catch the tones of objection, whether of the *vain man* or otherwise, does not think fit to notice this. He sees in the fulness of his theology only the fact of a new and gracious probation in which superabundant life is provided for the race , and speaks precisely as if the benefit was accepted by all who needed it   Not that he forgets the distinction between the provision and the application of it.   His precise use of the terms εἰς πάντας and οἱ πολλοί shows that he kept that in view. While he says that *many were made sinners*, meaning all men, he changes the tense when he adds *shall many be made righteous*, not meaning all   But in the verse preceding there is no such difference · *as by the offence of one judgment came upon all men to condemnation , and even so by the righteousness of One the free gift came upon all men unto justification of life.* It is true that our translation clothes the bones of the naked original here ; but the naked original still more strongly stamps the antithesis · *as by one offence, unto all men, to condemnation , even so, by One righteousness, unto all men, unto justification of life.* Rom. v 19.

Ver. 18.

III. Hence it follows of necessity that the benefit of the Atonement provided before *the foundation of the world* was a free gift to the coming race of mankind   That gift was the restoration of the Holy Spirit   not indeed as the indwelling Spirit of regeneration, but as the Spirit of enlightenment, striving, and conviction.   Man did not set out on his way of sorrow without this preparatory Comforter   This was as it were the χάρισμα πνευματικόν, the Spiritual Gift, which was freely bestowed on mankind before sin, strictly speaking, began its history, before the original sin of Adam had become original sin in his posterity ; which has therefore controlled and lightened the curse upon sin through all successive ages and generations.   That *blessing of Abraham* bestowed on the Gentiles through faith was the *blessing of Adam* also, bestowed as yet without faith   And as the Spirit has been from the beginning the *Spirit of Christ*, He is the true *Light which lighteth every man that cometh into the world.* When it was predicted that Christ should be for *salvation unto the end of the earth*, the prediction, like many others, was a step in the revelation of *the mystery which* The Spirit restored 1 Peter i 20.

Gal. iii 14 1 Peter i 11. John i. 9. Isa xlix. 6. Rom xvi 25

was kept secret since the world began   The *glory of His people*, the
new and sanctified race, is and has ever been *a light to lighten the
Gentiles*   There was an earnest or pledge of the Coming Spirit
given to the world as certainly as an earnest of the Incarnate Son
was given   But we have to do specifically with the effect of this
gift on the innate evil of our race. As it will finally for the
saved superabound, abolishing the principle of sin as well as all
innumerable transgressions, so from the beginning it restrained,
controlled, and mitigated that evil, whether in the mind of God,
or in the heart of man, or in the course of history.   Without this
there is no consistent exhibition of Original Sin.

IV The doctrine in the light of redemption receives certain
important modifications   This may be best shown by pointing out
a few apparent contradictions which it reconciles and explains
these being referred to the two heads of condemnation and
depravity and to the general relation of human nature to its
penalty of evil

1. The nature is condemned, and yet it is universally redeemed.

(1) However difficult it may be, we must receive the fact of a
human nature, abstracted from the persons who inherit it, lost or
marred in Adam and found or retrieved in Christ   It is said of
our Lord that He came, not only *in the likeness of men*, but also *in
the likeness of sinful flesh.* This impressively connects the Incarnate One with our fallen humanity, not as partaking of its sin—
for He was *God manifest in the flesh*—but as assuming our nature,
without its sin and with its infirmity   Now, that fact assures us
of the arrest of the effects of the Fall   In order that He might
take our nature, and be *made like unto His brethren*, the nature
common to Him and us must be saved from utter revolution.   It
may be said therefore that the first effect of the redeeming intervention was to preserve the nature of man from sinking below the
possibility of redemption: indeed rather that intervention was itself
its preservation   Hence, not only was the natural image of God
retained . the eternal sense of right and wrong and good and evil
was not suffered to be effaced, and thus the elements of the moral
image also were shielded from absolute violation.   It is impossible
to define what the difference was between the ruin of angelic intelligences and the fall of human nature · suffice that that difference

Luke ii.
32.

Modifica-
tions.

The
Race Re-
deemed

The Free
Gift in
Human
Nature
Phil ii. 7
Rom. viii.
3

1 Tim iii.
16.

Heb ii.
17.

is to us an infinite one ; our life is in it   The Fall was the utter ruin of nothing in our humanity ; only the depravation of every faculty.   The human mind retains the principles of truth , the heart the capacity of holy affections , the will its freedom, not yet the freedom of necessary evil.   All this we owe to the Second Adam.   It is said, indeed, that He came only in the likeness of men ; but He could not have come even in their likeness, if men had lost every trace of good.   He could not have even tabernacled in our nature, if it had been in the worst possible sense corrupted and doomed to destruction.

(2.) The condemnation resting upon the race as such is removed by the virtue of the one oblation beginning with the beginning of sin   The nature of man *received the Atonement* once for all ; God in Christ is reconciled to the race of Adam ; and no child of mankind is condemned eternally for the original offence, that is, for the fact of his being born into a condemned lineage.   Of this immunity baptism, conferred upon all who enter the race, is the sign and the seal   Personality, virtual in all who are born, does not actually begin until the will consciously assumes its responsibility.   And for individual personal guilt forgiveness is provided, which ratifies the pardon of the one original transgression and *superabounds for the many offences.* Hence, though we do not assume a second personal fall in the case of each individual reaching the crisis of responsibility, we must believe that original sin as condemnation in the fullest sense, and as an absolute doom, never passed beyond Adam and the unindividualised nature of man   It was arrested in Christ as it regards every individual, and changed into a conditional sentence   As it is the penalty of physical death it is in one sense without mitigation   *in Adam all die.* But in another sense the penalty is lightened, relieved, and abolished , for *in Christ shall all be made alive*

2   And as certainly as the Free Gift qualifies the condemnation of original sin, so certainly it mitigates the depravity inherited by man   That depravity is universally admitted to be twofold : the absence of original righteousness and the bias to all evil But these are one in the withdrawal of the Holy Ghost, the original bond of the soul's union with God.   Now the Spirit was as surely given back to the race as the Atonement was given to

Condemnation.

Rom v. . 11.

Rom. v. 19.

1 Cor. xv. 22.

The Free Gift and Depravity

it : given, that is, like the Atonement, as a provisional discipline of preparation for the fuller grace of redemption.

Remembrancer
(1) The Spirit's universal influence qualifies original sin as He is in every responsible soul a remembrancer of a forfeited estate, the prompter to feel after God and regain that communion which all history proves to be an inextinguishable yearning of mankind. He suffers not the spirit of man to forget its great loss. It is through this preliminary universal influence that guilt is naturally in man ashamed of its deformity. If the descendants of Adam and Eve inherit their nature despoiled of righteousness, they
Gen. iii 7.
inherit the sentiment also by which *they knew that they were naked ;* though this part of the inheritance comes from the original grace that the first offenders could not transmit. Shame, and the sense of despoilment and loss, are united with fear in the sacred phenomena of conscience, which must be essentially bound up with the doctrine of original sin

Prompter.
(2) But conscience suggests the thought, at least in man, of recovery, and the same Spirit who moves towards God in conscience, through fear and hope, universally touches the secret springs of the will. Original sin is utter powerlessness to good . it is in itself a hard and absolute captivity. But it is not left to itself When the Apostle says that the Gentiles have the law *written in their hearts,* and in conscience measure their conduct by
Rom. ii
14 15.
that standard, and may do *by nature the things contained in the law,* he teaches us plainly that in the inmost recesses of nature there is the secret mystery of grace which, if not resisted and quenched, prompts the soul to feel after God, and gives it those secret, inexplicable beginnings of the movement towards good which fuller grace lays hold on In fact, the very capacity of salvation proves that the inborn sinfulness of man has been in some degree restrained, that its tendency to absolute evil has been checked, and that natural ability and moral ability—to use the language of controversy—are one through the mysterious operation of a grace behind all human evil.

Original Sin, and the Covenant of Grace
3. Hence, in conclusion, the great antitheses of this doctrine are reconciled in the statement, carefully guarded, that original sin is the sin of Adam's descendants as under a covenant of grace. What it would otherwise have been we can never know · there

would then have existed no federal union of mankind. The souls of Adam and Eve would have only added two more to the spirits of evil. As we know the doctrine and the fact, it is the harmony of truths in our being otherwise irreconcilable Human nature is lost, and yet we are still *the offspring of God.* The natural and moral image—essentially one in creation—has departed in its glory, and yet it is recognised as in some sense still existing Every man is born condemned, and yet he is bidden not to put from him life He is by nature able neither to think nor feel nor act aright, yet he is throughout Scripture appealed to as if his duty were simply matter of his will In short, original sin and original grace met in the mystery of mercy at the very gate of Paradise.

Acts xvii. 29.

THE DOCTRINE OF ORIGINAL SIN IN ITS GENERAL RELATIONS

Theological relations

These points being established, we may view the doctrine that results from the combination: in its aspect towards the moral government of God and the vindication of His attributes; as explaining the Providential government of the human race; as related to the several doctrines of the Christian Faith; in its bearing on the constituent elements of human nature; and, lastly, in its effect upon the doctrine of sin generally, and in its particular manifestations, as under the discipline of the Gospel.

I Holy Scripture only in an indirect manner refers to the objections that may be urged against the righteousness of the Divine procedure in relation to the fundamental principles involved in the doctrine of original sin

Theodicy.

1. St Paul's thoughts, before and after the express treatment of the subject, seem to hover over this awful question of the vindication of God. But, under the guidance of inspiration, he leaves it where we must leave it,—among the unsolvable mysteries of the Eternal Will No one, however, can fail to see that in the strict connection of the doctrine of universal sin with that of universal grace he finds rest to his own soul, and teaches us to

St. Paul.

find rest also   Every express delineation of the universal evil of
mankind is, without exception, connected with redemption   This
is the only vindication of the Righteous God from the tremendous
charge brought against Him by the judgments of men   God's
own Theodicy, or vindication of Himself, is exhibited in the free
gift of the Second Adam.   Original sin sprang from the federal
constitution of the race   one in the unity of the unlimited many.
But the many are one in recovery as well as in sin.   As surely
as sin and death passed through to the race, so surely from Christ
did grace pass through.

The Three
Imputa-
tions.

2. Other expedients for the reconciliation of the Divine economy
with human judgments are adopted even by those who accept a
doctrine of original sin   we may say. other methods of stating
St. Paul's vindication   There are those who hold the THREE
IMPUTATIONS which lie at the basis of human history—the imputation of Adam's sin to the whole world, the imputation of the
sin of man to the Holy Representative of mankind, and the
imputation to man of the benefit of His redemption—who nevertheless so held them as to increase the great difficulty instead of
lessening it   The several reckonings are made to flow from an
absolute sovereignty in God, giving no account of His matters.
Though the word has a judicial sound it involves an arbitrary
idea, and one which adds a superfluous harshness to our doctrine.
The imputations are not equal and uniform : while the sin of the
first Adam is imputed to all his posterity, the righteousness of
the Second Adam is imputed only to a predetermined fragment
of mankind. If it is said that the sins of those only were reckoned
to Christ who receive the benefit, that does not lighten the gloom
of the subject   The want of correspondence between the imputation in Original Sin and the imputation in Christian Righteousness lays a tremendous burden on the doctrine common to the

Ezekiel
xviii. 29.

two.   *Are not My ways equal?*   This is the Lord's vindication of Himself; and, as to the theology which beclouds His
justice, He says to it, *are not your ways unequal?*

The two
Coven-
ants.

3. It may be rejoined, that St. Paul himself adopts the very
method which we denounce, by making the federal covenant with
man in Christ the correlative of the federal covenant with man
in Adam   But he invariably asserts the universality of the benefit

of grace, so far as concerns the intention of God As to the why of this federal constitution, and the why of evil generally in the dark background, there is no solution given to man, because it is not possible to the creature. That mystery. like redemption itself, will in some sense be for ever hid in the Divine nature. It is, however, a mystery that is not lightened by rejecting the doctrine of original sin.

II. Thus is explained the economy of God's providential government of the nations. If the exhibition of original sin is cut off from the universal gift, there can be no intelligible account given of the *times of this ignorance* which *God winked at*   All heathenism, past and present, is on that theory inexplicable. The world has been ever groping after God · universal sinfulness must be reconciled with that fact Not blank atheism, but the superfluity of superstition has been the law · a polytheistic superstition to which the nations were given up, because they resisted God's inner light; unspeakable degradation, and the almost unlimited change from dishonour to dishonour, marked the history of the heathen world ; but only as the result of a rejection of influences that have striven with men. And light has been seen rising in the deepest darkness. Neither the Saviour's intercourse with Gentiles, nor the Apostles', permits the supposition of such a total and unrelieved corruption, ruin, and abandonment of human nature as some theories of original sin and the "massa perditionis" assume Tertullian's "anima naturaliter Christiana" may be set against this, as the opposite exaggeration : the truth lying in the middle. The absolute corruption of the roots of our nature is a Manichæan error, revived in Flacianism, but contradicted by the whole doctrine of original sin as taught in Scripture. Apart from Christ, and in hard theory, the ruin of man is complete. But man has never been in such a far country as not to hear the appeal of the Father. the *far country* is still the land of Emmanuel.

III. The connection between original sin ard the Christian system is fundamental and universal. Upon it is based the necessity, the possibility, the universality of the Atonement, by the obedience of the last Adam, who bore in His own Person the consequences of the sin which He never shared. From original sin He was free: for, though His human nature was *made of a*

Government of Nations.

Acts xvii 30.

Luke xv. 13.

Connection with Christian Doctrine.

Gal. iv. 4.

woman, made under the law, as bearing the consequences of human transgression, it was not begotten of man, but of the Holy Ghost Hence the same Divine necessity that exempted Him from the sin of our nature demands that none other be exempt, not even His mother after the flesh   The sinlessness of Jesus is secured by the miraculous conception, His impeccability by the hypostatic union ; hence His active and His passive righteousness are united in one, the former rendering the latter possible and sufficient   Regeneration also derives its double character from the doctrine of original sin : it is the new creation of life in the soul, while it is at the same time the renewal of the original image of God ; it is regeneration as the Divine commencement of a new life, renewal as the resulting process   But, before this, apart from this, and yet concurrently with it, Justification meets original sin as the reversal of its condemnation with the guilt of all that flows from it at the bar of God   And Ethical Sanctification in its beginning, process, and final issues, is the full eradication of the sin itself, which, reigning in the unregenerate, coexisting with the new life in the regenerate, is abolished in the wholly sanctified

Human Nature
IV. It is expedient at this point to glance briefly at the constitution of man's nature as it is now found . of that nature namely, which alone we know as human.   A few leading terms give us the general character of the humanity that sin has transmitted unimpaired as human nature, but entirely corrupt in its unassisted development as fallen and sinful nature

Jas. iii. 7.
1 The term Human Nature is not used in this relation in Scripture   St. James alone speaks of ἡ φύσις ἡ ἀνθρωπίνη, translated *Mankind*   The word Nature signifies the condition or law of preappointed development, and thence the essential character and constitution with which every created thing comes into existence. It may therefore be applied to man in two senses, both faithful to the original meaning of the word   either to the constituent elements of his being, as differencing him from every other, or to the moral development of that being as growth from within, and apart from external influence   As to the latter, every individual of mankind is born with a nature which, without external influence upon it, is morally degraded and corrupt   The bias to evil—that is, to forget God, to serve the creature and to live for

self—is innate and congenital; and this makes it the nature of man, as being inherent and not accidental But, in the former sense of the term, sin is an accident of humanity · it came from without; it is not "das Gewordene" but "das Gemachte." It is not in harmony with the original constitution of man conscience, and the law written in the heart or reason which is its standard, being witness. The distinction is always remembered in Scripture

2. The disturbance in the very essence of human nature may be regarded as affecting the entire personality of man as a spirit acting in a body He is born with a nature which is—apart both from the external Evil One and from the external renewing power of the New Creation—under the bondage of sin. That bondage may be regarded with reference to the lower nature that enslaves the higher, and to the higher nature that is enslaved

(1.) Fallen human nature is Flesh or σάρξ · the whole being of man, body and soul, soul and spirit, separated from God, and subjected to the creature. The αὐτὸς ἐγώ of Self is *without God*, but only in the sense of being without Him as its God , and *in the world*, as its false sphere of life and enjoyment This is the slavery of sin to which man is naturally born, and to which he is naturally predetermined *For I know that in me, (that is in my flesh,) dwelleth no good thing* . this contains the truth concerning our fallen estate expressed by St Paul as its representative. It is slavery, or a yoke imposed *I am carnal, sold under sin ;* this *I* being the same person who can say, *with the mind, I myself serve the law of God,* and *what I hate, that do I.* It is, however, an innate or inborn or predetermined slavery . the Apostle calls himself σάρκινος, *carnal*, or fleshly, or fleshy, a strong word, which forbids the thought of his meaning the slavery of habit. If he wrote σαρκικός, this term, as the antithesis of πνευματικός, denoting an inherent characteristic of the law, would also point to an inherent quality of fallen nature. Again he refers to the *sin that dwelleth in me* not merely the sin that has gained an ascendency from without. And all this is confirmed by the strong words : *for I delight in the law of God after the inward man · but I see another law in my members, warring against the law of my mind, and bringing me into captivity to the law of sin which is in my members* Such is the meaning of the flesh as the designation of depraved humanity

Bondage

Of the Flesh.

Eph. ii 12.

Rom vii. 18.

Rom vii. 14
Rom. vii. 25
Rom. vii. 16.

Rom vii. 14.

Rom vii. 17.

Rom vii. 22, 23.

VOL. II.   F

enslaved to sense. Another use of the term, signifying human nature as mortal and frail, underlies the former, but this use is not directly connected with sin. In this latter sense *Jesus Christ is come in the flesh;* as to the former, He was sent only *in the likeness of sinful flesh.*

1 John iv. 3.
Rom. viii. 3.

(2.) This slavery, however, has its more spiritual aspect Starting from the same idea of the one personality in man, we may view the effect of original sin upon the αὐτὸς ἐγώ in its higher principle, distinct from the flesh, though not apart from it. The one spiritual agent in man, operating through the three elements of his nature, body, soul, and spirit, and the three functions of his rational soul, the mind, the affections, and the will, is fettered and impotent to good Hence its fallen dignity evermore utters the cry, ταλαίπωρος ἐγὼ ἄνθρωπος *O wretched man that I am!* The I of this wretched man is the personal representative of mankind, in whom original sin—*sin that dwelleth in me*—has been brought by the application of law from a latent state into activity. *In me* is qualified in two ways *that is, in my flesh,* and *with the mind I myself.* Therefore the one personality has a double character *the inward man of the mind,* to which *to will is present;* and *the flesh,* or *the body of sin,* in which *how to perform that which is good I find not* But the one person, to whom these opposite elements belong —an inner man, a reason, a will to good, a carnal bias, an outer man, a slavery to evil—is behind all these, behind even the inner man. And in him, in the inmost secret of his nature, is the original vice which gives birth to these contradictions. The Apostle adds three views of his own state with regard to this inherent sin, or, in other words, three views of that sin in regard to him. First, without the law he *was alive,* and *sin was dead.* whatever difficulty there may be in explaining this of St Paul, it precisely describes the sin that lies virtually latent in every human spirit, though abounding in *dead works,* until the consciousness of sinfulness is roused by the pressure of Divine law on the conscience. Secondly, the latent sin *revived,* or sprang into life, and he *died,* both under its depravity and its condemnation: *sin wrought in me all manner of concupiscence* the original evil in him put forth all its varieties of form, and overwhelmed him with the proofs of its despotism. The indwelling sin which the law revealed reduced

Of the Spirit.

Rom. vii. 24.
Rom. vii. 17.
Rom. vii. 18.
Rom. vii. 25.
Rom. vii. 22,25,18.

Rom. vii. 8, 9.

Heb. vi 1.

Rom vii. 8.

him to such impotence as could be defined only by death. the slavery of the natural man could not be more impressively exhibited   Thirdly, there is the state of deliverance *from the law of sin and death* in regeneration   One important fact runs through the whole description   the absolute bondage of the nobler faculty, here called the mind, to the flesh, rendering the will powerless to perform its ineffectual desire. Rom. viii. 2

(3) In this picture of the original corruption of human nature there are some features which must be intently regarded   they will be only mentioned in passing now, as their fuller consideration belongs to the economy of grace and the plan of salvation It teaches most distinctly the freedom of the will, and at the same time the inability of man to do what is good.   The harmony of these seeming opposites is most manifest. the faculty of willing is untouched in any case, and the influence of conscience prompts it to will the right, but this is bound up with a miserable impotence to good, and results in both a natural and a moral inability to do what the law of God requires.   It shows most impressively that man, in his natural state, or in the flesh, must be under the Divine displeasure as the voluntary agent of the sin that seems nevertheless a law in the members only.   Here there is a paradox in the Apostle's words   *Now if I do that I would not, it is no more I that do it, but sin that dwelleth in me* · this is the outcry and protest of the soul against its slavery, but it is slavery still, bringing the ME into captivity to the law of sin, and into a captivity to evil with which a sense of guilt is inseparably connected.   It shows that the corruption of the nature is consistent with the presence of an unextinguished sense of right, and even desire for it, which the Good Spirit through the law excites.   St. Paul may be said to be describing not a state of nature, but a state of conviction produced by the Holy Ghost   This is certainly true, though the Apostle does not make the distinction.   But it must be remembered that the *inward man* and the *law of my mind* are expressions which do not mean anything increated by Divine influence through the law   The Holy Spirit speaks to a dead or sleeping man within the sinner, and revives a law that may have been long silent, obsolete, and in this sense dead Bondage of the Will Rom. vii. 20.

3   Against this gentler interpretation arise two classes of Objections.

F 2

objectors. First, there are those who make original sin the absolute destruction of the image of God and of the capacity of good in man of these much has been already said, and it will hereafter be shown, when we come to the Gospel of grace, how inconsistent this view is with the universal benefit of redemption. Secondly, there are those who interpret the primitive Fall to have been the loss of the Spirit as an essential element of human nature, given sacramentally back through the incarnation of Christ applied these also must hereafter be referred to. Finally, in defence of our position generally, it may be said that the misery of the *wretched man*, bound to the body of death, is only aggravated by the fact that there is a better nature beneath the worse This does not mitigate original sin as misery, impotence, and the source of condemnation, but it makes the exhibition of it consistent with the universality of redeeming grace.

Development of Sin.

V. It remains now to trace the connection of this doctrine with the history and development of sin generally. Original sin cannot be distinguished from its personal and actual manifestation It is the source of all the varieties of sin that are known in experience and described in Scripture that other fountain originally opened for sin and uncleanness, the streams of which in human life are infinitely diversified

Habitual and Actual. 2 Cor. vii. 1. Gal. v. 19.

1. The sin of our nature, indwelling in the soul, is its HABITUAL state, as opposed to ACTUAL transgressions The former is sinfulness, the latter more properly sin. Hence there is a secret *filthiness of the flesh and spirit*, as distinguished from *the works of the flesh* which are *manifest* The habitual or original principle of evil may remain after its works have ceased, waiting for the act of grace which shall entirely extinguish it

Actual. Inward and Outward.

2 Actual transgressions may be variously summarised. (1.) They may be offences of the heart's desire and imagination, of the words and of the acts, or, since the words are at once expressions of the thought and themselves acts, we may say sins of the thought and of the deed (2) They may be viewed in relation to the Divine law, and be divided into offences against God, against our neighbour, and against ourselves. These three are really one, since there is no sin but against God, but the Decalogue. and the general strain of Scripture, suggest the distinction.

(3.) Estimating them by the temptation that leads to the act, we have the division of selfishness, carnality, and worldliness the first, however, according to St. James, being the root of all *every man Jas. i. 14. is tempted when he is drawn away of his own lust.* Every act of sin is the expression of the heart's consent to some solicitation, but the solicitation may appeal directly to the internal affection, or come through the medium of the eye which desires to have, or tempt the spirit alienated from God and absorbed in its own pride. Hence St. John's definition of the *lust of the flesh, and the* 1 John ii. *lust of the eyes, and the pride of life.* It is impossible to distinguish with certainty between the transgressions to which Satan directly tempts, and those to which inbred sin alone excites. Great spiritual skill, however, may be attained in this by those who, in the spirit of St. Paul's words studying the Tempter, *are not ignorant of his* 2 Cor ii. *devices,* on the one hand, and, on the other, remember his exhorta- 11. tion *prove your own selves* 2 Cor xiii. 5.

3 As it respects measures of guilt, there are two views which Degrees. the Scriptures harmonise He who breaks any commandment is *guilty of all;* and the distinction between MORTAL and VENIAL is Jas. ii. 10. essentially unfounded. Yet differences are marked, according as the will, the final principle of all transgression, enters into the act of the soul (1) Not only are there sins of OMISSION and Ps xix COMMISSION, but there are sins VOLUNTARY and wilful, and sins 12, 13 INVOLUNTARY, the result of ignorance and infirmity. The supreme Judge reveals Himself as taking those differences into account Hence there is an evangelical doctrine of mortal and venial offence All sin is mortal, as the wages of sin is death, all sins are venial, inasmuch as Christ died for the expiation of all (2.) But thrice the Scripture declares that there is the possibility of deadly and unpardonable sin in this world. Our Lord speaks of such a sin AGAINST THE HOLY GHOST, and that in three Evangelists. Matt. xii. the Epistle to the Hebrews adds another, and St. John gives his 31. final testimony in his First Epistle. In the Gospels, it is the Luke xii 10. state of the heart hardened against Divine grace, *blasphemy against* Mark iii. *the Holy Ghost,* and therefore of necessity hopeless : *in this world* 29. it refuses forgiveness, and in the *world to come* its eternal condemnation follows. In the Epistle to the Hebrews, it is the sin against the Atonement, the absolute rejection of which by

Heb. vi. 6. equal necessity shuts out all hope, *seeing they crucify to themselves the Son of God afresh.* In St John's words this last sin is simply against God who provided the rejected Atonement, and sent the despised Spirit : it is a sin for which intercession may be vain ·

1 John v. 16. *I do not say that he shall pray for it* (3) The stages by which actual and wilful transgression reaches this unpardonable height may be profitably marked. There is a condition in which the soul thwarts the influence of Divine grace, referred to throughout the Scripture as being constantly in opposition to the Spirit *ye do*

Acts vii. 51. *always resist the Holy Ghost.* This is perhaps the most universal characteristic of active sin, as the monitions of the Supreme Convincer are bound up with all the activities of conscience and the Word of God. Successful opposition to His influence produces two opposite effects, conspiring however to one result. The soul's sensibility declines, and that state follows which is described in Scripture as the sleep of indifference or carnal security : having

1 Tim. iv. 2. their *conscience seared with a hot iron,* entangled in *the snare of the*

2 Tim. ii. 26 *devil,* and *taken captive by him at his will,* and willing and able to *turn away their ears from the truth* St. Paul shows that this con-

2 Tim iv. 4. dition is consistent with a pretence to religion *speaking lies in*

1 Tim iv. 2. *hypocrisy.* The Saviour's denunciations of the hypocrites for whom His sternest woes were reserved, teach us what a fearful connection there may be between utter insensibility to Divine grace and devotion to the semblance of godliness. But the obverse of this self-engendered deadness to the Spirit's influence is the direct hardening of the soul through the judicial withdrawal of that influence Upon this follows the secret of utter antagonism to good . that decisive reprobation which overtakes those who in

1 Tim. v. 15. a special sense have *turned aside after Satan,* and learned like him to call evil good. But this specific sin against the Spirit can have been committed by none who have grace enough to dread its commission, or who have the slightest true desire of good

In the regenerate 4. Lastly, moral evil in the renewed soul has a distinct character. Here again we have a reconciliation of opposites. On the one hand, there is no sin in the regenerate spirit · *whosoever is born of*

1 John v. 18 ; iii 9. *God sinneth not* The evil of his nature still remaining is not reckoned to him, and he *keepeth himself* from actual transgression *that wicked one toucheth him not.* On the other hand, the new

spiritual life only makes his indwelling corruption more intolerable. The sanctified mind knows iniquity, through the revelation of the law of grace, as the unsanctified cannot know it.   Thus original sin is in reality perceived in its utter vileness only by those who are not condemned for it, and who, with all their hearts, are seeking its destruction   Here comes in the distinction between defects of infirmity or secret faults which do not exclude from grace, not having in them the true nature of sin, and offences committed in spite of His remonstrances which grieve the Holy Spirit, and if persisted in cause Him though slowly to take His departure   It is the sure characteristic of regeneration that it is impatient of indwelling impurity.   *He that is joined unto the Lord is one Spirit*. his deep desire, the strongest sentiment of his new nature, is to be delivered from that which cannot be common to himself and his Lord.   The penitent seeking his first pardon sets his expectation on *the Lamb of God which beareth the sin of the world*.   But the renewed and forgiven believer keeps his eye fixed on the perfect holiness of his Saviour.   The children of God know *that He was manifested to take away our sins,* and not only to bear away our guilt   They read the words that follow as containing the Divine encouragement of the ambition of faith · IN HIM IS NO SIN   He alone was and is without the original offence ; and by His grace we may come to the high experience that *as He is so are we in this world*   It is of this new commandment that the Apostle of perfected love says, or may be understood to say · ὃ ἐστιν ἀληθὲς ἐν Ἀυτῷ καὶ ἐν ὑμῖν.

1 Cor. vi. 17.

John i. 29.

1 John iii 5

1 John iv. 17.

1 John ii 8.

HISTORICAL.

The doctrine of Sin, especially of Original Sin, occupies a large space in historical theology, inasmuch as it touches at some points almost every other branch of the Christian system. There is, strictly speaking, no development of dogma : only the exhibition of a successive series of collisions between the Scriptural statements and the current opinions of the Church. A few points may be noted in their chronological order.

I. It may be said, at the outset, that the fundamentals of our doctrine have been most firmly held by mankind universally. This is a point of great importance, connecting the most profound revelation of Scripture with the theology of nature

1. The brief reference already made to the Theories of Evil has shown that Pantheism and Dualism have successively ruled ancient and modern thought on the subject   But it cannot have escaped notice that neither of these theories gave a good account of the unlimited influence of sin in the human race. Indeed neither of them could confront the question, inasmuch as the fundamental principles of both were opposed to an absolutely universal power of the evil principle.   Not attempting to define sin, and with a very vague idea of its true nature, the systems of ancient mythology — Egyptian, Phœnician, Vedic, Hellenic—all accepted a certain composite of light and darkness, good and evil, which made up to their imaginations the sum of things in Nature.   Forces of evil equally with forces of good were acknowledged and worshipped ; and the very same names, as in the case of the DÆVAS, came to be applied to both.

2. Meanwhile, it cannot be doubted that there was a gradual preparation in the human mind for the final teaching of the Word of God.   While the Eastern systems of thought shaped more and more distinctly, in Persia the idea of one Personal Righteousness, and in Buddhism the essential evil of existence as self-separated

from God, Hellenic thought, expressed in its drama especially, developed the conception of a stern and awful Nemesis, the Vindicator of moral order. Falling immeasurably below the ethical grandeur of the Bible, the tragedians and philosophers of Greece, and the historians of both Greece and Rome, abound in presentiments of the truth. As to the inherent sinfulness of the race, in particular, the following words are forcible. A line of Sophocles says : Ἀνθρώποις γὰρ τοῖς πᾶσι κοινόν ἐστι τοὐξαμαρτάνειν. As to the origin of this universal sin Thucydides makes the vigorous remark : πεφύκασι ἅπαντες καὶ ἰδίᾳ καὶ δημοσίᾳ, ἁμαρτάνειν. And one more striking still is found in a fragment of Euripides ἔμφυτος πᾶσιν ἀνθρώποις κάκη, rendered by Horace, Nam vitiis nemo sine nascitur. So Tacitus. Vitia erunt donec homines. But though the sense of sin is variously and unequally expressed in various nations and various literatures, in none is the testimony to its universality wanting. While so many traditions, however, point to a past age of uprightness and of man's declension, none contain hints of the great revelation of the Bible, that the whole race of mankind had its probation and fall in one progenitor.

Antig. 1005

Hist III. 45. 3.

Hist. IV. 47

II. The Ancient Church, both under the guidance of inspiration and in the Rabbinical age, has held the essentials of the doctrine of moral evil in itself, and of original sin in particular.

Jewish Church.

1. It has been seen that the Old-Testament Scriptures maintain one consistent and uniform teaching as to the nature of sin generally, and as to its universal power over mankind The history of the Flood gives its evidence both in clear testimony and in awful judgment The covenant rite of circumcision significantly declared the hereditary sinfulness of man. The entire system of the Levitical economy was based on this assumption : while its trespass-offerings had more specific reference to individual offences, its sin-offerings had general reference to the deeper root of universal sin. The Psalms and Prophets abound in testimonies to the same effect not only asserting the universality of past and present sin among men, but also asserting it with equal confidence concerning the unlimited future, One Being only excepted, the Righteous Servant of Jehovah Generally it may be said that on no one subject is the teaching of the ancient Scriptures at once more elevated above all extra-Biblical ideas, and more steadfast

Hebraism

and uniform in itself than on this. It proclaims that EVIL, or

Isa.xlv.7.
רָע, the permitted consequence of sin, is under the Divine disposal, and not independent of the Divine will *I form the light, and create darkness , I make peace, and create evil , I the Lord do all these things.* But the same evil, in respect to the SIN which causes it, is evermore traced to the wilful rebellion of the human

Gen. vi. 5.
will . *And God saw that the wickedness of man was great in the earth, and that every imagination of the thoughts of his heart was only evil* (רַע) *continually.* There is hardly here the usual development of Scriptural revelation   The progressive dispensations expand the doctrine into abundant details to meet the gradual development of the method of atonement , but the fundamental idea of SIN is unique in its hard simplicity throughout the Scriptures.

Rabbinical Judaism
2 But it is equally certain that the later Jewish doctrine exhibited the outlines of the truth, even in some respects more clearly stamped than in the ancient Scriptures themselves. Rabbinical authors make much use of the typical relation of Adam to Christ · Quemadmodum homo primus fuit primus in peccato, sic Messias erit ultimus ad auferendum peccatum penitus.

Ecclus. xvii. 16.
And Adamus postremus est Messias. The Book of Ecclesiasticus declares that *every man from his youth is given to evil ,* Philo abounds in mystical accounts of its origin and universal influence , and a long-descended ancient tradition is summed up by one of the Rabbinical commentators on Genesis The first man was the cause of death to all his descendants

Early Christian Church.
III The early Christian Church exhibits the truth as it has been deduced from Scripture, but with the germ of every subsequent error here and there appearing   Before the Pelagian heresy the Greek and Latin fathers generally held the Vitium Originis, as Tertullian first called it, but laid stress upon the co operation of the human will enlightened by teaching and grace. The Latins were still more decided as to both   For instance, Ambrose says . Omnes in primo homine peccavimus , and, Nulla species cujusquam virtutis occurrit, quæ vel sine dono Divinæ gratiæ vel sine consensu nostræ voluntatis habeatur. So Lactantius : Non necessitatis esse peccare, sed propositi ac voluntatis. With one consent they held the doctrine of Tertullian as to the image of God in

man, of which it is said that non tam extinguitur quam obumbratur. Origen broached the old notion of a pre-existent state and fall of the soul · this has been revived again and again, but adds to the difficulty which it seeks to remove

IV The PELAGIAN CONTROVERSY of the fifth century in most of its bearings and issues turned upon the doctrine of Original sin. Pelagius, and his followers Cælestius and Julian, taught that transgression can be regarded only as the independent act of the free will of the individual; that Adam was created mortal, his offence having hurt himself alone ; and that his descendants are born in precisely the same moral condition ; that the prevalence of sin in his descendants is the result of following his example : in eo quod omnes peccaverunt exemplo Adami , and by a longa consuetudo vitiorum it comes that vitia quodammodo vim habere naturæ   All the stress was laid upon the free self-determination of every man living to good or evil, the perfection of good being attainable by every independent individual through the grace of his nature and the law and the example of Christ St. Augustine, at the other extreme, taught that in Adamo omnes peccaverunt, omnes ille unus fuerunt · we all were that One, and SINNED IN HIM (by a mistranslation of ἐφ' ᾧ πάντες ἥμαρτον)   The corruption of nature — peccatum originis — beginning in Adam was concupiscentia, the ascendency of the flesh over the spirit , it introduced a certain necessity of sinning, the freedom of the will having no meaning save as opposed to external compulsion · and this, transmitted to his posterity, makes them sinners and guilty in themselves as well as in Adam.   SEMI-PELAGIANISM strove to mediate between these two extremes   It admitted original sin so far as concerns the weakening of the power to will and to do , limited the death of the Fall to physical death · regarded man's residual energies as sufficient to set him upon the beginnings of salvation, but the Divine grace as absolutely necessary to carry on and perfect it   The Augustinian doctrine gained the ascendency, and still reigns in all Predestinarian systems.   Pelagianism pure and simple has never held its ground, at least among those who have any faith in the Christian Scriptures.   Semi-pelagianism however has, on the whole, exerted the widest influence . it reappeared dogmatically in the Lutheran

[margin:] Pelagianism.

[margin:] Rom.v.12.

Synergism, and in the spirit at least of its teaching has pervaded all communions which have denied the dogma of individual pre-destination

Scholas-tic.

V The Mediæval controversies were mainly transitional. The Schoolmen spent all their subtilty upon the questions involved ; but they simply furnished the materials for future confessions. Among the new points which they raised are the following. The punishment of original sin was supposed by some to be the negative loss of the vision of God   the utmost that St Augustine, fairly interpreted, had in his day reached   But to the pœna damni, or loss, was added the pœna sensus, even in the case of children unbaptised   for strongly maintaining this Gregory of Ariminum was branded with the name of Child-tormentor. The law of the propagation of evil was also much contested. Peter Lombard advocated the theory known as CREATIONISM : the immaterial spirit infused into the begotten organism of the soul and body contracts defilement and becomes guilty.   Anselm and Aquinas asserted TRADUCIANISM · Persona erat Adam, natura homo ; fecit igitur persona peccatricem naturam   Adam's person corrupted the nature , and in his descendants the nature corrupts the person   In favour of the latter is the whole doctrine of origi-nal sin, and especially the incarnation of Christ, whose human nature was created and not transmitted to Him   Against the former is the danger of making God the author of human evil ; while it may be thought to be defended by the dignity of the

Heb.xii.9. rational soul, the name FATHER OF SPIRITS given to God, and the tendency of the opposite theory to Materialism.   The IMMACU-LATE CONCEPTION of the Virgin was early introduced into the question · it divided the Schoolmen, many of the best of whom recoiled from the thought that one member of the race should be made holy without the intervention of atonement , and was left among the "Pious Opinions" of the Church, until, in 1854, it was made an article of faith by Rome.   Freewill and its rela-tion to grace were largely discussed.   The distinction expressed in the terms "Meritum condigni et congrui" was invented in order to show the value set by God upon the workings of nature towards grace . they have a merit which it is congruous with the Divine justice to reward by further gifts, and this is a Meritum de congruo ; while, after his justification, the works of the Christian have a higher merit, a Meritum de condigno, earning eternal life. But the source of good in man since the Fall is the Divine Spirit, and all merit is excluded One of the authors of the distinction, Peter Lombard, left this noble sentence : Libertas a peccato et a miseria per gratiam est, libertas vero a necessitate per naturam. Ipsa gratia voluntatem prævenit præparando ut velit bonum, et præparatam adjuvat ut perficiat

VI. The dogma defined in the Council of Trent combines the Augustinian Realistic identification of Adam and the race with the semi-Pelagian negative idea of the effect of the Fall Adam, created in the image of God, with the endowment of freewill, and perfect harmony in the purely natural elements, had the gift of original righteousness added . "CONDITUS in puris naturalibus" he was then "in justitia et sanctitate CONSTITUTUS." Original righteousness was a supernatural added gift, and the loss of it threw the race back into its created condition of contrariety between flesh and spirit, without the superadded restraint. In baptism the guilt of the original offence which incurred the loss is taken away, and yet the concupiscence that sprang from transgression and leads to transgression remains untaken away, not having, however, itself the essential quality of evil : "this concupiscence, which the Apostle sometimes denominates sin, the Holy Synod declares the Catholic Church never understood to be called sin because it is really and truly sin in the regenerate, but because it is from sin and inclines to sin " Against this the Reformed Confessions all protested, asserting that concupiscence has in it the nature of sin For the rest, the Roman theory admits that the natural image has been clouded through the Fall : man's whole nature being wounded, and propagated as such These points were referred to when the First Estate of man was the subject, and we must again and again return to them. *[Tridentine]* *[Sess. v]*

VII. The Lutheran standards deny the Tridentine doctrine Under the influence of a dread of semi-Pelagianism as tending to the idea of merit in man, the formularies were constructed in the Augustinian spirit. Original sin is defect of original righteousness, and a depraved concupiscence in the higher faculties towards carnal things In the Smalkald Articles " the corruption of nature *[Lutheran Standards.]*

is so profound and dark as to be past human comprehension, but must be received as matter of revelation and faith " In the Formula of Concord two opposite tendencies are met and opposed. On the one hand, the Synergists, who insisted on a certain measure of co-operation in the human will, συνεργεῖν, were withstood by the affirmation that, while in natural things man may do good, in spiritual things his will is entirely bound ; on the other hand. the doctrine of Flacius, that original sin is a corruption of the substance of nature, the actual image of the devil, was opposed by the affirmation that sin is only an accident of the nature, the act and not the essence of the soul

The Reformed.

VIII Calvin and the Reformed Confessions make no distinction between the imputed guilt, and the inherent depravity of man's fallen estate   But much controversy arose afterwards as to the nature and order of the two imputations. The Reformed school of Saumur, represented by Placæus, held that " vitiositas præcedit imputationem ·" there is a MEDIATE or consequent imputation, following and dependent on individual corruption. But the other theory, IMMEDIATE or antecedent imputation, has predominated : this makes the sin of Adam, as the federal head of the race, the exclusive or prior ground of condemnation   The FEDERAL theology of the vicarious representation of mankind by Adam, in virtue of a covenant of nature or of works (fœdus operum, fœdus naturæ), is divided into two classes, according as it makes prominent the realistic identity of mankind with Adam, or otherwise : in the former case, there is a moral as well as legal imputation ; in the latter, the imputation is altogether forensic. But both separate too sharply the supposed covenant of works from the real covenant of grace in Christ. The more forensic and representative imputation has taken, in later years, the form of a forfeiture on the part of Adam of CHARTERED PRIVILEGES which, through his fault, all mankind have lost   this loss being original sin. But such speculations as these stand or fall with the general principle of a specific covenant with Adam as representing his posterity, a covenant of which the Scripture does not speak. There is but one Covenant, and of that Christ is the Mediator.

Arminian.

IX. The Arminian doctrine in its purest and best form avoided the error of the previous theories, retaining their truth. It held the Adamic unity of the race "in Adam all have sinned," and "all men are by nature children of wrath" But it maintained also "that the most gracious God has provided for all a remedy for that general evil which was derived to us from Adam, free and gratuitous in His beloved Son Jesus Christ, as it were a new and another Adam. So that the baneful error of those is plainly apparent who are accustomed to found upon that original sin the decree of absolute reprobation invented by themselves." This "evil" is "eternal death together with manifold miseries" "But there is no ground for the assertion that the sin of Adam was imputed to his posterity in the sense that God actually judged the posterity of Adam to be guilty of and chargeable with (reos) the same sin and crime that Adam had committed." These words of the Apology for the Remonstrant Confession are confirmed by those of Arminius "I do not deny that it is sin, but it is not actual sin. . . . We must distinguish between actual sin and that which is the cause of other sins, and which on that very account may be denominated sin" The Canons of the Synod of Dort (1618) gave the most concentrated Calvinistic contradiction to all these views. As to freewill and grace Limborch says . "Grace is not the solitary, yet is the primary cause of salvation; for the co-operation of freewill is due to grace as a primary cause, for, unless the freewill had been excited by prevenient grace, it would not be able to co-operate with grace" Accordingly, he and the other leaders of Arminianism asserted the universal diffusion of prevenient influences of the Spirit, the acceptance in every age of those who strive after natural uprightness, "honestati naturali operam dent"; and, above all, the free gift to the whole race in Christ, which is the foundation of their whole system

Apol. Remonst.

X. The Methodist teaching on this subject is sometimes set down without any qualification as Arminian; sometimes it is charged with being semi-Pelagian.

Metho-dist.

1. It differs from the Remonstrant doctrine, where that doctrine, in its protest against the decisions of the Synod of Dort, declined from the earlier teaching of Arminius. The later Remonstrants laid great stress on the physical impurity of our nature, denied that the corruption of that nature has in it the true characteristics of sin, and attributed too much to the "innate

Differ-ence

liberty of the human will," as able to co-opeiate of itself with
Divine law   Methodism accepts the Article of the English
Church · "Original sin standeth not in the following of Adam,
(as the Pelagians do vainly talk) , but it is the fault and corruption
of the nature of every man, that naturally is engendered of the
offspring of Adam ; whereby man is very far gone from Original
Righteousness [quam longissimè distet], and is of his own nature
inclined to evil, so that the flesh lusteth always contrary to
the Spirit ; and therefore in every person born into this world, it
deserveth God's wrath and damnation   And this infection of
nature doth remain, yea in them that are regenerated , whereby
the lust of the flesh, called in Greek Φρόνημα σαρκός, which some
do expound the wisdom, some sensuality, some the affection, some
the desire, of the flesh, is not subject to the law of God   And
although there is no condemnation for them that believe and are
baptised, yet the Apostle doth confess, that concupiscence and lust
hath of itself the nature of sin."   Hence it holds that whatever
power there is in the human will—in its ability as well as in its
choice—comes from the redemption of Christ.

Agree-
ment.

2 It holds, with the purest Arminianism, earlier or later, that
no ability remains in man to ietuin to God , and this avowal
concedes and vindicates the pith of original sin as internal.   The
natural man—whether his naturalness is described by the sin of his
flesh, carnal, as he is σαρκικός, oi the sin of his soul, sensual, as he
is ψύχικος—is without the power even to co-operate with Divine
influence.   The co-operation with grace is of grace.   Thus it keeps
itself for ever safe from Pelagianism and semi-Pelagianism

Peculi-
arity.

3 It has, however, more fully and consistently than the Remonstrant system connected the universality of grace with the
universality of redemption . knowing nothing of the Augustinian
COMMON GRACE.   A few extracts will make this plain

Wesley's
Original
Sin.

Mr. Wesley, whose treatise on Original Sin is one of the most
faithful and stern reflections of the Scriptural doctrine that our
language contains, dwells upon this universal gift in very many
passages of his writings.   For instance, in his sermon on the
Scripture way of Salvation · " So that the salvation which is here
spoken of might be intended to be the entire work of God, from
the first dawning of grace in the soul till it is consummated in

glory. If we take this in its utmost extent it will include all that is wrought in the soul by what is frequently termed natural conscience, but, more properly, preventing grace, all the drawings of the Father, the desires after God, which, if we yield to them, increase more and more, all that light wherewith the Son of God ' enlighteneth every one that cometh into the world,' showing every man 'to do justly, to love mercy, and to walk humbly with his God,' all the convictions which His Spirit, from time to time, works in every child of man, although, it is true, the generality of men stifle them as soon as possible, and after a while forget, or at least deny, that they ever had them at all" In another passage in the sermon on Working out our own Salvation : "For, allowing that all the souls of men are dead in sin by *nature*, this excuses none, seeing there is no man that is in a state of mere nature, there is no man, unless he has quenched the Spirit, that is wholly void of the grace of God. No man living is entirely destitute of what is vulgarly called *natural conscience.* But this is not natural it is more properly termed *preventing grace.* Every man has a greater or less measure of this, which waiteth not for the call of man" "That by the offence of one judgment came upon all men (all born into the world) to condemnation is an undoubted truth, and affects every infant, as well as every adult person. But it is equally true that by the righteousness of One the free gift came upon all men (all born into the world—infants and adults) unto justification." Finally : "I assert that there is a measure of freewill supernaturally restored to every man, together with that supernatural light" So Mr. Fletcher. "As Adam brought a general condemnation and a universal seed of death upon all infants, so Christ brings upon them a general justification and a universal seed of life." Mr. Watson, in his "Institutes," largely treats on this subject. The following are a few sentences from the close of his discussion.

Mr. Fletcher.

"But virtues grounded on principle, though an imperfect one, and, therefore, neither negative nor simulated, may also be found among the unregenerate, and have existed, doubtless, in all ages. These, however, are not from men but from God, whose Holy Spirit has been vouchsafed to the world, through the Atonement. This great truth has often been lost sight of in the controversy.

Richard Watson. Works, x 490.

Some Calvinists seem to acknowledge it substantially, under the name of ' common grace ;' others choose rather to refer all appearances of virtue to nature, and thus, by attempting to avoid the doctrine of the gift of the Spirit to all mankind, attribute to nature what is inconsistent with their opinion of its entire corruption. But there is, doubtless, to be sometimes found in men not yet regenerate in the Scriptural sense, in men not even decided in their choice, something of moral excellence, which cannot be referred to any of the causes above adduced, and of a much higher character than is to be attributed to a nature which, when left to itself, is totally destitute of spiritual life. Compunction for sin, strong desires to be freed from its tyranny, such a fear of God as preserves them from many evils, charity, kindness, good neighbourhood, general respect for goodness and good men, a lofty sense of honour and justice, and, indeed (as the very command issued to them to 'repent and believe the Gospel,' in order to their salvation, implies), a power of consideration, prayer, and turning to God, so as to commence that course which, persevered in, would lead on to forgiveness and regeneration. To say that 'all these are to be attributed to mere nature' is to surrender the argument of the semi-Pelagian, who contends that these are proofs that man is not wholly degenerate. . . . The Scriptural proof that the Spirit is given to 'the world' is obvious and decisive. We have seen that the curse of the law implied a denial of the Spirit ; the removal of that curse implies, therefore, the gift of the Spirit, and the benefit must be as large and extensive as the Atonement."

Consistency of this doctrine.

4. On the whole, it may be said that the doctrine, thus stated, is the only one that is in harmony with all the facts of the case : it omits nothing, softens nothing, evades nothing. This position may be further fortified by a comparison with some other leading systems which have been referred to.

Compared with Tridentine

(1.) With the Tridentine decisions it has many points of agreement, but more of difference. The teaching of Rome is not consistent with itself in its view of the actual state of man as affected by the Fall. It holds original sin, the corruption of human nature, and the imputation of Adam's offence as a condemnation of the race. The Roman Catechism affirms that we are oppressed by the vice

of our birth, "naturæ vitio premimur," and that the virus of sin pene-
trates to what is strongest in our souls, "rationem et voluntatem, quæ
maxime solidæ sunt animæ partes." Yet it more than hints that the
departure of Original Righteousness has simply thrown man back
into the position in which he was created, as if a natural antagonism
between flesh and spirit was the normal state of humanity in the
purpose of the Creator. The negative loss and the positive
strength of evil are not harmonised. Again, maintaining rightly
that the condemnation of the original offence is removed by
baptism — that is, more correctly, by the atoning efficacy of
which baptism is the seal—it further declares, as has been seen,
that concupiscence in the baptised, that is, the regenerate, is not
of the nature of sin : as if baptism could make that which is
essentially sinful cease to be such ; as if the perversion of the will,
which constitutes us formally sinners as soon as we feel and assent
to its operation, were not in itself sinful. The Council correctly
lays down that without the preventing grace of God men cannot
exhibit those graces which prepare for justification ; and that
they can co-operate with this preventing grace, can assent to or
reject it. So far well ; but the taint of semi-Pelagianism is seen
in the stress which Romanist divines lay on the negative character of original sin, and on the necessity that the absolute will
and consent of an intelligent agent should concur to constitute
sinfulness before God. Whether the formal teaching of the
Council asserted it or not, the current Romanist doctrine denies
that men are born into the world with anything subjective in them
of the strict nature of sin. The taint also appears in the merit
of congruity, as opposed to the subsequent merit of condignity,
the co-operator with Divine grace bringing the former to approve
him for justification. The doctrine we have established goes far
with the Romanist as to the non-imputation of the guilt of inbred
sin in the regenerate ; but altogether leaves it by asserting that
there is inherent and innate evil in every descendant of Adam,
that concupiscence, remaining in the believer, is offensive in the
sight of God, that it must as sin be abhorred and mourned over,
and as sin be put away by human discipline and Divine grace.

(2.) In virtue of this principle the true doctrine is opposed also
to every theory of sin which insists that it cannot be reckoned

Sin in the
Character.

G 2

such by a righteous God save where the will actively consents; and that none can be held responsible for any state of soul or action of life which is not the result of the posture of the will at the time.   There is an offending character behind the offending will. In St. John's definition of sin it is not only transgression, but want of conformity with the law.   Our Saviour speaks of the evil heart, and of the corrupt tree: and of men as being evil, even when giving good things to their children.   To teach that there is no such thing as a sinful state or condition or potentiality is semi-Pelagianism : an error which has deeply infected much modern theology in America and England.   Those who have been taught by the Scripture the depths of sin steadfastly refuse to admit this principle.   They believe that the race of mankind is ruled by a common generic will, which is averse from God; and that the application of the law only makes the discord manifest. The influence of the Spirit which appeals to the law written in the heart teaches every man who listens to His teaching that he is not only a transgressor of the specific commandment, but a transgressor in himself, and before he knows the law that he transgresses.

Compared with Calvinism.

(3.) In the light of this doctrine the harshest form of Augustinianism is condemned, while the principles of eternal truth which it contains are upheld.   That theory makes the soul of man passive as a stock or a stone, into which by the act of regeneration the principle of life is infused through a sovereign exertion of electing grace, and takes no account of the preliminaries of goodness which are wrought in man by the selfsame Spirit Who is afterwards the Spirit of regeneration.   The notion of "common grace" is a solution that the "common sense" of mankind will not accept.   One

Acts x. 15.

of the rebukes which Simon Peter received told him, *what God hath cleansed, that call not thou common.*   Though the manifestations of a better mind which human nature exhibits are not evidences of its thorough cleansing, they are tokens of a cleansing prepared for it.   While it is denied that they are good works, it is denied also that they are strictly speaking evil.   They are not fruits of the tree of life in man, yet they are not fruits of the corrupt tree as such.   But this subject, as well as the function of the human will in salvation, must be reserved : meanwhile, we must hold fast the truth of St. Bernard's aphorism : " Tolle liberum arbitrium, non erit quod salvatur. Tolle gratiam, non erit unde salvetur "

(4.) Finally, the Methodist teaching on this general subject derives its value from its strict conformity with the doctrine with which St. John's First Epistle closes the Scriptural testimony. In its third chapter we have the fullest and most exhaustive statement of the New Testament as to sin generally, its origin, its nature, its manifestations, and the process of its destruction The counterpart of St. Paul's fifth chapter to the Romans, it deals less with the human original of evil, but more with its entire destruction as the design of the manifestation of the Sinless One, and as accomplished in the perfectly regenerate   The purpose of redemption is *to take away our sins*, according to the good pleasure of the Eternal Love of the Father Who *sent His Son, the Propitiation for our sins ·* not *to be* or to become, but as already, the Propitiation from heaven. Also *for this purpose the Son of God was manifested, that He might destroy the works of the devil* . He came, not to relax but to fulfil all righteousness , the works of Satan He came to undo and destroy (*ἵνα λύσῃ*)   In St Paul's chapter the source of our evil is traced no higher than Adam, and the Fountain opened for our cleansing sends forth its streams parallel with those of the fountain of our defilement   In St John's chapter the source is traced still higher, to Satan the sinner from the beginning : and the Redeemer whom St Paul makes the Second Adam St. John makes the Antagonist of the Original Enemy of righteousness. The whole design of redemption is the abolition of sin as transgression of law the perfect vindication of law, whether by the judicial satisfaction of its claims or by the restoration of its authority. Neither of the Apostles speaks of the destruction of the works of Satan apart from their operation in man ; and neither speaks of any destruction of those works save as accomplished in believing mankind. But, omitting any reference to the vast residuum of Satanic works with which the Judgment will deal, both dwell with deep emphasis on the annihilation of sin in the regenerate St. John, however, is the more full and explicit   In his doctrine the design of the manifestation of the Son is the entire removal of iniquity from human nature in the present life , and upon this Methodist teaching fastens with strong tenacity. That design is to be

The End of Sin.

1 John iii 5
1 John iv 10.
1 John iii 8

wrought out in those who believe, through their conformity with the Saviour in Whom IS NO SIN   Every man in Christ is to be made *righteous, even as He is righteous,* to become pure *even as He is pure,* and, between his justification and his sanctification, the regenerate Christian *doth not commit sin, for His seed remaineth in him . and he cannot sin, because he is born of God.*   Thus, in the Divine court of law, and household, and temple, respectively, the dark history of sin in man has its end   And, despite every argument to the contrary, Methodism holds fast and proclaims this great hope.

XI   The Socinians, Modern Unitarians, and Rationalists generally revert to the old Pelagian theory, which is really not a doctrine of original sin, but a denial of it in every form   In rejecting the Scriptural teaching, however, they have no substitute to bring   They admit the facts of human depravity   They cannot deny that evil is universal, and that all the differences among men as its subjects and agents are only differences of degree.   They allow that the entire fabric of human legislation and government is based upon the postulate that universal man requires restraint ; that all men know and instinctively recognise each other as sinners , that the mortality of the race is not more confidently presupposed than its bias to evil; that education universally deals with children as having innate or inwrought principles of error , and that, in fact, a deviation from the perfect standard is hereditary in our nature   They can give no account of this that will bear a moment's consideration   The influence of example may explain much, but this of itself demands a reason for the facility with which example is followed.   In short, there is no doctrine of our most holy faith which so irresistibly and universally appeals for its confirmation to the common conscience and judgment of mankind.   It shines by its own light, though alas its light is as darkness.

Marginal notes:

1 John iii. 7, 3, 9.
1 John iii. 5

Rationalist.

THE MEDIATORIAL MINISTRY.

DEVELOPMENT OF THE DIVINE PURPOSE.

THE REDEMPTIONAL TRINITY.

THE PERSON OF THE MEDIATOR.

THE MEDIATORIAL WORK.

THE FINISHED ATONEMENT.

THE MEDIATORIAL MINISTRY.

PRELIMINARY.

THE most appropriate superscription of the department of Theology on which we now enter is THE MEDIATORIAL MINISTRY. This term defines the relation of our Saviour's Person to God and man, separated by human sin. as it is expressed in the word Mediatorial. It embraces also the whole compass of our Saviour's work on earth and in heaven: this is better described by the Lord's own word, Ministry, than by any other. A thorough survey of the subject includes, first, the historical development of the Divine eternal counsel of Redemption as exhibited in a series of dispensations or covenants of which Christ, whether unrevealed or revealed, is the sole Mediator. Secondly, it presents to us the full manifestation of the Mediatorial Trinity · the several functions and relations of the Three Persons in the incarnation and redeeming work. This leads, thirdly, to the Person of Christ as the Mediator, whose Divine personality continues in His assumption of human nature and gives its perfection to all that He does and suffers for mankind. Fourthly, what our Lord accomplished once for all, and is still accomplishing, must be viewed in its historical process through a succession of redeeming states and offices. Fifthly, we close with the study of the Finished Work of His objective mediatorial ministry as distinguished from the subjective application of it in the individual and in the Church through the Holy Ghost. In discussing these topics, the very fundamentals of the Gospel, we must adhere rigidly to the revelations of Scripture. But, in this as in other departments, and perhaps more than most others, it will be necessary as we proceed to study the ecclesiastical development side by side with the Scriptural.

THE DIVINE PURPOSE.

The
Divine
Purpose

We cannot approach the accomplished work of redemption save through the eternal counsel from which it sprang, and the successive dispensations which connected it with that eternal purpose. Before the world existed Christ was ordained to take human nature in order to its renewal; not therefore as a necessary incarnation for the perfecting of the idea of humanity apart from sin. The mystery of the Divine counsel has been gradually unfolded through a series of economics, which occupied the times of preparation for the Gospel. These may be viewed under two aspects. First, the whole world of mankind has been dealt with according to the terms of a covenant dating from the Fall, but not yet fully revealed : a covenant of grace given as a simple promise to our first parents, renewed to Noah, and once more ratified to Abraham, as each the representative of mankind. This may be called the economy of the Gentiles inasmuch as the world was undergoing a negative preliminary discipline for Christ, the Desire of the nations, and at the same time enjoying a certain measure of benefit from His mediation. Secondly, a series of positive dispensations or covenants were given supernaturally to a chosen people, in which the coming Redeemer was foreshadowed and prepared for : in the Mosaic covenant as the law with its expiations, and as prophecy with its Gospel promise. Both the law and the prophets of the Mosaic economy incorporated and carried on the older promise or decree of redemption until the fulness of time when Christ blended all into the unity of the new covenant.

THE ETERNAL DECREE.

Redemption is in the New Testament declared to have been a purpose of God in or from eternity. This design, having reference solely to the Saviour's work, and apart from its application by the Spirit, is regarded in Scripture as an absolute decree of man's salvation virtually accomplished from the beginning . a mystery reserved for gradual revelation, but a reality underlying all human history.

1 By many various terms is the original design of man's salvation set forth. Love is in the van and in the rear of the long array. *God so loved the world, that He gave His only begotten Son:* here οὕτω and ὥστε mark the design of love as accomplished in the mission of the Only-begotten. That love is viewed as the spontaneous, absolute, decretive will of God neither taking counsel nor giving account outside of Himself *The counsel of His own will* is simply the decree of His supreme volition · the βουλή is the expression of the θελήμα , it represents our redemption as the primitive norm or rule according to which God *worketh all things*, rather than as a scheme or expedient itself evolved in the Divine mind. Those passages which are sometimes quoted in the latter sense refer to the gradual evolution of the heavenly counsel, the conditions on which personal salvation is suspended, and the methods of the Spirit's administration In regard to these, there is certainly a plan of Salvation, but not so strictly a plan of Redemption the latter is as simply a fiat of will as creation · *Lo, I come to do Thy will, O God.*

2 This decree had its effect in itself and was virtually accomplished : we cannot say from the time of its origination, for it

Marginal notes:

The Eternal Decree

Love.
John iii 16.
1 John iv. 10, 11. 7

Eph. i 11.

Heb. x. 9.
Decree and Accomplishment one

was not a project of time.   The fall of the world and its recovery
were never separated   The history of mankind is a history of re-
1 Peter i.   demption.   The Lamb was both *foreordained before* and *slain from the*
20   *foundation of the world,* and the virtue of the Atonement, like death,
Rev. xiii.
8.   passed through to all men, the heritage of the race.   It was the
Tit. iii. 4.   *love of God our Saviour toward man,* His φιλανθρωπία, that *appeared*
             in Christ as a mystery revealed.   And another of St Paul's last
1 Tim ii.   testimonies speaks of *God our Saviour , who will have all men to be*
3, 4, 6.   *saved,* as proved by the mediatorship of Christ Jesus, *Who gave*
             Himself a ransom for all, to be testified in due time.   Under a decree
             of redemption virtually accomplished the whole world has lived
             and moved and had its being.   The self-devotion of the *One*
1 Tim ii.   *Mediator* dated back before He became *Christ Jesus Man :* His in-
5   carnation was the testimony in time of an eternal fact in the
             Divine counsel.   Man has no history apart from Him.

ITS PROGRESSIVE UNFOLDING

The Decree was, however, a mystery slowly revealed,
and in a variety of ways . by gradual prophecy and gradual
preparation, both of which assumed the form of a series of
covenants, or covenant economies.

Purpose   1. The eternal purpose was preserved in the remembrance and
Forean-   hope of mankind by constant FOREANNOUNCEMENTS.   The Gospel
nounced.   was preached from the beginning.   The Lord Himself declared it
             to our fallen parents in words which have therefore been called the
             PROTEVANGELIUM, or First Gospel.   It was said to the serpent :
Gen. iii.   *And I will put enmity between thee and the woman, and between thy*
15.   *seed and her seed , it shall bruise thy head, and thou shalt bruise his*
             heel   this first prediction of a coming Deliverer, who should undo
             the work of Satan, went forth into all the world, and was mingled
             with the traditional hopes of all the nations.   It was renewed in
Gen. xxii.   the new world to Abraham   *In thy seed shall all the nations of the*
18.   *earth be blessed.*   This promise was given in prospect of the Atone-
             ment on the mount, and, like that Atonement, must carry its
             meaning backward as well as forward : in the Seed of the woman,
             limited to the stock of Abraham, all nations, not only should be

but were and had been already blessed. Again, the Seed was further limited to the line of David, who transmitted to the prophets the decree which was declared to him. Thus the great prophecies which went before on Christ were restricted to one people who received them as their guardians for the world, and those prophecies kept the Oath and the Promise of God with always increasing clearness before the minds of men.

2. There was also a continuous PREPARATION. This was negative in the demonstration of the sin and impotence of the world, whether of Jews or Gentiles. as to the latter, when *the world by wisdom knew not God, it pleased God by the foolishness of preaching to save them that believe,* as to the former, the law given to them *was added because of transgressions, till the Seed should come to whom the promise was made,* they were *kept under the law,* which was a *schoolmaster . . . unto Christ* Hence the great preparation running through the ages is summed up. *the Scripture hath concluded all under sin* It was also a positive preparation. The history of the ancient economy was one long arrangement for the manifestation of the redeeming purpose. For that the peculiar people was chosen, for that the holy land was prepared, for that the entire system of typical and symbolical ceremony was ordered, for that both the land and the people were finally given into the hands of the heathen. *For of a truth against Thy holy child Jesus, whom Thou hast anointed, both Herod and Pontius Pilate, with the Gentiles, and the people of Israel, were gathered together, for to do whatsoever Thy hand and Thy counsel determined before to be done.* This first hymn of the Christian Church sings the fulfilment of a decree for which all events had prepared and in the accomplishment of which all the most diversified agents conspired.

Purpose prepared for 1 Cor. i. 21.

Gal. iii.19, 23, 24

Acts iv 27, 28.

3. The gradual development of the Divine counsel of human salvation is in Scripture the unfolding of a COVENANT OF GRACE. Reserving for the present the fuller treatment of this subject in its application to the work of Christ and its administration in the Gospel, we must now fix our thought upon its connection with the history of that development.

The One Covenant of Grace.

(1.) The term itself bears a special Messianic meaning, as always having in view the fidelity of God to the design of human redemption through the sacrifice of His Son. The Hebrew ‏בְּרִית‏,

Always in Christ

almost always translated in the LXX by διαθήκη, signifies, not a compact as between man and man, but the Disposition or Arrangement assumed by the One Supreme purpose of grace. It employs analogically the language of human covenants, and is an example of the anthropomorphic mode of speech which expresses the Divine dealings with our race, in Christ the Mediator Unlike human compacts it is invariably connected with sacrifice The original Hebrew word is derived from בָּרָה, or בָּרָא, in allusion to the custom of cutting and passing between the parts of a divided animal on the ratification of a covenant. hence the Greek ὅρκια τέμνειν, and the

Gen. xv 18

Hebrew כָּרַת בְּרִית. The first express revelation of the covenant to Abraham gives the key to all its history There all is based on a free Divine promise The animals divided denoted the two parties to the great transaction; and the flame passing through was God, in His future Son, the Shekinah, uniting the parties alone, and thus ratifying His own covenant The New-Testament term διαθήκη does not preserve the original allusion, but it is never disconnected from the idea. The one covenant of grace has been ratified by an eternal sacrifice; which is at the same time

Heb ix. 16, 15.

the death of the Testator, who disposes the *promise of eternal inheritance* according to the counsel of His own will

One Mediator.

(2) This covenant of redemption or of grace has been always connected with Christ its unrevealed Mediator. As its MEDIATOR or μεσίτης, He is the medium through Whom or rather in Whom all its blessings are conveyed : that GRACE, which is the one name and one blessing of the covenant, the free bestowment of favour on

2 Cor. xiii. 14.

sinful man, or *the grace of our Lord Jesus Christ* Therefore the term, which has a wider meaning than its relation to a compact, may be applied to Christ as the yet unknown Redeemer who was at once the ground of the covenant, and its promise, and its virtual administrator. After He came and was revealed, it is the term

Surety in the Gospel Heb vii. 22

SURETY or ἔγγυος that more precisely expresses His mediatorship in the order of grace . in His Divine-human atoning personality He is the Pledge to man of the bestowment by God of all blessings procured through His atoning work, and the Pledge to God on the part of mankind of compliance with all the conditions of the covenant In the Old Testament the future Redeemer is not termed either the Mediator or the Surety, though He was in

the profoundest sense both as the Angel or *Messenger of the* ·Mal. iii. 1.
Covenant, and Himself the embodied Covenant reserved for the
future · *I will preserve Thee, and give Thee for a covenant of the people,* ·Isa xlix.
having all its blessings committed to Him as a great Promise for   8.
the last days. What was thus given to Him *by promise* becomes
the heritage of His people through faith, who as *Christ's are heirs* ·Gal.iii.18,
according to the promise.   19, 29

(3.) This one Covenant has taken three forms in the history of   ·Various
revelation   (1) As entered into with mankind represented by   Cove-
Christ, its revelation began with the Fall, was ratified for the   nants.
world with Noah, and was confirmed to Abraham, as the representative of all believers to the end of time   (2) But the covenant
with Abraham for the world in all ages also introduced the special
compact with his descendants after the flesh   This latter was
established through Moses its mediator , and blended the covenant
of grace with a covenant of works. *The law was given by Moses,* and, ·John i. 17.
as an appended form or condition of the original institute of grace,
perpetually convicted the people of their sin and impotence, drove
them to take refuge in the hope of a future grace, the ground of
which was kept before them in the institute of sacrifice   (3.)
Finally, the New Covenant, *established upon better promises,* was ·Heb v
ratified in the death of Christ   It was at once the abrogation of   6.
the Mosaic or later Old Covenant, so far as concerns its national
relation and its legal condition, and the renewal unto perfection of
the more ancient covenant, always in force and never superseded,
with mankind · of which more particularly hereafter.

(4) This one institute of mercy, as progressively revealed, distri- ·The Dis-
butes the history of revelation under a series of DISPENSATIONS,   pensations
which are sometimes called the Patriarchal, the Mosaic, and the Christian.   Dispensation and Economy are translations of the one word
οἰκονομία : the former referring rather to the degrees of the Divine
bestowment, and the latter to the various forms it has assumed in
the arrangements of the one Church.   In relation to this, the
documents of the former economies are called, after the precedent
of the Mosaic *book of the covenant,* the books of the Old Covenant ·Ex xxiv.
or Testament, and those of the last dispensation, the New Cove-   7
nant or Testament.   But it must always be remembered that
through these dispensations the virtue of the one covenant of

grace flowed   They were all preliminary and imperfect, but substantially effectual, revelations of the Gospel.   Grace reigned through righteousness in every age.   All who have been saved, have been saved through the Atonement, unrevealed or revealed. And in this sense we may add to the series above given a GENTILE dispensation, of which something has already been said, and more will be said hereafter.

The Decree Accomplished.

ACCOMPLISHMENT.

The Divine Purpose was fulfilled in the Mission of Christ, including His incarnation and death: the Decree, that is, of the redemption of the world.   This fulfilment is the fulness of time; its consummate secret being the ratification of the new and better covenant: new, in contradistinction to the old which was in its final form limited to one people , and better, because revealing all the provisions of grace, for time and eternity, in Christ the Mediator made perfect, on behalf of the entire race of mankind.

Heb 1. 2.
Eph 1. 10.
Gal. iv. 4.
Eph iii 9.
Acts xiii. 33.
Rom. xvi. 25, 26

1 Pet. 1. 20
Heb. 1. 2.

Acts ii. 17.

1 Our Lord's advent introduced the *last days*, or the *dispensation of the fulness of times*, or the *economy of the mystery* (οἰκονομία τοῦ μυστηρίου), or the *fulfilment of the promise which was made unto the fathers*, or *the revelation of the mystery . . made known to all nations for the obedience of faith.*   Everything in the coming of Christ had its end.   The entire current of New-Testament revelation glorifies God in the full manifestation of the Eternal Purpose for the salvation of the human race.   The LAST DAYS are in the Epistle to the Hebrews connected with perfected Revelation . *God hath in these last days spoken unto us by His Son* , in St. Peter's First Epistle with the revelation of the Atonement · *the precious blood of Christ, as of a lamb without blemish and without spot, who verily was fore-ordained before the foundation of the world, but was manifest in these last times* , and in the Pentecostal sermon with the outpouring of the Spirit : *It shall come to pass in the last days, saith God, I will pour out of My Spirit upon all flesh*   But in all these three summary instances the accomplishment of a Divine decree of redemption is in the context.   What was set forth to Himself in the

Divine mind was set forth on the scene of human history in the Passion of Christ. This is the sense of St. Paul's classical passage on the subject : where we have the ETERNAL COUNSEL ($\delta\nu$ $\pi\rho o\epsilon\theta\epsilon\tau o$), set forth or proposed to Himself by God ; the gradual WITNESS OF THE LAW AND PROPHETS, on the one hand, and, on the other, the pretermission of sins in the Divine FORBEARANCE AS YET UN-ACCOUNTED FOR ; and, lastly, the NOW of the Gospel times, with the full revelation of the objective and subjective Redemption. This is the emphatic doctrine of those other words : *When the fulness of the time was come, God sent forth His Son* ($\iota\nu\alpha$) *to redeem them that were under the law,* where $\iota\nu\alpha$ must have its full force. The Son was sent to accomplish a predetermined design. And the new covenant is spoken of as a finished transaction *The days come, saith the Lord, when I will make a new covenant.* instead of the $\delta\iota\alpha\theta\eta\sigma o\mu\alpha\iota$ of the Septuagint we read $\sigma\upsilon\nu\tau\epsilon\lambda\epsilon\sigma\omega$, *and will complete or bring to perfection.* It is not *that which decayeth and waxeth old.* Rom. iii.
21, *seq.* Gal iv. 4. Heb viii.
13

2. It must be remembered, however, that this fulfilment refers only to the objective work of redemption. The great purpose was accomplished, and the Divine counsel exhausted, in the $T\epsilon\tau\epsilon\lambda\epsilon\sigma\tau\alpha\iota$, *It is finished.* In the death of the Mediator there was a fulfilment of the one great promise on which all others were suspended. The supreme secret of the ages was made manifest. The *mystery of the Gospel, or the mystery which from the beginning of the world hath been hid in God,* being *the mystery of Christ,* or, as elsewhere, *the mystery of God, Christ,* was in one sense a mystery no longer, though in another sense to remain for ever such a mystery as *the angels desire to look into* Eph vi.
19.
Eph. xi.
4, 9.
Col. ii. 2.
1 Pet. i.
12.

3. It is also true that the purpose still runs on, waiting for another accomplishment, which connects it with the Spirit's work in the administration of redemption. Often the accomplished purpose of human salvation is confounded with the final realisation of all the Divine Plans. We must endeavour to keep these two distinct The language of the New Testament when speaking of the actualisation of the Divine decree in the mission of Christ is different from that which is used concerning the gradual fulfilment of other purposes dependent upon that However difficult it may be to make the distinction it is necessary. The processes of the gradual administration of grace will issue in the

Eph. i. 4　salvation of a certain portion of mankind, *according as He hath chosen us in Him before the foundation of the world*　But the gradual gathering of the elect, and the gradual salvation of each of the number, is represented as the result of a plan and method in the Gospel. Whereas of the redemption of man's race or mankind, that is, of all who have ever borne or shall ever bear the name of man, the Scripture speaks in definitive terms as having been once for all accomplished. *We have seen*—said the last writer in the last document—*and do testify that the Father sent the Son, the Saviour of the world* · and not only *to be the Saviour*.

1 John iv. 14.

HISTORICAL.

Patristic.　1. The Nicene Creed expresses the sentiment of the first Christians, that Jesus Christ was incarnate FOR US MEN AND FOR OUR SALVATION, δι' ἡμᾶς τοὺς ἀνθρώπους, and that the Divine purpose united redemption and creation. So Athanasius · "The Restitution could take place only in that the original Pattern after which man was created was manifested for his salvation." A long series of divines, from Irenæus to the present day, assume that the Incarnation would have taken place if man had not sinned; an opinion of speculative theology which disturbs the free grace of the eternal counsel

2. The early Church held fast the universality of the object of the redeeming purpose. From the Apostolical Fathers downwards there is a clear testimony. "Ideo autem passus est, ut tolleret peccatum mundi. Si quis autem non credit in Christum, generali beneficio se fraudat" These words of Ambrose represent the strain of ante-Nicene theology, which knew nothing of a restriction in the Divine purpose of salvation

Augustine.　3. But in this St. Augustine did not follow his teacher. He first laid down the principle that God in His sovereignty decreed the separation of a certain number from the mass of fallen mankind unto salvation, including the special, irresistible, and inamissible grace that leads to it · for them and for them alone He provided and sent His Son　This view of the eternal purpose was exaggerated by the followers of Augustine; it gave rise to Pelagian and semi-Pelagian extravagance in the opposite direction. Early Augustinianism made grace dependent on the predestination of its object, semi-Pelagianism made grace dependent on the Divine prevision of man's good use of it. The Synod of Arausio rejected both, and at the same time condemned "cum omni detestatione," the doctrine of a predestination to evil; and that of Chiercy (853) under Hincmar spoke still more decidedly. The ninth century was full of this controversy, Gottschalk being the representative of Augustine, and the link between him and his still greater representative, Calvin

4 The Scholastic divines took opposite sides as to the Divine decrees. Thomas of Bradwardine, Archbishop of Canterbury (1349), and Wyclif after him, prepared the way for the rigorous doctrine which Calvin stamped with his name. But the general tendency of Mediæval doctrine was towards the universal redemption which the Council of Trent laid down, and from which the Greek Church had never deviated

5. Calvin carried the ancient theory of Augustine to its logical conclusion: cadit homo Dei providentia SIC ORDINANTE, sed suo vitio cadit. This is SUPRALAPSARIANISM. the doctrine that God predestined the fall of the race as well as the salvation of some to the glory of His grace and the reprobation of others to the glory of His justice. INFRALAPSARIANISM seems to have been the favourite form of putting the dogma of Augustine: it modifies the former so far as to connect the fall with the Divine permission, instead of His foreordination. But the admission of this distinction goes far towards the subversion of Augustinianism It renounces the absolute Sovereignty, which cannot consist with a mere permission to fall; the whole system is dissolved when the iron bonds of Sovereignty are withdrawn. Accordingly, many of the Reformed have sought to mitigate in various ways their master's severe dogma. France, especially, Calvin's own country, made desperate attempts to shake itself free from the yoke. What has been known as the theory of HYPOTHETICAL REDEMPTION originated in Saumur with Amyraut (1664) Its watchword was the DECRETUM UNIVERSALE HYPOTHETICUM that is, Christ has made the salvation of all men possible if they believe; but, though the Son's intervention is of universal value, God's efficacious grace is given only to a certain number. This unhappy compromise has found advocates in England also.

Marginal notes:
School- men.

Calvin

Supralap- sarianism.

Infralap- sarianism.

H 2

Armin-
ianism.

6 The Remonstrants of Holland, or Arminians, were the first who, in modern times, protested against the Augustinianism which had found its way into some of the Formularies of the Reformation   Their principle was that the decree of God in Christ was in favour of mankind as such ; and that that decree was accomplished in the offering of Christ for the redemption of the whole race. The Lutheran Formularies, especially the later, assert the same universality ; as also do the Methodists everywhere. Against this Calvinism or Augustinianism urges that the decree of redemption was in favour only of those who are actually redeemed ; that redemption in purpose had not and could not have reference to those who perish ; and that, if general appeals and exhortations are found in the Word of God, this anomaly is to be explained by the fact that there is a secret decree behind the open declaration of the Divine Purpose.

7. It is obvious that inscrutable mystery rests upon this whole subject   Its chief difficulty, however, lies in the Scriptural application of the doctrines of vocation and election in their connection with general redemption.   In other words, while the eternal will of the Love of God to provide a Deliverer and an atoning deliverance adequate to meet the ruin of mankind is placed beyond the possibility of doubt, the revelation of the Bible thus responding to the instinct of the human heart, it may seem hard to reconcile such a catholic purpose with the partial, progressive, and limited announcements of that supreme truth   But this branch of the subject has its appropriate place hereafter ; and it will receive fuller treatment.

THE REDEMPTIONAL TRINITY.

The gradual unfolding of the mystery of redemption is also the gradual unfolding of the mystery of the Triune God. While the Divine essence is revealed as unity of nature in trinity of personal subsistence, the work of human salvation is so related to the Triunity and to the several Persons that the Redemptional Trinity may be made a topic of separate discussion : with the reservation, however, that the Economical Trinity is only the Absolute Trinity as manifested in the present dispensation, and that all the New-Testament exhibitions of it are to be interpreted accordingly. We have to consider, first, the common relation of the Triune Godhead to the Mediatorial Work, and then the relation of each Person : both in the light of Scripture alone.

I. The redemption of mankind sprang from the eternal purpose of God the Triune . *Let Us redeem man !* was silently one with *Let Us make man !* God is not divided. As the creation is a Divine work, while each Person is Creator, so redemption is a Divine work in which the Three Persons unite. *God . . . hath visited and redeemed His people ·* words to the Jews which the Apostle confirms : *After that the . . . love of God our Saviour toward man appeared.* These are the key to all those passages which connect God absolutely and independently of the hypostatic distinctions with our salvation, down to the end *God shall be all in all*, the TRIUNE GOD From this some inferences follow.

1. The Divine attributes that required and provided an atonement are the attributes of the Three Persons : no distinction can be admitted between the holiness and love of the Father and the holiness and love of the Son There is a perfect περιχωρήσις in the Redemptional Trinity, even as there is in the Absolute.

Marginal notes:

Unity of Triune Purpose.

Luke i 68.

Tit. iii. 4.

1 Cor. xv. 28.

I John x.

and my Father are One is a testimony that may be carried higher than the foundation of the world

Pretemporal Covenant of Redemption

2. Hence there is no support for the theory of a COVENANT OF REDEMPTION between the Father and the Son, according to which the Three Persons concerted the plan of salvation the Son undertaking on His part to undergo the penalties of the law for His people, and the Father pledging Himself to give the Son His own glory and His people's souls as His recompense, and the Spirit witnessing in order to administer this covenant The Scripture speaks only of the will and purpose of God's love to redeem mankind, which will was the will of the undivided Trinity. The sayings of the Word of God on this subject do not sustain the representations sometimes made of a harmony effected between the mercy and the justice of the Father through the intervention of the Son in the eternal Trinity before the world was. The reconciliation of those attributes must indeed be regarded as preceding the manifested work of redemption; the Atonement was a reality in the Divine mind before it was accomplished on the cross But it was not an Atonement offered to one Person in the Trinity by Another and witnessed by a Third. The Son Incarnate came to do the will of God . His own will, and the will of the Holy Ghost, as much as the will of the Father. The words Covenant, and Scheme, and Plan belong to the manifestations of the redeeming economy in time. We must not transfer them to eternity There is an impenetrable veil over what is so often called the Council of the eternal Trinity ; and the Scripture does not take our thoughts behind it · save only when the Son speaks of a glory which He had with the Father before the world

1 Peter 1 20.

was, and His disciple of an atonement *foreordained before the foundation of the world.* When another writer introduces the actual

Rev. xiii. 8

atonement the πρὸ καταβολῆς becomes ἀπὸ καταβολῆς not *before* the foundation but *from* the foundation of the world was the

Gal iii. 20.

Lamb slain *Now a mediator is not a mediator of one , but God is One.* if such an application of St Paul's hard saying may be permitted. No interior mediation, in the strict sense of the term, can be conceived within the Godhead.

Trinity in Redemption.

II. The Three Persons of the Trinity are revealed in most strict and definite relations to the economy of redemption

1. These relations are so clearly defined that it is necessary at the outset to show that the Scriptural doctrine of the Trinity is really independent of the work of Christ The Three Persons are connected with creation almost as closely as with redemption; in this economical, though not as yet redemptional, Trinity the Word or the Son is the Agent of the Father's creating will, and the Spirit connects the Father and the Son with the visible universe. The same names are given to the Son and Spirit in their pre-temporal being as are given to them in the dispensation of grace in time The Word who was *with God in the beginning* was *made* *flesh,* and His Divinity is the *Spirit* in which His oblation was offered The baptismal formula conjoins *the Son* and not the Son incarnate with the *Father* in the unity of the *Holy Ghost* In the mystery of the internal relations there was the eternal possibility of the Absolute Trinity becoming the Redemptional : there is no deeper or more adorable secret in the Christian Faith than this. The Father could send the Son, while the Son could give Himself; and the Holy Ghost, neither the Sender nor the Incarnate Sent, could in His distinct personality rest upon the Son made flesh, and be the Minister to Him who ministered to us.

John i. 2, 14.
Heb. ix. 14.
Matt. xxviii. 19.

2 This being so, there is a never-failing consistency in the exhibitions of the Redemptional Trinity as distinguished from the Absolute.

(1) The eternal generation of the Son is the ground of the generation by which the Son was made flesh The words *This day have I begotten Thee* cannot refer either to eternity or to the resurrection of the Lord's human nature they express the profound truth that the Only-begotten was now the same eternal Son begotten again in our human nature. *this day* being the one day of the incarnation finished and made perfect in the resurrection. Hence the Father of this Incarnate Son in the Mediatorial Trinity is always the supreme Representative of the Godhead. God and the Father are terms used interchangeably . St John says that *God sent His Son* and immediately afterwards *The Father sent the Son.* This is a law of phraseology which may be traced through the New Testament. The entire economy of redemption is always referred to God or to the Father as its origin, fountain, and head What belongs to all the Persons of the Absolute Trinity alike is in the

The Father.
Acts xiii. 33.

1 John iv. 10—14.

Trinity Redemptional assigned to the Father alone.   Hence He receives the doxology of the Church, and prayer is generally offered to Him.

The Spirit.
(2) And the Spirit never assumes any relation to the person and work of Christ, but that of One who, consubstantial with the Father and the Son, is yet the Agent of the will of the mediatorial Father.   The Double Generation is taught in Scripture; and analogy would be almost enough to establish the Double Procession as the ground of the Temporal Mission of the Holy Ghost   He is always sent forth · Himself like Christ an ἀπόστολος.   Before the Incarnation He prepared the way of the Lord, as *the Spirit of the Christ*.   In the miraculous conception, He is the Agent by whom the Father begets His Incarnate Son, and by whom the Son partook of our flesh and blood.   During the Saviour's ministry He presides over all its processes as the Intermediary between the Son and His Father · precisely as if He were the Director and Disposer of a passive Christ.   It was *through the Holy Ghost* that our Lord *had given commandments unto the Apostles*.   Even after the ascension the Spirit in the redemptional Trinity is still the Agent of the Father sent by the Son, and never is represented as independently revealing Himself   But to the Holy Spirit in His administration we must again refer.

Heb.iii.1.

1 Pet i. 11.

Heb ii. 14.

Acts i 2.

The Son Subordinate
(3.) As to the Son incarnate His place in the Holy Trinity is for a season merged in His mediatorial relation to God and His Father.   He Himself never swerves from the language of subordination.   Even in those sayings which, as it were, undesignedly manifest forth His Divine glory, there is still the recognition of the Father's will which He has come into the world to finish, and a perpetual remembrance of the obedience which He must learn.   But of the Redeemer's humbled estate it is not needful to say more now   Suffice that throughout the entire economy of redemption, and until the end when the Triune God shall be all in all, and the mediatorial distinctions of office in the Trinity cease, the predominant character of the Second Person is and will be that of Mediator, through whom we draw nigh to God: under the authority of the Father, and having the Holy Spirit under Him.   The last Gospel, which is the most distinctively Trinitarian, is also the most express on this subject.   Its earlier chapters

exhibit Him *under authority*, of which such passages as these are
specimens: *as the Living Father hath sent Me, and I live by the
Father*, when the mediatorial life is signified, *for I came down
from heaven, not to do Mine own will, but the will of Him that sent
Me*   Its later chapters show that the Spirit is *under Him*, He
had always spoken before of Himself as declaring what He was
ever hearing of the Father, *as I hear I judge*, and now He uses the
very same language of the Spirit in relation to Himself· *whatever
He shall hear that shall He speak* . . . *for He shall receive of Mine*.
And intermediately we hear Him declaring the absolute unity
between the Father and the Son: *I and My Father are One*.

    3. It is important to remember this truth in the study of the
mediatorial economy.   Illustrations will hereafter be given of
what needs now only to be stated. that, with certain occasional
reservations and saving clauses which abundantly declare the
supreme Divinity of the Son and the Spirit, the general strain of
the phraseology of the New Testament represents the Second and
Third Persons of the Trinity in their economical subordination to
the Father as the representative of the Godhead.   It must always
be borne in mind that the theology of the Bible is the theology of
redemption   before the application of this principle that peculiar
difficulty which springs from the comparative rarity of direct
allusions to the Trinity as such vanishes   In fact the difficulty
becomes a help to faith when it is looked at in this light.   The
sublime theory of a redemptional subordination of the Two Persons
is maintained, generally and down to the minutest detail, with an
exact consistency of which only Divine wisdom could be the
author.

John vi.
57, 38.

John v.
30,
John xv
13, 14

John x. 30.

Subordi-
nation in
Trinity.

THE PERSON OF CHRIST.

The dogma of the Person of Christ has not been always defined and limited with sufficient strictness. It is the formal statement of what the Scripture teaches concerning the indivisible unity of the two natures in the One Christ. It is not therefore the doctrine of our Lord's Divinity as such, though that is included. Nor is it the doctrine of His perfect Manhood as such, though that also is involved. It simply treats of the Person resulting from the union as Divine-human or Incarnate. The Word of God does not assign a term to this union which might indicate its nature · it does not use the expression Person of Christ, any more than it uses that of Trinity. But the former has the same relation to the Redeemer that the latter has to the Triune Essence. Sometimes those who do justice to the distinct dogma of the Person of Christ enlarge it unduly : including in it much that belongs to the Estates and Offices of Christ as the Subject of an historical development. It will be well to confine our present topic to the Divine Personality of the Son who assumes our nature, to the verity of the human nature which He assumes, and to the Divine-human Person, with its new and eternal composite personality, which is the result. Whatever does not fairly come within this scope must be referred to a subsequent stage.

The doctrine of the undivided and indivisible unity of the Incarnate Person is taught by the Holy Ghost in two ways · first, by the language used concerning the Christ, and, secondly, by the ascription of the virtue and qualities of each of the two natures to the Saviour's work. As to the former: while neither of the two natures ever gives its attributes to the other, the one common Person is clothed with both classes of attributes interchangeably. As to the latter: in all that the Saviour does and suffers each nature has its distinct functions unconfounded, while both are the functions of the one common Person, whose Divine personality gives them Divine virtue: some are Divine, some human; but all are Divine-human. These general truths were anciently summed up as follows Christ is truly God, perfectly Man, unconfusedly in two Natures, indivisibly in one Person. Later developments of dogma pursue the subject into a multitude of subtilties which have made no real advancement towards the solution of what remains THE MYSTERY OF GOD EVEN CHRIST.

THE DIVINE PERSONALITY.

God became incarnate as the Second Person of the Deity. Hence the sole, continuous, abiding, and everlasting personality of the One Christ is that of the Eternal Son, who retains His unchangeable Godhead in His human estate, throughout His mediatorial history, and for ever. Christ is Divine; His Divinity is that of the Son; and it is the personality of the Son which is the Subject in the act and issues of the incarnation.

DIVINE.

Divine.

The Divinity of the Son eternal in the essence of God has been already established: now we have to do with the Divinity of the Son in the Person of Christ. As incarnate the Redeemer is called by Divine names; His mediatorial relation supposes His truly Divine nature, which is ascribed to Him in connection with human, and as distinguished from it; and the Divine attributes are ascribed to Him, with the homage which those attributes demand.

The Incarnate God and Lord

I. In some passages—few, but among the clearest in the New Testament—the Redeemer in His human manifestation is called GOD. And in a larger number He is called LORD, with all the meaning of the ancient JEHOVAH in the term   In a still larger number He bears the third of the early designations of the Deity, ADONAI or Lord · that is, in all those wherein the term Lord is not the representative of Jehovah, but indicates only the jurisdiction over all things which is given to the Eternal Son   It needs hardly to be said that neither the term GOD, nor the term LORD as Jehovah, ever defines in Scripture a dignity conferred on Christ

God.
Isa. vii 14
Matt i 23
Isa ix 6.
Ps. xlv 6
Heb. i. 8.

John i 1, 18.
John xx. 28
Acts xx. 28.
1 Tim iii 16
Rom ix. 5.
Titus ii. 13

1. The New Testament begins by applying to Jesus the prediction of *Emmanuel, which being interpreted is, God with us.* And the light of fulfilment thrown back upon the same prediction shows that the Incarnate Son is *the mighty God*   So with regard to the forty-fifth Psalm · *Thy throne, O God, is for ever and ever,* which the Epistle to the Hebrews refers to the Incarnate Mediator. In the beginning of his Gospel St John speaks of the Word made flesh as *God,* and, in the best reading, as *God Only-begotten,* he also gives prominence to the confession of Thomas *My Lord and my God*   Two passages are doubtful: *the church of God, which He hath purchased with His own blood,* may be perhaps read *the church of the Lord.* · *God manifest in the flesh* is rather *Who was manifest*   But it is scarcely permissible to read otherwise than that Christ is *over all, God blessed for ever.*   And the closing testimony of St Paul is that Christians look for the appearance of *the great God and our Saviour Jesus Christ*   These are only a few texts; but their fewness is in their favour as evidence. The mediatorial economy is based on a subordination of the Son Incarnate; and the name God is given to Christ only in occasional ascriptions serving to protect the eternal truth which, for a season, seems of necessity veiled, and therefore liable to perversion.

Jehovah

2 The Incarnate is JEHOVAH; and His name of LORD, not always, but sometimes, is therefore the name of His highest supremacy, attributing to Him an essential and necessary Divine

being Here again, and for the same reason, the instances are
only occasional. Perhaps, with the exception of Thomas's confession, which as it were prepared the way for what follows,—the
link between the confession of the Gospel days and that of the
Epistles—it was not assigned to our Lord until after His ascension.
The prayer of the church of the ten-days' interval was to Jehovah
Christ. *Thou,* LORD, *which knowest the hearts of all men, show whether* Acts i 24.
of these two Thou hast chosen. St. Stephen's testimony, strongest Acts vii
in death, is LORD *Jesus, receive my spirit* Believers *were baptised* 59.
in the name of the LORD *Jesus,* and afterwards *call on this name.* Acts viii
16 ; ix.
The Evangelists abound in fulfilments of Scripture which imply 21.
that the Jehovah of creation and promised redemption in the Old
Testament is Christ in His mediatorial Person. *Thou, Lord, in* Heb. i. 10.
the beginning hast laid the foundation of the earth. The Baptist *pre-* Matt. iii .
pared the way of Jehovah, that is, of Christ The prophet Isaiah ^3
Isa. vi. 1.
saw the glory of the Lord · *he saw His glory,* that of Christ. St John xii.
James terms Him *the Lord of glory.* He is the New-Testament 41.
prophet, the *King of kings and Lord of lords.* This passage, how- James ii 1.
Rev xix.
ever, may be classed with St. Peter's sublime parenthesis *He is* 16.
Lord of all, and St. Paul's *To us there is . . one Lord,* as the transition from the Jehovah of absolute lordship to the Adonai of as Acts x. 36.
it were delegated authority. In the great majority of passages, 1 Cor viii.
6
with which we have not now to do, Christ is Lord in the sense of
an exalted Divine-human representative of Divine authority over
all things. These passages unite the two in one. But, it may be
said that even these texts of a delegated lordship proclaim the
Divinity of Jesus : even as the Adonai of the Old Testament was
equally with Jehovah a Divine name.

3. The Incarnate is JEHOVAH AND GOD. He Himself did not Jehovah
assume these titles, for a reason that will hereafter be more fully and God.
seen. But He so spake as to give matter of pondering which
would ripen in due time into a full faith in His Divinity : as, for
instance, when He said that wherever His disciples might meet,
there am I in the midst of them, I AM ; *before Abraham was,* I AM. Matt.
xviii. 20.
And He kept silence also when these terms were ascribed to Him .
His silence was His acceptance Perhaps the grandest testimony John viii.
58.
to the Saviour is that given Him by His most doubting disciple :
MY LORD AND MY GOD, which was meant to express, and accepted John xx.
28.

as meant to express, the homage of his soul to the Jehovah and
God, the Searcher of hearts, the Witness of all human secrets, and
the Saviour of the most guilty and undeserving of men. This
was the last public confession, at least of any individual; and it
gave the note of all subsequent New-Testament homage. Of the
two supreme names which sprang from the lips of Thomas only
one was currently used, and that one capable of a lower meaning ·
the reason of this belongs to the subject of our Lord's mediatorial
subordination.

Antithesis
of Divine
and
Human
Natures

II. As Mediator between God and man Christ is necessarily
Divine   Having all that belongs to the one represented nature,
He must also have all that belongs to the other. What His
mediatorial work required His mediatorial Person supplies :
perfect equality and oneness with both parties between whom
He mediates   And the best demonstration of the Divinity of the
incarnate Redeemer is to be found in the passages which exhibit
His two natures in their combination and unity. Of these there are
several classes; but we must limit ourselves to those which in
express words unite while they distinguish the Divine and human
natures, after the incarnation   This excludes, for the present,
Old-Testament predictions, the testimonies at the incarnation,
and even the indirect allusions of our Lord and His Apostles :
these will be referred to when the one personality is the subject.
In fact, we have only for our appeal the three Apostles who are
the pillars of Christological doctrine.

The Flesh
and
the Spirit.
Rom 1.
3, 4.
John iv.
24.
2 Cor iii.
17.
1 Tim. iii.
16.
Heb. ix.
14.
1 Pet. iii
18.

1. St. Paul distinguishes in the Person of Christ the Flesh and
the Spirit; the higher and the lower natures   *made of the seed of
David according to the flesh, and declared to be the Son of God with
power, according to the Spirit of holiness.* That the Divine nature of
Christ should be termed Spirit is what might be expected . *God
is a Spirit. now the Lord is that Spirit.* He who was *manifest in the
flesh* was *justified in the Spirit.* The same distinction virtually
occurs in the Epistle to the Hebrews, though the human nature is
referred to only by implication : *through the eternal Spirit* Christ
offered His blood. St Peter also uses the same antithesis : *Being
put to death in the flesh, but quickened by the Spirit.*

The Flesh
and God.

2 St. Paul also makes the antithesis the Flesh and God : *of whom
as concerning the flesh Christ came, who is over all, God blessed for*

ever. To this might be added the mystery that *God was manifest in the flesh*, but the reading *Who was manifest* is preferred, and the antithesis is in the *Spirit* that follows He also conjoins while he distinguishes the Divine Being who was in the *form of God* and *equal with God* and the *likeness of men* which He assumed.

Rom. ix. 5.
1 Tim. iii 16.
Phil. ii. 6, 7

3. Both St. John and St. Paul collocate the two natures as that of the Son of God and Flesh. God sent *His own Son in the likeness of sinful flesh.* St. John in his Gospel adds the designation Word *The Word was made flesh, and dwelt among us, (and we beheld His glory, the glory as of the only-begotten of the Father).* And in his first Epistle *Jesus Christ come in the flesh* is, as the context shows, the *Son of God manifested.*

The Flesh and the Son of God.
Rom viii. 3
John i. 14
1 John iii 8; iv 2.

4 To these might be added many other passages in which the two natures are collocated by implication such, for instance, as those indirect statements in which our Lord was wont to indicate both His heavenly and His earthly origin These, however, must be reserved for the present, as they will be used to illustrate the unity of His person in the two natures It is better to fix attention upon the comparatively few texts in which the person of the Incarnate is resolved into its two elements These are probably the best and most obvious demonstrations of the Divinity of our Lord, and that for two reasons. In the first place, they clearly manifest the design of the writers to give prominence to the distinction; and, by so doing, to assert the reality of the Godhead while the manhood is asserted In other passages the supreme dignity of the Redeemer is only taken for granted, and impresses its stamp upon the texture of the language. But in these the set purpose to declare His Divinity is plain Secondly, they bring that Divinity into formal and express connection with the one person of the Christ, thus obviating the double danger against which we have so often to guard our thoughts the resolution of Christ into two distinct persons, on the one hand, and, on the other, the tendency to fuse the two natures into one new nature as well as person, neither God nor man.

Import-ance of this Proof.

III The incarnate Person is invested with Divine attributes and receives Divine honour. It will hereafter be seen what the limitation of this is, and the reason of this limitation. But, apart from and behind the reserve of our Lord's humbled estate,

Divine Perfec-tions.

and bursting through the veil of His self-humiliation, there are evidences most ample of His Divine attributes, and of the honour paid to Him and accepted by Him which only God can claim.

Attri-
butes.

1. It is enough to show that every class of the Divine perfections finds its representative in Him : in other words, that the Divinity which has been already established is such in the full sense of the word, and not a divinity subordinate and impaired. Nothing that pertains to the notion of God is wanting in the ascriptions to Christ as manifest in the flesh. The absolute attributes of God are His : spirituality and eternity of existence especially, as He is *the eternal Spirit,* and *the same yesterday, and to-day, and for ever,* and the *Alpha and Omega, the First and the Last.* The relative attributes, such as Omnipresence, Omniscience, Omnipotence, Wisdom, and Goodness, are asserted of Him even in His earthly condition, and much more in His exaltation · He is addressed as knowing *the hearts of all men* as the Omniscient, has *all power,* is the *Wisdom of God* in whom all its *treasures are hid.* And the attributes which connect God with the moral universe are His in the unity of the Father · He is *the Holy One, and the Just,* and His *Love, which passeth knowledge,* is always dwelt upon as entirely co-ordinate with the love of the Father . the same in its eternal depth, in the object it contemplates, and in the means it uses.

Heb. vii.
14
Heb. xiii
8.
Rev. i. 11

Acts i. 24.
Heb i 1,2
1 Cor. i.
24.
Col. ii 3
Acts iii.
14
·Eph. iii.
19

Divine
Honour.

2. The worship and honour due to the one God our Lord as incarnate was ordained to receive He claims it for Himself, and that it is given Him we have ample proofs derived from every part of the New Testament

Heb i 6,
3.

(1) *Let all the angels of God worship Him !* was said when He brought *the First-begotten into the world.* They had worshipped Him before, for He was the Son *upholding all things by the word of His power.* At the incarnation they adored the God Only-begotten made manifest in the flesh, and throughout His history their ministry was the ministry of adoration. But it was to the church of mankind that the ancient command was given: *He is thy Lord; and worship thou Him !* Him whom the Father addressed as on His throne *Thy throne, O God, is for ever and ever.*

Ps xlv.11,
6.

(2) Our Lord claims an honour due only to God He claims it throughout His life and ministry by the silent majesty of His Divine character, by His wonderful works literally *wrought in God,*

John iii.
21.

and by the plain declaration that the Father committed to Him, the Son of man, all judgment, that *all men should honour the Son, even as they honour the Father.* And He who taught afresh the first and great commandment required of His disciples perfect self-sacrificing love to Himself, which is the fulfilling of worship as well as of law. He accepted all kinds of homage from all kinds of worshippers: already on earth, and still more above, from *things in heaven, and things in earth, and things under the earth* John v. 23.

Phil ii. 10

(3) Accordingly, there is literally no reserve in the supreme homage paid Him by His servants. He is invoked as God for His Benediction, *the grace of our Lord Jesus Christ;* He receives as God the Doxology *over all, God blessed for ever, to Him be glory both now and for ever* The last book of Scripture gives the exalted Son the same tribute that the Father receives. But the best evidence is the unbounded homage, devotion, loyalty, and love that are concentred on the person of Christ throughout the Epistles. *Whom having not seen, ye love, in whom, though now ye see Him not, yet believing, ye rejoice with joy unspeakable and full of glory.* Such love could be given only to God, and only God could inspire such joy.

2 Cor. xiii. 14.
Rom. ix. 5.
2 Pet iii. 18.

1 Pet i. 8.

THE SON.

While the Incarnate Person is the God-man, or manifestation of God in the flesh, the Divine personality is only that of the Son, the Second Person in the Trinity. As a distinct Person in the Godhead He brings the entire Divine nature into humanity, and continues His eternal personality through all the processes of His development and mediatorial work for ever.

Personality that of the Son,

I. Into the mystery of the eternal distinction in the Deity which rendered it possible that the Father should send and the Son be sent we dare not enter. Nor into that of the intercommunion by which the whole Divine nature is in each of the Persons, and therefore descended to earth in the Son Nor into the specific relation of the Son in the Godhead, the Eternal Logos or Word, to the manifestation of God in the creature and in man. These questions lead into a province of speculative theology which

The Mystery.

VOL. II. I

is neither encouraged, nor guided, nor rewarded, by any sacred
oracle It is our wisdom to confine ourselves to what is revealed.

The Mis-
sion of
the Son.

II It has already been proved that the Eternal Son, as such,
was sent by the Father, in the Divine counsel and act of the
Trinity; that He came therefore spontaneously, to save mankind.
It is necessary now only to show that the one eternal personality
is continued in the new manifestation of God among men.

1. We naturally turn to the account of the incarnation itself
for the evidence of this But, in receiving this evidence, we must
remember that the subsequent Scripture, especially the prologue
of St. John, sheds its light upon that narrative Men here

John i
14, 18 ;
iii. 16,
17.
Luke i. 35.
Luke i. 32.

interpret the voice of angels. The *Only-begotten of the Father* was
the Word who was *made flesh ;* God gave His Son, *Only-begotten,* by
sending Him into the world, and of that Son, *Only-begotten,* it
was said in the great annunciation *That Holy Thing which shall
be born of thee shall be called the Son of God* This *Son of the Highest,*
therefore, did not become the Son of God in the incarnation ; He
brought His sonship into our nature with Him. No argument
can evade this conclusion It may be said that in many passages
which are sometimes pleaded in behalf of the Eternal Sonship the
term Son refers to the historical and manifested Christ : for

1 John i.
3.
1 John iv.
9, 14.

instance, *our fellowship is with the Father and with His Son Jesus
Christ.* But when we read that *God sent His Only-begotten Son into
the world,* and immediately afterwards *the Father sent the Son to be
the Saviour of the world,* the simple and obvious meaning ought not
to be mistaken The Father who is God, and God who is the
Father, sendeth. God does not become the Father by sending
the Son.

2 This gives the law for the interpretation of the names,
derived from that sonship, which the Lord Himself and His
servants habitually use Whatever titles He adopts or receives
in relation to His office, the term Son always enters into the
designation of His Person. His pre-eminent name is throughout
the New Testament the Son of God, or the Son absolutely. If He
calls Himself the Son of Man, we can hardly disjoin the Eternal
Sonship even from that title. For the Son of man literally He
never was : His true paternity and filiation were Divine : and as
the Son, even in the fashion of man, He was still the Son of God

in humanity. Hence, omitting the predicatives OF GOD and OF MAN, the simple name THE SON preserves to Him His eternal and everlasting character as the Second Person of the Trinity made manifest in the flesh. A Person in the Godhead continues His personality in the human nature, which is therefore of necessity itself impersonal or without any personal existence independent of the Divine. That Person is not the Father, nor the Holy Spirit, but the Son. Accordingly it will be found that in the greater number of passages in which the term Son, absolutely, is used, the reference is to the Incarnate Person, who is not only the Son of God and the Son of Man, but the Son uniting the two.

III. The importance of remembering that the Divine personality of the Son runs on, the same yesterday, and to-day, and for ever, is very great, and may be illustrated in many ways.

Import-ance.

1. It gives unity to the Person and unity to the work of the Redeemer. It preserves the Divinity of both. While it leaves to the human nature its perfection, it denies to it a distinct personal existence. The manhood was taken up into the Godhead, not the Godhead received by a human person. The Lord is not united in fellowship with a human subject. He does not hold communion with His lower nature as distinct from His Divine Self. It is true that in the humiliation of His impoverishment for us He speaks and acts from a human consciousness. But the condescension was voluntary, and all that belongs to it He makes His own Divine act. *Though He were a Son, yet learned He obedience* this statement has no such emphasis in it as the writer designed, if the voluntary condescension of a Son equal with the Father is not in it. Thus this truth, on the one hand, saves the Person of Christ from the unimaginable surrender of anything that belonged to Him as the Son of God, while, on the other, it prevents our assigning the humiliation of Christ to a human nature the sufferings and acts of which the Son made His own only by imputation. He learned all that His passion taught as in the flesh, but He learned it as the Son. Hence the simplicity with which the mission of the Son from heaven to earth is always alluded to. Sometimes reference is made to the nature He assumed in order to accomplish His work, but sometimes, indeed still oftener, the purpose of the Son's commission is represented

The Unity of the Person

Heb. v. 8.

I 2

1 John iv 10. — as if accomplished by that Son alone. God *sent His Son to be the propitiation for our sins ·* the nature that gave Him His sacrifice is not mentioned. In fact, the Scripture assumes that the SUPPOSITUM INTELLIGENS, the self-determining and responsible Agent, the Person who saved us, is the Son of God.

Christ's Sonship and ours — 2. And it shows us the bond between the Divine Sonship and our own. The perfect design of Christianity, and that which is so to speak its peculiarity, is to bring God near to man as a Father: to restore His Fatherly relation to mankind And the soul of personal Christianity is the adoption which makes us as regenerate

Gal iv. 6. — the sons of God *Because ye are sons, God hath sent forth the Spirit of His Son into your hearts, crying, Abba, Father.* By the virtue of His Divinity the Saviour redeemed us with His precious blood; by the power of the Holy Ghost He sanctifies us from all sin to Himself, but the new life with its privileges to which He introduces us in His Gospel is the virtue of His Divine Sonship in us His eternal filial life poured afresh into our human nature.

Manhood.

THE PERFECT MANHOOD

The human nature that our Lord assumed, the human conditions under which He appeared, included all that properly belongs to man. The integrity of His manhood admitted no defect in any of its elements, nor any superfluity; He was man, but in the sinless development of pure humanity. Human nature in Him was perfectly realised; and He subjected Himself to all the conditions of human life.

Perfect Man — I. The Manhood of Christ is declared in Scripture to be perfect in the sense of possessing all that belongs to human nature He

Tim. ii. 5 — is *the Man Christ Jesus,* or *Jesus Christ, Man* the strongest and clearest declaration on this subject in the New Testament He is

Gal. iv. 4 — *the Son of Man,* He was partaker of *flesh and blood,* and *came in*

Rom. viii. 3. — *the flesh,* being *made of a woman;* in *the likeness of men;* and in the *likeness of sinful flesh* Man, but in the likeness of men, Flesh, but in the likeness of sinful flesh

1. More particularly, His human nature had each of the con-

stituent elements of that nature. Our Lord was conceived of the Virgin, nourished of her substance during gestation, and born as other men His body was real even after the resurrection He said, *A spirit hath not flesh and bones, as ye see Me have.* He possessed a human spirit, the seat of intellect, sensibility, and will Of intellect, limited of necessity · *Jesus increased in wisdom,* and of some things was ignorant, of sensibility His *soul* was *exceeding sorrowful,* and He was *meek and lowly in heart;* of will . *not as I will, but as Thou wilt* And, so far as a threefold distinction may be admitted in human nature, He was, essentially and of necessity, what we become through His Spirit, sanctified wholly and kept blameless throughout body, soul, and spirit. Reason was in Him the limited reflection of His own eternal Logos, His spirit was the abode of the Eternal Spirit restored in Him to our race; and through His soul He allied Himself with the needs and infirmities of sensuous human nature He appropriated all its elements in their unity that He might redeem all

Without Defect

Luke xxiv. 39

Luke ii 52.
Matt xxvi. 38.
Matt xi 29.
Matt xxvi. 39.

2 From this it follows that as Man our Lord added nothing to His Manhood by assuming it into the Godhead The Divine Logos neither displaced the human spirit, nor raised it to a condition transcending human limits. Upon this truth rests, as we shall see, the possibility of the Saviour's language of subordination.

Without Excess.

II The human nature of our Lord underwent a sinless process : a development in common with other men, but, unlike that of other men, without sin That is to say, on the one hand, the union with Divinity did not arrest the natural evolution of the humanity; and, on the other, that union did avail to secure the perfect development of the lower nature, under the conditions, however, of making its infirmities the instrument and medium of the atoning Obedience and Passion These topics will be touched upon under the Mediatorial History at present it is required to state them only so far as they are essential to a right view of the Perfect Manhood of Christ.

Sinless Development

1. Our Lord was perfectly Man : τελείως His human nature was the perfect realisation of the eternal idea of mankind Hence He calls Himself the Son of man; and by St Paul is termed the *Second* and better, or *last Adam :* ὁ ἔσχατος Ἀδάμ While immortality in Adam was a gift conditional, in Christ it was absolute ·

Man τελείως.

1 Cor. xv. 45.

John i. 4.   *in Him was life.*   But He was sent to exhibit the perfection of a human existence in the world of sin, and therefore the course of His life underwent the common development. Reserving the mystery of His introduction into our race, He was ever after in all points as one of us.

Rom. viii. 3   2. But He came *in the likeness of sinful flesh* . in the flesh of infirmity and capability of suffering and death. He surrendered His right to the immortality of His holy Manhood, and of Himself laid down His life   But there is another meaning of the Flesh in Scripture which has nothing in Christ: that of the seventh chapter of the Romans.   In Him was the mystery of all the consequences of sin as the endurance of sorrow without the sin itself that causes sorrow.   The development of His human

Lu. i 25   nature was absolutely sinless   because it was *that Holy Thing* which belonged to and was called and is *the Son of God*

The Incarnate Person.

THE DIVINE-HUMAN PERSON.

The Divine-human Person is the union, the result of the union, of the two natures, or rather the personality that unites the conditions of Divine and human existence. This personality is one and undivided; as is testified by the phraseology which assigns both to the Person and the work of Christ attributes taken from either nature, while the Subject of all predicates is one. The two natures of the one Person are not confounded or fused together; this is guaranteed to reason by the eternal necessity of the case, as also by the fact that none of the attributes of either of the two natures is ever in Scripture assigned to the other.

Hypostatic Union.   This union of the two natures in one person receives no name in the New Testament. Theology designates it the HYPOSTATICAL UNION. This term is derived from the later use of Hypostasis to represent the Personal subsistences in the Godhead in contradistinction from their common Substance or Essence. Hence it signifies that only one Hypostasis or Person is the resultant of the union of the two natures. It defines no more than that. And it is therefore only the theological expression of the truth concerning Christ which, without a definition, pervades the Scripture. But there are two errors against which it must be guarded, or rather against which the two words of the term guard the doctrine respectively. As the union is HYPOSTATICAL, it is not the conjunction of two natures by any bond that allows them to be conceived of as separate. As the Hypostasis results from a UNION, there can be no blending of the two natures into a composite which should be no longer either, but something between God and man.

Hypo-static.

Union.

I. The undivided and indivisible unity of the ONE CHRIST stamps the phrascology of Scripture, in its references both to His Person and to His work. Let us consider each in its order.

One Undivided Christ.

1. Whether He speaks of Himself or His Apostles speak of Him, it is the rule that, whatever name may be given to our Lord as the subject, predicates are applied to it taken from both natures or interchangeably from either of them A few illustrations will be sufficient, but these must be carefully classified, as the induction by which we gain our general principle or formula.

One Person

(1.) In all those passages, already referred to, which unite in one sentence the Divine and the human, the subject is Jesus Christ, and the predicates are taken from both natures. *The church of God, which He hath purchased with His own blood* He, the subject, has for predicates God and the Manhood the blood of which was shed. So also when it is said that *they would not have crucified the Lord of Glory.* In fact, all the passages that have been quoted as illustrating the general proposition, and others that might be added, contain virtually attributives from both natures

Subject of both classes of predicates.
Acts xx. 28

1 Cor. ii 8.

(2.) In some, however, the one subject has specially a Divine predicate. *The Son of Man,* the subject, has for its predicate *which is in heaven.* *The glory which I had with Thee* comes under the same law ; and many others, such as *Before Abraham was, I am.*

John iii 13.
John xvii 5

(3.) In other passages—in the nature of the case the abundant majority—the predicate is simply and purely human. Jesus *was asleep, Jesus wept,* His soul was *exceeding sorrowful,* and He said after the resurrection *Touch Me not.* These enter of course into the very substance of the history of His humbled estate ; and the last

John viii. 58.
John xi 35.
John xx. 17.

Matt
xxvii
46

Luke
xxiii.
46

and most mysterious illustration is the double cry with which the Saviour finished expiation · *My God, My God, why hast Thou forsaken Me?* and *Father, into Thy hands I commend My spirit!*

(4.) If we carry this law with us into the New Testament we shall find that One Person everywhere appears, who speaks and is spoken of sometimes as God, sometimes as man, sometimes as both, and without the slightest care to obviate possible mis-apprehension. The One Christ, with His two classes of attributes, is always taken for granted as familiar to Christian consciousness

One Work
Media-
torial.

2. This unity appears also in all that is said of the Redeemer's work His entire mediatorial agency is not that of the Son of God only, not that of the Son of Man, but that of the Θεάνθρωπος, the GOD-MAN in His whole Person, undivided and indivisible.

(1) It is to be observed that, negatively, Scripture never draws a line of demarcation between Divine acts and human in the mission and functions of Jesus. It does distinguish, as we have seen, between the natures, and that in a very elaborate way, which makes the absence of the other distinction more marked.

(2) Every possible variety of names is given to the One Agent in redemption; and every aspect and act of His work is ascribed to each appellative the Word, the Son, Jesus, Christ, Jesus Christ, all represent Him who took flesh and became man, re-deemed the world, rules in the present dispensation, and will lay down His mediatorial authority when the end shall have come.

(3) Sometimes language is used which allies the humanity with the Divinity in the pre-existing state. The Incarnate Lord seems to be in heaven before the ascension, before the incarnation,

1 Cor. xv.
47.

before the world was · He, *the Second Man, is the Lord from heaven;* and the condescension of Christ Jesus, as the example on earth of self-sacrifice, St Paul carries up to the eternity of His existence

Phil. ii. 6.

in the form of God. In Him, the Incarnate Head of the mystical

Eph i. 5.

church, the saints are regarded as *predestinated unto the adoption* in an eternal purpose So the Lamb was slain, and redemption

1 Pet. i.
20.

wrought, *before the foundation of the world.* Sometimes, on the other hand, terms are employed which might seem to bring the eternal existence of the Author of redemption into time, as when

Acts xiii
33

the Son is said to be fully begotten this day in our nature . *This day have I begotten Thee.*

(4.) But always and everywhere the Agent is one . one in personality, one in the operation or ἐνέργεια θεανδρική   All that was done and suffered was done and suffered by the one Redeemer : the Son of God, the Son of man, the Son, Jesus Christ Man, the One Mediator. He is one   by a bond between His natures that has no similitude or analogy in the compass of human thought, save that of the union between the soul and body of man   And here lies the foundation of the whole superstructure of the redeeming work ⋅ all is Divine in its infinite virtue and efficacy, all is human in its validity for mankind. The One Christ who redeemed the world may be distinguished as to His natures ; but in His work the distinction vanishes again. Its Agent one

II. While the Person is one in the unity of Divinity and manhood, the Scriptures never confound the two natures themselves. This appears first in the fact that positively the two elements are placed in antithesis to each other , and, secondly, that negatively none of the attributes of one nature is ever applied to the other. Unconfused.

1. For the former we may refer again to the passages already cited as proving the distinction of the natures, of which St Paul has given, so to speak, the formula : *Jesus Christ of the seed of David according to the flesh , and declared to be the Son of God with power according to the Spirit of holiness*   The antithesis is to be assumed in all those texts which speak of the Son or the Word becoming flesh or becoming man   This applies to St. John especially, in whose language *was made* or *became* is equivalent to *come into*. *The Word was made flesh* is equivalent to *Jesus Christ is come in the flesh.* Flesh and Spirit are not more absolutely distinct in the unmaterialistic teaching of the Bible, and in the philosophy of common sense, than the two natures of the Redeemer. Rom. i 3, 4. John i. 14 1 John iv. 3.

2. Negatively, appeal may be made to the careful decorum of Scripture, which never predicates of the Deity of Christ in the abstract the attributes of humanity, nor of Christ's Manhood in itself the attributes of the Godhead.   When it is said ⋅ *to feed the church of God, which He hath purchased with His own blood*, God, or the Lord, as the reading may be, is the Person of Christ whose human blood and not His Divinity as such purchased the church. This phraseological rule has no exception. Acts xx. 28.

3. There needs, however, no proof of either of these positions

In the nature of things the Infinite cannot become the finite, save in the irrational speculations of Pantheism   The Divine nature and the human are essentially and eternally distinct.   It may be said that there is communion between us and God, and union between man and God in Christ.   But in the God-man Himself this union is communion too : communion of the natures in the union of the Person.

Scriptural

SCRIPTURAL DEVELOPMENT OF THE DOCTRINE.

The passages which have been cited in confirmation of the several propositions concerning the Person of Christ render needless any lengthened examination of the Scriptural testimony.   But it will be useful to take a general view of the several forms of the doctrine as gradually revealed by the Holy Ghost: of the course of development by which the MYSTERY OF GOD, CHRIST, was gradually made known to the apprehension of faith while still reserved as a mystery not to be comprehended of reason. The bare outline of the subject is all that will be given. first of the Old-Testament preparatory teaching; then of the Saviour's testimony to Himself; and, lastly, of the mature Apostolical teaching after Pentecost.   It must be remembered that we have only to do with the indivisible unity of the Saviour's Person in the two natures.

Old Testament
John v. 39
Luke xxiv. 27.

I. Our Lord on two occasions emphatically declared that the Old Testament testified concerning Himself.   First, when He gave this solitary commandment to *search the Scriptures,* this was the enforcement and reward of the injunction.   After the resurrection He Himself searched the Scriptures with two of His disciples as they were never searched by any other; and gave them in that unpreserved discourse the outline we have to fill up We find in the ancient records intimations of the human nature and the Divine running parallel but distinct at first, and in the later Old Testament these are united in the predictions of one Incarnate Person Who, as Servant of Jehovah, unites the two.

1 He is THE SEED a term which pervades the Bible as signifying the element of man's nature in its development, the symbol of its continuity as a race, and, as applied to Christ, has a specific relation to His position in mankind as its representative First, He is the Seed of the woman this First Gospel contains a promise of a Divine Conqueror of Satan, but it declares only as yet the representative manhood of Christ. Secondly, He is the Seed of Abraham: *in thy Seed shall all the nations of the earth be blessed.* Thirdly, He is the Seed of David. *I will set up thy Seed after thee . . . and I will stablish the throne of His kingdom for ever.* These several predictions are severally interpreted in the New Testament of the One Christ, who was the Son sent forth *made of a woman,* concerning whom it had been said by St. Paul just before that the promise to Abraham referred to ONE, *And to thy Seed, which is Christ,* who is the *Seed of David according to the flesh,* but the *Son of God with power.* They are three converging prophecies which recur in the Psalms and in the Prophets in various forms.

2 Concurrently and running parallel with these He is the ANGEL OF JEHOVAH who appeared to Abraham and promised to him the coming of Himself the Seed *My Name is in Him.* He is the ANGEL OF THE FACE OF JEHOVAH; and the prophet Hosea recalling His wrestling with the patriarch terms Him *Jehovah God of Hosts.* He is the *Angel of the Covenant* in Malachi; and this name looks back upon the earlier Theophany or manifestation of the revealing Son in angel form, and looks forward to His future appearance in His own elect form of Man Accordingly in the New Testament He is the Jehovah Who, as Incarnate, came to His literal temple, and whose voice Isaiah had heard in the temple mystical, *when he saw His glory and spake of Him*

3. The two natures are also united in the later Old Testament.

(1) Three Psalms may be selected as pre-eminently conclusive not as exhausting the subject, but as the key indicated by the New Testament for the solution of the ancient *mystery of Christ Thou art My Son; this day have I begotten Thee* the former part of this sentence is declared in St. John to refer to an eternal Sonship, the latter by St. Paul to refer to His revelation in the flesh perfected and demonstrated in the resurrection *The LORD said unto my Lord.* here Jehovah at the beginning and Adonai at the

Marginal notes:

The Seed.

Gen iii. 15.

Gen xxii. 18.
2 Sam. vii. 12, 13.

Gal iv. 4.

Gal iii. 16.
Rom i. 3, 4.

The Angel of the Presence

Ex xxiii. 21.
Isa. lxiii. 9
Hosea xii. 5.
Mal. iii. 1.
Isa. vi. 1.
John xii. 41.

The One Person.

Eph. iii. 4
Ps. ii. 7.
John i 14.
Acts xiii 33.
Ps cx. 1.

end both belong to the Supreme; and the Lord of David is in His Incarnate Person exalted to the right hand of God. *Thy* *throne, O God, is for ever and ever .   . God, Thy God, hath anointed Thee with the oil of gladness above Thy fellows* The name of God is here given to the Eternal Son, whose human excellence, in union with the Godhead, finishes the incarnate character and stamps the incarnate supremacy of Him concerning whom it is said to the Church *He is thy Lord , and worship thou Him*

(2) The testimony of Jesus through the Spirit of prophecy is still more distinct in the prophets proper. The Jehovah of Isaiah's vision is that Christ who is the *Child born* and the *Son given ·* as the latter THE MIGHTY GOD; as the former, or rather in His incarnate Person, *Wonderful, the Prince of Peace,* a wonder to the adoring contemplation of faith, the peace of its satisfied possession. *Behold, a virgin shall conceive, and bear a Son, and shall call His name* IMMANUEL : in this name, which our Saviour never bore as a personal designation, the full mystery of the Christ of God is announced. Micah speaks of the *Ruler in Israel, whose goings forth* *have been from of old, from everlasting   . And this* MAN *shall be* *the peace.* Jeremiah prophesies of the Redeemer, *And this is His* *name whereby He shall be called,* THE LORD OUR RIGHTEOUSNESS . raised up to David as the Incarnate Righteousness He is JEHOVAH , and gives His name to the Holy City, the Church, as inheriting the *righteousness of God in Him.* The Divine testimony to *the Man that is* *My Fellow, saith the Lord of Hosts,* in Zechariah, is plain in its profound meaning when connected with *they shall look upon* ME *whom* *they have pierced,* and with the New-Testament quotations both of the Redeemer and St. John. Daniel first gives Jehovah incarnate the title *Son of Man,* and exhibits Him as invested with supreme dominion *One like the Son of Man* must be paralleled with *The form of the fourth* *is like the Son of God* Our Saviour's application of Daniel's titles will vindicate for him perhaps the highest place among the ancient testimonies Malachi closes them in the Canon with the prophecy of that *Angel of the covenant* who in the fulfilment is Christ coming to His temple : this may be regarded as the last and crowning demonstration that the Jehovah of the Old Testament is the LORD of the New

(3.) It must be added that the Incarnate Person thus foreshadowed, and more than foreshadowed, in the earlier Scriptures

Side notes:
Ps. xlv. 6, 7.
Ps. xlv. 11.
The Prophets
Isa ix. 6.
Isa. vii 14
Micah v 2, 5.
Jer. xxiii. 6.
Jer xxxiii. 16.
Zech. xiii. 7
2 Cor v 12
Zech -xii 10.
Matt. xxiv. 30
Rev 1. 7
Dan vii 13.
Dan. iii 25
Mal. iii. 1
The Servant.

is both in psalm and prophecy exhibited as the subordinate Agent of the work of the Mediatorial Trinity. Reserving the fuller treatment of this for its own place, we need only to indicate that the future Christ is the Lord's *Anointed*, or *Messiah*, the Minister of God : *Behold My Servant, whom I uphold.* The *Word of the Lord* in Samuel's days is the eternal *Wisdom*, God Himself and yet distinct : personified in the Proverbs, He is incarnate by that name in the New Testament ; but in both the revealer of the Divine counsel. These latter terms, however, like that of the Angel, are not specifically connected in the Old Testament with the human nature of our Lord   They belong rather to His unrevealed Divine-human Person · the ANGEL-SERVANT or the SERVANT-SON of Jehovah.

Ps ii 2
Isa xlii 1.
1 Sam iii 21.
Prov viii. 30, 31.

(4.) The Old-Testament testimony, read in the light of the New, is thus most abundant and most clear   But the incarnation of the Son of God was a mystery until He came   Later Jewish theology does not indicate that it was anticipated by the nation   And St Paul tells us that Christ was *the mystery of God*, even as the revelation of salvation to the world was, until *the fulness of the time*

Incarnation concealed

Col. ii. 2.
Gal iv 4

II   Our Lord's witness to His One indivisible Divine-human Person is in the nature of things supreme : it explains the pre-intimations of the Old Testament, and it gives all the elements which, under the teaching of the Holy Ghost, were more or less developed by Evangelists and Apostles   It is to be sought simply and only in His own sayings upon earth and from heaven.

Testimony of Jesus.

1. The testimony given by Jesus concerning this mystery while on earth has been anticipated in the earlier treatment of the One Personality   It may be stated more fully, though in epitome, and with necessary repetition, as follows —

On Earth.

(1.) He adopts for Himself three names, THE SON OF GOD, THE SON OF MAN, and THE SON   The first, employed but seldom, refers to His Divine nature ; the second, habitually used, makes Him one with mankind , and the third is very generally if not always applied to His indivisible Person as including the two former.

The Lord's use of the term Son

(2) While this is generally true, it is true also that each of these three names is referred by the Redeemer to His One Person as pre-existing in an equality with the Father; as Man among men , and as one and the same in time and in eternity, in heaven and upon earth   His use of them may be studied with advantage.

2 This may be illustrated by a few passages which give our Lord's self-revelation as found in the Evangelists

Son of God. (1) The term Son of God He seldom Himself used , but He accepted the title, in its Divine significance, from His disciples and from His enemies   The latter understood Him to make Himself *equal with God,* and this our Lord confirmed, both then *John v 18—23.* and on many other occasions · *That all men should honour the Son, John x 30. even as they honour the Father.   I and My Father are One.   He that John xiv hath seen Me hath seen the Father.*   He was accused of blasphemy 9. for calling Himself the Son of God.   He had not given Himself the name ; but He accepted it, and appealed to His works for *John x. evidence that it was His right   the Father is in Me and I in Him.* 38. But, as the Son of the living God He is also the Son of Man ; *Matt xvi.* and, when Simon Peter uttered that confession, His Master 16, 17. declared the knowledge of His Divine-human Person to have been given by the revelation of the Father Himself.   Only once does the Lord as it were spontaneously term Himself the Son of God ; and then He offers Himself to the healed blind man in the *John ix.* Temple as a human speaker · *Dost thou believe on the Son of God ? . . .* 35, 37. *It is He that talketh with thee.*   Thus is a very remarkable instance

The Son. (2) Generally He speaks as The Son absolutely   always with reference to the Father, but always in His incarnate relation   It is needless to quote any other passages than those in which the One Lord, the Son, declares His pre-existence and equality with *John viii* God.   As the Son He said · *Before Abraham was I am,* declaring 58. both His pre-existence and His eternity.   So also when He claimed *John v.* to have from the Father *life in Himself* life originated in the 26. *Matt. xi.* Father, but eternal or without beginning   *Neither knoweth any* 27. *man the Father, save the Son*   the Son in His incarnate person as Man alone revealeth the Father.   And it is the Son approaching *John xvii* the cross as man who prays · *glorify Thou Me with Thine own Self* 5. *with the glory which I had with Thee before the world was.*

Son of Man. (3.) But, as the name Son of Man was that which the Redeemer elected for Himself, so it is that which brings into fullest expression the unity of the Incarnate Person.   He assumed it instead of the more limited Messiah or Christ · as being the Messianic designation that allied Him with all mankind.

And it is the subject of an endless variety of predicates taken
from His two natures interchangeably. This has been already
sufficiently shown. It may suffice to appeal once more to His
first use of the Name He loved so well. *And no man hath ascended* — John iii.
up to heaven, but He that came down from heaven, even the Son of — 13.
Man which is in heaven. Here are the pre-existence, the descent,
and the return of Him who in His one person is the Son of Man.
Another saying recorded by St. John as spoken at the end of the
Saviour's ministry transfers this to the Son absolutely · *I came* — John xvi.
forth from the Father, and am come into the world ; again, I leave the — 28.
world, and go to the Father. The entire doctrine of our Lord's
Divine and Divine-human Sonship is here.

3. The testimony given from heaven is the supplement of that — From
in the Gospels ; and it removes any slight vestige of doubt which — Heaven.
some of the sayings uttered in His subordination may have left.
Of it we may use the Apostles' words · *now speakest Thou plainly.* — John xvi.
The final Apocalypse, or Revelation concerning Jesus Christ, was — 29.
given by Jesus to St. John, and through him to the Church for
ever. The Redeemer Himself appears in His final and most
glorious manifestation in His human form, declaring *I am Alpha* — Rev. i 11.
and Omega, the First and the Last. And, after many words which
show that He is still the exalted Servant of the Trinity, He leaves
lingering in our ears the last of all His testimonies : *It is done. I* — Rev xxi.
am Alpha and Omega, the Beginning and the End, the First and the — 6 ; xxii.
Last. Thus the supreme witness is His own. — 13.

III. The testimony of the Evangelists and Apostles is that of — Apostolic
the Saviour Himself through the Spirit · it is the fulfilment of the — Testimony
promise, *He shall glorify Me.* — John xvi.
1 The Evangelists take precedence. But, as St John's must — 14.
be regarded as Apostolic testimony, there remains only that of the — Evange-
Synoptists. St. Matthew and St Luke give them in the Gene- — lists.
alogies. In the former, the Seed of David is *Emmanuel, God with* — Matt. i.
us, in the latter, the Seed of the Woman is *the Son of God ;* the — 23
former connects Him with Joseph, His reputed father, with — Luke i.35.
Judaism and the Old Testament, the latter with Mary, with the
World and the New Dispensation. The Synoptists and St John
perfectly agree ; though St. John, as will be seen, makes more
direct reference to the Divine nature of the Incarnate.

Apostles.   2 It is common to the Apostles to call their Master LORD, a title which bases the mediatorial supremacy of the Redeemer upon the fundamental dignity of Jehovah the LORD; and it is common to them also to assign to Him attributes and to demand for Him homage which imply His Divinity. The distinct types of their teaching as to the One Person may be briefly indicated

St Peter   (1.) St Peter, preaching in the Acts to strangers gathered into Jerusalem, proclaims the Messianic authority of Christ in general, and does not as yet dwell on the mystery of the Divine-human origin

Acts ii. 22 of the *Man approved of God.* He accumulates names which imply
Acts iii Divine dignity, such as *the Holy One and the Just,* the *Prince of life;*
14, 15. but the subordination of the Servant of God of whom Isaiah spoke
  is uppermost: *God, having raised up His Son,* παῖδα, not the Son
Acts iii. absolutely, but the Servant-Son In his Epistles he continues the
26. tribute to the mediatorial Messiah, and opens with a benediction
1 Pet i 3 of *the God and Father of our Lord Jesus Christ.* Afterwards he speaks
1 Pet. iii of Christ as *put to death in the flesh, but quickened by the Spirit;* here
18. bringing the two natures into conjunction by the same formula
2 Pet i. which St Paul uses In the Second Epistle we read of *the righteous-*
1—4; *ness of God and our Saviour Jesus Christ;* believers are said to par-
iii. 8. take of His *Divine nature,* and with *the Lord a thousand years are*
  as one day. Moreover St Peter closes his ministry with a Doxo-
2 Pet. iii logy, which only God can receive *Our Lord and Saviour Jesus*
18. *Christ. To Him be glory both now and for ever. Amen.* St James
James ii. calls the Saviour *the Lord of Glory* that *worthy Name* which belongs
1, 7 to Deity alone. And St Jude ascribes to *the only wise God our*
Jude 25. *Saviour glory and majesty.*

St. Paul.   (2.) St. Paul has an order of testimonies peculiar to himself. Most of them, however, have been already quoted; and those which belong to the subordination of the Person of Christ must be reserved. The Epistle to the Romans is pre-eminently the Mediatorial treatise, and contains the clearest expression of the unity and distinction in the two natures. In the beginning it is thus stated .

Rom. i. 3, *The Seed of David according to the flesh,* or the human nature, and
4. declared or defined to be *the Son of God with power, according to the*
  Spirit of holiness, or the Divine Here is a twofold sonship and a
Rom. ix. twofold nature. The same distinction is varied afterwards: *Of*
5. *whom as concerning the flesh Christ came, who is over all, God blessed*

for ever There cannot be a doubt that it is the express design of
the Apostle to unite the two natures here. Between these there
is another of great importance. God sent *His own Son*, the Son Rom viii. 3, 32.
of Himself, *in the likeness of sinful flesh*, that *own Son* whom He
spared not, where the ἰδίου υἱοῦ corresponds to the πατέρα ἴδιον
of the Jews' correct inference · He called God *His own Father*. In John v. 18.
the Corinthian Epistle, remarkable for the fullest expression of the
mediatorial subordination, there are some plain announcements of
the Divine-human dignity. Christ is *the Lord of glory* Whom as to 1 Cor. ii. 8.
His human nature the princes of this world crucified   And where
His subordination is most expressly taught He is *the Lord from* 1 Cor. xv 45—47.
heaven and a *quickening Spirit* in His Divine nature, while the
second Adam in His human.   *The Lord is that Spirit*, Who is God, 2 Cor. iii 17.
and it is at the close of these Epistles, in which *the head of Christ* 1 Cor. xi 3.
is God, that the Trinitarian benediction is pronounced, placing the
Incarnate in the Trinity as the channel of all the grace that
flows from the love of God, and is made the common possession
of believers through the Holy Spirit   The Epistles of the Roman
Captivity — the three Christological Epistles proper — contain
another type of expression in harmony with that of St. Paul's previous and subsequent writings but very different.   In that to the
Colossians the Person of Christ, the Son of the Father's love, is
the Image of the invisible God, the Firstborn of (or before) *every* Col. i. 15, 16, 17.
creature, in Whom *dwelleth all the fulness of the Godhead bodily* Now Col ii. 9
these wonderful words describe the Incarnate Person; not rising
however from the lower nature, as in the Romans, but descending from the higher. It is said of Him Whose blood redeemed
men that HE IS the Image of God: Himself invisible as Spirit
but manifesting the Godhead in the flesh; that HE IS the First-
begotten before every creature—*for by Him were all things created,*
and *He is before all things,*—but also the Firstborn of the created
human race as the heir and representative of all   Firstborn in two
senses. The Ephesian Epistle contains no express statement on
this topic But, as the special document of the Mediatorial Trinity,
it assigns to our Lord a place in relation to God and to the Church
and to the individual soul which belongs to no creature   It is
observable that here alone St Paul joins St. Peter in blessing the
God and Father of our Lord Jesus Christ, words that might seem Eph. i. 3.

to refer the former appellation to the humanity and the latter to
the Divinity of Christ, but really belong to the doctrine of His
subordination   The Epistle to the Philippians is peculiar as
giving the only passage in which St. Paul approaches the mystery

Phil ii 6 of the incarnation.   *Christ Jesus* is the one subject of every predi-
—8.   cate in that paragraph where the whole career of the Redeemer
is condensed into one sublime example of condescension.   As to
His Divinity He was, or rather is, *in the form of God* ὑπάρχων
establishes the consubstantial Deity, and μορφὴ Θεοῦ the personal
subsistence in the Trinity   As to His manhood, He is *in fashion
as a man*, rather, as Man *in the likeness of men*   The word *made*

Gal iv 4. connects the passage with those words to the Galatians, *made of a*
John i. 14. *woman*, and more remarkably with St John's, *The Word was made
flesh*, while St Paul's *likeness of men* shows us that St. John's
expression must not be misinterpreted into declaring a real change
from one nature into another.   The *form of a servant* expresses the
unity of the mediatorial subordinate Person   The Pastoral Epistles
contain the Apostle's final testimony. his FAITHFUL SAYINGS.

Titus ii. One or two new forms of the doctrine appear   *The glorious appear-
13.   *ing of the great God and our Saviour*. these words are not absolutely
unparalleled in St. Paul, they are the final echo of that early

Rom. ix. *God over all, blessed for ever.*   The words God and Saviour gram-
5.   matically belong to one person, just as the God and Father of
Christ is one in the Philippian Epistle   Theologically, they
belong to the one Person who is God, and, as Incarnate, our

Titus i. 3, Saviour   It must not be forgotten that *God our Saviour* has been
4.   before made synonymous with *Jesus Christ our Saviour*.   In the
First Epistle to Timothy there is a new example of the method of

1 Tim iii. conjoining the two natures   *the Mystery of godliness God was
16.   manifest in the flesh, justified in the Spirit*   And this throws its

1 Tim. ii 5. light back on those words. *for there is one God, and one Mediator
between God and men, the Man Christ Jesus*, or Christ Jesus, MAN.
The two passages mutually explain each other.   In the last of
these Pastorals the Apostle takes his farewell of the subject in the
doxology in which he invites the universal Church to say Amen:

2 Tim. iv. *And the Lord shall deliver me. . . .* TO WHOM BE GLORY FOR EVER
18.   AND EVER. AMEN.

(3.) The Epistle to the Hebrews adds nothing positively new

to the form of the doctrine, but it is abundantly clear in the Epistle to Hebrews. doctrine itself The first chapter is simply an exhibition of the Divinity of the Incarnate as such. It begins with another reading of St. Paul's teaching to the Colossians : the Son incarnate—for God *hath spoken in His Son*—is the *brightness of His glory, and the express image of His person*. He is called God by the Father, who seats Him on His mediatorial throne, and to Him is ascribed the production of all phenomena, which He creates and lays aside, being Himself THE SAME The second chapter exhausts the verity of our Lord's manhood *Both He that sanctifieth and they who are sanctified are all of one* He *took part of the same ;* the children's *flesh and blood*. After the two chapters have dwelt on the two natures severally, we are called upon in the third—the mystery of the junction of the two natures being behind the veil—to *consider the Apostle and High Priest of our profession, Christ Jesus*. This Person, from God to man Apostle and from man to God High Priest, *through the eternal Spirit offered* HIMSELF : that is, as Divine, His eternal Spirit offered His humanity as a sacrifice And the Apostle at the close revolves back into the thought which closed the first chapter, in words which condense the whole doctrine of the Indivisible Person *Jesus Christ, the same yesterday, and to-day, and for ever*.

Heb. i 2, 3.
Heb. i 8.
Heb i. 10
Heb. ii. 11.
Heb. ii. 14.
Heb iii. 1
Heb. ix. 14.
Heb xiii. 8.

(4) St. John's personal testimony—apart from his record of our Lord's—is found in the Prologue and Appendix of his Gospel, in his Epistles, and in the Apocalypse The Prologue assigns to the Divine nature of the Redeemer three names : the Logos, the Son, the God Only-begotten. The human nature is called Flesh. And the union is described as the *being made*, or becoming, *flesh ;* and as the dwelling in that flesh as a tabernacle He *dwelt among us*. The Logos is a term which signifies what Wisdom signified in the Old Testament ; it had become current in Jewish theology, and had been perverted, St. John vindicates it, and then uses it no more. The Son is the revelation of the only-begotten God in the flesh. He *became flesh ;* but not by any transformation, for He only *dwelt among us* · here the future Eutychian error is obviated. He *dwelt among us*, but not as a Stranger, for He *became flesh*, and is glorified in the flesh · here the future Nestorianism is condemned. The high words of the introduction to

St John.
John i. 1—18.

the Gospel must interpret the whole   After the Prologue St. John rarely speaks; but when he does it is nearly always to exhibit the

John i. 14.   Divine glory of the Incarnate which, he says, *we beheld*   Having

John ii 11   recorded the first miracle, he adds that Jesus *manifested forth His*

John ii 21.   *glory*   Again he comments on the words of the Lord, *He spake of the temple of His body*   an evident remembrancer of the tabernacling with us.   Similarly the private note on the Lord's symbolical teach-

John xiii   ing of the mystery of His incarnation ·   *Jesus knowing . . . that He*

3   *was come from God and went to God*   In the First Epistle St. John

1 John i 1,   takes up his Logos term, but combines with it the life :   *the Word*

2.   *of life.*   As in his Gospel, he soon passes from that designation, and rests on that of Son   The verity of the union of the two natures is declared by the whole tenour of the opening paragraph · *the Life was manifested and we have seen It*   He who in the Gospel

1 John iv.   is said to have *been made flesh* is here said to have *come in the flesh*

3.   It is remarkable that the Epistle, which begins with the Word of

1 John v   Life that was manifested, ends with the same · *This is the true God,*

20.   *and eternal life*   And who is the true God ?   St. John's answer is his last testimony, and perhaps the last testimony of the Bible *we are in Him that is true, in His Son Jesus Christ.*

(5) But, with regard to St John as to all the other recorders of the Saviour's history and work, the best argument of their teaching concerning the unity, uniqueness and supremacy of the Divine-human Person is the general tone and character of their common presentation   It is not so much the result of a fair esti- mate of the meaning of certain passages, nor the induction derived from a comparison of many, as the impression made upon the thoughtful reader, especially if he is a devout reader, by the spirit and manner of their communications   Wherever we enter the presence of Jesus we feel that we are before One who is God and yet not only God, man and yet not only man.   There is scarcely a page or an incident on a page which can be understood on the theory of either nature being alone in Christ: always some residuum requires the other nature.   There is nothing like this in all literature, it is a conception that has no parallel.   And that all the writers so wonderfully agree in their testimony as to One Person who is God and man must be ascribed to the fulfil-

John xv.   ment of His promise .   *He shall testify of Me*

26.

ECCLESIASTICAL DEVELOPMENT OF THE DOCTRINE.

Generally speaking, it may be said that discussion concerning the Two Natures of Christ has occupied the Christian Church more or less from the beginning; but the controversies that bore upon the One Person as such were limited to the first five centuries. The theories and opinions of those who have denied the Divinity of our Lord do not in strict propriety come into consideration here, since they admit no Person of Christ as our theology understands it. We have to mark, first, the heresies that erred concerning the Two Natures respectively; and, secondly, those which misapprehended the nature of their Union.

Historical

I. The controversy touching the question of the Divinity of Jesus enters here only in an indirect way

1 It took its first form in the Ebionites and Nazarenes, Christians with the old leaven of Judaism not purged out The EBIONITES derived their name either from Ebion or an adjective signifying poverty, and asserted that Christ was only man, the NAZARENES improved upon this abject view by adding that He was miraculously conceived and endowed Thus these primitive precursors of HUMANITARIAN doctrine were respectively the representatives of the Socinianism of the sixteenth century and the later Unitarianism of our own age. SOCINIANISM, akin to the Nazarene opinion, allowed that Christ was miraculously born, that He had transcendent fellowship with God in heaven during His life, and that after His resurrection He was exalted above every other creature It held the inspiration of Scripture, which however it endeavoured by a new translation and strange comments to harmonise with its views. By slow degrees this ancient Socinianism lost its distinctive and nobler features, and descended into modern UNITARIANISM, akin to the Ebionite view. Thus

Humanitarianism

The Nazarenes and Socinianism.

Ebionism and Unitarianism

the Humanitarian error has completed its circle, ending in these latter days where it began in the post-Apostolic age.

Second Century. 2 During the second and third centuries these primitive errors were revived and combined. Theodotus and Artemon in the second century, 180, asserted that Christ was mere man, ψιλὸν ἄνθρωπον, but supernaturally born of a virgin. Paul of Samosata, in the third century, 261, held the same view, but admitted that the Logos was in Him as a spirit in a higher sense than in the prophets. But the opinions of these heretics were bound up with their erroneous views of the Trinity, and vanished from the Church or were merged in other forms of error.

II Of the early heresies which assailed the natures of our Lord, while all retaining faith in His Person, some erred as to both the Divinity and the humanity, and others as to each of these respectively

Gnostic and Docetic Heresies 1 The Gnostic errors were very various, but they agreed generally in making the Godhead of Christ an emanation and His manhood a semblance only of man. The Divine in Him was an Æon, and the human not a material body, but a psychical or ethereal appearance that had nothing to do with the substance of the Virgin. These heretics were therefore termed Docetæ (from δοκέω). In the earliest form of Docetism, that of Cerinthus, condemned by St. John, the Man Jesus had a true body on which the Christ descended at his baptism, to abide with him only till his death. Hence the emphasis of the Apostolic statement that

1 John iv. 3 *Jesus Christ is come in the flesh* not in the mere likeness of flesh

2 The heresies of Arius and Apollinaris dishonoured the two natures respectively · the former denying our Lord's eternal con-substantiality with the Father, the latter denying to Him the human spirit ; the former impairing the Godhead, the latter the Manhood. These errors were, however, intimately connected

Origen. (1.) Both had their preliminaries in the ante-Nicene age Origen asserted the eternal generation of the Logos, and gave its due prominence to the doctrine of the Eternal Sonship , but by laying undue stress on the subordination of the Son in the Godhead he paved the way for Arianism. His followers forgot the eternity in his doctrine of the Sonship and his watchword God-man. And when once the Logos in Christ was regarded as a created essence it became in their theory only an earlier and nobler edition of the human spirit, which might well take the place of the reason and intellectual nature of man in man's great Representative.

(2) The doctrine of Christ's Person, as taught by Arius, a presbyter of Alexandria, assigned to the Divine Sonship an origination by the will of God before time and the world existed. the Son ἦν ποτε ὅτε οὐκ ἦν, and was generated not φύσει, but βουλήσει. He was the First Creature, though distinguished from the creation as the mediator between God and it   The Nicene Creed (A.D. 325) gives in its defensive clauses the best explanation of the heresy it condemned : BEGOTTEN NOT MADE, OF ONE SUBSTANCE WITH THE FATHER   The term ὁμοούσιον, OF ONE SUBSTANCE, became the watchword of orthodoxy as represented by Athanasius and the Nicene Council   The Semi-Arians softened this into ὁμοιούσιον, OF A LIKE SUBSTANCE.   The difference, however, between the two terms, though indicated by a single letter, is really unlimited : no creature can be in essence like God   From the Nicene Council downwards there has been no community of Arians, nor any creed of Arianism, in Christendom.

Arianism

(3) It was soon proved that the Homoousion, "of one substance," was as important for the human nature of Christ as for the Divine.   Apollinaris, Bishop of Laodicæa (A D 362), so defended the Divinity of Christ as to take from Him the integrity of His manhood   The human nature was in God before the incarnation, and brought with Christ from heaven   And the incarnation was only the assumption of the flesh and animal soul of man.   The Divine nature rendered the human spirit needless. the Person of Christ was a composite of God and two elements only of human nature.   Hence the true God was retained, but not the true nature of man.   It was urged against Apollinaris by the great divines of the fourth century that man could not be redeemed without the redemption of his spirit   The Article HE DESCENDED INTO HELL in the Apostles' Creed was in due time inserted for the defence of the separate spirit in Christ; but the condemnation of the doctrine was formally proclaimed at the Second Œcumenical Council of Constantinople, A.D 381.   It is observable that this Council, which asserted the integrity of the human nature of Christ,

Apollinarianism

proclaimed also the Divinity of the Holy Spirit The Apollinarian errors reappeared, as will be seen, in later forms

Heresies as to the One Person

III The heresies which assailed the union of the two natures of our Lord in His one person were two, the Nestorian and the Eutychian. the latter, confounding the Natures, was a recoil from the former, which divided the Person.

Nesto-rianism

1 Nestorius was Patriarch of Constantinople (A D. 428), and a bigoted opponent of heresy. He took offence, however, at one of the current watchwords of orthodoxy, which termed the Virgin the MOTHER OF GOD, θεότοκος He had been trained in the Antiochian school of theology, as a presbyter in Antioch he had imbibed the teaching of Theodore of Mopsuestia—the real founder of Nestorianism—who laid much stress upon the union of the Logos with a man who was born of Mary. Nestorius conceded to his opponents that the Virgin was MOTHER OF CHRIST; but he denied the personal union, taught that a perfect man became the organ and instrument of the Logos, or the temple in which He dwelt. The tendency—perhaps only the tendency—of his teaching was to represent Christ as two persons, united by a bond not essentially different from that which unites God with any other pre-eminent organ of His will. The two natures in the Redeemer were in this theory united by an ἀσύγχυτος συνάφεια : not in one personality, but by a conjunction merely, though of an undefinable nature Nestorius was formally condemned at the Third Œcumenical Council, held at Ephesus A D. 431. His chief opponent was Cyril of Alexandria.

Euty-chianism.

2. The followers of Cyril, who died A D. 444, exaggerated his statements as to "the union in one hypostasis of the Logos from the Father and the human flesh." The mystical Alexandrian school of thought, represented by Eutyches, refused to admit that anything pertaining to Christ was otherwise than Divine after the incarnation. His avowal was this: "I confess that, before the union, our Lord was of two natures (ἐκ δύο φύσεων); but, after the union, I confess only one nature." The tendency—perhaps here again only the tendency—of this doctrine was not to merge the Divine in the human, nor the human in the Divine, but to establish a composite nature, neither God nor man one Nature and one Person, not One Person in two Natures The history of

the controversies which led to the assembling of the Fourth
Œcumenical Council, held at Chalcedon A D 451, is a painful
record of human infirmity overruled by the Spirit of Truth.

3. The Formula drawn up at that Council gives in its careful
statements the best explanation of the two opposite errors
"Following the holy Fathers, we unanimously teach one and the
same Son, our Lord Jesus Christ, perfect as to His Godhead
and perfect as to His manhood, truly God and truly Man, of a
reasonable soul and human flesh subsisting . consubstantial with
His Father as to His Godhead, and consubstantial with us as to
His manhood : like unto us in all things, yet without sin , as to
His Godhead begotten of the Father before all worlds ; but, as
to His manhood, in these last days born, for us men and our
salvation, of the Virgin Mary, the mother of God , one and the
same Christ ; Son, Lord, Only-begotten, known and acknowledged
in two natures, without confusion, without severance, and without
division , the distinction of the natures being in no wise abolished
by their union, but the peculiarity of each nature being maintained, and the two concurring in one Person and Hypostasis.
We confess not a Son divided and sundered into two persons, but
one and the same Son, and Only-begotten, and God-Logos, our
Lord Jesus Christ, even as the prophets had before proclaimed
concerning Him, and He Himself hath taught us, and the symbol
of the Fathers hath handed down to us." The four terms in the
original Greek deserve careful attention The two natures are
said to be united, ἀσυγχύτως, without commixture, and ἀτρέπτως,
without transmutation or conversion : these as against Eutyches.
The One Person is retained, ἀδιαιρέτως, undividedly, and ἀχωρίστως,
inseparably : these as against Nestorius Thus was concluded, at
the Chalcedonian Council, the long controversy concerning the
Person of Christ "truly" God, "perfectly" Man, "inseparably"
One Person, "unconfusedly" in Two Natures. The Athanasian
Creed added an analogy : "One not at all from confusion of substance, but from unity of person For as a rational soul and flesh
is one man, so God and man is one Christ." Later controversies,
and later decisions, were but feebler reproductions of these bold,
strong, and incontrovertible statements

IV. The later developments of the Christological dogma have

[margin note:] Chalce-
donian
Formula.

to do rather with the doctrine of our Lord's Two Estates than with that of His One Person So far, however, as they affect the latter, they must have brief notice.

1. Eutychianism reappeared, or rather continued, in the Monophysite and Monothelite heresies which long disturbed the Eastern Church.

Monophysites.

(1.) The MONOPHYSITE theory is, as the name imports, that of "One Nature" in Christ It was held with many subtle distinctions by a number of sects, which concurred in blending the Lord's Manhood with His Godhead, and differed according to their views of it as a property or as an accident of the Divine nature. These sects have continued to the present day as represented by Jacobites, Copts, Abyssinians, and Armenians.

Monothelites.

(2) The MONOTHELITE variation turned upon the question as to the unity or duality of the Redeemer's will. The Sixth Œcumenical Council, at Constantinople, A D 680, condemned the doctrine of One Will in Christ the Catholic Church, East and West, agreed that in two natures there must be two wills, and that in Christ the Divine and the human wills harmoniously cooperated, the human following the Divine. Much controversy issued in the rejection of the Monothelite heresy, which allowed no place for limitation in knowledge and human temptation or moral test in Christ. With it was rejected also—in ecclesiastical formula at least—the compromise aimed at in the expression μία θεανδρικὴ ἐνεργεία, "one Theandric or Divine-human operation." But, though this term was not accepted generally, it alone expresses the truth of the one mediatorial agency of that Person in whom the Divine will governed the free volitions of the human. This heresy also has lingered among the Oriental sects to the present time.

Adoptianism.

2. Nestorianism reappeared, long after the Chalcedonian decision, in the West, as Eutychianism reappeared in the East. Two Spanish bishops, Elipandus of Toledo and Felix of Urgella, taught that in His human nature the Redeemer was Son of God only by adoption. an adoption which was the seal of His excellence, foreseen at the incarnation and consummated at the resurrection The arguments of Alcuin, and other theologians, based upon the impersonality of our Lord's human nature—"in ad-

sumtione carnis a Deo persona perit hominis, non natura"—were sufficient to secure the condemnation of this form of Nestorian heresy, which is known as ADOPTIANISM, at the Council of Frankfurt, A.D. 794

3 It may be said that no controversy concerning the Person of Christ has since the Sixth Œcumenical Council disturbed Christendom. The decisions of the Council of Chalcedon, the Fourth Œcumenical, were really decisive   Mediæval discussions revolved around philosophical and mystical theories of the incarnation, but issued in no new development of dogma and in no very definite new heresy.   The discussions in which the Lutheran and the Reformed Churches were engaged, and those which divided the Lutheran divines, touched rather the relation of our Lord's two natures respectively to His two Estates of humiliation and exaltation , and therefore belong to another section.   They were all agreed as combatants, and agreed with the Roman and Greek Churches, in holding the Unity of the Divine-human Person as in some inexplicable way resulting from the assumption of the human by the Divine   They differed only as to the measure in which the attributes of the Deity were hidden or suppressed.   It is true that the more modern forms of this controversy involve questions which, seeming to touch only the Humiliation of our Lord, really touch the perfection of one or other or both of His natures.   For instance, the theories of many German and French divines which regard the Son of God as literally limiting Himself for a season to the bounds of a human spirit are certainly reproductions of what has been described as Eutychianism.   But to this subject we must return when treating of the Two Estates of the Redeemer.

Modern Tendencies.

THE PROCESS OF THE MEDIATORIAL WORK.

The Mediatorial History.

Between the Person of Christ and the Finished Work of Redemption we must interpose the process of the Mediatorial Ministry. The New Testament is a history of the Redeemer's mission, delivered partly in facts and partly in commentary on those facts. It sets out with the Incarnation as the basis of the whole; pursues the progress of the Christ through His Two Estates of humiliation and exaltation; describes His assumption of His Mediatorial Work. and His accomplishment of the functions of its three offices of Prophet, Priest, and King. After considering these topics in their order, it will be well to close with a review of our doctrine on the unity of the Person of Christ in all His estates and offices and work, as exhibited in the variety of names assigned to Him in Scripture and theology. This will prepare for the doctrine of the Atonement.

The Life of Jesus.

There is no method of studying the theology of redemption at once so interesting and so effectual as that which connects it with the successive stages of our Lord's history. This does not, however, demand the presentation of what is commonly called THE LIFE OF JESUS. Modern literature abounds with attempts to depict the Life which is above every life · a career which was spent under conditions that must needs render the attempt abortive But to these we may apply the ancient apostrophe in another

Isa. liii. 8. sense *Who shall declare His generation?* and the words of the

1 Cor ii 11. Apostle also that *the things of God knoweth no man, but the Spirit of God.* Only the Holy Ghost is or should be the Recorder of that history. And He has given it in its own unapproachable and undefiled perfection as it hath pleased Him. It is true that the effort to exhibit the Holy Character has been made in some works of edification which have preserved the spirit of reverence, aiming to portray the Redeemer as at once a Saviour and an example

But often it has been the unbeliever who has undertaken the task ; and the replies which he has originated under the same title have sometimes fallen into the errors against which they protest. Yet there is an historical review of the Saviour's career which may be made the basis of the entire system of evangelical theology. The life of our Lord was the manifestation of His Person and of His work, as begun below and continued above, and, remembering that the Acts and the Epistles and the Apocalypse supplement the Gospels, even as the Old Testament is their preface, we shall pursue our study of the Mediatorial Ministry in strict connection with the stages and processes of the Lord's history on earth and in heaven, before and at and after the Fulness of Time.

THE INCARNATION.

The mystery of the Incarnation occupies its own solitary place in theology. It has been seen that in the fulness of time the Eternal Son assumed human nature, conceived by the Holy Ghost; that the mystery is revealed as a fact, and defined by a variety of expressions which leave it a mystery still: no theories availing to explain it. We have now to do with its relation to the entire work of Christ, a relation which is fundamental, and of such a character as to make it the basis of all other acts, and co-ordinate with none. this truth, however, needing to be carefully stated and guarded. The Incarnation, as the foundation of our Lord's redeeming ministry, with all its offices, is everlasting and unchangeable, common therefore to the two estates of humiliation and exaltation.

The Incarnation

THE INCARNATION A PERMANENT CONDESCENSION.

It is the infinite condescension of the Son of God and the glory of man that the union of the two natures in Christ is permanent. He became man once for all. our manhood is a vesture which He will not fold and lay aside IMMANUEL is His name for ever. This being so, it is scarcely right to speak of our Lord's alliance with our race as part of His mediatorial humiliation were it

Permanent.

such, His humiliation would never terminate. It is true that the effect of His condescension will never cease. He will be one with mankind to all eternity . as it were expressly to declare this, to keep it in the minds of His people and prevent misconception, 1 Cor xv. 28. that one profound saying was placed on record · *then shall the Son also Himself be subject*, or *subject Himself*. His union with us, which is the same thing as His kingdom or His tabernacle with us, shall have no end. We know Him only as Immanuel Every reference, or nearly every reference, to His pre-existent state connects Him with man as man's predestined Head. Certainly every one of our Lord's own allusions does this Let His last word stand John xvii. 5 for all *the glory which I had with Thee before the world was ;* where the I of Him who prays, addressing the Father and not man, is the Incarnate I, transferred as it were and carried up into eternity. It is true that the exinanition, or self-emptying, which St. Paul Phil. ii. 6. attributes to the Son while as yet *in the form of God*, preceded the incarnation in the Divine counsel But that surrender of the manifestation of His glory was only a purpose until the actual descent , and must not be included in the Messianic humiliation that followed upon earth. The estates of humiliation and exaltation belong to the Incarnate Person as He is the Christ, and in the world of human affairs. As the Eternal Son, *in the bosom of* Jno. i 18. *the Father*, He could not be abased, though He might be emptied of His glory There is a distinction between the acts of Divine con- Phil. ii. 8. descension and the acts of Divine-human humiliation · *found in fashion as a man*, the Lord might *humble Himself ;* but not before It belongs to the freedom of the Divine Being that He can, in a certain sense, limit Himself if He will : for instance, the Triune God becomes the Author of a universe that existed not before His will added it to His self-manifestation ; and He condescends to specific relations with the creature, though Himself the Absolute God. But in this condescension there is no humiliation So also, though the analogy is imperfect, One Person in the Godhead, Col. i. 16. by Whom *were all things created*, might condescend and has condescended to unite Himself with His creature. Hence His assumption of our human NATURE as such is not of the essence of His humiliation : it was His literal assumption of the FLESH in the miraculous conception that added the element of self-abasement.

THE FUNDAMENTAL BASIS OF THE REDEEMING WORK

The Incarnation is not so much one of the stages or acts of the Redeemer's history as the necessary basis of all. By incarnation is here meant, not the literal taking of our flesh, but that union with our nature to which the Scripture does not give a name The truth on this subject also may be stated in two propositions The assumption of our manhood by a Divine Person was the accomplishment of the purpose of salvation ; it was also the means in order to that salvation.   These two are inseparable. *[Incarnation Fundamental.]*

1 When the Son of God became man the human race was declared to be a saved race   The ancient predictions concerning His advent into the flesh always announced His coming as that of a Redeemer and Deliverer who had already saved the world in purpose and in effect   The first Gospel declared that the Seed of the woman should bruise the Serpent's head   The entire strain of the Psalms and Prophecies predicts the coming of One whose coming was deliverance : so the great Fulfilment says, *He hath visited and redeemed His people.*   The most distinct and emphatic prophecy of the birth of Jesus unites in one sentence *Unto us a Child is born* and *His name shall be called The Mighty God, The Prince of Peace.*   The first New-Testament name of Jesus is *Emmanuel, God with us.*   The song of the angels heralds a Saviour whose advent is the pledge of an accomplished salvation.   To say all in one word, the incarnation of Christ is never regarded as one stage in a work that is to be wrought, however true that may in a certain sense be.   Certainly there is no hint of any uncertainty or contingency in the issue *thus it must be* reigns over all the mission which He who voluntarily came in the flesh undertook. *[End Virtually Attained.]* *[Luke i 68.]* *[Isa ix 6.]* *[Matt.i.23.]* *[Matt. xxvi.54.]*

2. But the other proposition is no less true. the Incarnation was a means to an end.   Though the early announcements dwell rather on the accomplishment of the Divine purpose in the gift of His Son, we find as the history of Christ proceeds more and more distinct intimations that the Saviour entered the body prepared for Him in order to achieve the reconciliation by an atoning death. He who was the Mediator in His incarnate Person, exhibiting in Himself the union of God and mankind, must also be the Mediator in His sacrificial work, effecting or realising that ideal union *[Means to an End.]*

Matt. xx. 28. *The Son of man came not to be ministered unto, but to minister, and to give His life a ransom for many* Hence, when we reach the Epistles we find that the Incarnation is always closely connected with an atoning design . not indeed generally as one stage towards the Atonement, but as essentially connected with it. JESUS is not the

Gal. iv 4, 5. perfect Saviour until He becomes CHRIST. *When the fulness of the time was come, God sent forth His Son, made of a woman, made under the law, to redeem them that were under the law.* Our Lord is our

Heb ii 14. Representative, *forasmuch then as the children are partakers of flesh and blood He also Himself likewise took part of the same, that through death He might destroy him that had the power of death* This passage with its entire context impressively shows that the Incarnation was the way to the cross Three terms are used, each of great importance It was to abolish death, by taking his power from its representative and lord, *that is, the devil* This, however, required that He should take our flesh in order that He might

Heb ii 9. *taste death for every man,* and thus *deliver them who through fear*

Heb. ii. 15, 17. *of death were all their lifetime subject to bondage ·* this deliverance being accomplished by His sacrifice of reconciliation, as the words ἀπαλλάξῃ and ἔνοχοι sufficiently prove Only as man could He be a *merciful and faithful High Priest in things pertaining to God to make expiation for the sins of the people,* εἰς τὸ ἱλάσκεσθαι. In order to accomplish these results—the destruction of death, the reconciliation of offenders subject to death, and the propitiation required

Heb.ii.16 in order to both—He *taketh hold of the seed of Abraham.* He taketh to Himself, ἐπιλαμβάνεται, not angels, but men, mankind, however, being viewed here as the saved church of humanity, or

Gal iii. 9. the *blessed with faithful Abraham,* and *the seed of Abraham My*

Isa. xli. 8. *friend.* But it was that He might taste of death ὑπὲρ παντός.

Errors. 3. A careful attention to the language of Scripture will help us to avoid some prevalent errors · that of those, on the one hand, who regard our Saviour's assumption of the flesh as His first step in an experiment for human salvation, translating the cry

John xix. 30. at the end *It is decided* instead of *It is finished*, and that of such, on the other, as make the Incarnation itself the bestowment of salvation on mankind. the death of the Saviour being needed chiefly for its moral influence as an example; and, lastly, of many who, on Sacramental principles, give the Incarnation of our

Lord an undue preponderance, and regard the extension of that Incarnation in the life of believers as the essence—as the fountain and process and end—of the Christian life These errors are only alluded to here . they will meet us again.

THE INCARNATION IN SCRIPTURE.

The Scriptural references to the Incarnation are comparatively few; but they refer to it as a mystery which had more than any other been hidden from the mind of man. In the Old Testament it is the subject of dim and mysterious prophecy which only the Fulfilment has explained In the New Testament it is historically recorded by two of the Evangelists; and, their record being pre-supposed, it is then theologically stated in a considerable variety of phrases which may be profitably studied and classified As these, however, have been considered under the Person of Christ, it will be sufficient to refer to them only in a very general way.

I The Incarnation of the Son of God, the supreme fact in human history, bringing the Eternal Generation into a human birth in time, was an event which the Spirit of prophecy never revealed until it took place. There is no one word in the Old Testament which plainly declared that God would become Man. On the other hand, there is no event recorded in the New Testament which is more expressly and variously announced as the accomplishment of ancient oracles. *Prophecy and Fulfilment*

1. This paradox is partly solved by an examination of the pre-dictions themselves which foreannounce the coming of a Divine Seed born NOT OF THE WILL OF MAN, BUT OF GOD Only the *fulness of the time*—therefore the fulness of time because this was its great secret—declared why it was said, not of the seed of Adam but of the seed of Eve, *it shall bruise thy head ,* and now we know that the Incarnation was the first accent of prophecy. Many later predictions spoke of the Seed of Abraham and of David; but the New Testament explains that the line of Abraham and David furnished only the human mother of our Lord Isaiah, who sheds so clear a light on the earthly end of the Messiah, sheds a light equally clear on His earthly beginning . *Behold, a Virgin shall conceive, and bear a son, and shall call His name Immanuel.* This oracle also veiled its own meaning A certain ambiguity in *John i 13. Gal. iv. 4.* *Gen. iii. 15.* *Isa vii.14.*

the term עַלְמָה has always been wrested by the Jews to the suppression of the truth, as by Kimchi "non est virgo sed puella. Puella vero hæc uxor prophetæ, vel uxor Achazi, quod probabilius videtur." It was never charged against the enemies of Christ that they misunderstood this and some other passages : such as,

Isa ix. 6 *Unto us a Child is born, unto us a Son is given*, and the testimony of
Isa xlix.1. the Servant of the Lord to Himself, *the Lord hath called Me from the womb, from the bowels of My mother hath He made mention of My name* But these are all with the utmost exactness explained in the New Testament of the Incarnation of the Son of God.

Theophanies.   2 Another solution may be found in the fact that the ancient revelation was pervaded by a certain presentiment of the appearance of God in human form. The early Theophanies, or manifestations of the Supreme, were in the likeness of men The Angel of Jehovah, or the Angel of the Face, had, so to speak, the form of the Son of man The general anthropomorphic style of the Old Testament was a perpetual indirect prophecy of the Incarnation. The same Jehovah who constantly interdicted the forma-

Deut. iv. 12. Ps. cv. 4   tion of any image of Himself—*ye saw no similitude, only ye heard a voice*—nevertheless commanded His people to *seek His face.* The WISDOM of the Proverbs is so described as to suggest the coming revelation of a Personal Representative of the Godhead

Prov viii. 31.   dwelling by more than a mere Divine influence *with the sons of men.* The supreme SERVANT OF JEHOVAH in Isaiah is all but declared to be Jehovah in human form. It is certain that the later Judaism did, in a confused manner, grope its way towards this truth ; misinterpreting these hints and the symbols with which they were connected Not to dwell upon this, the Christian reader of the Old Testament—and only to the Christian reader does it yield its true teaching—feels everywhere that time is labouring with a secret that is ready to be revealed IMMANUEL,

Matt. i. 23.   GOD WITH US. This, however, must not be carried too far When the Dayspring arose the world was not prepared to comprehend it St. Paul furnishes his testimony in a remarkable passage which

2 Cor. iv. 6.   looks both ways. *God, who commanded the light to shine out of darkness, hath shined in our hearts to give the light of the knowledge of the glory of God in the face of Jesus Christ.* This is the Face or Divine Presence which shines everywhere by anticipation in

the Old Testament but its revelation in the New is, as it were, light arising in darkness.

3 There are some passages in Scripture which suggest the question how far the uncorrected traditions of men, perverting the original promise, expected an incarnate God as *the Desire of all nations,* or that the gods might *come down to us in the likeness of men.* It cannot be doubted that no thought is more universal in mythology than that of the union of Divinity with humanity whether by the apotheosis of man, ascending to the fellowship of the gods, or by the descent of Divine beings to earth The science of Comparative Theology is able to adduce evidence from all parts of the world, and from every age, that a dim presentiment of the Incarnation has existed among men ; but, generally speaking, strangely blended with the notion of metempsychosis and transmigration. Among the Egyptians animals, rather than man, were the medium. The mythology of the Hindoos exhibits a boundless variety of incarnations or avatars one of which, that of Krishna, represents the Deity as man bruising the head of a serpent, while the serpent bites his heel Buddhism was based upon a Pantheistic evolution of the Infinite in the finite the object of which was to destroy sacrificial religion, and lead the spirit back to its original abyss. Lamaism in Thibet added the idea of hereditary incarnations The classical metamorphoses exhibited the notion in its most degraded form, though the name given to Jupiter, $Ze\dot{v}s$ $\kappa a\tau a\beta\acute{a}\tau\eta s$, maintains the truth that underlay the perversion. Scandinavian mythology has its many variations on the same thought. And so also have the American religions, especially that of Mexico, which contains unmistakable traditions of an incarnation of the highest god through a human mother. The thoughtful study of all these, and numberless other, fantasies of heathenism, will force upon the mind a conviction that the original promise of the Seed of the woman had been diffused among all nations, responding to the profound instinct of mankind longing for communion with a personal God, but left to its unregulated gropings until the fulness of the time.

II The Incarnation as an accomplished fact was in due time committed to record by two chosen writers, St Matthew and St. Luke, who, under the guidance of the Holy Spirit, collected

Traditions.

Hag. ii. 7.
Acts. xiv. 11

In the New Testament.

L 2

and made permanent the sacred tradition of the first disciples : the one representing the Jews, the other the Gentiles.

The Narrative.

1. The narrative itself is the most wonderful in human annals. It is given in two forms · by St Matthew, less as an historical account than as an exhibition of the fulfilment of prophecy , by St Luke, as an avowed narrative of the fundamental event in human redemption   The most searching criticism is constrained . to admit that the chapters of the Incarnation have precisely the same authority as the rest of the books in which they appear. No history in Scripture is more clear and explicit than that which narrates the miraculous advent of the Son of God as the Divinely-begotten Son of a human mother.   Superficial objections may be raised against the narratives themselves, especially as compared with each other; but, to those who believe in the Incarnation first, and who believe secondly in the superintendence of the Spirit over the preservation of its record, those objections vanish. St. Matthew begins with the Abrahamic and Davidic descent of the Messiah , and then describes His birth and infant history as the fulfilment of five distinct Old-Testament prophecies, omitting much that a mere chronicler would have inserted.   He gives the

Matt. i. 20.

public registry of the Davidic descent of *Joseph, son of David,* his privileges being inherited by Jesus, concerning Whose birth of Mary, however, the language suddenly changes : τὸν ἄνδρα Μαρίας, ἐξ ἧς ἐγεννήθη Ἰησοῦς, IMMANUEL, God with us.   St. Luke adopts a new and evangelical method of his own in giving the genealogy.   He traces it upward through Heli, the father of Mary, through all generations of men to God Himself · we must

Luke iii. 23

read his words, *being a son (as was supposed, of Joseph) of Heli ;* the son being the grandson, through Mary.   St. Luke makes Mary the centre, and the Incarnation is for all the world, that of the Seed of the woman.   St. Matthew makes Joseph the centre, and the Incarnation is that of the Son of David, the Christ. The details of the harmony need not here be entered into. Suffice that the two records may be woven into one continuous history of the supernatural advent, conception and birth of the Son of God in humanity.   And this history records an event which, in its essential character, had never entered into the mind of man.

2. It is remarkable that after this most full and explicit Subsequent Silence narrative, the mystery of the miraculous conception by which God became incarnate is never once alluded to   But it is always presupposed, and in such a variety of ways as to confirm the truth of the record which the subsequent silence of the New Testament is supposed to contradict.   In fact, the decorum of Scripture treats this supreme Miracle with a reticent dignity that gives a law to us : proofs are abundant of the death and of the resurrection and even of the Divinity of the Redeemer, but His generation in the flesh of man is left to the vindication of God   Direct evidences we are forbidden to seek for, the indirect abound everywhere in the Gospels themselves.   *For with God nothing shall be* Luke i. 37. *impossible*   this one word should be a sufficient answer to all possible preliminary objections that sense or reason may urge. *But Mary kept all these things, and pondered them in her heart .* this Luke ii 19. sentence sheds light upon much that follows.   The blessed Mother of our Lord was the human custodian of the mystery, nor did she depart until the light of Pentecost confirmed her witness ; though a veil, which we must not penetrate, falls upon her communications   It was part of our Lord's lowliness to bear the reproach which sprang from the paradox of His human birth : His cross began from His conception, and His mother bore it with Him, the sword piercing her soul also from the beginning as well as Luke ii. 35 at the end   This reproach He has endured at the hands of both Gentiles and Jews to this day, but reverence forbids our further examination of it.   Once more, the silence of our Lord and His disciples as to the fact may be explained on the general principle that the Divinity of the Redeemer was to be independently demonstrated, and that again would demonstrate His Divine birth.   Lastly, the supreme evidence of the Human Conception was reserved until it was perfected in the resurrection, with which birth from the dead St. Paul connects the ancient word   *Thou art* Acts xiii. 33. *My Son, this day have I begotten Thee !*   The Person and the Work of the Incarnate Son were both consummated then   He was at length perfectly raised up and begotten in our nature.   Meanwhile, whatever His disciples knew, Jesus Himself always spoke and acted as One who *made of a woman* knew that God was His only Gal. iv 4 Father . evidence of which abounds from His first testimony to

Luke ii 49
John xiv. 9.

Himself, *Wist ye not that I must be about My Father's business?* down to the end, *He that hath seen Me hath seen the Father!*

3. The Fact of the Incarnation is throughout the later Scriptures referred to in a variety of ways : always as the basis of the entire Mediatorial economy. The classification which is theologically most useful is perhaps that which views it in relation to the Three Persons of the Holy Trinity respectively

The Father.

Gal. iv 4
Rom. viii. 3
Acts iii. 26.
Acts xiii. 33

1 Cor. xv 47.
The Son.

(1.) The Father, or, what is in the New Testament the same, God, is connected with the miraculous entrance of the Son into human nature only in a general manner. He is said to have *sent forth His Son, made of a woman* and *in the likeness of sinful flesh ;* and, especially, to have *raised up His Son* among men. *This day have I begotten Thee* refers to the incarnation only as it is perfected in the resurrection the raising up of the advent and the raising up from the dead thus encircle the whole historical manifestation of the Son of Man Who is *the Lord from heaven*

John i. 14.

1 John iv. 3.
Heb. ii 14, 16

(2) The relation of the Son Himself to His Incarnation is carefully to be studied It was His voluntary act He condescended to be *made flesh,* but only as God who *dwelt among us .* these sayings must be blended, as mutually qualifying each other. He *came into the flesh* and *He came in flesh* these also have their several shades of meaning. He *taketh hold of the seed of Abraham* and *took part of the same flesh and blood* of which the *children are partakers ·* these also are mutually complementary. It must be noted that in this series of counterparts the active and the passive side of the Son's assumption and submission are made emphatic.

Heb x. 5.
John vi. 38.
Heb. x. 7.

As to the latter He says, *a body hast Thou prepared Me ,* as to the former, *I came down from heaven not to do Mine own will,* and *Lo, I come (in the volume of the book it is written of Me,) to do Thy will, O God*

The Spirit

(3.) That Body was prepared by the Third Person of the Trinity whose relations to this mystery of godliness is theologically the most important. The Son sent of the Father, and voluntarily coming to His own new nature, is yet CONCEIVED OF THE HOLY GHOST Into the subordinate question which here arises, as to the relation between the Son's assumption and the Spirit's preparation of the Humanity, we dare not enter at large. A few suggestions only may be reverently made. The human nature of our Lord must be *separate from sinners* . in the Christian economy Heb. vii. 26 the Third Person is the Sanctifier; He hallowed the flesh into which our Lord entered, and also so sanctified the Virgin Mother as to make her meet for her high function   Again, the act of the Holy Ghost demonstrated that the Redeemer became literally Man among men, and did not bring from heaven His pre-existing humanity, as many affirm that He did.   Once more, the Spirit's relation to the new manhood laid the basis of the Redeemer's subordination   In the unsearchable mystery of our Lord's Person, while His human nature is His own, and one with His Divinity, it is also a human nature which is to be led of the Spirit through all its processes to the end.   Hence, lastly, the Holy Ghost has a specific relation to His humanity as it is received on behalf of the race with which He is allied.   The Spirit of the Son, out of Whose fulness we all receive, is the Holy Ghost Who created and dwells in His human nature from the beginning ; and is the sacred link between us and our Head, even as He is the sacred bond between us all and the Father.   These are interior subtilties of the Redemptional economy of the Triune God which none who would understand the Scriptures may despise, though none can find them out unto perfection

THE HISTORICAL MANIFESTATION OF THE REDEEMER

Historical Process

The process of the Saviour's history passes through two stages of Humiliation and Exaltation, and His mediatorial work divides into three branches as He is Prophet, Priest, and King.

THE TWO ESTATES

The Two Estates

The history of the Redeemer is the history of redemption ; and the history of redemption fills, so far as concerns man, both eternity and time, both heaven and earth.   The stages of the Lord's progression, most comprehensively viewed, have, to speak paradox, no beginning and no end. His goings were from everlasting.   From His pretemporal, eternal existence, He descended to become the second

Head of mankind; was for ages an unrevealed Reality in human affairs; in the fulness of time became incarnate; finished His work upon earth; ascended into heaven; and will, when His work is a second time finished, assume a final manifestation which only the day will declare. Thus His estates are manifold. But as the revealed Redeemer, as the Christ under the burden of His Messianic office, His estates are two: that of Humiliation and that of Exaltation.

THE ESTATE OF HUMILIATION

The Estate of Humiliation may be viewed, first, with regard to our Lord's Person, and, secondly, with regard to His work: a distinction, however, which must not be too precisely maintained, inasmuch as the two are inseparable.

HUMILIATION OF THE INCARNATE PERSON

The humiliation of the Person of Christ began with His miraculous conception, and ended with His session at the right hand of God. But it may be unfolded as the humble development of His human nature, and the obscuration of the Divine and personal Sonship.

I. Our Lord took our manhood in its sinless perfection; but under the law of its development, and with the natural infirmities to which sin had reduced it.

1 The term Development, as applied to human nature in contradistinction from the Divine, and also as differenced from the angelic, is of wide application Humanity has a purely physical development the beginning of which was not in the first man, who passed only through its later stages. It has an intellectual development, pertaining to the soul as acting in bodily organisation. It has a moral development . which, though we know it only as a restoration from sin to holiness, may be predicated of sinless human nature. It has an historical development · the

union of all the former processes in the accomplishment of the end destined for mankind in the eternal idea   To all these our Lord submitted.   He might have assumed our nature in its ultimate perfection , but then the design of redemption would have been either unpurposed or unaccomplished.   He took into personal union with Himself the germ of all that is called Man ; and in His sacred Person the human nature was unfolded to its final perfectness in His ascension   He was *found in fashion as a man ,* Phil. ii. 8 even as we shall hereafter be found conformed to the fashion of His glorified humanity.

2 Our Lord's manhood was subject to the infirmities of our Infirmity mortal condition   He was sent *in the likeness of sinful flesh.* Sin Rom. viii. 3. bruised His heel before He bruised its head.   He was a *Man of* Isa liii 3. *sorrows, and acquainted with grief,* in a lower as well as in a higher sense : He experienced, that is, the griefs and sorrows of our common human condition which we can understand as well as the griefs and sorrows of His Messianic burden which pass our knowledge.   After recording His descent from the Mount, St. Matthew begins his record of His miraculous cures of human disease by quoting the prophecy concerning the Righteous Servant *Himself* Matt. viii. *took our infirmities, and bare our sicknesses.* This passage has no 17. Isa liii. 4 other design than to include our physical distress in the benefit of the great vicarious intervention.   The Scripture preserves the silence of Divine decorum as to the literal participation of our Lord in the ills of the flesh   But it reveals to us His humiliation in assuming a nature of itself unshielded from infirmity.

3 The communion of natures, or their incomprehensible union Both in one Person, requires us to regard both the development and Humiliation of the the infirmity of the lower nature as the humiliation of the Son Son. Incarnate.   That an integral part of Himself should pass from stage to stage towards perfection, and in that passage should be marred as well as perfected, was the voluntary abasement of the Eternal Son : after *being found in fashion as a man, He* HUMBLED Phil. ii 8. HIMSELF ; and that particular element of humility, which preceded and was the condition of every other, did not cease until the heavens received Him to glory

II Nor must we shrink from applying the term humiliation to Obscuration of our Lord's Person as Divine : not to His Divinity, which is a Divinity mutable Eternal Spirit, but to His Person as Divine-human, and therefore to the Divinity as hiding for a season the manifestation of its glory under the veil of the flesh.

Godhead Immutable. 1 We must begin with a qualification. If, in the Person of the Mediator, we require the verity of the unchanged Manhood, much more must we insist upon the verity of the unchangeable Godhead Sound theology is as tenacious of the Divine as of the human reality in the One Christ. Any theory of the Redeemer's humiliation which assumes the possibility of His relinquishment or even suppression of any Divine attribute is self-condemned Much more must we reject any theory that would make the Eternal Son voluntarily reduce or retract His Divine Self into an abstract potency or principle made concrete in human nature. It is only **1 Tim. iii. 16.** due honour to the God *Who was manifest in the flesh* that this proposition should be left undefended God in Christ is immutable, **Heb. xiii. 8.** *the Same yesterday and to-day and for ever*

2. But the Person of the Christ was humbled , during His sojourn on earth ; and that humiliation continued until He finally **Veiled** entered the heavens Hence while the Son tabernacled with us He did not in the exercise of His ministry and in the work of redemption manifest His Divine attributes beyond the extent to which His perfect human nature might be the organ of their **John i 14** manifestation The *glory as of the Only-begotten* witnessed by the Apostles was only what might be seen in the Incarnate Person · **John ii 11.** He *manifested forth His glory*, but not to the uttermost. This may be more clearly formulated in three ways.

Under the Father. (1.) The Incarnate Son was SUBORDINATE TO THE FATHER in a specific humiliation which did not continue, as touching His Person, after the ascension. Undoubtedly there is a sense in which His subordination still continues, as there is a sense also in which it will continue for ever in His fellowship with human nature But, **Matt. xxviii. 18,** until the hour when He could say, *All power is given unto Me in heaven and in earth*, He was, as the Servant of God and of man, in a deeply humbled and very special state of subjection. From the **Luke ii. 49.** first words concerning His mission, *I must be in My Father's will*, down to the last, *My Father is greater than I*, this truth rules all **John xiv. 28.** the Redeemer's relations to His God and our God.

(2.) He was UNDER THE GUIDANCE OF THE HOLY SPIRIT during

His earthly life rather than under the independent agency of His *Led of the* Divine personality. Our Lord's human nature was sealed and *Spirit.* consecrated and enriched with sevenfold perfection by the Spirit given to Him not *by measure.* This particular subordination ceased *John iii.* when He who received became the Giver of the Holy Ghost . *34* indeed. it may be said to have ceased when the Redeemer laid down His life OF HIMSELF, and *through the* ETERNAL SPIRIT, His *Heb. ix* own essential Divinity, *offered Himself* to God for us. Until then, *14* however, the Son as such did not act through His human nature alone His own Divine supremacy is in abeyance, and, as the Representative of man, He is, like us. *led of the Spirit.* *Gal. v. 18*

(3) Hence the marked prominence which He gave always to *Humanity* His HUMAN NATURE as the organ of His self-revelation Until the *His* ascension, He spoke of Himself chiefly as the Son of Man a title *Organ.* which at once declares His unity with the human race as its Representative and His submission to humanity as the sphere, and as it were the only sphere, of His temporary and temporal self-manifestation.

These are the elements and factors in the humiliation of the *Humilia-* Divine-human Person. Their combination presents to us an un- *tion of the* fathomable mystery. Separately and conjointly they pervade the *Person* evangelical narrative, and equally the later Scripture based upon it. From deeper and bolder investigation we are repelled by the limitation of our faculties. Moreover, all that can be further said must needs occupy attention when the humiliation of the Redeemer's work is considered, and the historical controversies on the subject rise before us.

HUMILIATION OF THE REDEEMING WORK

Viewed in relation to His work the humbled estate of Christ began with His baptism and ended with His descent through death into Hades. It may be regarded as His personal submission to be the Representative of a sinful race ; and as His obedience to the Father's redeeming will. These converge to His Passion and Death, in which the Redeemer's humiliation was perfected.

THE REPRESENTATIVE OF SINNERS.

Repiesentative of Sinners
Gal. iv. 4.

That our Lord humbled Himself to be the REPRESENTATIVE OF SINFUL MAN is the first key to the solution of His entire history on earth. *God sent forth His Son, made of a woman, made under the law;* made *under law* generally, the Mosaic only included; and *made* under law · γενόμενον, the same aorist participle that is used for the Incarnation, thus showing that He was born under conditions of law. Now Christ was man, the Seed of the woman, before He was Jewish man, the Seed of David: as the Seed of Abraham He was both in one

Cncumcision.

Luke i 35

1. The history of the Messiah gives us His humiliation as exhibited in His Israelitish relations first, or rather His human humiliation first under its Israelitish aspect Of this His CIRCUMCISION was the sign and seal. THAT HOLY THING—our Lord's human nature—underwent the rite that signified at once initiation into the Hebrew covenant and the obligation to put away human sin. This rite was in the case of our Lord the symbol of all obligation to the old law until He Himself abrogated it, and His unconscious submission to the imputation of sin even as His baptism was His conscious submission to it Hence He was presented in the Temple, though Greater than the Temple, became in His twelfth year a Son of the law, and honoured down to the end every Divine ordinance and legitimate tradition in the old economy

Baptism

John i.29.

Isa liii 12.
Matt. iii.
15

2. But He was the Representative of sinful mankind. When He appeared unto Israel He appeared to the race of man His Baptism and Temptation were of universal import in this respect. He came to His BAPTISM as the *Lamb of God which taketh away the sin of* THE WORLD · though sinless, and incapable of sin, He was in the river Jordan already *numbered with the transgressors.* Not until He had thus fulfilled the requirement of *all righteousness* did He receive the attestation from heaven which declared that sin had nothing in Him otherwise than as imputed. In the TEMPTATION, also, He represented the sinning race, while He demonstrated that *in Him is no sin,* nor the possibility of sin. He repelled temptation as the Son of God incarnate, Who, by the necessity of His Divine personality, could not be *tempted with evil,* but He repelled it in terms of human rejection, giving His

Temptation.
1 John iii

James i
13.

example to tempted mortals by the use of Scripture appropriate to sinners   He was made under law in this sense too, that He underwent the human probationary test in which He was not found wanting.   In the SINLESS HOLINESS of His life, also, He was the Representative of sinful humanity   presenting to God the perfect obedience due from mankind, and to man the perfect example which, through the virtue of His expiatory death, man should be able to imitate.   But here we must modify the sense in which He was under law.   It is the characteristic of evangelical righteousness that it is *not under the law ;* that its obedience is from within , and if this is true of the servants, much more was it true of the Master.   His holiness was not the fulfilment of duty imposed on Him ; but the new and Divine expression in His life of the commandment itself.   In Him, as in us, it was the perfect love of God and perfect charity to man : love in Him, as in us, was *the fulfilling of the law.*   Finally, in His VICARIOUS PASSION, in His voluntary endurance of the penalty of human sin, He was the Representative of sinners   literally *made under the law.*   How literally is proved by three passages, which may be combined into one : Christ was made *sin for us, who knew no sin ,* hath *redeemed us from the curse of the law, being made a curse for us ,* was *made under the law, to redeem them that were under the law.*

3   *Being found in fashion as a man, He humbled Himself*   the voluntary humiliation which made the Holy One a Representative of sinners extended over His whole life   It is impossible to point to any crisis when it began   The shadow of His cross fell upon His entire path, though it did not betray its influence on His thoughts and feelings and words until the hour approached ; until about the period when from the Tabor of His transfiguration He lifted up His eyes and saw the Moriah of His sacrifice, after which He began to speak to His disciples of His coming betrayal and death   Nor dare we curiously inquire into the secrets of our Lord's internal consciousness as bearing this relation to mankind. Suffice that through this *His visage was so marred more than any man ;* that this made Him *a Man of sorrows, and acquainted with grief.* To be *numbered with the transgressors ;* and that, not only by the transgressors themselves, but by His Father, who *put Him to grief !*

Marginal notes:

Holy Obedience

Rom vi 14

Passion Rom xiii. 10.

Gal iv. 4. 2 Cor. v. 21. Gal iii.13. Gal. iv. 4, 5.

Phil ii. 8.

Isa. lii. 14. Is. liii 3, 12, 10

OBEDIENCE.

All this finds its fuller Scriptural expression in the OBEDIENCE which the Incarnate Son rendered to the Mediatorial Will of the Father. The term is generally limited to the active and passive righteousness; but, before considering it in that more restricted sense, we may refer it to the general subordination of the Redeemer during the whole course of His humbled estate

Subordination.
John vi 38.
John x. 18.

1. He who is the Lord of all entered the world as the Servant of God *I came down from heaven, not to do Mine own will, but the will of Him that sent Me* He was under a discipline of submission peculiar to His person and office. The commandment *received of My Father* was one not written in any code of laws appointed for man, but belonged only to Himself. In keeping that great Messianic commandment He was alone: the law was one and unique, the obedience one and unique. This supreme submission is the theory of the Redeemer's history on earth. It explains His invariable deference to the Father · *My Father is greater than I;* His references to God as distinct from Himself *there is none good but one, that is, God ,* His abnegation of the use of Divine names and attributes . *but of that day and that hour knoweth no man, no, not the angels which are in heaven, neither the Son, but the Father;* His calling the Father His God . *I ascend unto My Father, and your Father, and to My God, and your God ;* and His habitual adherence to the title *Son of Man* All this is profoundly consistent with His Divine prerogatives apart from the subordination As the Son of God He is equal with God, knoweth all things, and claims equal honour with the Father. In His mysterious subordination He is the Servant of the Holy Trinity, and the current of His self-revelation is faithful to that fundamental principle of His mission.

John xiv 28.
Matt xix. 17.
Mark xiii 32.
John xx 17.
Passim.

Reparation to Divine Law.

2 But the Obedience of Christ may be more specifically viewed as the one great act of reparation to the Divine law which He accomplished on the behalf of mankind . His Active and Passive Righteousness, which are one. In His active obedience He perfectly fulfilled the obligation of righteousness as the love of God and man , and thus it was proved that His atonement was not needed for Himself. In His passive obedience He endured the penalty of human transgression. But the relation of His one

obedience to the Atonement and our justification must be reserved for a later stage   Meanwhile it is sufficient to mark the three cardinal passages in which it is referred to.   *For as by one man's* Rom.v.19. *disobedience many were made sinners, so by the obedience of One shall many be made righteous:* this includes the whole mediatorial work of Christ as the Second Adam, superabounding against the sin of the race in the First Adam   *Though He were a Son, yet learned* Heb v. 8. *He obedience by the things which He suffered*   this makes His great submission the voluntary act of the Eternal Son, who needed it not for Himself.   *Being found in fashion as a man, He humbled* Phil. ii. 8 *Himself, and became obedient unto death, even the death of the cross* this makes it the Divine-human act of the Redeemer consummated in death.   Uniting the three, we gather that the entire obedience of our Saviour was one work, that it was the act of the Divine Son, but voluntarily rendered in the nature of mankind

THE PASSION AND DEATH.

THE DEATH of Christ was His perfect humiliation. Its atoning Death, character will be hereafter dwelt upon.   For the present we must consider it as an act of supreme submission, self-renunciation, and abasement   It was His Passion generally, and His Crucifixion in particular.

1. The Passion or Suffering of the Redeemer must be sepa- The rated in thought from the precise manner of His decease.   He Passion. *was obedient unto death*   His soul was *exceeding sorrowful, even unto* Phil ii. 8 *death.*   He was made *a little lower than the angels, for the suffering* Matt *of death.*   This was the penalty of human sin . not the destruc- xxvi 38 tion of soul and body merely, but that severance of the spirit Heb. ii. 9 from God the uttermost terrors of which no mortal has ever known.   It was this which our Lord underwent   His physical dissolution was after the manner of men . not of that did He say, *Behold and see if there be any sorrow like unto My sorrow !*   His Lam. i 12. passion, or suffering, as a voluntary sacrifice for sin, brought with it the death of the body as one of its effects.   That crisis would have taken place in Gethsemane—for there its awful signs began —but His hour was not yet come.   In His Old-Testament lamentation the future Redeemer cries, *Reproach hath broken My heart.* Ps. lxix 20.

John xix. 34.
John xix 36.
The *blood and water* which followed the piercing after death gave token that this was literally true. Though it was ordered that *a bone of Him shall not be broken*, this did not extend to the fleshy protection of His sacred heart, rent by the pressure of intolerable woe. Thus far our own human experience gives us light. But no

Mark xv. 34.
further the appeal, *My God, My God, why hast Thou forsaken Me?* was the exceeding bitter cry that sprang from the Redeemer's infinite perception of what lies in eternal abandonment by God. That was the death of redemption

The Crucifixion
Phil ii 8
2. The death of the Redeemer cannot, however, be separated from His Crucifixion. He *became obedient unto death*, EVEN THE DEATH OF THE CROSS. The sacred details of the scene of which the cross is the centre are given by all the Evangelists, who here at last converge to a perfect unity · the harmony of their narrative is broken by a few seeming contradictions, which appear on a superficial view, but vanish before deeper investigation. The only one of these that deserves mention is the apparent difference between the Synoptists and St John as to the actual day of our Lord's death. Collating their several accounts with St Paul's to the

1 Cor. v 7.
1 Cor. xv. 23.
Corinthians—*Christ* OUR PASSOVER *was sacrificed for us*, as it were on 14th Nisan, and rose THE FIRST FRUITS, as it were on the 16th Nisan—and marking that the Synoptists speak of the day

Luke xxiii 54.
Matt xxvi. 5
John xiii. 1
Matt. xxvi. 17.
of crucifixion as the *Preparation* of the great Sabbath of 15th Nisan, and *not on the feast day* itself, we are led to the conclusion that the Last Supper was, as St. John records, *before the feast of the Passover*, and that the Crucifixion took place on Friday, the 14th Nisan. The disciples who, according to the Synoptists, on *the first day of the Feast of unleavened bread*, put their question, *Where wilt Thou that we prepare for Thee to eat the Passover?* prepared the meal on the 14th Nisan, but before the 13th had ended, that is, on the evening of Thursday, the 13th Nisan, and on that same evening the Lord anticipated the Passover which

Luke xxii. 15.
He so much *desired to eat* with them. The exact date of the world's redemption may, with near approach to absolute certainty, be assigned to the Friday, 18th March, 14th Nisan, in the year of Rome 782, A.D. 29.

The Cross in Theology.
3. Viewing the Passion in its relation to the Crucifixion, we may venture to make a few further remarks.

(1.) As entering into the fulfilment of the *determinate counsel and foreknowledge of God*, the crucifixion may be said to have been an accident of the Passion The Father made the soul of His Servant *an offering for sin*, and His Son *sin for us*, but in what way that oblation should be offered was predetermined only in the foresight of human malignity The immolation on Calvary is never spoken of save as the act of man. The shame and ignominy of the cross was endured by Jesus as the expression of man's rejection by *wicked hands* He was *crucified and slain* The *princes of this world*, in their ignorance and in the infamy of their pride, *crucified the Lord of glory*. But this was foreseen and made the subject of type and prophecy; though of such type and prophecy as required the event for their full explanation. It was the death that was predestined; the cross was only foreknown : a distinction sustained by the usage of Scripture.

The Cross.
Acts ii.23.

Is liii. 10.
2 Cor. v. 21

Acts ii 23.
1 Cor ii. 8.

(2) The crucifixion of our Lord was, therefore, the fulfilment of prophecy · whether the acted prophecy of .type or the spoken prophecy of prediction. Isaac, the only son of Abraham, bore the *wood of the burnt offering* to Mount Moriah, even as the Only-begotten bore His cross. The *serpent lifted up in the wilderness* was the type of the *Son of Man lifted up*. While the prophets foreannounced the sacrifice of the Lamb, they indicated that His death would be unlike that of the ancient victim. *He was* WOUNDED *for our transgressions. They shall look upon Me Whom they have* PIERCED ; and *they* PIERCED *My hands and My feet* These words were spoken as from the heart of Jesus in the Old Testament. It was reserved for Himself to utter the first express prediction of the Cross, which He had hinted at to Nicodemus, but began to speak of, for Himself and all His followers, when He was about to ascend the Mount on which He lifted up His eyes and saw His Other Mount in the distance. The history of the crucifixion shows that the minutest details were ordered as it had been written concerning Him : *signifying what death*, ποίῳ θανάτῳ, *He should die.*

Predicted.

Gen xxii 6
John iii. 14.

Is. liii 5.
Zech. xii 10.
Ps. xxii. 16.

John xii. 33.
John xviii. 32.

(3) The Providence took up into its plans the death of the Cross as that which alone could unite the whole world in its perpetration. *To this end was I born*, He said—and we may add for this purpose He died—*to bear witness unto the truth.* He was a Martyr to the eternal truth of God. And His martyrdom was

The World at the Cross.
John xviii. 37

John viii. 44. the act of the world which, like Satan its prince, *abode not in the truth.* It was the deed of the Jews, for they delivered Him to Pilate; it was the deed of the Gentiles, for they alone crucified their malefactors. The combined wicked hands of mankind universal cast out the Eternal Word. They CONSCIOUSLY rejected the Divine Witness; they UNCONSCIOUSLY offered up the Eternal Victim, and consummated the world's iniquity in the very act which obtained the world's salvation. He who knew what was in man prayed for them: *they know not what they do!*

Luke xxiii. 34.

The Cross the Altar. 4. Hence the cross was to our High Priest simply the awful form which His altar assumed. *His own Self bare our sins in His own body to the tree.* ἐπὶ τὸ ξύλον, as St. Peter invariably terms the Cross, and he only. The most affecting type of the Eternal Son incarnate bore the wood on his shoulders to his Calvary, and that wood became the altar on which *in a figure* he was slain, and from which *in a figure* he was raised again. St. Peter has indicated this in the most impressive phrase of the New Testament, and the Epistle to the Hebrews, not mentioning the cross, alludes to it when it says that Jesus *suffered without the gate,* and that *we have an altar.* On that altar our High Priest offered His oblation; and *put away sin by the sacrifice of Himself.*

Peter ii. 24.

Heb xi. 19.

Heb. xiii. 10, 12

Heb ix. 26.

The Curse. 5. But, while the cross on which human malignity slew the Holy One is really the altar on which He offered Himself, and we forget the tree in the altar into which it was transformed, the Cross still remains as the sacred expression of the curse which fell upon human sin as represented by the Just One. God *made Him to be sin for us Who knew no sin;* and, though it is not said that He made Him a curse for us, it is said. *Christ hath redeemed us from the curse of the law, being made a curse for us, for it is written, Cursed is every one that hangeth on a tree* In His Holy Person sin was represented, and its penalty endured. It was *condemned in the flesh.* But, He who *endured the cross, despising the shame,* thus cast down the powers of evil, *triumphing over them in it.* His Cross is now the glory of Christianity. It is the seat whence the Prophet teaches His highest lessons. It is the altar of His continually availing sacrifice. And it is the throne of His Power as King in the universe. But the Cross is no longer His or His alone. It is Divinely *in a figure transferred* to us. All our religion

2 Cor. v. 21

Gal. iii. 13.

Rom viii 3.

Heb xii. 2.

Col. ii. 15.

1 Cor. iv 6.

is the *fellowship of His sufferings, being made conformable unto His death,* and *bearing His reproach.* Our sub-exemplar said, *I am crucified with Christ.*

Phil iii. 10. Heb. xiii 13

LIMITS OF THE HUMILIATION

The humiliation of the Redeemer, therefore, embraces the whole process of His incarnate life, from His Conception to His Burial These two extreme terms, however, must be carefully defined The first requires a distinction to be made between the Incarnation and the Conception ; the second, between the Burial and the Descent into Hades. (1.) The Son of God might have exhibited His incarnate Person in majesty from the beginning ; in which case the Transfiguration glory would have been the rule and not the exception. But, condescending to become incarnate, He was conceived of the Holy Ghost and born after the manner of man. The distinction between the Incarnation generally, and the humble manner of His assumption of flesh, is subtile but not unimportant (2) And the end of His abasement was reached when He became *obedient unto death.* Obligation went no further than the dissolution of soul and body That separation was attested by His entombment. But the burial itself has two aspects. It was the descent of the body to the sepulchre ; where the flesh of the Holy One of God saw no corruption, being still part of His incarnate Person Humiliation was arrested at the moment that Death received the sacred Form, as the Baptist received the Heavenly Candidate for baptism · COMEST THOU TO ME? Meanwhile the exaltation of the Redeemer had already begun For, His spirit, also part of His incarnate Person, quickened by the Spirit of His Divinity, went down to the nether world and received at the very moment of its severance from the body *the keys of Hades and of death.*

Limits.

Phil. ii 9

Matt. iii. 14.

Rev. i 18

HUMILIATION OF PERSON AND WORK ONE.

Having distinguished between the humiliation of our Lord's Person and that of His work, it is expedient that we efface the distinction and regard His Person and His work as one. Apart from the ministry of redemption there is, theologically, no Person of Christ Some important results follow from this truth first, the

Person and Work One

M 2

redeeming submission makes the personal humiliation a profound reality, secondly, the inalienable Divine dignity of the Redeemer gives its glory to the submission.

Humilia-
tion a
Reality.

1. There is a sense in which the Person of the Incarnate, as such, was incapable of abasement His assumption of a pure human nature, by which the centre of His being, that is His Personality, was not changed, was an act of infinite condescension, but not of humiliation strictly so called. The self-determining or self-limiting act of the Godhead in creating all things cannot be regarded as a derogation; nor was it such in the specific union of Deity with manhood. But, as we shall hereafter see that the Descent into Hades was the moment which united the deepest abasement and the loftiest dignity of the Christ, so the moment of the incarnation in the womb of the Virgin united the most glorious condescension of the Second Person with His most profound abjection His work began as a suffering Redeemer, with the submission to conception and birth. Hence the Person and the work cannot be separated. And the humiliation which the Redeemer underwent must be regarded as the humiliation of the God-man. He assumed it, even as He assumed the nature that rendered it possible.

Glory not
Hidden

2. As the glory of our Lord's Divinity was manifested forth in His Person and work, so that glory shines through all the narratives of His humbled estate Many lesser evidences might be adduced, but we may be content with the three testimonies given by the Father from heaven at the three great crises of that humiliation, and occasional assertions of our Saviour as to the voluntary and Divine character of His submission

The Three
Testi-
monies
Matt. iii
17.

(1.) At the Baptism, which has been hitherto viewed only as it was received by the Representative of sinners, the Divine attestation was given: *This is My beloved Son.* Here was more than the perfect complacency of the Father in His Son now incarnate, and the acknowledgment of the sinless development of the past; it was also a symbolical exhibition of the Holy Trinity as to be revealed in redemption, and the Triune glory, though it vanished from human observation, rested for ever on the Saviour's work. Midway in His career, or rather when preparing to enter the

2 Pet i.17 path of final sorrow, our Lord *received from God the Father honour*

and glory on the holy mount. That glory rests, slanting along
a double perspective vista, upon the two intervals, backwards to
the Baptism and forward to the Passion. Whatever other lessons
the Transfiguration taught, it certainly declared that the Holy
Sufferer was the Divine Son, and that the brightness of the
Father's glory in Him was only withdrawn or hidden, or veiled
for a season Finally, the hour of our Saviour's preparatory
passion was magnified by a third demonstration of the Father's
honour put upon His Son He heard the Voice which others
did not distinguish, the Voice which declared that all the past of
the Redeemer had glorified the Divine Name, and that the still
greater future would still more abundantly glorify it *I have both* John xii.
glorified it and will glorify it again. 28

(2) On many occasions He asserted for Himself the Divine
dignity which coexisted with His humiliation. A *Teacher come* John iii 2.
from God, He re-uttered the law on the Mount as His own, and
the entire fabric of the Sermon asserts His supremacy While
He vindicated His own observance of Sabbatic ordinance as
real and true, He declared Himself *Lord also of the Sabbath,* and, Luke vi 5
honouring the Temple prescriptions, proclaimed Himself *Greater* Matt. xii.
than the Temple. Complying with an exaction of men as subject 6.
to the powers that be, He intimated that as the Son He was free Matt. xvii.
from tribute. He ever made it known that His life was in His 26.
own hands, that He did not and could not renounce the prerogative of *life in Himself,* that He laid down His life with Divine John v 26
freedom, that He had *power to lay it down,* and *power to take it* John x 18
again. And what He declared in life He proved in death · for,
though the Father's rebuke of sin broke His heart, He spontaneously yielded up His soul, or *gave up the ghost,* ἀφῆκε τὸ John xix
πνεῦμα, even as He voluntarily gave up His body to those who 30.
came to capture Him. It was part of the commandment *received* John x.
of My Father that our Lord should sometimes assert, what His 18.
consciousness could not be bereft of, His absolute independence Divine.
of the creature with which, for the sake of redemption, He had
so closely bound Himself. Hence He declares His self-abnega-
tion to be the *example* which He gave His disciples, nor does He John xiii
ever once speak of it save for that purpose. Before He be- 13.
queathed His peace He left them this legacy, showing by its

most affecting illustration in Himself the eternal connection between humility as the source and peace as the result. The Feetwashing was the symbolical representation of His entire way of lowliness; and in it the *Master and Lord* set the seal of Divine dignity on His earthly condescension When, drawing very nigh to the lowest limit of His abasement, He said, *Believest thou not that I am in the Father, and the Father in Me?* and, more than that, *He that hath seen Me hath seen the Father,* He Himself declared that the whole of His past career had been a manifestation of God in the flesh. *I and My Father are one.* We have not, however, isolated passages only to rely on. The whole history of our Lord's humbled estate in the Gospels, and the exposition of it in the Epistles, alike proclaim that in the mystery of His condescension to the lowest depth His glory was revealed As the Incarnate Son He said of Himself: *Ought not Christ to have suffered these things, and to enter into His glory?* But the glorification of Divine love waited not for the ascension. The Divine majesty of the Son was most richly and blessedly manifested IN the redeeming sorrows and not alone AFTER them To the Christian sentiment the obscuration of the Cross is the very *darkness* which God makes His *secret place*

John xiii. 13.

John xiv. 10, 9

John x.30

Luke xxiv. 26.

Ps xviii. 11.

Exaltation.

THE ESTATE OF EXALTATION.

The Redeemer's Estate of Exaltation may be viewed in its historical stages as a process: the Descent, the Resurrection, and the Ascension; and with reference to its completeness as affecting the Person and the Work of the Redeemer. These, however, need not be separated: the latter branch may be merged in the former, partly because it has been anticipated in the Humiliation, and, partly, because it enters into the discussion of the Three Offices.

Process.

The process of the Redeemer's exaltation, like that of His humiliation, is matter of Scriptural testimony alone. We are taught that it began with the Descent into the invisible world;

that it was continued in His Resurrection; and that it was consummated in His Ascension and Session at the right hand of God.

THE DESCENT

Between the lowest point of our Lord's humiliation and the beginning of His glorification there was, there could be, no interval. In fact, the critical instant of His death was at the same time the critical instant of His commencing triumph. Here we must consider what the Descent into Hades imports, and how it belonged to the exaltation of Christ: but in few words, as the light of Scripture here soon fails us.

1. The phrase Descent into Hell, Descensus ad Inferos, is not in the New Testament. St Peter, bearing witness to the Lord's resurrection, quotes the words of David : *Thou wilt not leave My soul in hell , neither wilt Thou suffer Thine Holy One to see corruption* The Greek ῞Αδης, Hades, answering to the Hebrew Sheol, signifies the Unseen State , which again corresponds with the English Hell, according to its simple original meaning of Covered or Hidden Depth, and without reference to punishment endured in it   Into this State of the Dead our Lord entered   as to His body it was buried and concealed in the sepulchre or visible representative of the invisible Hades into which He entered as to His soul. It is observable, however, that St. Paul, making the same use of the Psalm, does not distinguish between the grave and Hades. He speaks only of the body: they *laid Him in a sepulchre ;* and thinks it enough to quote, *Thou shalt not suffer Thine Holy One to see corruption.*   Undoubtedly the entombment of our Lord, and His passing into the condition of the dead, are the one meaning of these passages , and they signify that His death was a reality, and that so far His burial belonged to His humbled estate.

2. But that this descent into Hades was at the same time the beginning of His exaltation is evident from the following negative and positive considerations .—

The Descent.

Acts ii. 30, 31. Psalm xiv. 10.

Acts xiii 29, 35.

John xix. 30.　(1.) Negatively, when our Lord cried *It is finished !* the abasement of the Representative of mankind ended. The expiation of sin demanded no more : it did not require that the Redeemer should be kept under the power of death. After the tribute of Rom. vi 9.　His voluntary expiation death had *no more dominion over Him.* He triumphed over all the enemies of salvation on the cross. Death was at once His last sacrifice, His triumph, and His release; *it was not possible that He should be holden of it* · not only Acts ii 24; iii. 15.　because He was *the Prince of Life,* but because the law had no further claim. When He offered up His holy spirit, wrath to the uttermost was spent upon human sin; but He Himself was never the object of wrath, and the Father received the spirit commended to Him as a sufficient sacrifice. The Holy One could not endure the torments of the lost. the thought that He could and did is the opprobrium of one of the darkest chapters Is liii. 9.　of historical theology. Not in this sense did He make *His grave with the wicked*

(2) Positively, He triumphed in death over death. First, in His one Person He kept inviolate His human body, which did not undergo the material dissolution of its elements. not because, as it is sometimes said, He was delivered from the grave before corruption had time to affect His sacred flesh, but because the work of death was arrested in the very instant of the severance Rom vi 9　of soul and body. As His spirit *dieth no more,* so His body *saw* Acts xiii 37　*no corruption* The unviolated flesh of our Lord was, till the moment He was quickened, a silent declaration of perfect victory. His Divinity never left His body, any more than it forsook His spirit in its passage to the world of spirits. Secondly, according to the testimony of two Apostles, our Lord triumphantly descended into the lower world, and took possession of the kingdom Rom. xiv 9　of the dead. *To this end Christ both died, and rose, and revived, that He might be Lord both of the dead and living* · these words indefinitely distribute the mediatorial empire over man into its two great provinces. He died, and in death took possession of the Rom. x. 7.　Dead, He revived, and ruleth over the Living. *Who shall descend into the deep ? (that is, to bring up Christ again from the dead)* · here Eph iv. 8, 9　the deep, or the abyss, must refer to the great Underworld. *Now that He ascended, what is it but that He also descended first into the*

lower parts of the earth? whence, in the strong figure of Scripture, Col ii 15
He led captivity captive Triumphing over all the enemies of our
salvation—sin, death, and Satan—*in it,* the cross, He declared His
triumph in the Descent *Quickened by the Spirit* of His Divinity, 1 Peter
by which also He went and preached unto the spirits in prison; the iii 18,
historical sequence—*He went, by the resurrection, Who is gone into* 19, 21.
heaven—indicates, and will allow no other interpretation, that in
the Interval the Redeemer asserted His authority and lordship in
the vast region where *the congregation of the dead* is the great Prov xxi
aggregate of mankind, the vast assembly to which also we may 16
apply the words, *in the midst of the congregation will I praise Thee.* Ps xxii
22.

THE RESURRECTION

Resurrection.

The Resurrection of our Lord, viewed in its widest import, is His exaltation. It is the perfect opposite of His
humbled estate. As a fact in His history it is only a stage
in the process of glorification; but the general strain of
the New Testament teaches us to regard it as absolutely
the counterpart and antithesis of His humiliation. If His
death is the limit and measure of the Obedience, His resurrection is the substance and sum of His dignity and
reward. The preaching of the Apostles everywhere gives
prominence to these two truths as the pillars of the
Christian faith; and the evidence of the supreme miracle
of the resurrection of Jesus is, both as internal and
external, sufficient to establish the dignity of His Person
and the authority of His work. This point of view alone
commands all the elements of the doctrine of Christ s
resurrection.

IN ITS DOGMATIC RELATIONS

The Resurrection was the glorification of the Redeemer's
Person and the seal of His atoning work.

I. His rising from death Divinely vindicated the Redeemer's As to the
Person As such, it was the demonstration of His Divinity, as Person.

effected by His own power; and, as effected by the Father, the declaration of His Incarnate dignity: both, in the unity of the Holy Ghost, merged into the Godhead generally.

His own Power.

1. It is remarkable that in all our Lord's predictions of His resurrection He makes Himself the Agent. His first allusion to

John ii. 19.

it was among His earliest predictions *Destroy this temple, and in three days I will raise it up,* and His last was among His latest:

John x.17, 18.

I lay down My life, that I might take it again. No man taketh it from Me, but I lay it down of Myself. I have power to lay it down, and I have power to take it again It may be objected that the words follow: *this commandment have I received of My Father* But the mediatorial law of obedience included both death and resurrection; and, as certainly as the commandment implied a personal voluntary surrender of life, the offering of Himself in death, so certainly it implied the personal voluntary resumption of that life The mediatorial authority is distinct from the Divine power inherent in the Son. this latter being the foundation of the former He who was the Seed of David after the flesh was

Rom i 4

declared to be the Son of God with power, the Son of God no longer in weakness and obscuration, *according to the Spirit of holiness,* His Divine nature, *by the resurrection from the dead* Hence the most

1 Cor. xv. 4

general statement is that *He rose again the third day.* the words containing rather an active than a passive meaning

By the Father

2 Like every other event in the history of the Mediator, the resurrection is ascribed to God the Father.

Rom vi 4.

(1.) He *was raised up from the dead by the glory of the Father ·* that *Father of glory* whose glory had its utmost manifestation in

Eph i 20

the power wherewith it *wrought in Christ when He raised Him*

1 Peter i. 21.

from the dead, and, as St. Peter adds, *gave Him glory.* Hence the glory of God the Father is His power in its exercise; and its result is the Son's resurrection. He to Whom the Incarnate offered the sacrifice of His humiliation bestowed upon Him the reward of His resurrection. When the Redeemer prayed, *Glorify*

John xvii. 1.

Thy Son, that Thy Son also may glorify Thee, He had in view both His death and His rising again from the dead. As the crucified and risen Son He was glorified by the Father.

The Finished

(2.) It was not only, however, the resurrection to glory and reward. it was also the Father's testimony to the perfection of

His Divine-human Person as the Son   St. Paul gives the final *Incarna-* *tion.* interpretation of the memorable words of the Psalm : *Thou art* *Acts xiii.* *My Son, this day have I begotten Thee.* The manhood of the In- *33.* carnate Son was never perfected until the resurrection, which was therefore the consummating ˙period of the Incarnation. The *Luke ii* *glad tidings* announced at the first birth are perfectly declared at *Acts xiii* the second birth of the Incarnate Son : *this day* is the One Day *32.* of the Lord's incarnate history from the miraculous conception to the rising from the dead, which was the moment of His perfection both as an Incarnate Person and as the Christ.

3 Generally, God absolutely, without distinction of Persons, is *By God.* said to have raised up the Saviour.

(1) This is in harmony with the tenour of Scripture, which speaks everywhere of the processes of the mediatorial history being under the arrangement and ordering of God   The resur- rection of the Mediator is ascribed to God always when the Messianic subordination is implied or made prominent : *Him God* *Acts x 38,* *raised up the third day,* the Same who *anointed Jesus of Nazareth* *40.* and *was with Him.* It may be said generally that the processes of the Redeeming Work of the Three Persons are ascribed to God as the term of Deity representing each

(2) It is referred to God also when Christ's resurrection is connected with ours , the demonstration of Divine power being made emphatic : *the exceeding greatness of His power to us-ward who* *Eph i 19,* *believe, according to the working of His mighty power, which He wrought* *20.* *in Christ, when He raised Him from the dead.* So in that remarkable passage . *but if the Spirit of Him that raised up Jesus from the dead* *Rom viii.* *dwell in you, He that raised up Christ from the dead shall also quicken* *11.* *your mortal bodies by His Spirit that dwelleth in you.* This text, thus read, seems to imply that the Holy Ghost was the Agent in the quickening of Christ, and will be the Agent in ours   But another reading is to be preferred : διὰ τὸ ἐνοικοῦν, *on account of the* *Spirit that dwelleth in us*   The Holy Ghost is, strictly speaking, the Agent in spiritual quickening alone

(3) But it must be remembered that here, as everywhere in relation to the Mediatorial Trinity, all actions proceeding ad extra are referred interchangeably to the several Persons of the Trinity The Father and the Son and the Holy Ghost are one in the send-

Col ii. 2.
Luke ii
26.

ing and raising up and dominion of Him who is, not the Christ of the Father, but THE CHRIST OF GOD or THE LORD'S CHRIST.

As to His
Work.

II. The resurrection was the seal and glorification of His redeeming work. This may be viewed in regard to the three offices hereafter to be mentioned individually, and to the claims and character of the Messiah generally   Reserving the latter for

His Three
Offices

the next Section, let us mark how the Author and Finisher of the Christian Faith was in the several offices in which He laid the foundations of that Faith justified or approved by His resurrection.

Prophet

1. As the Prophet or the Apostle of revelation He appeals to all His works for the authentication of His teaching generally, and to His resurrection in particular as the crowning work by which He would vindicate His claim to be the Supreme Oracle to mankind. His first emphatic and distinct prediction to the people at large was that concerning the raising of the *temple of His body.* He again and again foreannounced it, calling attention

John ii 21
Matt xvii.
23.

to *the third day;* and His resurrection on that day was the seal and confirmation of His prophetic mission   Not only so, however: it was also the entrance of the Prophet on a wider sphere of teaching and influence for the whole world, and the preliminary seal of that new function. It confirmed at once the words already spoken *on earth,* and the words that should be spoken

Heb. xii
25

from heaven Thus, viewed in relation to the past, it was the ratification of His claim as a prophetic Teacher, viewed in relation to the future, it was the credential of His eternal teaching after its first principles had been given below

Priest.

2. As the High Priest of the atoning sacrifice our Lord was justified in the resurrection   It declared that His propitiatory offering was accepted as salvation from death, the penalty of sin, and that the Spirit of a new life was obtained for all : both these in one, and as summing up the benefits of the Atonement.

Rom iv
25

(1.) As the Divine-HUMAN Representative of mankind Christ *was delivered for our offences;* as the DIVINE-human Representative He *was raised again for our justification.* The strong evidence both of the vicarious character and of the validity of our Lord's sacrifice is given in His resurrection. His release from death declared that He died not for His own sin, and that His atone-

Rom viii.
34.

ment was accepted for mankind · *who is he that condemneth?   It is Christ that died, yea rather, that is risen again* The resurrection establishes the atoning character of the death.

(2) His resurrection is the pledge of life—perfect and consummate life in every definition of it—to His people On it depended the gift of the Spirit of life, the fruit of the Ascension The Lord rose again as the Firstbegotten from the dead, the *Firstfruits of them that slept. If we be dead with Him, we shall also live with Him Because I live, ye shall live also* **1 Cor. xv. 20 2 Tim ii 11 John xiv. 19**

3. As King our Lord was sealed, anointed, and crowned in the resurrection. In virtue of His Divinity, on the one hand, and, on the other, in anticipation of His atoning work, He was King even in His humiliation, and taught and acted as such. Though He spoke of the kingdom of heaven, and of the kingdom of God, He also spoke of His own kingdom · My *kingdom is not of this world,* He said to His judge; to His disciples: *and I appoint unto you a kingdom, as My Father hath appointed unto Me; that ye may eat and drink at My table in My kingdom.* But it was not until His resurrection that He was clothed with mediatorial authority, according to the set time and order of the economy of grace. From the sepulchre He went to the mountain in Galilee, where He clothed Himself with His final authority, and said: *All power is given unto Me in heaven and in earth.* **King John xviii 36. Luke xxii. 29, 30 Matt. xxviii 18.**

EVIDENCES OF THE RESURRECTION

The Resurrection was the assurance and infallible proof of the Messiahship of Jesus. It was the Divine demonstration of the truth of the Christian revelation, and itself was demonstrated by sufficient evidences. **His Messiahship**

I Generally, His resurrection is referred to as the crowning evidence that Jesus is the Christ, and therefore of the Divine authority of His religion

1. The one great argument of the New Testament is that Jesus of Nazareth, rejected and crucified by the Jews, was their Messiah and the world's Christ, the Son of God and the Son of man. Before His death His Divine credentials of word and work approved Him. To them He made His appeal. But He also appealed by

anticipation to His own future resurrection. This was His first public pledge laid down in the Temple, and it was repeated when He gave the sign of the prophet Jonas: *so shall the Son of man be three days and three nights in the heart of the earth.* He had His own resurrection in view when He convicted the Sadducees of *not knowing the Scriptures.* Hence He further prepared for its evidential force by making the raising of the dead the crowning miracle of His many wonderful works, reserving the greatest for the last.

Matt. xii 40.

Matt. xxii. 29.

2. But for all ages and all times the one demonstration of the Christ and His religion is His rising from the dead. This is the view taken of it by the preachers of the Gospel in the Acts and the teachers of the Christian Faith in the Epistles They point to it in every discourse as their own great credential, and as confirmed by the Holy Ghost accompanying their words They preached *Jesus and the Resurrection* St Paul speaks for the whole company when he says that all human hope depended upon the verity of this event. *If Christ be not risen, then is our preaching vain, and your faith is also vain*

Acts xvii 18.

1 Cor. xv. 14.

II Hence the evidences of the Fact are sufficient. They are of two classes · first, the witness of those to whom our Lord appeared; and, secondly, the witness of the Spirit after His final departure : these, however, are to be combined for ever. The external evidence is not alone ; nor is the spiritual evidence of the Christian Faith or demonstration of the Holy Ghost without a basis of facts which He thus demonstrates to be true.

Evidences of the Fact

1. No part of our Lord's history is more minutely recorded than the history of the Forty days, which must chiefly be regarded under this aspect, as a continuous practical proof of the verity of His resurrection to His own chosen witnesses.

The Record.

(1) These witnesses were selected as such : *Him God raised up the third day, and showed Him openly; not to all the people, but unto witnesses chosen before of God, even to us, who did eat and drink with Him after He rose from the dead.* The Lord never appeared to the Jews after their rejection of Him : the day of their visitation was over This also was foretold *I go My way, and ye shall seek Me. Neither will they be persuaded, though one rose from the dead.* The witnesses were, in fact, all the members of the Lord's discipleship : expanding in number from the solitary Mary Magdalene to the

Acts x 40, 41.

John viii 21.

Luke xvi 31.

Five Hundred. But they were *chosen* in the sense that special demonstration of the reality and of the nature of His risen body was given to the Apostolic company.

(2) Though the witnesses were chosen, Christ was, according to St. Peter, openly shown of God, and the four Evangelists record the reasons of His prearranged appearance. Five times He showed Himself alive on the day of His resurrection: to Mary Magdalene, to another company of women, to Peter, to two disciples on the way to Emmaus, to the Eleven. To these must be added another Jerusalem appearance for the conviction of St. Thomas. Two manifestations took place after long silence in Galilee, to the Seven and to the Five Hundred. Two again in Jerusalem: one to James, the Lord's brother, and another at the Ascension. These Ten are all the appearances that are recorded: probably all that took place.

(3.) The Risen Lord Appearances were accompanied by *many infallible proofs;* by many signs, τεκμηρίοις, which could not deceive those who witnessed them. First, He distinguished the day of His resurrection, the third day, by a more abundant exhibition of those signs. The third day was connected with the ancient type of the wave-offering, as the three days and three nights with the prophet Jonah: both meaning, according to Hebrew computation, one whole day and two fragments *On the morrow after the sabbath the priest shall wave it;* the firstfruits of harvest were waved before the Lord, and the lamb sacrificed, thus typically uniting the paschal atoning sacrifice of Christ and its Easter acceptance On the fourteenth Nisan our Lord died, having eaten His passover on the preceding evening. The paschal sabbath was the day of His rest in the grave; on the sixteenth He rose; and to give evidence of the honour put on this third day, which was to become the first, He appeared many times. Secondly, He took more than one opportunity of showing the marks, τεκμηρία, of His hands and His feet, and of exhibiting the verity of His body even eating and drinking with His disciples. Into the mystery of His double relation—to the present world in a body that might be nourished, and to the spiritual world in a body which suddenly appeared within closed doors—we cannot penetrate. Suffice that the Lord added this special miracle of an occasional resumption of His

The Witnesses
Mark xvi 1.
John xx. 1.
Matt. xxviii. 1.
Luke xxiv. 13, 33, 34
John xx. 19, 24.
John xxi. 1
Matt. xxviii. 16.
1 Cor xv. 6, 7.
Luke xxiv 50.
Acts i 3

Lev xxiii 11

Luke xxiv. 39.

physical relations in order to demonstrate the reality of His resurrection. He could undergo the Transfiguration at will, and by it closed every interview, and all His appearances, until the ascension. Thirdly, the tokens of the reality of His resurrection were the perfect identity of His human affections He tarried to convince the doubters by the Old Testament, and by exhibition of Himself; to pardon the transgressors who had forsaken Him, especially Peter, who had added denial to his abandonment, and had a private interview for his personal pardon before the public interview for his official pardon; and to teach the things concerning His kingdom.   He thus showed Himself to be the same Jesus

Assaults.   2. The evidence of our Lord's resurrection contained in the New-Testament records is unimpeachable. Its assailants have always employed one of three methods of resisting it.

(1) They sometimes adopt the transcendent principle of scepticism: the absolute rejection of this supreme miracle, simply because it is miracle. To this all assaults on this fundamental fact of Christianity come at last.   The cumulative force of the evidences of every kind is such that it cannot be resisted by those who believe in revelation and the possibility of miraculous intervention. Those who reject the Lord's resurrection on this ground therefore reject with it all Divine revelation; they persistently refuse to consider the evidences of it not persuaded, incapable of being

Luke xvi. persuaded, *though One rose from the dead.*
21.
Sceptical   (2.) Certain theories are devised which may account for the
Hypo-   universal acceptance of the fact on the part of the disciples. These
theses.   may be reduced to two: either the first preachers of Christ's resurrection were impostors, or they were enthusiasts, who. having once listened to the visionary tale of a supposed appearance of Christ, propagated the delusion, and recorded it in legendary narratives.   But a careful consideration of the character of the Apostles, of the simplicity of their faith in the resurrection of their Lord, of the self-sacrificing labours by which they sealed their testimony even unto death, will teach every candid mind that neither of these can be the solution.   And the narratives themselves in their coherence and tranquil consistency irresistibly plead their own cause.

(3) These narratives are sometimes subjected to a process of

examination which detects in them inconsistencies   It is true that
there are certain differences in the minute details of the day of the
resurrection, even as there are differences in the accounts of the Lord's
earlier history.   But it must be remembered that the witnesses give
independent evidence, and that each records something not mentioned by the others.   Every Evangelist has his own design · St.
Matthew, for instance, keeps the final Mountain and Commission in
view, St Luke Emmaus and the Ascension, St. John the more
public appearances of the Risen Lord, concerning which he says that
he records as the third what was really the eighth St Luke's Gospel
seems to make the Lord's final departure take place on the evening
of the resurrection ; but he himself, in the Acts, mentions the forty
days.   The third Evangelist has two accounts of the Ascension,
entirely different in detail but the same in fact ; just as he, a careful
historian, gives three narratives of Christ's appearance to Saul,
in which the minute differences—such as that the companions
of the Convert in one account see without hearing, and in another
hear without seeing—only confirm the accuracy of the narrative

3 The supreme Witness of the resurrection of Christ was
the Holy Ghost.   To His evidence our Lord referred before He
departed.   The Spirit accompanied the testimony of the Apostles,
He has made the Christian Church the abiding demonstration of
the life of its Head ; and He gives His assurance in the hearts of
all to whose penitent faith He reveals the ascended Saviour   *Witness of Spirit*

(1) The Apostles preached the Lord's resurrection as witnesses
who were sustained by the Spirit's higher testimony   literally, a
witness through, and in, and with their preaching   *And we are
His witnesses of these things ; and so is also the Holy Ghost, whom God
hath given to them that obey Him*   While St. Peter preached the Risen
Jesus to Cornelius *the Holy Ghost fell on all them which heard the Word*
This was the reason that *with great power gave the Apostles witness of
the resurrection of the Lord Jesus*, it was because they declared it with
the confidence of personal assurance, *God also bearing them witness,
both with signs and wonders, and with divers miracles, and gifts of the
Holy Ghost, according to His own will.*   *Apostles.*   *Acts v 32*   *Acts x. 44.*   *Acts iv. 33*   *Heb. ii 4.*

(2.) The history of the Christian Church, with its institutions,
is one continuous and ever-enlarging demonstration of the unseen
life of its Ruler   The Lord's Day, which has been kept as the   *The Church.*

memorial of the resurrection from its very morning, is itself testimony that there was never a time when the clear faith in that vital Fact was not held   Similarly, the Eucharistic celebration has from the beginning avowed reliance on a Death once suffered and in a Life which has not been continued upon earth. From the Day of Pentecost the Church has been opposed by principalities and powers, human and superhuman ; but never has the resurrection of its Head and Defender been successfully assailed.

Internal.

(3.) The most universal and best evidence is the influence of the unseen Redeemer by His Spirit in the hearts and lives of believers. The later New Testament dwells on the working in us of the

Eph. 1. 19, 20

mighty power which He wrought in Christ when He raised Him from the dead. The spiritual life of those who accept the Saviour is to themselves a ground of assurance that needs nothing to be added. They receive the records because they are bound up with the Scriptures of truth ; they believe the Event recorded because it took place in harmony with ancient prediction, according to the Lord's own word, and in consistency with His own Divine power   They know that no argument was brought against the fact by those who were most interested in denying it at the beginning, and that no argument has been brought since that has any force   But their infallible evidence is the life of their own souls

Ascension.

THE ASCENSION AND SESSION.

The Ascension of our Lord is the historical term and end of His Exaltation; and, as such, may be viewed in its preliminaries, recorded by all the Evangelists; as an actual event recorded by St. Luke mainly ; and in its sequel including the entire Apostolical testimony to His Session and Intercession.

Preliminaries.

I. The narrative of the Forty Days describes, not only the sequel of the resurrection, but also the preparation for the ascension. The seven weeks of interval corresponded to the seven weeks

1 Cor. xv. 23.

numbered from the wave-offering, the type of CHRIST THE FIRST-FRUITS   But nothing in Old-Testament symbol or type points to the fortieth day as that of the Saviour's going up.   That day was chosen by our Lord . but not arbitrarily. In His love to His disciples

and in His wise provision for the future He gave to them the
larger part of this time It may be supposed that His main
purpose was to wean them from their dependence on His personal
and visible presence. Hence the gradually diminishing appearances Hence that one preliminary note of the ascension . *Touch*   John xx.
Me not, for I am not yet ascended ! This explains the blended   17.
remembrances of the past and anticipations of the future : of
which the last chapter of St. John is an impressive example Of
any preparation of His body for the day of His glorifying there is
no hint. It was simply the set hour , but the hour set by Himself . no change passed upon Him during the interval. The
resurrection was the final removal from the conditions of human
life ; and, so far as concerned Himself, there was no reason to
keep Him on earth. His tarrying so long in a midway condition
was due to His tender concern for His disciples And the
result was that when He finally departed they were fully prepared
for the new economy of His spiritual manifestation , they sur-   Acts iii
rendered Him resignedly to the heavens which *must receive* Him ,   21
and they *returned to Jerusalem with great joy.*   Luke
   xxiv.
II. The history of the Event is recorded only by St. Luke.   52.
His account in the Gospel describes it rather as the end of the   The
Lord's life on earth, in the Acts with reference rather to His   Event. ¯
mediatorial work in heaven and final return to finish redemption.

1. The Ascension was the end of the Saviour's earthly course.   As to the
(1.) Until that day Jesus *went in and out among us ,* and His   Past.
life had been spent amidst unglorified human conditions. The   Acts i 21
forty days were also *days of His flesh*, for all His manifestations   Heb. v. 7.
were in many respects like those of former times · the spiritual
vanishings were anticipations of the ascension, and are not alluded
to save as marking the appearances themselves.

(2.) Hence the clear historical narrative which runs on with a
continuous detail of what *Jesus began both to do and to teach until the*   Acts i 1,2.
day in which He was taken up. The Lord *led them out as far as to Be-*   Luke
thany. He went before them as He was wont to do, but now for the   xxiv.
last time. He led them out designedly that they might be witnesses   50, 51.
He was parted from them and carried up into heaven , or, as elsewhere,
far above all heavens, far above the gradational heavens to which   Eph iv.
St. Paul himself, and other saints, had been rapt. It was not, as   10

before, a disappearance into Hades—between which and the upper world the Forty Days alternated—but a local withdrawal into what is called *the Presence of God,* concerning which we cannot and we need not form any conception. During His life He spoke of His ascent as belonging to His incarnation : the Son of Man was in heaven, and had *ascended up to heaven,* in virtue of the hypostatic union   But in this final going up the *heaven must receive* Him   words which must retain their full significance, though they are quite consistent with His receiving the heavens.

Heb iv 24.

John iii. 13 Acts iii. 21.

Witnesses

(3.) The Apostles were witnesses of this event   The Resurrection neither they nor any mortal witnessed ; but the Forty Days were a continuous evidence to them that their Lord had risen. The entire community of believers was not summoned to Bethany : for, though it was necessary that the resurrection should be attested by all, the ascension had not the same evidential character   In this respect it was only the natural conclusion, as it were, of the resurrection itself; and is never referred to in the Epistles save in its theological, experimental, and practical bearings. The Apostles had been with their Master in His temptations, and they were permitted to behold the honour and glory which He received in His ascension   Only three of them witnessed the Transfiguration earnest, the same, namely, who witnessed the agony of the garden , but all are admitted to the second holy mount   only, however, the Apostolic company, for there is selection still.   Their evidence is sufficient to assure us of the reward conferred on the human nature of our Lord, and of the fact of His entrance into the invisible world.

As to the Future.

Heb. ix. 24, 28.

2   As the beginning of a new life the ascension was the passing into a new sphere of mediatorial action, the taking possession of *the Presence of God* for His people, in a departure from earth which preceded a return from heaven or His appearing *the second time.*

Intercession and Rule

1 John ii 1, 2

Heb. iv 14.

Heb. ix. 25.

(1.) With the Lord's ascension is always connected the priestly office of intercession wherein as the High Priest He pleads His *propitiation for the sins of the whole world,* and as His people's Surety pleads especially for them. *We have an Advocate with the Father, Jesus Christ the Righteous, Who is passed into the heavens,* even as His type *entereth into the holy place every year*   And the government of the Church is in His hands, a s   t on the mediatorial throne:

to exercise the dominion He went up, even as He came down
to obtain it through death   Hence it is said to be a dignity
with His right hand conferred on the Son by the Father, and to be   Acts v. 31
the reward of His humiliation unto death.   In this sense heaven
is the centre of the universe, from which the heavens. the earth,
and things under the earth are surveyed and governed by the
Incarnate Lord.   But the further consideration of this subject
belongs to the doctrine of the Offices of Christ.

(2.) The account of the Acts connects the departure of our Lord   Return.
with His return . hence the prophetic *Mount called Olivet*, the new   Acts i. 12
angelic announcement which in every word respects the future   Zech. xiv
and not the past, and the emphasis laid upon the first Promise of   4
the perfected Christ   *This same Jesus, which is taken up from you*   Acts. i
into heaven, shall so come in like manner as ye have seen Him go into   11
heaven.   The Second Coming is predicted as soon as the first is
past ; this being the link of continuity between the old covenant
and the new : in both there is a great expectation of the Saviour
Meanwhile, the theological bearing of the Ascension of our Lord
is most affectingly taught in connection with the doctrine of His
people's union with Him   In virtue of this, believers are blessed
with all spiritual blessings in heavenly places in Christ   They seek   Eph i 3.
those things which are above, where Christ sitteth on the right hand of   Col. iii. 1.
God   And, according to the last words of the New Testament, their
one deep longing is to see Him again : *Even so, come, Lord Jesus !*   Rev xxii.
III   The sequel of the Ascension is the Session at the right   20.
hand of God in heaven, with its attestation on earth, the Pente-   Its Result.
costal descent of the Holy Spirit, the Promise of the New Covenant.

1. The Session was the subject of our Saviour's prophecy,
equally with the events that preceded it   His first reference to   The
it was indirect · *He saith unto them, How then doth David in Spirit*   Session.
call Him Lord, saying, The Lord said unto my Lord, Sit Thou on My   Matt.
right hand, till I make Thine enemies Thy footstool ?   Afterwards, in   xxii.
His own day of judgment, when He was adjured by the high   41—44
priest and confessed Himself the Son of God, He varied the
phrase : *Hereafter shall ye see the Son of man sitting on the right*   Matt
hand of power   This emphatic twofold allusion of Christ is echoed   xxvi.
throughout the New Testament, and rules all that follows   64.

(1) The Apostle Peter speaks of Him as raised by the right   Acts ii.
33.

1 Pet. iii. 22.

hand of God to sit *on the right hand of God* And he constantly refers to the Session, sometimes with and sometimes without the term, to express the mediatorial authority of Christ as an administration of the power of God · to shed forth the influences of that Holy Ghost Who represents upon earth the Lord's administration in heaven. But St. Paul is the elect expositor of this authority, and he sums up the entire doctrine in his Ephesian Epistle · *He raised Him from the dead, and set Him at His own right hand in the heavenly places, far above all principality, and power, and might, and dominion, and every name that is named, not only*

Eph. i 20, 22, 23.

in this world, but also in that which is to come, and hath put all things under His feet, and gave Him to be the Head over all things to the Church, which is His Body, the Fulness of Him that filleth all in all.

(2.) Hence the Ascension is described as the beginning of a supreme authority which is to end when He *hath put all enemies*

1 Cor xv 25.
Heb. x. 12, 13.

under His feet Until then our Lord's Session is passive also, as in the attitude of expectation *This Man, after He had offered one sacrifice for sins for ever, sat down on the right hand of God; from henceforth expecting till His enemies be made His footstool* But

Acts vii 56.

Stephen, for his assurance in death, saw *the Son of Man* STANDING *on the right hand of God*

(3) But, lastly, this delegated and terminable authority is based upon an eternal prerogative of Session He who *sat down on the right hand of the Majesty on high* was THE SON, *Whom He hath appointed heir of all things, by Whom also He made the worlds;*

Heb i 2, 3.

before His incarnation *being the brightness of His glory, and the express image of His person, and upholding all things by the word of His power.* Nor could He have sat on the right hand of God, in universal supremacy, had He not in His eternal dignity been in

John i. 18.

the Bosom of the Father.

Pentecost

2. The Pentecostal gift of the Holy Ghost was at once the immediate proof of the verity of the ascension, and demonstration of the authority to which it led. The prediction of the

Ps lxviii 18.

Psalmist, *Thou hast received gifts for men; yea, for the rebellious also, that the Lord God might dwell among them,* was interpreted both by our Lord and by St. Paul of the supreme Gift of the

John xvi. 7.

Spirit. *I will send Him unto you* was the promise before the Saviour's departure : it was confirmed after His resurrection;

and it was fulfilled on the Day of Pentecost once for all and for ever.

(1.) For this there were Ten days of preparation   Whether or not the disciples connected the promised Gift with the Fiftieth day, the end of the seven weeks, we cannot tell : probably they did.   The indefinite *not many days hence* might suggest to the presentiment of some among them what others were not prepared to infer.   Evidently their Master's purpose was to make this interval a period of discipline   without His personal presence in the flesh, and without His spiritual manifestation by the Holy Ghost, they were reduced for a season to a midway condition of which there is no parallel   But these days were days of prayer, of personal and united preparation for the most glorious revelation heaven had ever sent down to earth   The circle of the Apostolic company was made complete by the choice of St Matthias , and this by lot, as in an intermediate dispensation between the Lord's departure and the coming of the Spirit   Thus the organic body prepared for the Spirit by the Lord Himself was made whole after the great breach that had been made in it   And the individual believers were prepared for the high Gift by meditation upon their own powerlessness and need, and by fervent prayer for its bestowment.   Hence the history of the Eve of Pentecost is narrated in the Acts with careful precision as the record of the final preparations for this consummate fulness of time, the descent of the Holy Ghost

(2) The Gift itself was the demonstration of the Session of Christ at the right hand of God.   *Having received of the Father the promise of the Holy Ghost, He hath shed forth this, which ye now see and hear*   St Paul speaks of the Ascension *gifts unto men* with special reference to the dispensation of *the ministry for the edifying of the body of Christ*, which began with the Day of Pentecost.   But the great prophecy in the Psalm, *that the Lord God might dwell among them*, had its plenary fulfilment when the Holy Ghost came down as the Shekina, the symbol of God manifest in the flesh, resting upon the Church and abiding within it as the indwelling presence of the Holy Trinity.   Thus the glory within the veil, and the candlestick outside, symbols of the Son and the Spirit, were blended when the veil was removed, into one and the same FULNESS OF GOD

Ten Days
of
Interval

Acts i. 5.

Eve of
Pentecost.

The Gift.

Acts ii
33.

Eph iv 8,
12

Ps. lxviii.
18

Eph. iii.
19.

The Two Estates of the Redeemer are exhibited throughout the Scriptures with the same precision and uniformity as that which we have marked in the doctrine of the Two Natures in the Incarnate Lord But we need not trace so carefully the process of Biblical teaching on this subject, as it has been to a great extent anticipated in the development of the doctrine of Christ's Person.

Old Testament. I In the Old Testament the history of the future Minister of redemption is foreshadowed as a career leading through deep humiliation to glory , the Messiah being a mediatorial Person, whose attributes are Divine and human, but who always occupies a subordinate position in carrying out the Divine counsel The first distant intimation of this is the phrase Angel of Jehovah, where Jehovah is the Agent of Jehovah. In due time the term Messiah, or The Anointed, prophetically designated the same Angel as incarnate · the future Revealer of the Divine Will, Propitiation for human sin, and Ruler of a saved and ransomed people But this Messiah is described as consecrated for God by God, first to a state of the deepest depression and then to a state of the highest majesty In Isaiah's prophecy, which gave our Lord His own term Minister, the coming of the Incarnate is predicted as that of a Servant All the Psalms and the Prophets, however, agree in ascribing to the Redeemer a subordination to God which is made mysteriously consistent with Divine titles and honours In Him the Alpha and Omega meet

Our Lord's Testimony II. Our Lord never defines the secret of His incarnate Person ; never speaks of His two natures as united in one ; nor does He once propose the mystery of His exinanition and its results to the acceptance of His disciples. He reveals it distinctly but does not distinctly explain it, thus tacitly rebuking beforehand the future presumption of speculative theology We must consider only therefore the kind of testimony which He gives as to the two Estates respectively.

Subordination 1 In many ways He declares His subordination in His humbled state , but always speaks of it as a voluntary submission

(1.) He terms Himself the Son of Man rather than the Son of God, though not refusing the latter name   He speaks of Himself as come *not to be ministered unto, but to minister ;* of His doctrine as *what My Father hath taught Me,* and the *things which I have heard of Him .* of His mediatorial work as a commission or commandment *received of My Father,* for the strength to accomplish which He prayed, while for its gradual disclosure, or the hour of each crisis, He waited   *Of that day and that hour knoweth no man, no, not the angels which are in heaven, neither the Son, but the Father.* He spoke of God as apart from Himself   His God as well as ours He said, *My Father is greater than I,* when speaking of His going to Him through the way of humble suffering.   Not so much in individual passages, as in the uniform tone of His self-disclosure, we mark the Redeemer's strict subordination to the Father as the God and Head of the redeeming economy.

Son of Man.

Matt xx 28

John viii 26, 28 John x. 18 Mark xiii. 32

John xiv. 28.

(2.) That the incarnate Jesus in His humbled estate voluntarily made Himself subject, while retaining the eternal dignity of His Divinity, is obvious from these assertions of His oneness with the Father to which reference has already been made, from His demand of honour equal to that paid to the Father, and especially from His anticipation of a return of the glory which He surrendered in His incarnation.   There are some passages in which the voluntary subordination and the coequal dignity are combined in a manner that ought not to be misunderstood   *For as the Father hath life in Himself, so hath He given to the Son to have life in Himself   I proceeded forth and came from God ; neither came I of Myself, but He sent Me*   The profoundest word, however, is not in St John, but in St. Matthew   *All things are delivered unto Me of My Father ; and no man knoweth the Son, but the Father , neither knoweth any man the Father save the Son.*

Dignity and Subordination.

John v 26. John viii 42 Matt. xi 27.

(3.) Hence we are constrained to interpret our Lord's testimony to His exinanition in a sense that shall make it consistent with His consciousness of equality with the Father.   This is the great difficulty of the subject , but it is a Scriptural difficulty, committed to humble faith , and this doctrine of a relative and only mediatorial inferiority is much more consonant with the Christian idea of God than the theories of a contracted or depotentiated Divinity which are invented in its stead

Mystery.

Exalta-
tion
2. The Saviour's testimonies to His state of dignity are in word before His ascension, in word and manifestation afterwards.

Antici-
pated
(1.) It is important to consider in what way our Lord was wont to look forward to His future dignity. Here we mark the same twofold strain that we find throughout the subject. On the one hand, He speaks of His exaltation as simply the avowal to the universe of His true character and dignity John iii
13 *No man hath ascended up to heaven, but He that came down from heaven, even the Son of Man which is in heaven ·* the Saviour, foreseeing His ascension, speaks of it as adding nothing to His real dignity, because He is never out of heaven. Human nature in contact with Him is already exalted He who heard these words had just John ii
19. before heard the Lord say : *Destroy this temple, and in three days I will raise it up* But when the Lord at the close prayed for His Heb. xii
2 coming glorification we understand that Jesus, *for the joy that was set before Him, endured the cross,* anticipating His reward

After the
Ascension
(2) After His ascension the Redeemer most expressly teaches us the continuance of a mediatorial subjection in harmony with the essential Divinity of His Divine-human Person As to the fact of the abiding subordination, He speaks of Himself as the Minister of redemption precisely in the same terms as while on earth. There is literally no difference He bids His servants Acts v
31. speak of Him as the Prince and the Saviour whom God *exalted with His right hand,* as the Son or the Servant *sent to bless.* There Acts iii.
26. is no more glorious manifestation of Christ than that to Saul in his conversion, and there we hear our Lord saying that his office Acts xxvi
18 should be to turn men *from the power of Satan unto God . . . by faith that is in Me.* So in the Epistle to the Church of Phil-Rev iii
12 adelphia He speaks of *the temple of My God* and *the name of My* John xx
17 *God ·* reminding us of the words before the ascension, *My Father and your Father, My God and your God* But that this con-tinuing ministry is consistent with His supreme Divinity, we have the Apocalyptic testimony. When St. John was in Rev i 11. Patmos, and *in the Spirit,* he heard the voice of the Redeemer, saying, *I am Alpha and Omega, the First and the Last ·* than these words none more expressly declare in Scripture the necessary, Rev i. 17,
18. absolute being of God That the Risen Saviour spoke of Him-self evident from what follows after the human manifestation ·

Fear not , I am the First and the Last   I am He that liveth ! Deep
meditation on these and all other such sayings of our Lord must
constrain us to understand His secret   the FELLOW of God made
the SERVANT of redemption.

III. The Two Estates occupy a prominent place in the Aposto-   Apostolic.
lical theology   It will be expedient to refer only to a few salient
points : the subordination generally , its continuance until the
last day ; its continuance for ever.

1. The subordination of our Lord is in one sense limited to the   Subordi-
days of His flesh, and ends with His exaltation at the ascension.   nation.
One passage is entirely dedicated to this subject : that in the
Epistle to the Philippians which makes the voluntary condescension of Christ the example of Christian humility. The Eternal
Son, retaining His equality with God, and still being *in the form*   Phil ii.
of God, yet *made Himself of no reputation*, or emptied Himself   It   2—8.
is too often forgotten that the subjection of Christ is here altogether
voluntary , that it is matter of self-imputation rather than of an impossible reality   As *in the form of God*, Christ was still the possessor
of Divine attributes, but He did not use or manifest them   *He*
thought it not robbery to be equal with God . He did not, as to His
human nature, think fit to arrogate the display of His equality
with God. But it was *in the form of a servant* that *He humbled*
Himself · while His exinanition was that of the God-man, in respect, however, to His Divinity as making the manhood its organ.

2. The exalted state is, however, not described as the resump-   In
tion of our Lord's pretemporal glory apart from His incarnate   Heaven
subjection. Though the *fulness of the Godhead* is in Him, it is in   Col ii 9.
Him *bodily,* and as flowing from the pleasure of the Father   the   Col i 19
eternal generation was not an act of the Divine will, but in the
necessity of the Divine essence , but *it pleased the Father that in Him*
should all fulness dwell after the ascension   Hence in the Corinthian Epistles we have some distinct exhibitions of the subordination   *The Head of Christ is God ·* this is perhaps the most   1 Cor. xi.
striking expression of the fact that even in heaven the Incarnate   3
is mediatorially subject. *And Christ is God's* declares the same   1 Cor iii.
truth. But it is the current doctrine of the Epistles , and finds   23
its reason as well as its expression in the sequel of the passage
above quoted . ·   ·   *God at h* ·   ·   ,   ·   Phil ii 9

3 There is a sense, however, in which the subordination is represented as abiding eternally   Only one passage expressly refers to this, but it is one which is exceedingly explicit, and gives so much prominence to the subject that we must not pass it by as belonging to the hidden and reserved mysteries of the Christian faith.   *Then shall the Son also Himself be subject unto Him that put all things under Him*   αὐτὸς ὁ υἱὸς ὑποταγήσεται. Here, let it be remembered, the verb has a middle signification. the Son shall *subject Himself.*   It is indeed as if, at the close of the redeeming economy, He reaffirms His original assumption of our nature.   He will not fold it or lay it aside as a vesture. Remaining in the unity of the Father and the Holy Ghost—God shall be *All in all*—He will end the whole history and mystery of redemption by ratifying His incarnation for ever.

1 Cor. xv.
28.

No
Formula

4. Before leaving the Scriptural view of this subject we should observe that the sacred writers give no formula to express the mediatorial relation of the Son incarnate to the Father and to the Holy Trinity.   All that is meant by subordination is asserted, but the word is not used, nor is any synonym employed until the subjection of the last day is referred to.   This is a remarkable circumstance and points to a striking theological paradox. It might seem that the following was the order of the Lord's historical process   The Logos in the Trinity, the humiliation of the incarnate state, the elevation to supreme dignity after the resurrection, the abdication at the close of all mediatorial authority as such, and the voluntary continuance of the Son as incarnate in a subordination to the Eternal Trinity that does not impair the dignity of the Son as God in the unity of the Father and of the Holy Ghost   The union of man with His Creator is thus made perfect   not by Pantheistic absorption into the Godhead, but by union with God in the Son   The Lamb *is in the midst of the throne ;* and He is *the Head of the Church, the Saviour of the Body.* for ever.

Rev. vii
17
Eph v. 23.

Historical
Develop-
ment.

ECCLESIASTICAL DEVELOPMENT

The earlier developments of historical Christology were limited to the relation of the two natures in the one Person of the Christ. Subsequent controversies had reference rather to the nature of the subordinate estate into which the Redeemer descended At the Reformation the characteristics of the Divine-human humiliation on the one hand, and on the other its reversal in the ascended dignity, were profoundly studied and became the ground of many divisions A few general remarks will be enough to indicate the direction which theological study here takes first, in mediæval theology ; then in the theories of Lutheranism , and, lastly, in some miscellaneous tendencies of modern thought

I. After the settlement of the Four Œcumenical Councils the Christological discussions reappeared in controversies referring rather to the degree in which the Divine Person partook of the humiliation of the human nature. Four speculative tendencies may, without violence, be brought into relation with each other. *The Four Councils*

1. First the Monophysite and Monothelite errors made our Lord's humbled estate a real renunciation of the Divine nature, without seeming to do so. These were simply the reflex of the Eutychian heresy, which has never vanished from theology. *Monophysitism.*

(1) The Monophysite dogma has been called Theopaschitism, because its tendency was to assign one nature as well as one Person to Christ, who therefore as a composite God-man was crucified the emphasis of course resting on the Divine nature which absorbed the human, the passion was exaggerated into a suffering of God. Hence the name. This error was held in a great variety of forms , in its one general principle it was the link of transition between pure Eutychianism, which absorbed the man in the God, and the philosophical Eutychianism of modern Lutheran theories. Monophysites are supposed to linger only among the Eastern sects · in reality the divines of the Depotentiation school are their representatives. *Theopaschitism*

(2.) The Monothelite heresy was the same with a difference . the former error just mentioned had reference to the human nature of Christ generally , this latter to His single will only. Now if there was in Christ only one will, there could be only one nature ; for the will cannot be divided. Hence the humanity was abolished in this dogma, and the humiliation of the Son of God was His sinking to such a point as to say NOT AS I WILL. The true doctrine taught indeed NOT AS I WILL, OR TAKE IT , but as the *Monothelitism.*

result of two wills, the human being of necessity submissive to the Divine or necessarily one with it in act

Adoptian-
ism.

2 The heresy sometimes called Adoptianism was taught by two Spanish divines in the eighth century, and was condemned at the Synod of Frankfurt, A D. 794. It was really a revival of Nestorianism, as it kept apart the Divine and the human sonship of our Lord, making the human nature partaker of the Divine Sonship only by an act of heavenly and gracious adoption. Thus the humbled estate of the God-man was merely the expression of His alliance with a human person of consummate and more than human excellence   Alcuin and other opponents of this view laid great stress on the fact that the humiliation of Christ was His union with our nature, not with a human individual   "In absumtione carnis a Deo, persona perit hominis, non natura."

Nihilian-
ism.

3 The term Nihilianism is suggested by a controversy once vigorous, but of little importance save as the expression of an erroneous protest against a still greater error   It took up the word that defeated the error just mentioned—that is, the IMPERSONALITY of our Lord's human nature—and defended the position that the Second Person underwent no change whatever through the assumption of flesh.   The notion was condemned by the Lateran Council of A D. 1215, as tending to reduce the Incarnation to a nullity. It was the very opposite of Theopaschitism before, and of the Depotentiation theory that followed, the Reformation. these errors both being based on the assumption that God in one of the Divine Persons is capable of being reduced to such a point as to combine with a finite personality as its power and energy.   But error cannot cast out error; and this theory perverted the true dogma of the impersonality of the human nature of our Lord by excluding the reality of a human presentation of His Divine human Person.   It went far towards abolishing the Humbled Estate, and leaving only a Docetic Christianity.

Reason of
the Incar-
nation.

4. Very much more interesting was the mediæval discussion as to whether the suffering of the God-man was essentially necessary, or whether His union with human nature was attended with humiliation only on account of sin.   While the question is confined to these limits the answer is plain enough. we know of no manhood as the object of the Redeemer's condescension apart

from sin, and of no Mediator who was not made sin for us.   But
the question does not rest there

5. This beautiful speculation involves another topic of very
great importance   The question is not simply whether or not
human sin rendered necessary the Incarnation, but whether
man was not really the created expression of God's eternal idea in
His Son.   The Infinite and the finite were one in Him.   The
universal Spirit in God found its incarnate embodiment, realised
itself, in humanity as conceived in the historical Jesus.   The
Pantheistic Christology of Duns Scotus in the early middle ages
laid the foundation for modern German transcendental philosophy, which, whether in Kant or Hegel, is intimately bound up
with the necessary evolving of the Trinity through Christ.   But
from these speculations we must turn away

II   At the Reformation the Lutheran and the Reformed dogmas
concerning our Lord's Two Estates widely disparted

1   The Lutheran was based upon the principle of a COMMUNIO
NATURARUM, or COMMUNICATIO IDIOMATUM   the latter implying
that the attributes of the Divinity were imparted to the manhood
in the unity of the Person , the former implying further that the
one nature is interpenetrated by the other, that what one nature
is and does the other is and does.   The "Natura humana est
in Christo capax Divinæ."   The Reformed doctrine denied this:
"Finitum non est capax Infiniti."   It asserted that the humanity
of Christ never was nor ever could be possessed of Divine attributes   It may be well to consider more at large the Lutheran
dogmatics on this subject   It divides the Communicatio Idiomatum, or interchange of attributes, into three branches   (1)
The GENUS IDIOMATICUM   this signifies the use of predicates
taken from either nature and applied to the whole Person.   (2.)
The GENUS AUCHEMATICUM SEU MAJESTATICUM : this signifies
the ascription of Divine attributes to the human nature, in the
POSSESSION from the conception, in the full USE from the ascension.   (3) The GENUS APOTELESMATICUM : this signifies the ascription of mediatorial acts to the One Agent.   It is obvious that the
second of these contains the peculiarity of Lutheran doctrine.
The Reformed theologians, and the great body of the Christian
Church, have always denied the communication of examples n e,

Pantheis-
tic Incar-
nation

Reforma-
tion.

Commu-
nicatio
Idioma-
tum.

omniscience, and omnipotence in any sense to the human nature of our Lord

Lutheran Theories.

2 The application of the theory to the Two Estates may be traced in two opposite directions: first, in regard to the deification of the human nature generally in the ascension, and particularly the ubiquity of that nature in the Eucharist; secondly, in regard to the more modern theories of retraction or depotentiation of Divinity in the Incarnate Man

Ascension.

(1.) In the Lutheran theology the ascension of Christ is regarded as the assumption of His human nature into the full dignity and use of all Divine perfections During His humiliation He possessed the attributes of omnipresence, omniscience and omnipotence, but voluntarily declined to exhibit them. After the ex-

Col. ii. 9

altation there was in Him *the fulness of the Godhead bodily.* His body became not merely the organ of these attributes, but itself possessed them. He entered not into the local heaven, but into the immensity of God. The heavens did not receive Him, but

Acts iii. 21.

He received the heavens so are the words ὃν δεῖ οὐρανὸν μὲν δέξασθαι translated by the advocates of this view.

Ubiquity.

(2) Hence the soul and body of Christ have the ubiquity of the Godhead Not, however, that the actual flesh of the Redeemer can be literally extended to infinity; but that the hypostatic union gives the Divine power and knowledge to the Glorified Man, and therefore the omnipresence also The application of this doctrine to the Saviour's offices will be hereafter seen. Suffice here to observe that it is made to explain the anomaly in the prophetic office that the Divine-human Revealer was ignorant of some things while on earth: in Him now are hid all the treasures of wisdom and knowledge. The Glorified King now sways the destinies of the universe as God-man while on earth He had no such authority save in the unity of the Triune God As Priest the Redeemer gives, the virtue of omnipresence now to the sacrifice He offered for sin, dispensing to the communicants at the Eucharist His glorified body and blood at every altar. The theology of Lutheranism generally attaches much importance to the physical aspect of redemption. It seems to regard corporeal embodiment as " the end of all God's ways " to use the favourite language of some of its modern exponents

(3.) In the beginning of the seventeenth century a controversy on this subject sprang up in Lutheranism One party maintained that the humiliation of Christ was the hiding of Divine attributes which in His human estate He possessed · this idea of κρύψις, or concealment, gave them their name of Kryptists. Another party affirmed that there was an actual κένωσις, or emptying Himself, of the Divine attributes which belonged to the human nature in virtue of the hypostatical union hence they were Kenotists. The former view invested Jesus as man with omnipresence, omniscience and omnipotence from the moment of the Conception ; but this possession was veiled during the earthly life, and avowed only after the Ascension The latter regarded Him as having the κτῆσις or possession of these attributes from His birth, but as utterly renouncing their χρῆσις or use until He was glorified. The former view, held by the Tubingen theologians, made the ascension the first display of Christ's Divine attributes in humanity ; the latter view, held by the Giessen theologians, made it the first resumption of them The controversy was one of infinite subtilty, but concerned only the Lutheran theologians · they alone asserted a communication of Divine attributes to the manhood, and they alone were involved in the embarrassments resulting. The general bearing of the question is well seen in the following words of Gerhard :—" Not a part to a part, but the entire Logos was united to the entire flesh, and the entire flesh was united to the entire Logos ; therefore, on account of the hypostatic union and intercommunion of the two natures, the Logos is so present to the flesh and the flesh so present to the Logos that neither is the Logos EXTRA CARNEM, nor is the flesh EXTRA LOGON ; but wherever the Logos is, there it has the flesh most present, as having been assumed into the unity of the person " The controversy led to no definite results indeed, to us who look at the question from the outside, there is but little difference between them.

(4) During the present century the condescension of the Son of God in the Incarnation has been profoundly studied by German and French divines under the influence of a certain Eutychianism that has never ceased to cling to Lutheran Christology, but modified by the transcendental philosophy which sees in Christ the developing body of the Spirit of the Godhead coming to perfect

Marginal notes:
Lutheran Controversies.

Krypsis.

Kenosis

Depotentiation.

personality in the Holy Ghost The various theories to which the names of individual men are attached need not be discussed at length; that would be to exaggerate their importance. It will be enough to mention the one element common to them all: namely, that of a literal merging of the Divinity of the Son into the finite Spirit of the Man Christ Jesus. The general idea takes many forms sometimes simply Pantheistic, the Eternal Spirit thinking itself as a Person in Christ, sometimes purely Eutychian, God the Son contracted into humanity, and both growing together to perfection; sometimes Apollinarian, the Potency of the Son working dynamically in the psychical soul and flesh of Jesus. But all these hypotheses have been shown by anticipation to be incapable of resisting the simple argument of the essential Immutability of the Divine nature.

Pretemporal Humanity

III. Many modern theories have been revived from antiquity or invented afresh which have striven to break the fall of the Divine into the human, the chief of these being the interposition of a human pre-existent soul of Christ

The Root idea.

1. The one fundamental principle in these sporadic speculations —they have never been formulated in any Confessions—is that the pure humanity of our Lord was as independent of the race of man as that of Adam was when he came from the Hand and Breath of his Maker. Denying, with the Scripture, that Jesus owed anything to a human father, they deny, without or in opposition to Scripture, that He derived anything from a human mother. The Virgin was no more than the instrument or channel through which a Divine humanity, existing before the foundation of the world or from eternity, was introduced by the Holy Ghost into human history. The passages relied upon for the maintenance of this notion are such as that in which our Lord says,

John vi. 38
1 Cor. xv. 47

I came down from heaven, and *the Second Man is the Lord from heaven,* which, with some like them, are made to signify that the human nature as well as the Divine was pre-existent in eternity

Modern Mysticism.

2. Modern Mysticism has furnished in Behmen, Poiret, Barclay, Œtinger, Goschel, Petersen, and others, the most attractive forms of this theory. In them the pure ideal humanity of Jesus—which it is hard however to conceive as purely ideal— was one with the Word from eternity, as it were in a pretemporal

incarnation. After the fashion of that humanity man was created : and the incarnate Jesus of history literally *came unto His* John 1. 11. *own* Œtinger, one of the most unexceptionable of Mystics, says : "Because Wisdom, before the Incarnation, was the visible Image of the invisible God, therefore the Son, in comparison with the Being of all beings, is something relatively incorporeal, although He too is a pure spirit. The heavenly humanity which He had as the Lord from heaven was invisibly present even with the Israelites. They drank out of the rock" But in all these speculations the Incarnation is antedated; or, rather, it is not the Son of God who becomes flesh but the Son of God already in the heavenly nature of mankind.

3 Swedenborgianism, in its theological system, has on this sub- Sweden-ject as on every other, a peculiar revelation. Swedenborg asserted borg. the unity of God, and strove to reconcile with that the Deity of Christ His theory established a kind of hypostatic union between the Father and the Son in the One Christ, the only God in the universe The Incarnation he viewed in an Apollinarian way : the eternal God, eternally God-man, manifested Himself in the animal soul and psychical body derived from the Virgin , but the material body was finally absorbed and glorified. This is literally a composite of nearly all the heresies of antiquity. But its peculiarity as to the person of Christ is that it gives Him, like all other men, both a material body and a spiritual, the former corresponding with the world of sense, the latter with the spiritual world which He never left. The Christ of this system is the one eternal Jehovah, God and Man in one

4. Others, of whom Isaac Watts may be regarded as the repre- More sentative, have held similar views as to the pre-existent humanity Modern of Christ. Their starting-point is the same as the Lutheran, that views. the human spirit is capable of expansion to infinity Now the pre-existent soul of Christ was, in their view, created and personally united with the Logos · here Orthodoxy and Arianism unite. This already incarnate Logos became incarnate on earth by assuming the animal life of a natural body . here Apollinarianism, as so often elsewhere, steps in. Accordingly, all the humiliation of our Lord consisted in this transcendent human spirit being bereft of its knowledge and passing through all stages of exinanition until

the ascension restored it to its perfection   But in this case the Man Christ Jesus is not strictly one of us.   There is an enormous addition made to His Person; but there is no relief afforded to the difficulties of His humiliation.

THE THREE OFFICES OF THE CHRIST.

Three Offices.

Jesus is, in virtue of His incarnation, the Anointed Mediator between God and man.   To the offices of His mediatorship His incarnate Person was specifically anointed at His baptism, and thus He became the perfected Christ of God.   His work was the fulfilment and consummation of the ancient prophetical, priestly and regal functions to which the typical servants of God under the old economy were anointed.   These offices He began to discharge on earth, and continues to discharge in heaven.   While considering them as distinct, it is important to remember that they are one in the mediatorial work; and that the integrity of evangelical truth depends upon the faithfulness with which we give to each its due tribute in the unity of the two others.

In Theology.

The division of the mediatorial work into Three Offices is based, as will be seen, on the Scriptures, both of the Old and of the New Testament, but it is not formally stated in them   It was current in later Judaism; is distinctly to be traced in the early Fathers, especially Eusebius, Cyril of Jerusalem, and Augustine, and in the Middle Ages was elaborated by Thomas Aquinas.   It was introduced into their theology both by Luther and Calvin, and, though contended against by some writers who object to the too systematic distinction of the several offices, it has become current in modern theology   There are many reasons why it is inexpedient to make the Three Offices the basis of an analysis of the mediatorial work.   But their consideration is most appropriate in the present review of the process of historical redemption.

THE CHRIST OF PROPHECY

The Redeemer of mankind, whose advent in the fulness of time is the supreme verbal and typical prophecy of the Old Testament, was marked out as THE LORD'S ANOINTED or THE CHRIST. This appellation was not at first given to Him directly, but indirectly as He was represented by those who in the Theocracy were anointed to their office In some passages however the future Saviour is predicted by this name ; and when He came into the world He was the fulfilment of a general expectation of the Messiah as hereafter to come in one or all of these three offices.

The
Symbol
of Oil

I Anointing was from early times a symbol of consecration to God . to the Divine possession and to the Divine service.

1 Generally, it signified human dedication and Divine acceptance So, in the first recorded instance of its use, Jacob *took the stone that he had put for his pillows, and set it up for a pillar, and poured oil upon the top of it*, because it was revealed to him, *the Lord is in this place.* More particularly it was the symbol of light and peace and joy : of light for prophetical illumination, of peace for priestly atonement, of joy for legal government as the presence of God with His people

Gen.
xxviii.
18, 16

2 This anointing oil was the emblem of the Holy Ghost, the Spirit of consecration. As blood was the expiatory symbol, water that of purification, and light of God's accepting presence, so oil was the symbol of sanctification generally as mystically combining all these This symbol in its most perfect form, the *holy anointing oil*, was a peculiar confection, like everything pertaining to the sanctuary after a Divine pattern, and never to be used save in connection with Divine uses, for the priesthood and the sanctuary, it was not to be privately prepared, nor to be *poured upon man's flesh or the stranger. It is holy, and it shall be holy unto you* Thus the precious ointment, the ointment of the apothecary, was the elect typical emblem of the Holy Ghost in His special relation to the unction of Christ, and in His general relation to that of the saints who share the sacred unction

Ex xxx.
22—33.

II Anointing oil was used for the consecration of the priesthood and of the prophets and rulers . especially of the high priest and the kings in the ancient economy.

Its Use

Priest-
hood.

1 The priests were anointed, as also the furniture of the sacrificial service : all things were both sprinkled with blood and anointed with oil. *And thou shalt anoint Aaron and his sons, and*

Ex. xxx.
30.
Lev viii.
30

consecrate them.　And Moses took of the anointing oil, and of the blood which was upon the altar, and sprinkled it upon Aaron, and upon his garments, and upon his sons, and upon his sons' garments with him ; and sanctified Aaron.　The anointing oil was therefore as essential and as pervasive as the blood, its correlative symbol the expiatory atonement and the consecration of the Holy

Lev. iv 3.

Ghost being co-ordinate　After the first institution *the priest that is anointed* signified the High Priest . it is to be supposed that the successors in the ordinary priesthood were not consecrated

Prophets

by this symbol.　The prophets were set apart in the same way. Moses, the head of the prophetic order, who anointed the priests.

1 Kings
xix 16

did not himself undergo the rite　The Spirit anointed him without the emblem.　But Elijah was commanded to anoint Elisha to be prophet in his room　As to the kings, the testimony is more

1 Kings.

clear　Elijah anointed Hazael to be king, which points back to an earlier ordinance　The judges were not thus instituted

Num.
xxvii
18, 23
1 Sam. x.
1.

Joshua received the imposition of Moses' hands as one on whom the Spirit of consecration had already fallen.　But, when Saul was given to Israel, *Samuel took a vial of oil. and poured it upon his head, and kissed him, and said, Is it not because the Lord hath anointed thee to be captain over His inheritance ?*　David, however,

1 Sam
xvi 13.

was the specific regal type of the Messiah　*Then Samuel took the horn of oil, and anointed him in the midst of his brethren , and the Spirit of the Lord came upon David from that day forward*　Designation and endowment with gifts were the two elements in the regal consecration　the former making the Lord's Anointed a sacred and inviolable person, and the latter insuring him every requisite grace for the administration of his office.

Ancient
Meanings
one in
Christ.

2　Thus the anointing oil, the symbol of the Holy Ghost, had various meanings in the typical economy : meanings which were afterwards one in Christ　The prophetic anointing signified rather the setting apart of an organ for occasional influence　it pointed out one in whom the Spirit was already present.　The priestly anointing indicated not so much mere appointment as consecration to the Divine service.　The regal anointing superadded to the other meanings that of the permanent Divine indwelling: the king was God's representative alone. The prophet and the king represented God and not man : the former, occasionally; the latter, permanently The priest represented God to man, and man to God; his consecration was abiding, and affected all things connected with him. As in the case of the altar, *whatsoever toucheth them shall be holy.*

Ex. xxx 29

III There are a few remarkable passages in which the future Redeemer is foreannounced as the Anointed One, the pre-eminent מָשִׁיחַ, and in relation to these three offices distinctively

The Predicted Messiah

1. The Psalms open with the Great Name of the future, which was to be sanctified for ever as common to Christ and His people . *The rulers take counsel together, against the Lord, and against His anointed.* Here is the regal office , and this is echoed in a later Psalm . *God, Thy God, hath anointed Thee,* where the prophetic office is also referred to, and the priestly consecration is scarcely hid.

King

Ps. ii. 2

Ps. xlv 7, 2, 8

2 The Anointed One speaks of Himself through Isaiah . *The Spirit of the Lord God is upon Me , because the Lord hath anointed Me to preach good tidings.* Here is by our Lord's own interpretation the prophetic office : the only passage of this class which He quotes. Others He left for the use of His Apostles.

Prophet.

Isa. lxi. 1. Luke iv. 18.

3. Daniel closes the Messianic prophecy proper by giving the name Messiah to the Future Redeemer, specifically as High Priest, but including His other offices. Three times he mentions the word. *After threescore and two weeks shall Messiah be cut off, but not for Himself : seventy weeks are determined . . . to make reconciliation for iniquity . . and to anoint the Most Holy* But He is *Messiah the Prince ,* and His coming was to *seal up the prophecy.* Here are all the offices combined , this distinction and combination are the glory of Daniel's predictions.

Priest.

Dan ix 24, 25, 26

IV. Hence in later Judaism a clear testimony was borne to the union of the three functions in One Supreme Person; and the Saviour when He came found among the people a general expectation of the Messiah or Christ. He appealed to it as everywhere latent.

General Expectation.

1. The Targums, or Chaldaic paraphrases of the Scripture substituted for the Hebrew text in public reading after the Captivity, exhibit in very many passages a clear view of the Messiah in His offices. ' They call Him God , the King; the

Later Judaism

Prophet; the High Priest upon His throne; the promised Shiloh. They apply to Him all the passages which Christians are wont to apply. They make His two advents one, however, and regard the delay of the Messiah as caused by the sins of the people; at least this is the explanation of some of later date, when the critical periods indicated for the coming of Messiah were evidently over-past. Some Jewish authorities, it is true, invented a double Messiah; one, the Son of Joseph, in humiliation; the other, the Son of David, in glory Others referred the predictions of sorrow to the Hebrew race, not to the Messiah · the People being the afflicted Servant of God. But before the time of Christ Jewish expectation took very much the form which is sketched in our own exposition of the Old Testament.

In the
Gospels

John vii
42.
Matt. xii
23.
Matt xvii.
10.
Matt. ii 4
Luke ii.
26.
John i 41.
John vii
31.

Matt ii.
2, 4.
Luke
xxiii 2
John vi
14, 15.

John vii.
40, 41.
John iv.
25

2. The state of Messianic expectation in the time of our Lord may be gathered from the Gospels with great precision The Christ was to come *of the seed of David* and *out of the town of Bethlehem where David was.* The people were wont to ask, *Is not this the Son of David?* He was to be heralded by Elias *Why then say the scribes that Elias must first come?* He was to be the Anointed · *He demanded of them where Christ should be born,* Who had been announced to Simeon as *the Lord's Christ.* Andrew's word to Simon was · *We have found the Messias, which is, being interpreted, the Christ.* So the people were accustomed to say, *When Christ cometh, will He do more miracles than these which this man hath done?* He was expected in His three offices. As King especially, for the state of the Jewish people would endear that character: *Where is He that is born King of the Jews . . . the Christ?* with which corresponds the final charge · *saying that He Himself is Christ a King!* As Prophet also of Him whom they would take by force *to make Him a King,* they testified, *This is of a truth that prophet that should come into the world.* There was no real difference between those who said, *Of a truth this is the Prophet!* and those who said, *This is the Christ!* Samaria shared the expectation of Christ as a prophet · *I know that Messias cometh, which is called Christ . when He is come, He will tell us all things.* We have not the same direct evidence that the Messiah was expected to be a priest. It is plain, however, that the representatives of Judaism who welcomed the Child Jesus waited for a priestly Messiah.

Zacharias, Simeon, and the Baptist all regarded Him as the incarnation of God Who *visited and redeemed His people*, not by the right hand of His power simply, but *by the remission of their sins*, through the sacrifice of the *Lamb of God which taketh away the sin of the world*. But here the popular expectation faltered and failed. The Christ was expected as *the Son of God which should come into the world*, that *abideth for ever* upon earth as the pledge of the Divine presence, and life, and power among men, as the Head of a new kingdom of heaven and as the vindicator and redeemer of God's ancient people But as the High Priest, Himself the Offerer and the Offering, they did not recognise their Messiah Hence no part of our Lord's sayings was more offensive than those in which He spoke of His flesh given *for the life of the world*. The common people were one with the Pharisees and Scribes, and the disciples themselves differed little from them, in the carnality of their hopes. *Be it far from Thee, Lord!* said Simon Peter, when under the teaching not of the Father but of flesh and blood, and in these words the Lord perceived not only the timorous loyalty of one who loved Him, but also the blinding agency of Satan, whose object was to merge the priestly office of the Messiah in the two others to induce the nation to regard Him only as a supreme Teacher and a mighty King. Peter's Ἵλεώς σοι, κύριε was not from above but from below. Such theories of the Messiah holding the prophetic and regal offices alone and without the priestly bond between them, have been the watchwords of most of the errors of the Christian Church concerning the work of Christ.

Luke i 68
Luke 1. 77.
John i. 29.
John xi. 27
John xii 34

John vi 51, 52.

Matt. xvi 22

3 It is well known that at the time of our Saviour's advent the world at large was familiar with the Jewish expectation, and even shared it. The Desire of the People was the Desire of the Nations also. The coming of the Magi was a testimony to this . the blessing of the Spirit resting upon the seed sown in the Captivity Outside the Scripture we read : "Percrebuerat Oriente toto vetus et constans opinio esse in fatis ut eo tempore Judæa profecti rerum potirentur" So also "Pluribus persuasio inerat antiquis sacerdotum literis contineri eo ipso tempore fore ut valesceret oriens, profectique Judæa rerum potirentur."

The Christ of the Nations.

Suet. Vesp c 4

Tac Hist v 13

4. Finally, all this will explain the appeals of the early

Apostolic Appeals.

preachers of the Faith. Contending with the Jews the Apostles constantly made it their aim to prove that Jesus was the Messiah : so St. Paul reasoned *that this Jesus, whom I preach unto you, is Christ.* Here was to the Jewish people, always and everywhere, the theme of all argument and preaching. Preaching to the Gentiles, they skilfully touched the same great Messianic desire, known to be latent in all hearts · there are glimpses of this in the New Testament, but much more evident illustrations in the Apologetics of the first two centuries. The history of Christian Missions in all ages adds its tribute The Gospel never fails of a response when it speaks to the indestructible hope of a Deliverer, whose coming the world has longed for ever since it began its career of wandering from God

Acts xvii. 3

THE CHRIST OF FULFILMENT.

The Christ of Fulfilment.

As the Messiah or Christ of Fulfilment our Lord accomplished in Himself all the types and symbols and prophecies of the Old Testament. The holy oil of unction is in the New Testament the Holy Ghost, the Spirit of Christ's anointing in two senses : first, as consecrating His Person in the Incarnation ; and, secondly, as consecrating Him to His offices at the Baptism.

THE PERSONAL UNCTION

ncarnation.

Our Lord in His Person is the Lord's Anointed. As such He is the Messiah of the Old Testament come in the flesh ; and the Mediator between God and men in both natures as united in one Person.

I. At the Saviour's birth He was declared to be *a Saviour, which is Christ the Lord,* Simeon saw *the Lord's Christ.* And He was so called, not in anticipation only, but because in His incarnation or conception His human nature was sanctified and consecrated, essentially separated from the sin of our race by the Holy Ghost The body of humanity thus prepared for Him He assumed before it came to personal and independent subsistence, and insured its eternal sinlessness. He was the Lord's Christ, even

Luke ii. 11, 26.

as He was Jesus, from the instant of His conception And, as the term Mediator is bound up with the term Christ, He was the Mediator in His incarnation, before the mediating act of atonement was accomplished.

Christ Mediator in the Incarnation

II Hence all the future functions of the Christ must be attributed to neither of His natures distinctively, but to His one Person Our Lord, as Mediator, is not divided

The Christ one Incarnate Person

1. He sustains no office which is not based upon His Divinity, and executed through His human nature As Prophet He is still the Only-begotten God, *which is in the bosom of the Father*, Whom as Man He hath *declared* to men. As Priest He is the Son who *learned obedience by the things which He suffered*, *it behoved Him*, as the Son, *to be made like unto His brethren*, and, *taken from among men, to make reconciliation for the sins of the people* The *Church of God*, or the Lord, was *purchased with His own blood*, and the High Priest offered Himself *through the Eternal Spirit* of His Divinity. So also His Kingly authority, exercised in human nature, requires as its foundation the Divine dignity of the Son *Who upholdeth all things by the word of His power* The first verses of the Epistle to the Hebrews contain the three offices of the one Incarnate Person in their most complete and grandest exhibition.

Divinity underlying all Offices.
John i.18
Heb. v.8
Heb. v 1
Heb ii 17
Acts xx. 28
Heb. ix 14
Heb i 2

2. The Incarnate Person is the one Mediator not the human nature as some Romanists have affirmed, not the Divine nature as Osiander and some other Protestants maintained, but the one Theanthropic Agent whose mediatorial volition is one in the unity of the Divine and human wills Hence the word Mediator has a unique meaning as descriptive of the Christ *There is one Mediator between God and men*, rather, *of God and men, the Man Christ Jesus*, rather, *Jesus Christ Man*. This passage, solitary as marking the union of the two natures in relation to the Christ as such, is supported by others testifying that He became afterwards the Mediator of the New Covenant, in which Moses was His type. In the former—His incarnate mediation—He had and could have no type. As the one Mediator His Person Incarnate is the Agent of all His doctrine, of all His sacrificial acts, and of all His authority as King. He teaches as the Word speaking in human language; He atones and intercedes as the High Priest taken from among men, but first given to man as the Son; and He

One Mediator

1 Tim ii 5.

rules as the Eternal Son to Whom in the flesh all power is mediatorially and economically committed

Unity of all Offices. 3. It follows that our Lord, as in His own Person the fulfilment of the promises concerning Christ, gathered all types into one before He entered upon the distributive functions of His several offices. He is the unity of God and man; and the unity of all the distinct elements of the predicted Mediatorial Ministry. No one man ever united the three offices Moses was prophet or law-giver, but, strictly speaking, neither priest nor king David was king and prophet, but not priest Melchizedek was priest and king, but not prophet Ezekiel was prophet and priest, but not king And where the functions were united in one person, they were still distinct · he who occasionally prophesied might occa-sionally act as priest. Though each office was permanent in some cases, as in Moses, Aaron, and David, never were two or three of these offices permanent in one officebearer. But in the one Person of the Incarnate all these offices are united, in their perfection, in their constant exercise, and each as necessary to the other He is always the Light of the world, always the Life of redemption, always the Ruler of mankind

Official Unction.

OFFICIAL UNCTION AT BAPTISM.

Our Lord's second or official unction was received at His Baptism, which was His public designation or sealing to the Messianic office, and the full equipment of His human nature for its discharge. After His baptism He assumed at successive intervals the three offices distinct-ively; and began to fulfil them. After His ascent He continued them all in perfection; and will not lay them down until the end. The beginnings of the Messianic work are recorded in the Gospels; its consummation is exhibited in the Apostolic testimony.

Baptism I The Baptism of Christ to His office was the effusion upon Him of the Holy Spirit marking Him out as the Messiah, and at the same time replenishing Him, as to His human nature, with all Messianic gifts This outpouring from heaven was preceded by a baptism of water, shared by our Lord with men generally as the baptism of repentance, but which had a special twofold significance in regard to Him

1. Jesus was baptised by His Forerunner, who was both the representative of the old economy and the preacher of repentance for the new. (1) In the former relation the Baptist performed on the Person of the Christian High Priest the washing which preceded His anointing with the Holy Ghost. The typical high priests in particular were washed before they were anointed, and anointing generally was preceded by baptism (2.) In the latter relation the preacher of repentance administered the baptismal pledge of penitent waiting for the Messiah, to One who, though the Messiah Himself, was also the representative of sinful man. Thus in the case of our Lord's descent into the Jordan two ends were accomplished on the one hand, He was baptised as the Head and Surety of the human race assuming in its symbol the transgression of mankind, and, on the other, He was designated as the Messiah in whom were combined all the offices to which His types were of old anointed. In the former sense His baptism represented a sin assumed but not shared ; He was already *numbered with the transgressors* at the Jordan, and *came by water* before He came by *blood*. The Baptism was a prelude of the Crucifixion. In the latter, it represented the perfect purity which His pre-eminent ministry required ; the water represented not the cleansing from sin but the absence of the need of purification.

2 The Baptism of the Holy Ghost must be viewed as the designation of Christ to His work as the Representative of the Holy Trinity, and the equipment of His human nature with all the gifts necessary for His mission.

(1.) When John was sent to his ministry he was told that the Messiah would be indicated to him by a higher baptism than his own. *Upon whom thou shalt see the Spirit descending, and remaining on Him, the same is He which baptiseth with the Holy Ghost.* The symbol was beheld by the Baptist, who came, *baptising with water,* that the Baptiser with the Spirit *should be made manifest to Israel ;* and of the token of the Spirit's descent he says, *I saw, and bare record that this is the Son of God.* The Holy Trinity united in this

By the Baptist

Isa liii. 12.
1 John v 6

With the Holy Ghost.

Sealing

John i. 31, 33, 34

Matt iii 16, 17.   designation. The *voice from heaven* was that of the Father; it proclaimed that the Man Christ Jesus was at the same time His *beloved Son;* and John saw *the Spirit of God descending like a*

His Fore-runner John i. 31.   *dove and lighting upon Him* Thus was the Lord marked out to His forerunner, who before *knew Him not*, and that forerunner in his turn marked Him out to the world, which also in another sense as yet knew Him not.

Equipment.   (2) According to the ancient prophecy, the Spirit was to descend upon the Messiah in the sevenfold unity and distribution of His perfect gifts It was said of the Branch of the root of

Isa. xi 2.   Jesse: *and the Spirit of the Lord shall rest upon Him, the Spirit of wisdom and understanding, the Spirit of counsel and might, the Spirit of knowledge and of the fear of the Lord.* Concerning this gift which replenished the human nature of the Redeemer, or His

John iii. 34.   Person as represented by His humanity, the Baptist said: *God giveth not the Spirit by measure unto Him* And it is this gift that He distributes to His people · what He has for us without measure He distributes by measure to us Long afterward he who testified of these things gave the first and the last formal expression of the privilege of believers to share their Master's anointing :

1 John ii. 20   *ye have an unction from the Holy One,* where the χρῖσμα is from the Holy One who needed no anointing for His own soul but reserved it for ours · that we might be Christians as He is the

Acts xi 26.   Christ. *The disciples were* CALLED—but not MADE—*Christians first in Antioch.*

Assumption of His Offices.   II. Our Lord formally assumed His three offices at certain set times, each of which is solemnly recorded by an Evangelist.

1. As the Messiah generally He always spoke and acted as having in Himself the unity of these functions from the beginning. But during His humbled estate, and until He had fulfilled His chief office, that of making atonement, He maintained a certain reserve, and only by degrees declared the full mystery of His work. He began by declaring Himself to be the Lawgiver and Teacher · that is, by assuming His prophetic office And this function He discharged alone until the eve of His departure ; when, in His self-consecrating prayer, He assumed the ministry of His High-priesthood, and offered Himself a sacrifice for sin. Having accomplished that, He assembled His disciples around

Him after the resurrection and assumed His royal authority : the power given to Him in heaven and upon earth.

2. But this was also IN heaven FOR earth ; the Saviour ascended to discharge all His offices above ; and the Acts and the Epistles contain that full theological development of their meaning which was not possible until the Holy Spirit had come down at Pentecost. The later New Testament is no other than the expansion of the Saviour's own doctrine concerning His Messianic work We must therefore take each several office and consider our Lord's own testimony and that of His Apostles based upon it.

In Heaven.

3. The offices of Christ will be laid down at the last day Though He will for ever retain the hypostatic unity of His Person, the mediatorial economy will cease   Not the regal office alone will terminate, but all His offices. He will come *without sin* . that is, without His priestly relation to sin. He will no longer be the Revealer ; for God shall be *all in all*. But this will be viewed hereafter with respect to the several functions.

End.

Heb. ix. 28.

1 Cor. xv. 28.

THE PROPHETIC OFFICE.

Prophet.

Christ as Prophet is, generally, the perfect Revealer of Divine Truth to mankind : as such He comes with His supreme credentials, the Truth, and the Light of men. More particularly He was, during His earthly ministry, the Lawgiver and the Preacher of the Gospel · each distinctly, but both in one. This office, filled by Himself, was fulfilled through His word by the Holy Ghost.

A distinction must be noted here between the absolute or universal office of Christ as Revealer, and His economical office as the Minister of His own generation. It may serve a good purpose to consider the latter first as being transitional to the former.

THE PERSONAL MINISTRY

St. Paul affirms that *Jesus Christ was a Minister of the Circumcision for the truth of God, to confirm the promises made unto the fathers, and that the Gentiles might glorify God for His mercy* These words have reference to the office of Christ generally, but particularly as the Revealer of the Divine will to the Jews and for

Personal Limited Ministry. Rom xv. 8, 9.

the Gentiles : as to the former, in the re-enactment of the Law , as to the latter, in the preaching of the Gospel. Here, then, we may consider the Ministry generally, and then its two branches.

Minister of Circumcision

I. Our Lord's personal prophetic ministry constitutes the substance of the teaching of the Word in the Four Gospels.

Acts vii 37.

1 It was strictly a continuation of the ancient prophetic economy, according to the argument of St. Stephen · *This is that Moses, which said unto the children of Israel, A Prophet shall the Lord your God raise up unto you of your brethren, like unto me , Him shall ye hear* So far as concerned His relation to the old dispensation

Luke vii. 16
John iv 19
Lukexxiv 19
Matt xi 9.

Christ was the last of the prophets ; as the people said, *that a great Prophet is risen up among us* Jesus accepted the woman's word . *Sir, I perceive that Thou art a Prophet ,* as also the similar language of the Emmaus disciples. He intimated, indeed, that *all the prophets and the law prophesied until John,* and that even John *was more than a prophet.* How much was He greater Himself !

Heb. 1 1, 2

So also in the Epistle to the Hebrews a distinction is made between the prophets by whom God spake to the fathers and the Son by whom or in whom He speaks to us But all this does not interfere with the fact that our Lord was a Minister of the

Luke iv. 24.

Divine will to His own nation. *No prophet is accepted in his own country.* these words, spoken when He opened His ministry, paralleled His own coming with that of Elijah to Israel.

Limited.

2. Hence the Redeemer's mission was confined to the ancient

Matt xv 24

people : *I am not sent but unto the lost sheep of the house of Israel* The Light visited Galilee and Samaria, but it did not go beyond Israel and its lost sheep the Prophet of the whole world took

Matt. iv. 15, 16.

up His abode in *Galilee of the Gentiles,* so that *the people which sat in darkness saw great light* Anticipating the time when He would draw all nations to Him, He nevertheless strictly limited Himself to the Holy Land, and never had the dust of heathenism to shake from His feet. He was never called a Jew, nor did He so term

Rom. xv 8

Himself, but He was a Messenger to the Jews, a MINISTER OF THE CIRCUMCISION, and, in a sense, AS ONE OF THE PROPHETS

Our Lord His own Prophet.

3. The Saviour's personal ministry was that of an extraordinary Prophet raised up to introduce a new dispensation of which He was Himself the herald. He blended in His own Person the

ancient Prophet and the more modern Rabbi sent sometimes suddenly under a Divine extraordinary afflatus, like a Zealot responsible only to God ; or lifting up occasional burdens, subsequently written down, after the more ordinary though still extraordinary manner of the prophets ; and also gathering around Him a body of disciples whom He taught out of the law, according to the usage of the Rabbinical schools

4. The style and methods of our Lord's teaching were such as to mark Him out from every other teacher Its characteristics were unshared . as His form and features, for ever lost to human knowledge, were His own and no other's, so was it with His ordinary communications. He possessed or rather condescended to assume in its perfection the gift of persuasive speech : as it was predicted that He should be *fairer than the children of men*, so also it was said of Him, *Grace is poured into Thy lips.* They confessed it who were *astonished at His doctrine, for His word was with power*, as also those who were disarmed by its grace *never man spake like This Man.* His method of teaching by parable was original and unrivalled . there is scarcely any trace of its use in the Old Testament; and such allegories as are found in other Oriental teaching and in the Talmud are in perfect contrast to our Lord's. His illustrations from nature and life are confessed to be the most beautiful in literature even by those who are unwilling to admit that they sprang from One Who knew the mysterious symbols of nature because He ordained them and Who was perfectly acquainted with the human heart His method of dealing with enemies, or captious censors, betrays the presence of every element of dialectic or Socratic skill And, like almost all great teachers, He had the esoteric instruction for the more susceptible and humble, to unfold the mysteries which were veiled from the prejudiced in parabolic disguise Moreover, He aptly appropriated the good of the Rabbinical theology, and knew how to accommodate Himself to current delusions while correcting them, as in the case of His appeal concerning the casting out of the demons by the children of His enemies. Jesus also was the supreme Master of the symbol and symbolical action, and to that Christianity owes much But, on this whole subject it is difficult to speak with fulness or precision, as our Saviour's personal instructions have come

Characteristics

Ps xlv 2

Luke iv. 32

John vii. 46.

to us through the medium of His servants. He has left us nothing under the direct impress of His own hand.

Transition to the World. 5 It is important to remember that throughout our Lord's ministry He was at once the Minister of the circumcision and the Revealer of all truth for the world The blending of these gives an indescribable and most wonderful grace to His teaching. But this leads us to a higher view than that which has hitherto been taken.

Law- Giver or Preacher II. Jesus Christ was the last Lawgiver, and the First Evangelist of His own glad tidings ; His whole ministry united the Law and the Gospel in their essential elements

Deut xviii. 15. 1. As the LAWGIVER, *like unto* Moses but greater than he, our Lord assumed His function on the Mount of Beatitudes. He rose up out of the Old Testament as the Witness and Embodiment of its truth, and was in no sense its destroyer. He came not to abolish but to fulfil ancient Scripture, and that in three senses first, to fulfil its meaning in Himself as it was all one prophecy of Him ; secondly. to discharge it of its functions as it was the law of a transient ceremonial economy which He appeared to end , and, thirdly, by republishing its moral teaching in harmony with the new dispensation as a dispensation of the Spirit and of love.

Fulfil- ment of all Law. (1.) All previous lawgiving, whether engraven on the fleshly tables of the heart of universal mankind, or on the Mosaic tables and in the Mosaic books, was fulfilled in the revelation of Jesus, the Incarnate Expression of God's will to man. *Christ is the end of the*

Rom x. 4. *law :* and in this sense pre-eminently, that all revelation, both of the wrath and of the mercy of God, was complete and fulfilled in His Person He came as the Representative of all written and unwritten revelation so entirely to take its place that in His presence there was necessity for nothing more · whether He would or would not supersede all, it remained for Him to show. On earth as well as in heaven there was no need of the sun, the Lamb was

John viii. 12 the light thereof. He said, *I am the Light of the world,* and *I am*

John xiv. 6 *the Way, the Truth, and the Life.* But He was pleased to continue still the dispensation of word and ministry that He for a time suspended. The ancients gave Him their books, and He re-sanctified them for His Church. When He retired He continued His function by a more enlarged revelation through His Apostles.

(2) Our Saviour, the final Lawgiver, abolished the old law,

and all that it contained, so far as it was the basis of a covenant between God and a peculiar people. As a code of the Theocracy, the law was political, ceremonial, and moral: three in one and inseparably in one. This law our Lord came to abrogate : it was done away in Him, because the new covenant was to be no longer with one nation, and no longer based upon types, but to be confirmed in Christ with all nations on the basis of the accomplished redemption The entire economy commonly called the Law, as one, and therefore as such including the moral law in its statutory form, was abolished in Christ, who established a new legislation, known variously as the *perfect law of liberty*, the *law of faith*, the *law of the Spirit of life*.

(3.) But the moral law, written on the heart and on the two tables, Jesus reuttered Extracting it from its place in the Legal Economy He gave it all its honours in the Economy of Grace. Though He abolished it as a condition of salvation, He confirmed it as a rule of life. To be more particular · He renewed it first as it was a schoolmaster, to teach the sinner his sin, and bring him to his Saviour ; and then as a rule and standard of holy living , but, for both purposes, the whole law is exhibited in its internal character as a spiritual rule and in its great principle as perfect love. As the Lawgiver our Lord expanded ethical teaching into an infinite extent and breadth by a spiritual interpretation , and condensed it all again into a perfect simplicity by reducing it to love. The spiritual application multiplies the precept past all limits ; the reduction of all to charity makes all simple and comparatively easy again. But the Saviour as Lawgiver presides over another department of theology, that of Christian Ethics, to come hereafter.

2 The New Legislator opened His ministry on the Mount ; but as the Prophet, preaching his own Gospel, greater than Isaiah but like him, our Lord announced His function formally in the Synagogue at Nazareth *where He had been brought up.*

(1.) The Gospel proper, as the glad tidings of redemption through atonement and the forgiveness of sins, could not be fully preached before the Cross. Jesus, during His life on earth, was rather a Lawgiver than an Evangelist. But when He said in His own synagogue, *This day is this Scripture fulfilled in your ears*, He

The Jewish Law

James i. 25.
Rom. iii 27.
Rom. viii. 2

The Moral Law.

Preacher of Gospel.
Luke iv. 16.
Anticipated.
Luke iv 21.

P 2

began to preach the great deliverance. The text He chose was the most comprehensive that prophecy afforded for the description of the effects of redemption as finally administered to its objects Concerning this opening stage of His ministry St Matthew records that *Jesus went about all Galilee, teaching in their synagogues, and preaching the gospel of the kingdom* From that time the republication of the Law and the anticipation of the Gospel alternated or were combined in the Saviour's works and words He spoke of the perfect law that convinces of sin, and also of a free forgiveness: always being a jealous assertor of the Divine claims even while frankly and abundantly promising and even imparting remission. But it was not till the sacrifice had been offered that our Lord preached Himself as the perfect Lawgiver and the finished Saviour. When He sent His Apostles forth He bade *that repentance and remission of sins should be preached in His name among all nations*, who were to be taught to *observe all things whatsoever I have commanded*.

Matt iv. 23.

Luke xxiv. 47.
Matt. xxviii. 20

Prophecy of Kingdom

(2) The preaching of the future Gospel was always predictive; but Christ was more expressly the Prophet of His own kingdom in His foreannouncements of its history and destiny. As all prophecy from the beginning of the world had respect, directly or indirectly, to the kingdom of the Messiah, so the Great Prophet and consummator of the prophetic word constantly spoke of the future of His Church. Towards the end of His ministry almost all His discourses were directly prophetic; and His last utterances were almost entirely limited to predictions

Predictions

John xiv. 12

Acts i 1.

(3.) Both the preaching and the prophecy of the Gospel kingdom our Lord continued after His departure by the ministry of His Apostles. As they wrought *greater works* than He, so they spoke greater words than His; but as in the former they were only the instruments of His higher and more spiritual energy, so they were only the speakers of His words, which could not be spoken until He had accomplished His work on the cross. St. Luke speaks of the Divine-human ministry as of *all that Jesus began both to do and teach*. After His ascension He continued all His offices: all through His own activity, but with a difference. The High-priestly function He discharges alone · the Kingly by the Holy Ghost, the Prophetic by the Spirit through the

Apostles   In the nature of things He could not perfectly preach His own Gospel ; nor could He give explicit prophecies of the last dispensation until the former dispensation was fully ended.   He Himself in His own Person only began . He perfected nothing. His words were seed in the hearts of the Apostles, to bear fruit in due season.   The Spirit Whom He would send was *the Spirit* of *truth,* and would guide them into all its developments; but only as bringing their Master's own words back to their memory. Precisely what the Redeemer did for the old Law—bring it to the people's remembrance with enlarged interpretation—the Spirit did for the Redeemer's own ministry   This has reference to every part of His prophetic office.

John xvi. 13.

THE UNIVERSAL MINISTRY

Jesus never formally assumed the ʃprophetic office in its highest meaning, in that meaning which was peculiar and unshared · which He could not indeed assume because He was never without it.   He spoke as One who not only brought the final revelation with Him, but as being Himself that revelation ; He distinguished Himself from all other teachers by the assertion of absolute personal authority , He accompanied His teaching with credentials of miraculous works wrought in His own name , and, lastly, He came as the Prophet of mankind, making provision for the continuance of His doctrine for ever.

The Supreme Prophet

1. While He appeared as a second Moses Jesus distinguished Himself from human teachers as being Himself the revelation of all truth.   He never appropriated the name Prophet, or Rabbi, or Seer, though He did not decline these titles when given to Him But again and again He asserted concerning Himself such prerogatives as could belong to no human agent of Divine instruction. He said of Himself, *I am the Way, the Truth, and the Life.*   All things pertaining to man's life, present and future, to his salvation and spiritual interests in time and eternity, our Lord connects with His own Person and manifestation   Not only is He the Giver and the Medium of the gift   He is the Gift itself Receiving what is His depends upon receiving Himself.   He is all the truth, as it respects our race, concrete and personified.   All revelation is in His Person · He is the union of all that is God

Himself Truth

John xiv. 6

and all that is man, and nothing beyond this has vital concern for mankind. Here is the great distinction between Christ and every other prophet He is God and He is Man ; and His Person is the compendium and substance of all that may and must be known concerning both. In this highest sense He is neither a prophet nor a seer He declares Himself. Even God is revealed only as connected with Him : as His Father. This glorious distinction pervades our Lord's words. When He promises the Spirit to guide His disciples, it is Himself whom the Spirit is to expound : we must connect *I am* THE TRUTH with *the Spirit of truth* and *He will guide you into all truth.* I AM THE TRUTH was the loftiest word of Christ the Prophet

John xiv. 6, 17 ; xvi 13.

2. In His mediatorial person, however, our Lord condescended to be literally a Prophet. He used His human nature as the organ of His revelation, and as Man speaking to men was the consummate agent of Divine counsel for mankind. He was the perfect נָבִיא, which means the Interpreter of God, or One who pours forth the Divine words. Thus He said of Himself, *My doctrine is not Mine, but His that sent Me* not meaning literally that it was not His, but that it was not His as distinguished from God. *As My Father hath taught Me, I speak these things* words which must be connected with what follows, *and He that sent Me is with Me* He was also the perfect רָאָה, Seer, or, more poetically,חֹזֶה. *What He hath seen and heard, that He testifieth ·* this was declared by the Baptist concerning Christ, of Whom he also said, *He that cometh from heaven is above all* Through the eyes of His human spirit the God-man saw the mysteries of His own kingdom As Prophet and Seer in His incarnate Person He was in some sense limited. In the unity of His Father and the Holy Spirit He was a Revealer to Himself in His own human faculties of *the treasures of wisdom and knowledge, hidden* in Himself for a season from His own humanity, and gave His mortal vision to behold what He communicated. In His prophetic knowledge and utterances we see what the human mind is capable of knowing in union with the Divine. After His resurrection, or rather after His ascension, there was no longer any restraint, and the human faculties of the Divine-human person were the organ of the perfect revelation of all such knowledge as man can ever have or need

Divine-Human Prophet.

John vii 16.

John viii 28, 29.

John iii. 31, 32.

Col. ii. 3.

3. The Credentials of our Lord's prophetic office were in harmony with His twofold character, as sent first to His own generation and thus raised up for the world. *Credentials.*

(1.) As a Minister of the Circumcision He gave such demonstration by miracle as became an authoritative messenger from God precisely so much and no more. The leading wonders and signs of the ancient prophets were types of His miraculous works, which as performed by Himself or His Apostles—for their works were His—ended the reign of evidential miracle. *Miracles*

(2) But, as the Supreme Revealer, He did not lay stress on His miracles, because He was Himself the Miracle of miracles All that preceded and followed were only faint preludes and echoes of His one great Wonder, the manifestation of God in the flesh, His resurrection from the dead, and His glorification of human nature *If ye believe not that I* AM, *ye shall die in your sins,* and, *when ye have lifted up the Son of Man, then shall ye know that I* AM Here was the secret of the authority with which He spoke His words and His actions had in them a Divine and irresistible self-evidencing attestation He never used the language of an Old-Testament prophet, *The Word of the Lord came unto me,* or *the Spirit of the Lord came upon me,* but *Verily, verily, I say unto you !* He did not lay claim to inspiration, the influence under which the prophets poured forth their words and the seers saw their visions : He was not God-inspired but God Incarnate Hence the constant tenour of His declaration to the effect that *every one that is of the truth heareth My voice,* and that *if any man will do,* or *wills to do, His will he shall know of the doctrine* HEAR HIM ! was spoken concerning the Revealer when His Divine nature was made more intensely *manifest in the flesh* at the Transfiguration *Himself.* — *Self-evidencing.* — John viii. 24, 28. — John xviii. 37. — John vii. 17. — Luke ix 35. — 1 Tim iii. 16.

4 Finally, the Ministry of Jesus as the Apostle of our profession was the final revelation for the world. It is important to mark this, as it has a close connection with the ultimate appeal on every theological subject and the rule of faith in the Christian Church In Him all past, present and future teaching was one *For the World*

(1) Our Lord always assumes a tone of absolute finality With Him the prophetic office ceased prophecy, like the law, found its end in Christ. There is no other revelation, no other messenger from God after Him Whatever other teachers arose were simply *End of the Prophetic Office*

men from His feet, bearing His words and expounding them more fully under the influence of the Spirit   Nothing can be more express than His assertions that every future word of instruction should be only His own word continued and developed.

Abiding

(2) Before He departed He made provision for the continuance of His own function in the Christian Church   Without doubt He executes His prophetic office from His throne in the heavens. His Apostolic company perpetuated such of His words as were of permanent value for mankind.   One of that company was brought under teaching who ever declared that what of new or enlarged doctrine he had for the world was given him by revelation of Christ, and it was he who said, *Let the word of Christ*

Col iii. 16.

dwell in you richly. Our Lord Himself repeated from heaven His direct instructions   the Seven Churches received them for all   By His last inspired Apostle, however, He has said that all Christians

1 John ii. 20.

have an unction from the Holy One, and ye know all things.   Thus by His Spirit, who is this Unction, the Supreme Revealer continues to execute His prophetic office in the Church generally, and in every individual Christian.

High Priest

THE PRIESTLY OFFICE

The central and most important office of our Lord's mediatorship is His priesthood, of which the high priest, as the representative of the Levitical system of expiations, was the type. As Prophet our Lord predicted and asserted His sacrificial work ; but He more formally assumed it on the eve of His passion, and after His ascension revealed its full import by the Apostles. According to their teaching the Saviour's priestly office consists of Offering and Presentation of Himself the sacrifice, answering to His death and ascension; also of Intercession and Benediction, both based upon the sacrificial Atonement, and connected with the administration of salvation.

His Own Testimony.

Much of our Lord's prophetic ministry as the Prophet of His own dispensation was occupied with the announcement, prediction and exposition of His priestly atonement.

1 When He began to preach He took up His forerunner's word, which was twofold *Repent ye for the kingdom of heaven is at hand!* and, *Behold the Lamb of God, which taketh away the sin of the world!* Very gradually, and by hints left for future enlargement, He unfolded the doctrine both of His priesthood and of His kingdom Though He never called Himself a Priest—not even indirectly, as He called Himself Prophet and King—He constantly used language which only this office explains. He did not actually say that He was the High Priest, the Sacrifice and the Offerer; nevertheless He applied to Himself and His mission almost every sacrificial usage and every sacrificial idea. This will appear evident from a cursory examination of the Gospel of St. John, in which we find the sacerdotal office made prominent: the Synoptists keep rather in view the regal.

Matt iii. 2
John i. 29

2 It is observable that our Lord before the Transfiguration did not dwell much on His coming death According to St John He had spoken of Himself as *the Bread of God which cometh down from heaven and giveth life unto the world,* this however was based rather upon the *manna in the wilderness* than upon the sacrificial feasts, though the transition to the latter is found in the words. *the bread that I will give is My flesh, which I will give for the life of the world.* On the Holy Mount our Lord was evidently prepared for the last stage of His mediatorial history on earth. The subject of discourse was the *decease which He should accomplish at Jerusalem.* The decease referred to His exodus or departure generally; but we may suppose that, as the victim was anciently examined by the priest, in order to ascertain its integrity, so the glory of heaven searched Jesus through and through · the result was, *This is My beloved Son, in Whom I am well pleased.* He was approved by the Father as the Spotless Sacrifice for the world From that time our Lord began to predict the fact, the circumstances and the results of His death. Now He began to testify of His Cross, to those who much wondered at His words. Still, while His language and teachings revolved around the altar, they were not directly sacrificial, even when He spoke of the Son of Man come *not to be ministered unto, but to minister, and to give His life a ransom for many*

The Crisis of the Holy Mount John vi. 33.
John vi 49
John vi 51.

Luke ix 31.

Matt. xvii. 5.

Matt. xx. 28.

3 It was on the eve of the Sacrifice of the Cross that our Lord

Final
Assump-
tion

solemnly assumed His sacerdotal function : first, by the institution of the Supper, the memorial sacrifice of Christianity ; and,
secondly, by what is sometimes called the High-priestly prayer ;
the symbolical Feetwashing having been interposed with an affecting relation to both.   The sacramental institute is pervaded by
sacrificial ideas it exhibits the true paschal Lamb Whose blood
is at the same time shed for the remission of sins in virtue of a
new covenant ratified by blood of propitiation, and the benefit of
Whose death is celebrated in a continual peace-offering feast The
High-priestly prayer was the self-consecration of Jesus to the final
endurance of the sorrows of expiation.   All the Messianic offices

John xvii.
14, 2,
19

are hallowed in that supreme Prayer   The prophetic . *I have
given them Thy word,* the regal . *as Thou hast given Him power over
all flesh,* the priestly: *I sanctify Myself, that they also might be
sanctified.*   But it is pre-eminently the consecration prayer of the
High Priest · the formal assumption. in the presence of the cross,
His altar, of His atoning work

After
Pentecost

4. After Pentecost the sacerdotal office of Christ, previously the
least prominent, takes the leading place.   Its full exposition is
mainly to be found in the Epistle to the Hebrews , but every
other document of the New Testament contains explicit references
to some of its relations.   Taking that Epistle as the text, and the
rest as illustrative, we may view all under the two aspects of
Sacrifice followed by Presentation, and Intercession followed by
Benediction.   But first the mediatorial character of the Redeemer
as High Priest must be viewed as the foundation of the whole, its
leading elements being these : in the presentation of the sacrifice
the High Priest represented the people to God , in the benediction
He represented God to the people.   He was in ancient times, and

Heb. v. 1.

is in Christ, *taken from among men ;* but then as now his function
looked towards both heaven and earth.

High
Priest

THE HIGH PRIEST AND CHRIST.

The High Priest represented the priesthood generally, and was
the type of Christ as the universal Antitype of all sacerdotal
persons and ministries.   We need only observe the points of
correspondence, as also the points of difference, between type and

Antitype . especially in regard to the high-priestly vocation, consecration, and functions

1 The vocation of the priesthood generally, and of the high priest in particular, was connected with the Levitical typical service alone. Before the time of Moses, the natural head of every family was also its religious head wherever Abram went he *built there an altar unto the Lord ;* and when the paschal sacrifice was instituted, the father of the family discharged the priest's function. Moses absorbed for a season all offices into himself, that they might be again distributed. He was not only the lawgiver but the priest also · as it is written, *And Moses took half of the blood, and put it in basons ; and half of the blood he sprinkled on the altar.* He assigned the priesthood to his brother Aaron, as the head of an hereditary sacerdotal order : the rest of the same tribe being set apart to subordinate ministries. Hence there were Levites not priests , ordinary priests of the Levitical tribe , and the hereditary high priest or head of the family of Aaron. This Chief Priest was therefore the representative of all, called from out of the people to represent the people as seeking approach to God by sacrificial gifts. In the New Testament we are told that *no man taketh this honour unto himself, but he that is called of God, as was Aaron. So also Christ glorified not Himself to be made an high priest , but He that said unto Him, Thou art My Son, to-day have I begotten Thee.* The eternal Son, begotten of the Holy Ghost in human nature, was fully constituted the Messiah, and given to the world as such, in the Incarnation as finished in the resurrection. Hence He was *called of God an high priest after the order of Melchisedec .* his high priesthood was solely of Divine origin, it was that of a king also and it was eternal

2. The ceremonial of consecration, as used by Moses, began with washing at the door of the tabernacle , followed by investiture with the high-priestly array ; and upon the sacred person thus washed and clothed the oil of anointing was poured forth. In connection with this a sin-offering was sacrificed for removal of guilt, a burnt-offering to express entire consecration, and a peace-offering to show God's acceptance. But the oil was the sanctification : *and he poured of the anointing oil upon Aaron's head, and anointed him, to sanctify him* The high priest was הַמָּשִׁיחַ : *the priest*

Vocation

Gen xiii
18

Ex xxiv.
6.

Heb. v.
4, 5

Heb v.10.

Consecration.
Ex. xxix.
Lev. viii.

Lev. viii.
12

Lev. xxi. 10.   *who is higher than his brethren, upon whose head the anointing oil was poured,* poured in abundance.   Our Lord was consecrated to His office by the Holy Ghost Whom He received without measure :

John vi 27   *Him hath God the Father sealed.*   All other particulars of the typical consecration fell away, unless the baptism of Christ responded to the washing of the High Priest   But the essential difference was in this, that Christ, while He received as incarnate the Spirit of

John xvii 19.   anointing, did also consecrate Himself : *for their sakes* I SANCTIFY MYSELF.   By the Divine glory of His Sonship He dedicated His Person and His being to the propitiation of the sins of men

3 The function of the High Priest requires careful consideration in its typical reference to the Great Antitype.

Function   (1.) As to his person and his office a mediator generally, for all the people and for every individual he was the one and only priest.   He was the embodied unity of the priesthood : he alone virtually represented the people to God and God to the people.   His garments indicated this : without his distinctive vestments he was a common man.   The breastplate, as also the shoulder-pieces attached to the ephod, bore the names of the tribes upon it . he who wore this sacred symbol represented all the tribes of the congregation, bearing them as it were both on his heart and on his shoulders.   Hence also upon his diadem was the inscription

Ex xxviii. 36—38.   HOLINESS TO THE LORD . . . *And it shall be upon Aaron's forehead, that Aaron may bear the iniquity of the holy things, which the children of Israel shall hallow in all their holy gifts, and it shall be always upon his forehead, that they may be accepted before the Lord.*   The antitypical High Priest, the Redeemer of mankind, was the Representative of the whole world, bearing the sins of His people upon His heart, and the government of them upon His shoulders, presenting them before God as expiated and reconciled.

Urim and Thummim.   (2.) But the high priest represented God also to the congregation : the breastplate with its inscription was called the Urim and Thummim, that is, Lights and Perfections, being the same precious stones which bore the names of the tribes regarded as pledges of light by inspiration from above on all occasions of public appeal to God.   In this prerogative of the high priest he was the type of the prophetic as well as priestly office of Him who

Heb iii. 1.   came as the *Apostle and High Priest of our profession.*   The office of blessing the congregation was common to the priesthood, but in its highest annual discharge on the day of atonement, when the nation was accepted as a whole, it was the high priest's act alone, as will be hereafter seen. The Epistle to the Hebrews—the Temple Epistle—shows at length that Jesus is the supreme High Priest, the Antitype of Aaron, not only for men in things pertaining to God, but also for God in things pertaining to men, the former and the latter being included in one sentence : *A merciful* and *faithful High Priest in things pertaining to God, to make reconciliation for the sins of the people.* Heb.ii 17.

THE GENERAL PRIESTLY FUNCTIONS

Priestly Function.

The offering of the sacrifice by the Christian High Priest exhibits the unity and consummation of all the sacrificial elements in the ancient offering, as also of all the kinds and seasons of sacrifice, including the whole economy of the Levitical institute

THE RITES OF SACRIFICE.

The Levitical sacrifice consisted of the presentation of a victim, with imposition of hands ; the slaughtering, and sprinkling of the blood , the burning of the victim, and the sacrificial feast. These were not combined in every sacrifice ; but they all belonged to the expiatory ceremonial, viewed as complete in itself and as hereafter to find its perfection in Christ, the Compendium of all oblations.

I. The PRESENTATION of the victim and LAYING ON OF HANDS were both the acts of the guilty offerer of the sacrifice.

1. The place was the court of the sanctuary, whither the transgressor came indicating his desire to find his offended God in His holy dwelling-place. The victim was spotless, examined and approved as such : it was provided by the offerer himself, according to the prescription of the law, as the substitute of his own forfeited life. Its spotlessness was simply typical of the perfect sinlessness of the *Lamb without blemish and without spot.* That Holy Victim *offered Himself without spot to God,* being Himself the representative of the sinner who offered , but He was also *delivered up for us all* by the Father, who provided a sacrifice for the guilty race The New Testament does not speak either of the Church or

Presentation.

1 Peter i. 19
Heb. ix. 14
Rom viii 32.

of the individual as providing an oblation   It is the prerogative of the Divine love to furnish sinful man with his sin-offering · as

Gen xxii. 8. on that early typical mount it was said, *God will provide Himself a lamb for a burnt-offering.* JEHOVAH-JIREH is the eternal law of the atonement between God and man.

Imposition of Hands. 2. The imposition of hands was not so much symbolical of the transfer of sin or guilt as of submission to the Divine appointment and consequent dedication of the animal to be the medium of atonement. It was essentially therefore the deed of the delinquent,

Lev. i. 4 who not only touched but leaned on his victim · *and he shall put his hand upon the head of the burnt-offering, and it shall be accepted for him to make atonement for him.* It was his act of faith in the ordinance of God; and has its fulfilment in the faith of the sinner who makes the death of Christ his own.

II. The SLAUGHTERING and SPRINKLING OF THE BLOOD followed   these being universal and always united.

Slaughtering. 1. The Slaughtering, or שְׁחִיטָה had for its object the obtaining of the blood, to be presented to God for expiation : it was perhaps also the expression of a pœna vicaria ; though it was the offerer himself who slew the victim, and not the priest, except in the case of offerings for the nation. The victim was slain by the transgressor as the acknowledgment of his own desert of death.   Our Lord laid down His life of Himself, and gave up His spirit voluntarily as a

Acts ii 23 sacrifice ; but *by wicked hands* He was *crucified and slain.* The sinful world consummated its sin by slaying the sacrifice for its sin ; its greatest iniquity was in that deed, but the Saviour made His

Heb ix. 26. death His own act. *He put away sin by* THE SACRIFICE OF HIM-

Heb. vi. 6 SELF. Though it is only the apostates who *crucify to themselves the Son of God afresh,* yet every penitent believer presents the death of Christ as representing His own death, and the Church in the Holy Supper commemorates it as suffered for all

Sprinkling 2 The priest alone sprinkled the blood, or applied it to the purpose of expiation, around the altar, first towards the curtain that concealed the mercy seat, and then, in the highest expression

Lev xvii. 11. of the symbolical act, on the Kapporeth or mercy-seat itself. *For the life of the flesh is in the blood · and I have given it to you upon the altar to make an atonement for your souls ; for it is the blood that maketh an atonement for the soul.* Two terms are here observable.

לְכַפֵּר, *to make atonement,* is literally to cover that is either the soul of the offerer as guilty, so that he is seen as under the pure life that on the altar screens him, or the condemning sentence of the covenant-testimony deposited beneath the mercy-seat Again, *the blood maketh an atonement,* בְּנֶפֶשׁ, *by means of* or *in virtue of the soul in it.* This is the true rendering, and it signifies that the inno-cent life which had been taken before the altar as the vicarious representative of the offerer is on the altar accepted of God repre-sentatively. Thus the sprinkling was the second or more effectual PRESENTATION without which the first was not perfect. The Redeemer's atonement was fully accomplished when His blood was shed, but it was not declared to be accepted until He pre-sented it in the heavens : *By His own blood He entered in once into the holy place, having obtained eternal redemption for us* And He *through the Eternal Spirit* OFFERED HIMSELF *without spot to God* The symbol of sprinkling is used with two applications, heaven-ward, for the propitiation of Divine displeasure ; earthward, for the expiation of guilt. The sprinkling of the conscience signifies the application of the virtue of the expiation to the believer whose guilt is cancelled or negatived for the sake of Christ But the term is sometimes varied in the evangelical use · occasionally it is the washing away of sin, or the purging of the conscience.

III The sacrificial idea was completed by the BURNING OF THE OFFERING and the SACRIFICIAL MEAL or FEAST, which are closely united in their symbolical significance

1. The term used for burning is one that signifies to make to go up in vapour the essence of the sacrifice ascends to God with acceptance. Therefore it could not directly symbolise the punish-ment of perdition : though as burning on the altar it was a symbol of the punitive justice as well as the sanctifying power of the Divine Spirit. The fire that consumed the offering, or parts of it, came from God : on that great first day of Levitical sacrifice *there came a fire out from before the Lord, and consumed upon the altar the burnt-offering and the fat. which when all the people saw, they shouted, and fell on their faces* It was kept up continually by the morning and evening sacrifice *the fire shall ever be burning upon the altar, it shall never go out* This signified that the entire service of sacrifice was to be well-pleasing for ever, from generation to

Margin notes:
Lev. xvii. 11

Heb. ix. 12, 24.

Burning.

Lev. ix. 24.

Lev. vi. 13

Eph. v. 2　generation, for His sake Who *hath loved us, and hath given Himself for us an offering and a sacrifice to God for a sweet-smelling savour.* Although the symbol had its highest fulfilment in the perfect self-surrender of Jesus, it had reference also to us and our oblation of ourselves. The beneficiary of Christ's atonement must be sprinkled with His blood for the covering of his person as guilty, and he must yield himself with Christ as a whole burnt-offering made acceptable by the Holy Ghost . the one without the other can never

Gal. ii 20.　avail. No less than this is meant by, *I am crucified with Christ.*

Sacrificial Meal　2 Every sacrifice surrendered its life in its blood ; some sacrifices were wholly destroyed, but in the peace-offering part was burnt and part reserved for a feast This was the highest result of the ceremonial as expressing the communion between heaven and earth In other sacrifices Jehovah received through the priests part of His portion . and what was burnt was also *the bread*

Lev. xxi 6　*of their God. And the priest shall burn it upon the altar . it is the*

Lev iii. 11.　*food of the offering made by fire unto the Lord.* St. Paul tells us that

1 Cor x 17　*we are all partakers of that one bread* The Lord's Supper is spread on the Lord's table : an altar to God, a table to us. Jesus is our great Peace-offering, as well as our Passover , and the highest expression of Christian faith in the evangelical sacrifice is thus to partake of the *bread of their God*, and sup with Him.

THE VARIOUS OFFERINGS

Various Sacrifices.　The various sacrifices themselves may be blended into unity. They were divided anciently into burnt-offerings, peace-offerings, and bloodless gifts : to these were added, in the Levitical economy, sin and trespass offerings. All oblations of every kind were under the jurisdiction of the high priest, and were consummated and summed up in the one sacrifice of Christ

I The primitive sacrifices, which prefigured the Atonement long before the Levitical service, and corresponded therefore to the Gospel before the Law, are to be traced up to the earliest times, even to the very gate of Paradise

Origin of Sacrifice.　1. The origin of sacrifice is not matter of express revelation. But the almost universal prevalence of oblations, bloody and un-bloody, indicates its Divine appointment The primitive record in Genesis is as dim in its utterance on this subject as it is upon sin generally and the atoning Redeemer. We read of sacrifices offered by Cain and Abel by the former unbloody gifts, by the latter slain victims *The Lord had respect unto Abel and to his offering: but unto Cain and to his offering He had not respect* The reason of the difference lay in the disposition of the offerers. *By faith Abel offered unto God a more excellent sacrifice than Cain:* his offering was a gift, but it was also an expiatory typical sacrifice, which Cain's was not. And there can be little doubt that the faith which rendered that primitive oblation acceptable was faith in the Great Sacrifice of the future Thus the first account of approach to the Supreme by sacrificial offerings teaches, when interpreted by the New Testament, that it was not enough to draw nigh with gifts betokening gratitude and self-surrender, but that every oblation of thanksgiving must needs have in it a propitiatory element This primitive oblation therefore gave the law for all subsequent worship as culminating after long and various developments in the Christian atonement

2. The BURNT-OFFERING, עוֹלָה, was the earliest, most common, and most comprehensive of the oblations dedicated to Heaven as Korban or Gift. Its pre-eminence was its symbolical meaning, that combined in one the expiatory shedding of blood and the perfect offering of the self: hence it underlay, surrounded, and perfected all other oblations from the beginning of sacrificial communion with God down to the Perfect Sacrifice It was this which Noah presented at the second beginning of propitiatory oblations He *offered burnt-offerings on the altar. And the Lord smelled a sweet savour, and the Lord said in His heart, I will not again curse the ground* Jehovah accepted the expiation of the Patriarch; and smelled afar off the sweet savour of the Perfect Sacrifice for the guilty world. Abraham was commanded to take his only son Isaac *into the land of Moriah; and offer him there for a burnt-offering* the type of the same far distant oblation of the Only-begotten. The covenant of Sinai was ratified by burnt-offerings. They pervaded also the subsequent Levitical economy, constituted the daily or continual sacrifice which typified the eternal atonement, and always maintained their preeminence. The double character assigned to them is stated at the outset of

Gen. iv 4, 5

Heb xi 4

Burnt-Offerings.

Gen. viii 20, 21.

Gen xxii 2, 7

Ex xxiv 8

VOL. II.   Q

Lev. 1 4, 15 Leviticus *And he shall put his hand upon the head of the burnt-offering, and it shall be accepted for him to make atonement for him.* After the sprinkling of the blood fire was put upon the altar, the wood laid in order, and it became an *offering made by fire, of a a sweet savour unto the Lord.* This twofold character further gives it special significance as it respects the Supreme Antitype and His people. *Christ also hath loved us, and hath given Himself for us an*

Eph v 2 *offering and a sacrifice to God for a sweet-smelling savour.* Here the propitiatory sacrifice of Christ is the freewill burnt-offering of His perfect love And in that it is the example of the offering of His people as the sin-offering proper He does not admit us so directly to share or continue or fill up His sacrifice

Peace-Offerings. 3. The PEACE-OFFERINGS—whether thank-offerings, vows, or freewill gifts—were combinations of expiatory and dedicatory sacrifice ; but they represented the gifts of the offerer rather than himself the giver   Like the burnt-offering they signified at once the consciousness of sin and the thankfulness for deliverance from it   They were presented, so far as they were expiatory, for the re-establishment of a state of grace ; and, that being accomplished, as the joyful expression also of acceptance with God   These all

Eph ii. 14. found their antitype in the Paschal Lamb · *He is our Peace,* Whose oblation we present in faith for the forgiveness of sins, and receive sacramentally as the pledge of that forgiveness   It may be added that the meat-offerings and drink-offerings which were connected with the daily burnt sacrifice, as also with the other peace-offerings, belong to the general idea of Divine acceptance and communion with the worshippers   Our present purpose does not require a minute investigation of them   Suffice that they in some sense mitigated the sternness of the ancient institute , and that they all find their end and perfection in the Christian Supper.

Sin-Offerings II Peculiar to the Levitical economy were the SIN-OFFERINGS, and their modification, the TRESPASS-OFFERINGS. These were intimately connected with the giving of the law, as containing the more express revelation of the nature of sin, and as the basis of a preparatory covenant of typical sacrifice for its expiation   We have here chiefly to do with these offerings, including their more stern and their more joyful accompaniments, as the preeminent type or prophetic symbolical foreshadowing of the Christian Atonement.

1 It is impossible to formulate with precision the difference between the sin-offering and the guilt-offering in the Levitical institute. Both were expiatory sacrifices for SIN, as being offence against positive law and ceremonial ordinances, committed in ignorance and inadvertence, that is, not with a high hand and in deliberate rebellion. But the trespass-offering was always presented for individual error. the sin-offering not always. The former respected violation of the rights of the covenant, the latter rather neglect of its precepts Hence the former had more to do with transgressions touching property, the latter with transgressions of law The trespass-offering connoted the idea of SATISFACTION · *and he shall bring his guilt-offering to the Lord, a ram without blemish out of the flock, according to thy estimation, for a guilt-offering, unto the priest; and the priest shall make atonement for him before the Lord, and it shall be forgiven him.* The sin-offering connoted rather the idea of EXPIATION through the sacrifice of a pure life. But in the supreme and universal oblation of Christ the distinction is done away for ever. He is at once the Satisfaction of every Divine claim, and the Propitiation for every human offence

2 The sin-offering, of which the guilt-offering was only a species, brought into distinct prominence the expiatory character of the sacrificial institute, which, before the giving of the law, was to a certain extent veiled and hidden. It was from the beginning itself called SIN, חַטָּאת, LXX. ἁμαρτία, περὶ τῆς ἁμαρτίας, *for sin,* even as the guilt-offering was itself called GUILT, אָשָׁם. Hence our Lord is said to have been made *sin for us, Who knew no sin,* and, at His second coming, will *appear without sin unto salvation* The sacrifice was, so to speak, the embodiment or incarnation of sin, and, where the offering made atonement for all the people, the flesh was *burned without the camp. No sin offering, whereof any of the blood is brought into the tabernacle of the congregation to reconcile withal in the holy place, shall be eaten.* But in the lower and more individual grades of the sin-offering there was a marked difference *In the place where the burnt offering is killed shall the sin offering be killed before the Lord:* IT IS MOST HOLY *The priest that offereth it for sin shall eat it* though not the transgressor himself. It might seem that when the flesh was eaten by the priests their official sanctity neutralised the impurity of the victim. Our Great High

Sin and Guilt-Offerings

Lev vi 6

Distinction.

2 Cor 21
Heb ix. 28.

Heb xiii 11

Lev vi. 30

Lev vi 25, 26.

Q 2

Priest was MOST HOLY though bearing the sins of the world ; and, though He represented the sin-offering that must not be eaten, He was nevertheless the Offering of which we all partake as priestly offerers. *And the Lord hath laid on Him the iniquity of us all.* This gives the idea both of expiation and of substitution His soul was made *an offering for sin* Jesus was the reality of that which the sin-offerings only typified *But in those sacrifices there is a remembrance again made of sins every year ·* a remembrance made, not only every year, but on every occasion of their presentation. They only taught the evil of sin and the need of atonement · there could be nothing homogeneous between an animal victim and a human transgressor They accustomed the people to the thought of a SUBSTITUTE ; but we, in the Fulfilment, see that the Supreme SIN-OFFERING has expiated sin itself, and not merely offence against the Levitical institute ; that He is the atonement even for those offences with a high hand of whose perpetrator it was said : *that soul shall be utterly cut off, his iniquity shall be upon him* In Him is all the virtue, and none of the defect, of the ancient types.

Isa lии 6, 10

Heb. x. 3

Num. xv. 31

3. The distinction between two kinds of sin-offering, one for the whole congregation, the other for individual transgressions, must be constantly borne in mind.

(1) The latter had less direct relation to the Christian Sacrifice being designed to make atonement for offences against the Theocratic code not wilfully committed but through ignorance or rashness or levity. This qualification perpetually occurs as restricting the efficacy of these offerings for sin. *If any one of the common people sin through ignorance,* בִּשְׁגָגָה, *while he doeth somewhat against any of the commandments of the Lord concerning things which ought not to be done, and be guilty, or if his sin, which he hath sinned, come to his knowledge, then he shall bring his offering. . . And the priest shall make an atonement for him, and it shall be forgiven him* Here it is to be observed that the Hebrew word used signifies transgression or ERRING through the predominance of the evil principle within, in contradistinction to sinning presumptuously or *with a high hand,* בְּיָד רָמָה For the latter class there was no sin-offering. Hence the Psalmist's prayer · *Who can understand his errors? cleanse Thou me from secret faults. Keep back Thy servant also from presumptuous sins* For the former there was cleansing ; from the latter the petitioner sought only restraint. And in the

For Individuals.

Lev. iv. 27—31.

Num xv. 30. Ps. xix 12, 13.

Epistle to the Hebrews it is said that the high priest offered *for* Heb ix.
7
the errors of the people, for their ἀγνοήματα, and not for their wilful
violations of the covenant   Herein the type fell immeasurably
below the Antitype   The expiation of Christ avails for every
sin that is confessed over the Atonement · *if any man sin, we have* 1 John ii
1, 2.
an Advocate with the Father, Jesus Christ the Righteous: and He is
the propitiation for our sins.   Yet the severity of the restriction in
the type is also pressed into the service of Christian caution.
Though the Great Sacrifice avails for all sin, there is no atone-
ment for the obstinate rejector of that sacrifice.   *If we sin wilfully* Heb. x
26.
after that we have received the knowledge of the truth, there remaineth
no more sacrifice for sins.   As there were sins unatoned for in the
Theocracy, so also *there is a sin unto death* under the Gospel. 1 John v
16.
For the
People

(2.) The daily and annual sacrifices for the sin of the people
covered the guilt of all the congregation as such, and availed, on
behalf of all who put their trust in the Divine ordinance, for the
expiation of every kind of offence not already punished by excision. Lev. iv
6—17.
The blood of these was sprinkled *before the Lord* towards the Holiest,
and *upon the horns of the altar of sweet incense ,* on the great day of
atonement *upon the mercy-seat*   But of this more hereafter. Lev xvi.
16
Purifica-
tions

4 The sin-offerings of the Levitical economy had sometimes
connected with them certain peculiar Purifications of the individual and of the community, regarded as having contracted
defilement : leprosy ; contact with dead bodies , suspected crimes,
such as adultery and murder ; the bloodguiltiness of the community when the manslayer was not discovered.   The diversified ceremonies superadded to the sacrifice which generally
accompanied them pertained to what the New Testament terms
the purifying of the flesh.   They had mainly to do with the Heb. ix.
13
Theocratic relations of the parties , but were all typical of the
defilement of sin, and are often referred to as illustrations of the
purifying effect of that Atonement   They have done much to
mould the phraseology of the Christian covenant , but of themselves
belong rather to the archæology of the ancient people.

III The Redeemer of mankind represented in Himself every The Unity
of all
Sacrifices.
expiatory offering of every kind, and in His one oblation offered
once all other oblations have found their end and spiritual per
fection.   He is the One Sacrifice for sin presented by Himself, the

High Priest, for and on behalf of mankind represented by Him. He is the VICTIMA SACERDOTII SUI ET SACERDOS SUÆ VICTIMÆ.

Rom. x 1 As, in the Epistle to the Romans, He is the *end of the law for righteousness,* so, in the Epistle to the Hebrews, He is the end of

Heb ix. 12 the sacrifices for *eternal redemption.* But here two important cautionary suggestions must be made

Only Figures 1. The entire system of ancient sacrifices was but the shadow of an eternal substance   The Epistle which gives us the authentic

Heb x 4. valuation of the old economy tells us that *it is not possible that the*

Heb x 1, 2 *blood of bulls and of goats should take away sins;* that the law could not *make the comers thereunto perfect* in freedom from the *conscience*

Heb ix 13 *of sins*   They sanctified only *to the purifying of the flesh*   On the one hand, they availed only for the maintenance of a national and individual relation to the Theocracy   On the other, they made no provision for deliverance from guilt as violation of the moral law.   The true secret of the peace which was pronounced upon penitent and sincere offerings was reserved · to be made known

Heb ix 9 when *the figure for the time then present* should be superseded by the Reality   And, with regard to this, the sincere Hebrew and the sincere Gentile were on a level : only that the former had the revelation that constantly announced a future Redeemer, and might mingle with his merely carnal ordinances a dim faith in the yet unrevealed Atonement

But containing Eternal Truth 2   But, this being true, the figurative and typical institute gave profound suggestion of the nature of that future propitiation   It told of the exceeding sinfulness of sin, which in its endless varieties was so rigorously watched by the Holy One of Israel, and demanded such varieties of sacrifice.   The meaning of the sacrificial phraseology must not be lost when it is transferred to Christian times, as many vainly affirm : that meaning is glorified in the spirit, but its body and its letter is still of Christ.   Patterns

Heb ix 23 only, they were still *patterns of things in the heavens.*   Many terms are given to oblivion in the Gospel ; but EXPIATION as the ground of REMISSION through the shedding of SACRIFICIAL BLOOD are words to be had in everlasting remembrance.   If the economy of typical propitiations had no permanent significance, but introduced a system in which no atonement was offered to justice, the New-Testament Epistles must have been written in a totally different style

THE SACRIFICIAL SEASONS.

The various holy seasons and festivals of the old covenant were also summed up and abolished in the one High-priestly function of Christ   There were the Daily Service; the Sabbatic Days; the Three Feasts, and the Great Fast   In the year there may be said to have been two main cycles. the Passover, with the days of Unleavened Bread, and the Feast of Weeks or Pentecost for the spring; the Day of Atonement, the Feast of Tabernacles, with its Azereth for the autumn   All these were under the supervision and control of the high priest; and they were all done away by being glorified in the mission and work of the Redeemer. The Passover and the Day of Atonement will for our purpose adequately represent the entire series.

Seasons

THE PASSOVER.

The Passover was at once a sacrifice for sin and a peace-offering   Unless we admit this combination we miss the design of the institute and lose its profound connection with the Christian Sacrifice.

The Passover.

1. The Angel of the Lord passed over or spared all the houses which were sprinkled with the blood of the paschal lamb, but sprinkling generally, at least sprinkling with blood, connoted the idea of expiation   The representative of the household confessed that deliverance was of the grace of God alone; and the people as a whole at the beginning of every ecclesiastical year renewed the covenant with God by sacrifice. As a sin-offering it was also a peace-offering : celebrating as a national expression of gratitude the redemption from Egypt as well as the deliverance of Israel's firstborn. Subordinate to this was its acknowledgment of the goodness of Jehovah in the gifts of the earth. The slaying of the victim and the partaking of it went together from year to year, and from generation to generation   hence the Passover was a sin-offering and a peace-offering in one

Origin

2. *Christ our Passover is sacrificed for us   therefore let us keep the feast.* These words, though standing alone in this form, must be understood according to their plain import as throwing a flood of

Christ
1 Cor v 7
8.

light on the ancient institute and on its spiritual significance. In virtue of the blood of Jesus the spiritual Israel are redeemed from worse than Egyptian bondage and blessed with a better inheritance than Canaan. In the first reference to the Lord's sacrifice John i. 29 the Baptist termed Him *the Lamb of God, which taketh away the sin of the world,* where it is certainly the paschal lamb that is referred to, but with the expiatory and substitutionary idea of later prophecy added and made prominent The Lord's own constant reference to the sacrificial and sacramental food of His flesh would seem to imply the presence in His thoughts of the paschal feast, which indeed was the main characteristic of the Passover. It was a communion, and in this different from every other sacrifice : not a feast in which the offerer partook with the priest, but one in which the families of Israel united. At the close of His life the Redeemer instituted the Eucharist, as the Evangelical Passover, in which His Church should for ever keep the feast · first, as a commemorative Sacrifice, celebrating the expiatory death ; secondly, as a symbolical Sacrament, representing Christ, the Passover, as the nourishment of His people , and, thirdly, as an emblem of the unity of His New Israel in Himself.

3 The Passover was prolonged for seven days to give the feast the covenant character of perfection : the seven days were the FEAST OF UNLEAVENED BREAD which gave it its name. On the first day after the proper Passover was the offering of the wave-sheaf. Seven full weeks after that wave-offering came the FEAST OF WEEKS, the celebration of the completed harvest · hereafter to be abolished and glorified in the outpouring of the Holy Ghost on the day which was known as the Pentecost With this feast the fulfilment of the Old-Testament paschal festival was complete. The characteristic of the whole solemnity was the festal commemoration of deliverance from Egypt , a deliverance which typified the Great Redemption. And its connection with the Eucharist, the abiding sacramental commemoration in the Christian Church, makes the Passover in a certain sense the preeminent typical institute of the Old Testament. The Lord's Supper is, so to speak, the antitype of the Paschal Feast as it included the whole cycle of seven weeks : it therefore is the Christian Feast which celebrates all the events of the Fifty Days

The Paschal Week.

THE DAY OF ATONEMENT.

The Day of Atonement, on the tenth of Tisri, the seventh month, effected an annual reconciliation between God and the collective people ; and was the chief, inasmuch as it was the most comprehensive, typical and symbolical Old-Testament prefiguration of the Christian mystery. As such it combined most of the other elements of the sacrificial economy, and added not a few of its own. It was the day of the high priest pre-eminently, when his function culminated. On other days acting by delegates, on that day—THE DAY, יוֹמָא, of the Talmud—he administered his office almost alone . the sublimest of all typical figures

1. The sacrifices he first offered for himself showed the distinction between the type and the Antitype . as the representative of the people, and also one of them, he needed atonement for himself and his priestly order and the very sanctuary *that remaineth among them in the midst of their uncleanness.* The holy places however were purified by the sprinkling of the blood of the victims offered for priest and people, probably mingled, and not by any distinct sacrifices ordained for that purpose . their uncleanness resulted from the sins of those who entered them.

2 The high priest's typical relation to Christ was shown in his transaction with the two goats respectively. One, chosen by lot, he offered for a sin-offering. Its blood availed for universal expiation for all the transgressions of all the people, as sprinkled upon the mercy-seat seven times ; for the altar and sanctuary without as sprinkled also upon them   The counterpart victim, the Scapegoat, was the symbolical BEARER AWAY of the iniquities which the other goat BORE   Upon its head the high priest confessed *all the iniquities of the children of Israel, and all their transgressions according to all their sins,* and it was driven forth *unto a land not inhabited · into a separated land,* אֶרֶץ גְּזֵרָה, symbol of that utter separation from God which is the punishment of sin   Though the two goats were distinct, they made up one expiatory idea. The victim which was slain represented the sacrifice for sin and the remission of penalty. The victim which was not slain, but driven into the desert to die, symbolised the absolute removal and Divine oblivion

Day of Atonement

Peculiarities

Lev. xvi 16.

Lev xvi 8—34

Lev. xvi. 21, 22.

of guilt : לַעֲזָאזֵל, TO AZAZEL, or *for the Scapegoat,* means literally *to utter forgetfulness* or *complete dismissal.* The double symbol declared that all penalty was remitted and all sin forgiven and forgotten : cancelled as though it were not.

Into the Presence.

3 But that which made this the Supreme Solemnity of the Levitical economy was the fact that then only was the blood of

Lev xvii 11.

expiation, of which Jehovah said, *I have* GIVEN IT TO YOU *upon the altar to make an atonement for your souls,* brought within the veil, into the very presence of God where the law within the ark testified against the transgressors   Then were all the other forgivenesses of the year confirmed, then all defects in forgiveness repaired, saving only as touching those high-handed acts of rebellion which found no place of repentance   The assurance

Lev xvi. 30

was *that ye may be clean from all your sins before the Lord*   Hence in the Great Fulfilment the Christian High Priest hath entered

Heb. ix 24, 25.

into heaven itself, now to appear in the presence of God for us.   But the typical high priest went out again from the face of Jehovah. The process of expiation must be repeated annually.   Jesus needs not to *offer Himself often*.   His one oblation covers the whole sphere of human sin from the beginning to the end of its continuance on earth   And His abiding within the Veil is our security.

THE PASSOVER AND DAY OF ATONEMENT COMBINED.

Combina-tion.

The entire doctrine of the Atonement is based upon the Christian fulfilment of the prophetic and typical meaning of these two solemnities, the Paschal Feast and the Atoning Fast.   A combination of their elements is necessary.   Neither is sufficient of itself.   But, united, they furnish a most impressive and comprehensive view of the central Christian mystery.

1. As the Passover predominates in the Gospels, so the Day of Atonement takes the lead in the later New Testament :

Rom iii 21—28.

especially in the Epistles to the Romans and the Hebrews, neither of which alludes to the paschal solemnity.   The former points every allusion to the subject with a reference to the great Fast day it makes Christ Himself the propitiatory, or mercy seat, or propitiation, set forth in the mind of God and upon the scene of transgression, for the remission of human sins in the past and the present and the future . while it does not exclude the intercession of Christ, it dwells rather on the offering in the outer court. Moreover, it connects the whole rather with the idea of righteousness than with the idea of sanctification . combining in one the evangelical court and the evangelical temple. In the Epistle to the Hebrews the great day of expiation occupies a very large place The sacrifice in the outer court and the presentation within the veil fill up the central chapters of the treatise.

Heb ix , x

2 As united they demonstrate typically what the Christian atonement demonstrates really, the absolute necessity of satisfaction to Divine justice in order that the Divine love may be glorified , that therefore the God who is offended Himself provided the Supreme Sacrifice; that the virtue of the atonement, apprehended by faith, secures the perfect abolition or cancelling of sin and its punishment , that the one Redeemer who offered His life on the altar of the cross ever liveth to present His intercession for His people on earth.

Justice and Love

3. They further teach in their unity that the benefit of the supreme expiation belongs to the company of Christ's people as such   That is the general lesson taught by the types of the Levitical economy If we would seek the universal effect and influence of the redeeming Sacrifice we must go behind and beyond the Mosaic institute, to the primary sacrificial oblations which were before the Law   There we find Him in Whom should *all the nations of the earth be blessed.*

The Church and the World

Gen xxii. 18.

4. When combined they also proclaim that the redeemed estate of the people of God, the children of redemption and of the sacrificial covenant, is one of mingled fasting and feasting. If the Passover was the Great Feast, the Day of Atonement was the Great Fast but they are united in the Cross and its commemoration In other words, there is a foreshadowing of the truth that stamps its solemn impress on the writings of the Apostle Paul the Christian life is a union with Christ in His suffering and in His joy, in His life and in His death, in the process and in the result of His atonement. The joy, however, predominates; for *He hath borne our griefs, and carried our sorrows ;* borne them away into the land of forgetfulness. The Day of Atonement has no

Feast and Fast

Isa. liii. 4.

1 Cor v 7 sacramental commemoration as such . *Christ our Passover is sacrificed for us ; let us keep the Feast.*

INTERCESSION AND BENEDICTION.

It was the preeminent function of the high priest to present the blood of atonement, and thus silently to intercede for the whole congregation once in the year; though the priestly service generally was one of perpetual mediation and intercession. The Blessing of the people was also the special office of the priests, to be discharged after and on the ground of the sacrificial offerings. Our Lord's Intercession is the presentation of Himself in heaven to the Father after His self-oblation on earth; not without special prayer for its objects. His Benediction is imparted by the Holy Ghost, and is bound up with the administration of all the blessings of the new covenant. While Intercession is more directly connected with the sacrificial office, Benediction is linked with all the offices of the Christ. It is the final consummation of each.

INTERCESSION

Incense

I The intercession of the high priest was expressed typically by the incense before the mercy seat in the Holiest on the day of
Ps. cxli 2 atonement David says generally · *Let my prayer be set forth before Thee as incense ;* and in the New Testament we read
Rev. v 8 generally again of the *golden vials full of incense, which are the prayers of saints* But the incense offered by the high priest was
Num xvi 46 strictly connected with his typical mediatorial relation . *And Moses said unto Aaron, Take a censer, and put fire therein from off*
Ex xxxii 11, 32 *the altar, and put on incense, and go quickly unto the congregation, and make an atonement for them.* Moses himself, without the incense, had interceded in words. This was an extraordinary, and, as it were, irregular procedure , and is the solitary instance of the incense-cloud representing the atonement The prayer of Moses and the

censer of Aaron alike typified the intercession of Christ, Who intercedes both by the presentation of His sacrifice and by the virtue of His prayer. At first the high priest himself burnt *sweet incense every morning* as also *at even . . . a perpetual incense before the Lord* on the altar for that purpose which was *before the vail that is by the ark of the testimony.* Hence we read in the Epistle to the Hebrews of the *Holiest of all, which had the golden censer, and the ark of the covenant* This discrepancy is to be explained by the fact of the intimate connection between the two. The daily incense was the symbol of the intercession that daily allayed the Divine displeasure; but it was on the day of atonement that this symbol had its highest meaning *That the cloud of the incense may cover the mercy seat that is upon the testimony, that he die not:* these last words belonged to the type only, but the general truth remains that the incense of intercession covered the mercy seat simultaneously with the blood of atonement, and blended with the thick cloud of the Divine glory. So the mystical temple of the Prophet's vocation *was filled with smoke.* the smoke of the same intercessory incense which fills the temple where Jesus the High Priest presents His eternal sacrifice

II This antitypical intercession of Christ is variously set forth in the New Testament, especially in the Temple Epistle.

1 It is the presentation of HIMSELF before the Father on our behalf. *By His own blood He entered in once into the holy place, having obtained eternal redemption for us.* Not that He is represented as carrying His sacred blood with Him · the exhibition of His Sacred Person is enough. A careful consideration of the classical passage in the Epistle to the Hebrews will shed much light upon this. The English Authorised Version mentions three appearances of Christ as marking the historical process of the Atonement The three terms in the original are different and carefully chosen the middle one expressing the fact that the Son of God in our humanity manifests Himself before His Father and our Father without a veil. *In the end of the world He appeared to put away sin by the sacrifice of Himself·* πεφανέρωται, was manifested as God in the flesh. This is closely, indeed indistinguishably, connected with His entering *into heaven itself, now to appear in the presence of God for us:* ἐμφανισθῆναι, to present Himself boldly and abidingly

Marginal notes:

Ex xxx 6, 7, 8.

Heb ix 3, 4

Lev xvi 13

Isa vi 4.

Christ's Intercession

Himself
Heb ix 12.

Heb. ix 26, 24, 28.

without any protecting cloud of incense   This silent intercessory appearance shall end when He will *appear the second time without sin unto salvation* ὀφθήσεται, He will be seen of angels and men in His majesty, without the humiliation of His sacrificial connec-

1 John ii. 1.
tion with sin   St. John expiesses the same truth *if any man sin, we have an Advocate with the Father, Jesus Christ the Righteous; and He is the propitiation for our sins.*   He is Himself the Pro-pitiation and the Advocate   Himself, which is more than His blood or His life.   The virtue of His sacrifice is the value of His Person.   The MERIT of Christ is the power of His intercession; and that merit is not simply the fact of His voluntary self-sacrifice, but His self-sacrifice as that of the Son of the Father's infinite complacency   His merit is the worthiness of His Incarnate Self   His Presence in heaven is His all-effectual plea   Three important truths arise here to our notice.   (1) The intercessory presenta-tion of Himself in heaven is not, as the Socinians and those who

Heb. ix. 28
follow them assert, the beginning of His priestly function.   *Christ was once offered to bear the sins of many* ἅπαξ προσενεχθεὶς εἰς τὸ πολλῶν ἀνενεγκεῖν ἁμαρτίας, sacrificial terms which had their full meaning already in the Cross   (2.) There is, however, no continua-tion of the sacrifice in heaven; and there can be no continuation of it

Acts x. 4
upon earth   The Atonement is gone up FOR A MEMORIAL BEFORE GOD for ever, and the Romanist Sacrifice of the Mass has no sanction, but is utterly condemned, in the Epistle to the Hebrews.

Heb ix 27
As it is appointed unto men once to die for their sins, so Christ was in the deepest truth APPOINTED TO DIE ONCE for expiation of sins, but only once.   (3) Lastly, the unity of the Atonement on earth and the intercession based upon it in heaven must be most care-

Heb ix 24
fully maintained.   The NOW *to appear* marks the whole period from Calvary to the Judgment as the Day of Grace, and of the

Heb. ix 26
PUTTING AWAY OF SIN, the ἀθέτησις ἁμαρτίας

His Prayer
2 The intercession of our Lord is also direct supplication on behalf of its beneficiaries   the words which describe it prove this

Rom. viii 27
He maketh intercession for us   the term ἐντυγχάνειν is generally used of oral supplication either for or against its objects.   And

1 John ii 1.
Jesus Christ the Righteous is called our παράκλητος *with the Father*, our Advocatus or Intercessor, fulfilling His promise that He

John xiv. 16.
would *pray the Father* for His disciples, and thus continuing in

heaven the High-priestly prayer begun on earth. As to the speech of the glorified Son Incarnate, the tongue not of men nor of angels, the unspeakable words which it is not yet lawful either to hear or to utter, it is needless to inquire. Suffice that the Saviour's intercession has all the effect of what below is called intercessory prayer As we must not refine away the truth of His being *touched with the feeling of our infirmities,* so we must not make the God-man above a Silent Representative of our humanity. Heb iv 15

III. The objects of His intercession are the world, the mystical Church of His people, and every individual who appeals to Him. Objects.

1. By His presence in heaven Christ is the Pleader for the world, that is for the humanity, human kind, or human nature, which He represents. The high priest entered into the inmost sanctuary of the temple on behalf of the covenant people. the blood which he sprinkled was accompanied by incense, which he waved, without a word, not to protect himself from the insufferable glory of God, already dimmed by the *thick darkness* of the cloud, but to prevent the Divine justice from causing his death as the representative of the people. This incense signified the intercession of Christ, whose presence in heaven keeps the sinful earth in being; *I bear up the pillars of it* It availed from the beginning by anticipation; on no ground can we understand how a guilty race should be propagated under the moral government of God save that the intercession of the Second Adam began when first it was said · *the plague is begun* Hence Isaiah, going beyond the Levitical economy, says that *He made intercession for the transgressors* this in the widest meaning of the word. The World

1 Kings viii 12

Ps. lxxv 3

Numb. xvi. 46. Isa liii. 12.

2. It is true, however, that the specific intercession of Christ is limited to His prayer for His own people. Before He departed He poured out an intercessory supplication which was the earnest and the type and the pledge of His future pleading for His Church as united by faith with its Living Head For the Church

(1) This intercession is only for His own not because the Redeemer forgets the world which He came to save, but because it is of a character distinct, and appropriate only to His people's relation to Him It is not only request on their behalf, but the sacred demand of Christ on behalf of Himself as represented in His people. They are His other Self, YET NOT ANOTHER *Father, I* Not for the World

John xvii. 24.

will that they also, whom Thou hast given Me, be with Me where I am.
It is rather stipulation than intercession. θέλω rather than ἐρωτῶ.

Heb vii 24, 25

Hence Jesus, *because He continueth ever, hath an unchangeable priest-hood Wherefore He is able to save them to the uttermost* (or perfectly and evermore) *that come unto God by Him, seeing He ever liveth to make intercession for them.* He hath brought them to God, but also brought them to Himself; and only asks the portion that falleth to Him He demands rather than asks for them, as united with Himself

John xvii. 26

and part of Himself, all that is His · *that the love wherewith Thou hast loved Me may be in them, and I in them* The Father's love is arrogated for them as of necessity, because the Beloved Son of the Father is in them both collectively and individually.

Giving its Virtue.
Eph. 1 6.
1 Peter ii 5.
Rev. viii 3.

(2.) The Saviour's intercession as High Priest makes accept-able both the persons and the worship of His people. They are *accepted in the Beloved* They *offer up spiritual sacrifices, acceptable to God by Jesus Christ* He is the *much incense, that He should offer it with the prayers of all saints* · the angel to whom it was given was only a ministering priest or Levite under this great High Priest And in order that all the service of those who are priests with Christ may be well pleasing, the Holy Ghost represents the

Rom viii. 26, 27.

Supreme Intercessor within their hearts *The Spirit itself maketh intercession for us with groanings which cannot be uttered. And He that searcheth the hearts knoweth what is the mind of the Spirit, that He maketh intercession for the saints according to the will of God* according to the will of the High Priest also There is no more impressive view of the heavenly pleading within the veil than that which makes the voice of the Holy Ghost within our hearts its echo. This concert of the Two Intercessors—the one within the shrine above, the other within the shrine of our spirits, but both agreeing in one—is the infallible guarantee of our communion with God and acceptable prayer.

Sym-pathy.

(3.) This intercessory pleading is the Scriptural expression for that perfect sympathy of our Lord with His members on earth which His community of nature gives Him, in virtue of which He is their Paraclete or Advocate or Helper, succouring them in temptation, strengthening them for duty, and imparting to them seasonable help He knows the secrets of all hearts as God · but His humanity gives Him a knowledge that He could not without it have, and the Scripture lays much stress on the benefit of this *Wherefore in all things it behoved Him to be made like unto His brethren . . For in that He Himself hath suffered being tempted, He is able to succour them that are tempted* His sympathy does not spring from remembrance of sin or fall or danger of falling, but from His human experience of the devices of Satan haunting the accesses of our nature In His atoning passion He Who knew no sin yet became acquainted with it as only God incarnate could become, so also in His administration of His atoning grace He knows, as only God incarnate can know, our need [Heb ii. 17 18]

3. But this leads to the individual bearing of our Saviour's intercession *The Head of every man is Christ* the High Priest over the whole house has a special relation to every worshipper. He is the Representative of the whole Church, and of every several branch, in His intercession it was the Church of Laodicæa, neither hot nor cold, concerning which He said, *I will spue thee out of My mouth*, or drop its name from His heavenly Litany. But His heart is also the faithful Friend of sinners, and faithful to every mortal transgressor as his own High Priest. As surely as the Atonement availed for the entire family of Adam, so certainly the pleading of Christ on the ground of the atonement may be appealed to by every representative of that family [For the Individual. 1 Cor. xi 3] [Rev iii 16.]

(1.) This is the strength of the penitent's heart in approaching the God of justice. The *one Mediator between God and men* makes intercession for all *that come unto God by Him For through Him we both*—Jews and Gentiles, saved and unsaved—*have access by one Spirit unto the Father* Every man living and sinning on earth has, if he will only use it, an introduction, προσαγωγή, a right of humble approach to God. He has not only the ground of confidence that an accepted propitiation for his race gives, but also the assurance of a Divine-HUMAN Representative who loves his own individual soul, and has left on record this unrevoked and irrevocable word *him that cometh to Me I will in no wise cast out* If He will not cast him out, most surely the Father behind Him will not. [For Every Man. 1 Tim. ii. 18] [Heb. vii. 25.] [Eph ii. 18.] [John vi. 37.]

(2.) Especially is this true of the believer. On the basis of the Atonement he is accepted in Christ; but he might be tempted to think, nor would it be an unreasonable temptation, that, having sinned against the grace of that Atonement, his hope must perish [For Every Believer.]

But his Head above is a living, unchangeable, ever available
Pleader for him   *If any man*—any Christian man—*sin, we have
an Advocate,* Who, in the court of heaven. vindicates the rights of
His sacrifice offered on earth.   For every believer He is at once a
Propitiation and a Paraclete in the presence of the Father.

1 John ii. 1

BENEDICTION

Benediction.

I. The solemn Benediction which attested Divine acceptance
was expressly provided for in the Levitical service   It was an
integral part of the high priest's duty, which, like almost all
others, was committed in due time to the priesthood generally.
At the first consecration of Aaron and his sons, after the offerings
were presented for the host, *Aaron lifted up his hand toward the
people, and blessed them   .   and the glory of the Lord appeared unto
all the people.*   The evidence of that verbal blessing was that *there
came a fire out from before the Lord, and consumed upon the altar the
burnt-offering and the fat   which when all the people saw, they shouted,
and fell on their faces*   Of *the priests the sons of Levi* it was afterwards said, that them *the Lord thy God hath chosen to minister unto
Him, and to bless* IN THE NAME OF THE LORD.   The stress must be
laid upon these last words   God alone is to be blessed in Doxology,
and God alone blesses in Benediction, whether in Old Testament
or New   The blessing was not only, however, in the name of the
Lord , it was also the name of the Triune God Jehovah impressed
upon the people, making them His own   *Speak unto Aaron and
unto his sons, saying, On this wise ye shall bless the children of Israel,
saying unto them, The Lord bless thee, and keep thee : the Lord make
His face shine upon thee, and be gracious unto thee   the Lord lift up
His countenance upon thee, and give thee peace   And they shall put*
MY NAME *upon the children of Israel , and I will bless them*   Here
are united the blessings of universal providential care, of mercy
for sin, and of internal peace · for the people generally and for
every individual worshipper prepared to receive it.   Two things
are to be observed in passing

Lev ix 22—24.

Deut xxi. 5.

Benediction and Doxology

Triune.

Num vi 23—27.

1. As we have seen that the symbols of sacrifice within the veil
pointed mysteriously but certainly to the Triune God, so also did
the Benediction which sealed to the worshippers the acceptance of

The Trinity.

those sacrifices. Three names, yet to be revealed, are alone
wanting to make the Levitical Blessing the distinct benediction
of the Holy Trinity. The benediction IN ACT, the effusion of the
Divine glory, found its great realisation, though itself a reality,
when God *shined in our hearts to give the light of the knowledge of the* 2 Cor iv.
glory of God in the face of Jesus Christ. His is the Face of God 4.
turned on the penitent in GRACE, whether in this world or the
next The benediction IN WORD found its highest fulfilment in
the testimony of the Divine Spirit, giving PEACE through the
assurance that we are *accepted in the Beloved* Eph i 6.

2 The ancient Benediction was not only typical , it was more Its Value
than a mere form of words , it was a reality, pronouncing over
the people, and every individual who sincerely complied with the
conditions of the old covenant, an acceptance the true and eternal
ground of which was as yet not made known It has already
been seen that the Levitical economy, as such and in its specific
prescriptions for the atonement of individual and national offences,
aimed only at the maintenance of external legal relations to the
Theocracy But, underlying and surrounding all these, was the
great typical system of sacrifice that was accepted for the sake of
the Coming Atonement, the undisputed virtue of which secured
the effectual acceptance of God There was a pretermission or
πάρεσις of all sins for a season, until the fulness of time confirmed Rom iii.
this into an ἄφεσις, or full forgiveness. 22.

II. It is the prerogative of the One Mediator between God and Fulfil-
man that He is not only the Minister of blessing, but that He ment.
is also its Source He is God and the High Priest in one. He Heb vii
is the Antitype of Melchisedec, who *met Abraham*, higher than 1—11.
he, and *blessed him* and all the Levitical priesthood in him. The
benediction of Jesus is the benediction of God Incarnate, and it
is no less than the administration of all the benefits of the evan- Heb. ix.
gelical covenant : *the promise of eternal inheritance.* 15.

1. The blessing of our High Priest is deliverance from sin. It
is *the blessing of Abraham*, that is, *the righteousness of faith*, and *the* Gal iii 9
promise of the Spirit through faith · that Spirit being the sanctify- —14
ing power of the Gospel. *God, having raised up His Son Jesus,* Rom. iv
sent Him to bless you, in turning away every one of you from his 13
iniquities. Comparing these passages, which are one in the unity Acts iii 26.

R 2

of the blessing of Abraham, we gather that the Christian High-priestly benediction is our deliverance from all sin.

Eph. 1 3.
Blessing a word un-definable
2 Hence it is the impartation of *all spiritual blessings in heavenly places in Christ.* The term BLESSING is one that cannot be defined : it is the gracious mystery of the manifestation of the Supreme to His people in grace It is a gift without a definition , including all the individual benefits that may be put into words, it surpasses each in particular and surrounds the whole. It is the unbounded sum of all that has been procured for the redeemed children of men first, as the restored prerogative of the creature resting in the Creator, and, secondly, as the superadded blessedness of a nearer than creaturely union with God in Christ.

The Holy Ghost
3. This Benediction is imparted through the Holy Ghost. He is the Vicar of Christ, and the Agent of His will, and the Medium of every benefit of His passion Therefore the more full consideration of this subject belongs to the next department of our Theology Meanwhile, it must be remembered that the Blessing of the Gospel is obtained by Jesus the Priest, announced by Jesus the Prophet, imparted by Jesus the King, through the Mediatorial Spirit of the new economy of grace.

THE JEWISH AND THE CHRISTIAN TEMPLE

Before we pass to the Kingly Office of Christ we must linger for a while on the scene of His High-priestly function, which is, whether on earth or in heaven, the Temple, or Tabernacle : the place of special Divine revelation to man.

Type
The Altar
I In the Old Testament we see the progressive stages of the history of sacrificial worship converging towards the Christian Temple.

Gen viii. 20.
1. Before the Levitical economy the Altar stood alone under the heavens . the מזבח, the first record of which is that *Noah builded an altar unto the Lord,* a θυσιαστήριον, so termed from the burnt offerings SLAIN before it From that time the patriarchs raised altars where God revealed Himself, as Abram *builded an altar unto the Lord, Who appeared unto him.* When the law was given on Sinai Jehovah said to His people : *Ye have seen that I have talked with you from heaven Ye shall not make with Me gods of silver, neither shall ye make unto you gods of gold. An altar of earth*

Gen. xii 7.

Ex. xx. 22, 24.

*thou shalt make unto Me, and shalt sacrifice thereon thy burnt offerings,
and thy peace offerings, thy sheep and thine oxen in all places where I
record My name I will come unto thee, and I will bless thee.* From
that time there was to be no longer an altar in every tent.

2. The Mosaic Sanctuary was a Tabernacle, אֹהֶל מוֹעֵד, the
Tent of congregation, where God met His people; also the
אהל הָעֵדוּת, the Tabernacle of Testimony, or of Covenant
revelation The innumerable details of the economy of this
domain of the high priest's function belong to archæology : only
the leading points need to be referred to here, and those only
as pertaining to the Mosaic Sanctuary There was a threefold division In the Court, surrounding all, the Covenant People
assembled , and this, in the later Temple, made silent provision
for the future ingathering of the Gentiles Here was the Altar
of Burnt-offering The sanctuary proper, the Holy Place, הַקֹּדֶשׁ,
admitted the priests only , it had the Table of Shewbread, the
twelve loaves of which renewed every sabbath were a permanent
meat offering in acknowledgment of the Divine gifts , opposite to
this the Golden Candlestick, with seven lamps, the symbol of
God in His Holy Spirit for ever enlightening the Temple ; and
between them, over against the ark of the covenant, the Altar of
Incense, representing the daily intercession of the priesthood and
the daily prayers of the congregation. Into the Holiest of All,
the Most Holy Place, קֹדֶשׁ קָדָשִׁים, the high priest alone entered
once in the year. There was the Ark, the most comprehensive
symbol in the ancient worship the Ark of the covenant, because
it contained the roll of the law, the conditions of God's good will
towards His people, and at the same time the testimony of His
people's sinfulness ; the Ark of the throne of God, because His
glory as a thick cloud rested on the Kapporeth or Mercy-seat,
which covered the record of transgression from the Divine eyes
Over the Propitiatory were the Cherubim, so important in the
symbolical drapery of the curtains, of which it was said . *O Shepherd
of Israel, Thou that dwellest between the Cherubim, shine forth !* These
represented all the Divine attributes in their universal manifestations : barring the entrance to Paradise and watching the way of
return. But they have faded away in Christ

3. The Tabernacle, with all its divisions, was one under the

The Taber-nacle

Ps. lxxx
1.

supremacy of the high priest   Every figure, symbol, and act within it—from the laver at the entrance to the thick cloud of the Divine glory never seen but by faith—paid its tribute to the great Fact

Ex. xxv. 22.
there I will meet with thee, and I will commune with thee from above the mercy-seat, from between the two cherubims.   It may not always be possible to trace the connection ; nor is it necessary.   We must be content with observing the typical allusion of the whole to the Christian temple in which the Supreme Sacrifice was once offered WITHOUT the veil, and then presented WITHIN it.

Antitype
II   The new temple is as conspicuous in the Evangelical revelation as the old temple was in the Levitical economy

Christ the Temple
1. It is the glory of the Christian Offerer that He is the Antitype not only of the typical high priest, and of all the offerings He presented, but of the place itself in which He offered   Nor is there anything more impressive in the Great Fulfilment than the truth that the Incarnate Son is as incarnate Himself the Temple.

John ii. 19, 21
His first prediction concerning His own Person declared this . *destroy this temple, and in three days I will raise it up :   . . He spake of the temple of His body*   His human nature—our human nature—is the shrine

John i. 14
in which the *Word,* Whose *Glory* was *as of the Only-begotten, became flesh and dwelt among us.*   This central truth throws its beams backwards to Paradise and forwards to the Consummation . giving unity to all the Scriptural records of God's dwelling among men   In Eden the Divine Presence, with the guardian Cherubim, had its ark.

Gen. iv. 16.
After the Fall *the Presence of the Lord* was retained upon earth until the Flood   It then became the *Glory of the Lord,* כָּבוֹד, over the Ark of the Covenant   permanent, as distinguished from occasional Theophanies, and as the type of the final indwelling of God in our nature.   The later Jewish theology gave it the name SHEKINAH, as the tabernacle was formerly called מִשְׁכַּן יְהוָה, the dwelling-place of Jehovah   But now in Christ Jesus, the

1 Tim iii. 16.
Incarnate Son, God is abidingly *manifest in the flesh*   The ancient symbol was the object only of faith   the Reality is object of faith

John i 14.
also, but the Apostles could say, *We beheld His glory,* and He Himself said, *he that hath seen Me hath seen the Father*   When He

John xiv. 9
appeared it was already true that *the tabernacle of God is with men,* though another fulfilment was in the future.   The true theology

Rev. xxi. 3
of our Lord's Person holds that He inhabited human nature as

His temple : He enters or *is come into* or *in* the flesh   Not that the | 1 John iv. 2.
Divinity is the High Priest and the flesh the temple.   There are
indeed two passages that seem to warrant such a view   Jesus is
said to have consecrated for us a new and living way of access to
God *through the veil, that is to say, His flesh*   in His human nature | Heb. x. 20
He suffered, and the rending of that veil opened the way into
the Holiest.   But the rending of His Holy Flesh did not rend
asunder His one Personality   He *through the Eternal Spirit offered* | Heb ix 14
Himself in heaven when that sacred curtain was repaired.   But it
must be remembered that He *offered* HIMSELF.   We must beware
of the temptation to refine upon these distinctions, and not think
it necessary to harmonise all the various sayings of Scripture on
the great mystery which rises above all figures and analogies.

2 The Body of our Lord, in another view, is the mystical fellow- | His Church the Temple.
ship of His saints.   In that Jesus is High Priest, and all who are
His partake of His priesthood.   (1) First, the Church as such is the
sphere of the High Priest's function.   He is Himself its Shekinah,
and His rays from the Holiest, blending with the Sevenfold Light
of the Spirit from the Holy Place, is the FULNESS OF GOD for | Eph. iii 19.
which the Apostle prays   Whosoever is in Christ lives and moves
in Him as a Temple   *ye are the Temple of the living God*   In Him | 2 Cor vi 16
all the building fitly framed together groweth unto an holy temple in the | Eph ii. 21
Lord.   Thus is fulfilled the mystic prophecy of the precious
ointment *that ran down upon the beard, even Aaron's beard.* The | Ps cxxx. iii 2.
unction of the High Priest descends upon all His members, for
He and they are one; while, in the sublime confusion of figures,
those who form the *spiritual house,* and *holy priesthood,* offer up | 1 Pet ii 5.
themselves as *spiritual sacrifices.* (2) And every individual Christian is said to be a temple in which our High Priest dwells · the
whole economy of communion with heaven being translated into
the believer's heart, in which he is exhorted to *sanctify the Lord* | 1 Pet iii. 15.
God.   This indwelling of the High Priest is the highest and
deepest characteristic of personal religion : it is that ABODE WITH | John xiv. 23.
HIM which the Saviour reserved for His last promise to any
individual on earth, as well as His last promise to any individual
from heaven : *I will come in to him.* | Rev. iii. 20

3 But there is a yet wider view.   Heaven and earth make the
New Temple in which our High Priest ministers   It is a sanc-

Heb ix. 11

tuary *not made with hands*   Heaven is the Holy of Holies, into which He has entered with the virtue of His sacrifice   There are the cherubims of glory without the symbol, beholding not the mercy-seat sprinkled with blood, but the Person of Jesus Who without blood and without the incense presents Himself boldly for us that we also may come with boldness.   Following out the symbol to its issues, the expositor of the Christian temple says that

Heb. ix 23

it was necessary that *the heavenly things themselves* should be purified with the *better sacrifices*   not that heaven itself needs sprinkling, save through the One Propitiation of its God.   The Holy Place is done away in a certain sense   there is but one Priest, and all believers are a royal priesthood who offer up spiritual sacrifices acceptable to God through Jesus Christ   In that outer court our

Heb. xiii 10

Lord's altar, the Cross, was once erected.   It is gone, and yet the Apostle says, *We have an altar* /   disguising, and yet scarcely disguising, his allusion to the cross.   In this outer court there is no

Eph ii. 14.

distinction of Jew and Gentile   Christ hath *broken down the middle*

2 Tim ii 20

wall of partition   Nor is there any other distinction.   The whole family of believers as yet in probation occupies the GREAT HOUSE

John xiv. 2.

in which there *are many mansions*   But the strange paradox remains that, while Christian men in the militant church are on

Eph i 3

the pavement of the outer court, they are at the same time *in*

Heb x 19.

heavenly places in Christ   Hence they are exhorted *with boldness to enter into the Holiest* above almost in the same sentence which bids

Heb. x 25.

them not *forsake the assembling of themselves together* below   But these subjects belong rather to the doctrine of the Church.

The Atonement of the High Priest.

4 There is one other application of the High-priestly function of our Lord to which it is important in this place to refer, however slightly   The entire scheme of the Christian atonement belongs to this office of the Messiah   Not as the Teacher, nor as the Ruler, does He save the world   save as teaching the principles of His sacrificial work, and administering the blessings it has purchased.   It will hereafter be seen how much the doctrine of the Atonement is bound up with the Divine government of a Lawgiver Who administers His law in a new court, the Court Mediatorial.   There He exacts and receives what theological language terms satisfaction   But it must always be remembered that the Temple is the true sphere of atoning sacrifice.   The

evangelical Hall of judgment is no other than a Court of the Temple   And it is something more than a mystical fancy which regards the Veil as separating between the outer sanctuary where the oblation that satisfies justice is offered, and the Holiest where it is presented for Divine acceptance.   Our Lord's Atonement is the Sacrificial Obedience or the Obedient Sacrifice which hath put away sin   the Obedience was rendered in the outer court where blood reigns unto death, the Sacrifice was offered on the inner shrine where mercy reigns unto life   In Christ all these things are one   And this unity is the main object of the Evangelical discussion of the Epistle to the Hebrews   On all other matters, even of an economy that was Divine, it is very brief and never solicitous to expatiate   *of which we cannot now speak particularly.*   Heb ix 5.

THE REGAL OFFICE.

Kingly Office.

The Kingly authority of Christ is grounded on His sacrificial death: as its high reward; as the medium of carrying out its ends; and in its highest exercise the bestowment of the blessings purchased by His Atonement.   This mediatorial dignity was arrogated by Himself on earth by anticipation and in virtue of the Divinity of His Person.   After the resurrection He formally assumed it on the Mountain in Galilee, He then ascended to His throne in heaven for its exercise, and thence sends forth His Apostles to declare and enforce His royal prerogatives.   The Kingdom of Christ is exhibited in their writings as the kingdom of grace   administered in the world by His Providence, in the Church, and in the hearts of believers.   As such it will terminate with the final judgment; but as the kingdom of glory, already begun, and to be consummated at the great day, it will be everlasting.

I   Understanding by the title King the Redeemer's mediatorial government generally, we may say that it occupies the foremost place in the Old-Testament prediction, and was accordingly assumed by our Lord as His own from the beginning   The   Predicted.

Old
Testa-
ment.

Gen iii.15,
xxii 17,
xlix 10.

2 Sam.vii.
18.

Pss ii.
xlv,
lxxii,
cx.

Luke
xxiv 26

1 Pet i
11

Isa liii,
liii.

earliest and most glorious prophecies which went before on the Deliverer proclaimed His supreme authority. Such were the Protevangelium; the promise to Abraham; the blessing of Jacob, and the predictions to David The Psalms open with the kingly supremacy of the Christ, and make this their ever recurring key-note. The Prophets set out with this theme it begins prophecy proper in Isaiah and, as has been seen, runs through the whole series of the Messianic prophets, who invariably connect the announcement of the Saviour's SUFFERINGS with THE GLORY THAT SHOULD FOLLOW The teachers in Judaism, after the Captivity, introduced a different view. They took the sufferings of the Servant of Jehovah to themselves and their own nation, and a carnal view of the reign of their Christ predominated · their favourite name for Him was KING MESSIAH. The Jews of Egypt differed from those of Palestine in not localising the scene of the Messiah's government in Jerusalem, and generally in understanding His kingdom to be moral and spiritual.

Our Lord
Himself

II Our Lord opened His mission by proclaiming, not His own kingdom, but the kingdom of heaven and of God On the nature of that spiritual government He discoursed largely; but it was not until the close of His ministry that He represented Himself as the Supreme Ruler in it His authority till then was that of the Teacher only · as exercised upon the Mount of Beatitudes, and vindicated for Him on the Mount of Transfiguration. His mediatorial kingdom as such was to be specially based upon His atoning death as the Divine-human Representative of Mankind. The relation between His regal government and His expiatory humiliation was declared by Himself on the eve of His passion, and is much dwelt upon by His Apostles. It is placed before us under two aspects.

Founda-
tion
of His
Kingdom.

Judicial
Right.
2 Cor. iv
4

John xii.
31, 32.

1. By undergoing a substitutionary death for mankind the Redeemer obtained both a judicial and a moral right to the human race. (1) He redeemed it from the bondage of sin and the doom of death. But in His own language and in His servants' Satan represents that bondage as the *god of this world* Approaching His cross our Lord said *Now is the judgment of this world, now shall the Prince of this world be cast out. And I, if I be lifted up from the earth, will draw all men unto Me.* The alien power was

cast out in the court of judgment, and it was decided that the world belonged to Him Who *died and revived, that He might be Lord both of the dead and of the living* But this was only the vindication of an authority which had been virtually His from the beginning; since He had been the King uncrowned, because *the Lamb slain, from the foundation of the world* (2.) His moral right is that which the infinite benefit of His passion confers, and it is this which draws men to His feet It is the gracious and effectual sway of the atoning sacrifice on all who accept its propitiation : *ye are bought with a price.* Rom xiv 8, 9

Rev xiii. 8. Moral Right

1 Cor vi. 20

2 The self-renunciation of Jesus receives universal government as its reward He obtained as a gift the dominion over mankind *Glorify Thy Son, that Thy Son also may glorify Thee · as Thou hast given Him power over all flesh, that He should give eternal life to as many as Thou hast given Him* But He also received the mediatorial government of the universe. *Wherefore God also hath highly exalted Him, and given Him a name which is above every name.* Whether or not the virtue of His passion extended to other worlds, certainly its reward and honour extends to them. Reward

John xvii. 1, 2.

Phil ii. 9.

III. After His resurrection He formally assumed His regal sway. Assumption.

1. It was on the Mountain of Galilee, to which He summoned His Apostles and disciples, and virtually the whole company of believers, that He for the first time announced His absolute authority in human affairs. Above He had said, *All Mine are Thine, and Thine are Mine,* with a wider and deeper meaning, but now He declares, *All power is given unto Me in heaven and in earth* all power in heaven AND earth, in heaven FOR earth. Having already proclaimed His rule below as *Lord of the dead,* and having declared it in the midst of His brethren on earth, He then ascended up to exercise it for ever. John xvii. 10

Matt xxviii. 18

Rom. xiv. 9.

2. Hence it is obvious that the regal office of Christ must not include His government of the universe as the eternal Son. And further we are prepared for the doctrine of St Paul, that the jurisdiction obtained by the Mediator will, after all its designs are subserved in the salvation of the saints and the subjection of His enemies, be surrendered to the Father, and mediatorial authority shall cease It began after the Cross, and will therefore end when the redeeming design is fulfilled. Divine-Human only

Kingly
Function.

IV The formal analysis of the Redeemer's regal office, set forth in the Acts as exercised on earth, in the Apocalypse as exercised in heaven, and in the Epistles theologically described, can only be summarised here. Almost every topic finds its more appropriate place hereafter in the Administration of Redemption.

In the
Church

1 The kingdom of Christ is the Christian Church or the kingdom of grace. As such its treatment must be reserved for a later stage. Meanwhile, some points of importance require brief notice

Spiritual
Passim

(1.) This kingdom is in its widest meaning the re-establishment of the Divine authority over man It is *the kingdom of heaven*, because its Ruler is ascended into heaven, and there sits upon the throne of saving authority; because its object is to restore the principles of heavenly obedience upon earth, according to our

Matt vi.
10

first great prayer · *Thy kingdom come. Thy will be done on earth, as it is done in heaven ,* and because it will be consummated when earth becomes heaven and heaven earth to mankind It is *the kingdom*

Passim.
Rev xi
15

of God, because the Incarnate Ruler is Himself Divine , and it is thus also distinguished from *the kingdoms of this world* which are ordained of God to be the types and reflections of His supreme rule Hence the Church, as the kingdom of Christ, is essentially a spiritual authority over spiritual subjects. Whatever relation it may sustain to the transitory governments of time, it is entirely independent of them And, whatever externality it may assume for a season, its profound and abiding character is the internal and spiritual reconstruction of the THEOCRACY in which God, now the God-man, rules over a saved mankind. (2) It has indeed an outward organisation laws and administration of law, rulers and submission to rulers, terms of admission and penalties of excommunication. But all these are connected rather with the Visible Church, or visible Churches, than with the Kingdom of Christ, which is the glorious restoration of Divine authority over man · one, spiritual, ever enlarging and tending to its consummation in heaven. The KINGDOM has a meaning which the CHURCH has not.

Within
the
Heart

2 This will be further apparent if we consider how habitually the kingdom of our Lord is declared to be set up within the individual heart It is the interior life of religion, and coincides with the imparted blessings of personal salvation under the New Covenant, and the ethical relations which result from them. There

is no view of personal religion more comprehensive than that which makes it the absolute sway of One Ruler within the heart.

3. It is the jurisdiction over the world for the sake of the Christian Church. The New Testament abounds with testimonies, which find their highest expression in St Paul's words, concerning the mighty power which *hath put all things under His feet, and gave Him to be the Head over all things to the church, which is His body, the fulness of Him that filleth all in all* The providential government of human affairs is in the hands of Christ for the sake of the Body of a new mankind which He is gathering and sanctifying to Himself (1) Hence the kingly office of the LORD OF ALL is exercised in the protection of His people; He is the *Captain of their salvation*. *He hath on His vesture and on His thigh a name written* KING OF KINGS, AND LORD OF LORDS (2.) It is the Headship of a conquering Gospel which must in some sense win the world, subjugate and suppress Satanic powers, and rescue mankind as such. When our Lord first announced His authority He added · *Go ye therefore, and teach all nations, baptizing them in the name of the Father, and of the Son, and of the Holy Ghost, teaching them to observe all things whatsoever I have commanded you, and, lo, I am with you alway even unto the end of the world* He whose Name is ABOVE EVERY NAME here pays fealty to the Holy Trinity whose Representative He is But the final accomplishment of the designs of Heaven is bound up with obedience to Himself For that He waits on His throne. With this Lo we may connect another in the Old Testament. *Lo, My Servant, Whom I uphold! He shall not fail nor be discouraged, till He have set judgment in the earth.*

4. The last function of mediatorial sway will be the final judgment; when the High Priest shall no longer intercede for the world, nor the Prophet teach mankind, but the *Son of Man*, who is also *the King*, shall *sit upon the throne of His glory, and before Him shall be gathered all nations*. gathered for the first and last time that He may *separate them* again to be united no more

5 While the Mediatorial King will lay down His authority, the same King, as Head of the Church, shall reign for ever. *And of His kingdom*—as the indwelling of the supreme glory of the Godhead in mankind—*there shall be no end.* But these are subjects that belong to Eschatology.

Provi-
dence

Eph i 22,
23

Acts x.
36.
Heb.ii.10

Rev. xix.
16

Matt
xxviii.
19

Phil. ii 9.

Isa xlii.1.

Judgment

Matt xxv.
31, 32

Luke i. 33.

Names of
Redeemer

THE NAMES OF THE REDEEMER

Almost all the elements of Christian doctrine may be connected with the appellations which the Scripture gives to our Lord, as they are supplemented in some cases by theological nomenclature. What the names of God are in Theology proper, the names of Christ are in Christology. They define all we know of His pretemporal being, of His general Mediatorial relations, whether as the humbled or as the exalted Christ, of His specific Messianic offices, and of His relations to the Church in administered salvation. They have passed in review already, but may with considerable advantage be classified.

Pretem-
poral.

I. The names of the supra-human, supra-creaturely pretemporal Being who became man are twofold those which belong to Him absolutely as Divine, and those which belong to Him as the Second Person in the Deity

God.
Rom ix
5
1 Cor ii 8.
Rev 1
8—11.

1 He is GOD absolutely, or the GREAT GOD, GOD BLESSED FOR EVER He is JEHOVAH or LORD , the LORD OF GLORY , the FIRST AND THE LAST ; the ALMIGHTY, as the term representing both the Shaddai and the Adonai of the Old Testament, both the interior self-sufficiency and the external omnipotence of the Divine Being

The
Second
Person.
John i. 18.
Heb 1 2
Col. 1 15.
Rev iii.
14

2. As the Second Person in the Godhead He is the SON, the SON OF GOD, GOD ONLY-BEGOTTEN, WISDOM, the ANGEL OF JEHOVAH, the WORD OF LIFE, the WORD OF GOD, the WORD, the IMAGE OF GOD, the BRIGHTNESS OF HIS GLORY, the FIRSTBORN before every creature , the BEGINNING or Author OF THE CREATION OF GOD, of His own creation as God   With reference to most of these names it may be said that, while they are based upon the original dignity of the Son, they are given to Him in His incarnate relations ; not one of them but has some indirect reference to the Divine-human estate.

The
Person
Incarnate.

II. The names that expressly formulate the union of the two natures in the One Person of Christ are in the Scriptures few.

1. Obviously IMMANUEL, *God with us*, takes the lead a name once used symbolically and typically in the Old Testament; in the New so applied as to become personal, yet never adopted after its first proclamation. It is the first in the Gospels, and will in reality be the last, surviving as the expression of an eternal truth when most others have become historical. Some descriptions of the one Incarnate Person found in the prophets have not been transmitted to the New Testament   Such is the term THE BRANCH   This belongs to our Lord's human nature : *And there shall come forth a rod out of the stem of Jesse, and a Branch shall grow out of his roots*, but also to His Divine . *In that day shall the Branch of the Lord be beautiful and glorious, and the fruit of the earth shall be excellent and comely*, where the human is the fruit of the earth and the Divine the Branch of the Lord.   THE SON is one of those Divine names of the eternal Second Person which connect Him with the temporal Manifestation : so in the baptismal formula, where it is difficult to detach the word from its connection with the Incarnate.   With special reference to His Person as including the Manhood the name SON OF GOD is also sometimes used

2 One designation stands out with peculiar prominence, as derived from the Redeemer's relation to mankind : THE SON OF MAN. Once occurring in Daniel, it was adopted habitually by our Lord; under peculiar circumstances it was used by St Stephen, and then is heard no more. It suggests that instance of the term MAN where He is called MEDIATOR, the solitary example which permits us to employ the word as describing the Person of our Lord . ἄνθρωπος Χριστὸς Ἰησοῦς, Christ Jesus, not a man or the man, but MAN.

3 None of the phrases used in Scripture has been retained in the language of theology to express the union of the two natures in the Person of Christ. The source of the word GOD-MAN is lost in obscurity · Origen's claim to it is doubtful. In theological language such terms are used as THE INCARNATE, the DIVINE-HUMAN PERSON, the THEANTHROPIC PERSON.

III The designations of the Son of God in His official aspect towards the universe and to mankind are of course the most numerous and the most important   They are based on a variety of principles, and require arrangement.

Margin notes: Immanuel Isa vii 14 Matt i 1. Isa xi 1. Isa iv 2. Matt. xxviii. 19. John ix 35. The Son of Man. Passim. 1 Tim. ii. 5. God-Man. Official Names

Αρχηγός or Prince.

1 First, those names of our Lord's Divine and eternal nature which connect Him with the creation generally must be distinguished; especially as they form a transition to His redeeming relations   Going back to the pretemporal titles, we find that the Eternal Word is the PRINCE OF LIFE.   As the Author of all life, He is THE LIFE absolutely.   Thence He is OUR LIFE , the PRINCE or Captain OF SALVATION, the PRINCE or Author OF THE FAITH, 'Αρχηγός in these passages meaning nothing less than that He is the eternal Source and Beginning of that life which is to us salvation, and is obtained in faith . whence, combining them all, He is a PRINCE AND A SAVIOUR   Though these titles bring the Lord within the redeeming economy, they have their ground in an eternal relation of the Son in the Trinity as the Originator of all creaturely existence.

Acts iii 15. Heb ii 10 Heb xii. 2.

Acts v 31.

Prophetic

2 There are some which belong to the times of prophetic preparation, and are not continued in the New Testament   such are the ANGEL OF JEHOVAH, the MESSENGER of the Covenant, and the SERVANT OF THE LORD.   These three should be marked in their unity and gradation : the last of them reappears in the New Testament when Christ is called a MINISTER, and in the words of St Peter, who speaks of God having raised up in our nature for His Messianic work His SON Jesus, where παῖς is used as in some sense intermediate between Son and servant.   Reference may be made to the names, or the cluster of names, given to the coming Redeemer in Isaiah : *And His Name shall be called* WONDERFUL, COUNSELLOR, THE MIGHTY GOD, THE EVERLASTING FATHER, THE PRINCE OF PEACE   In earlier times He was foreannounced as SHILOH, PEACE, which suggests the PRINCE OF PEACE, and *He is our* PEACE : there is no word more intimately and sacredly bound up with the Lord and His work.   And earliest of all we find Him designated the SEED : of the Woman, of Abraham, and of David.

Mal. iii 1. Isa. xlii —xliii. Rom. xv. 8.

Acts iii 26

Isa ix 6.

Gen xlix. 10. Eph. ii 14.

Gen. iii. 15.

3 The names which denote the relation of the Incarnate Son to His work generally occupy the central place in this classification.

Official Names.

(1.) Some of them define His office in its widest range and in its universal issues   The largest and broadest of these is JESUS, from the Hebrew Jehoshua or Joshua, Help of the Lord, or Lord-Saviour   the NAME OF JESUS has a supreme meaning in the New Testament.   He is the PRINCE OF SALVATION, THE SAVIOUR . of

Phil ii. 10 Heb ii.13.

all men from the penalty of original sin ; and, of those who believe, from all evil from its guilt and from its indwelling, that is from sin and from sinfulness He is the SALVATION of His people : *Say ye to the daughter of Zion, Behold, thy Salvation cometh, behold, His reward is with Him, and His work before Him* He is the Hebrew MESSIAH, and the universal CHRIST, as the Anointed Agent of the Divine will, and the source of the anointing of His people by the Spirit. In both Testaments He is the HOLY ONE, as THE LORD'S ANOINTED. In the execution of all His offices combined He is our REDEEMER from the penalty and power of sin, and from Satan its representative, and the world its sphere ; but this name is not generally given to Him in Scripture, though constantly applied to His work. When our Lord, approaching His passion, said, *The Son of Man came not to be ministered unto, but to minister, and to give His life a ransom for many,* He all but called Himself THE MINISTER OF REDEMPTION, which is the New-Testament form of the Old-Testament SERVANT of God. In His whole manifestation He is the LIGHT of the Gentiles, the GLORY of Israel, the DESIRE of the nations, and the SALVATION of the ends of the earth.

(2) Besides these appellatives, which have become, as it were, proper names, we find almost every aspect of the benefit of His work providing a title for Him. He is not called the Justifier · *it is God that justifieth ;* but as both the ground and the administrator of that justification He is THE LORD OUR RIGHTEOUSNESS , and He is Jesus Christ THE RIGHTEOUS. In the temple where holiness reigns He is Himself emphatically THE SANCTIFIER, and THE HOLY ONE, sharing these titles with the Father and the Spirit. Between our justification in the court, and our sanctification in the temple, comes in our new life in the house of God; and Christ as the Only-begotten is THE PRINCE OF LIFE, of that life which springs from union with Himself. As to the covenant ratified in His blood, He is THE MEDIATOR as its ground in His Person and work ; the SURETY, as the living Pledge in heaven, both for God and man, of the observance of its conditions and the bestowment of its blessings ; the TESTATOR, as appointing to His household those blessings by His will on death Looking at the ultimate accomplishment of all its designs Hs is THE

Side references:
Isa. lxii. 11.
1 John ii. 20.
Isa. lix. 20.
Matt xx 28.
Isa xli. 6
Isa. xvii. 3.
Haggai ii. 7.
Ps. xcviii. 3
Rom. viii. 33.
Jer. xxiii. 6
1 John ii. 1.
Heb ii 10.
Acts iii. 14.
Acts iii 15.
Heb ix 13.
Heb. vii. 22.
Heb ix 16.
Heb. xii. 2
John xiv

FINISHER of the Faith, and THE LIFE of believers · the life under its two aspects gives Him two names He is THE RESURRECTION from universal death, and He is ETERNAL LIFE in its everlasting issues.

John xi. 25.
1 John i. 2.

His Specific Offices.

IV The specific offices of the Redeemer yield Him a variety of titles, each of which describes one aspect of His work, and is inappropriate as applied to the Person of Christ generally Of course those only are referred to which are limited to each office, and for the most part such as are found in Scripture or in the exact reproductions of Scriptural language. Some of them are too limited for common application.

Prophet

1. The Lord as the Revealer of the Divine will is pre-eminently the PROPHET. This was one of the earliest prophetical designations, but, when once shown that in Him the fulfilment had come, the term is no longer applied it is left to His servants the prophets, whether of the Old or of the New Testament. For the same reason those titles have been disused which were given to our Lord with special reference to His Israelitish mission such as RABBI, MASTER, TEACHER, MINISTER OF THE CIRCUMCISION. Once, and once only, is He the APOSTLE, that is, the antitype of Moses, as He is the HIGH-PRIEST and antitype of Aaron the only place in which our Lord is directly connected with these two persons as united. It might have been expected that here He would have been termed the Prophet, but the mission of Moses is referred to as the type of that more than a prophet, Who said, *As My Father hath sent Me, even so send I you.* It is with reference to His prophetic office that He is THE WISDOM OF GOD, THE LIGHT OF THE WORLD, THE TRUTH . from God, to enlighten men, and perfect human knowledge. There is an emphasis on His being the TRUE LIGHT that enlighteneth every man, as also on His being the Truth, both as its substance and its Teacher.

Heb. iii. 1.

John xx. 21.

Priest.

2. As the atoning Representative of mankind, that is, in His sacerdotal office, Jesus has many titles, both descriptive and personal He is the HIGH-PRIEST: first, as the Antitype of Aaron, and, secondly, as the Head of a fellowship of priests, *the High-priest of our profession.* But as He is now the only Offerer for sacrifice, the offerings of His people being presented by Him, He is the PRIEST absolutely: the great Sacrificer and Intercessor for

Heb iii. 1

man   Thus the former sanctions the universal priesthood of Christians, while the latter abrogates every special ministerial priesthood   From His sacrificial work He derives many appellatives which have become almost personal names. He is the living PROPITIATORY or Mercy-seat, or atoning Sacrifice.   He is the Victim of His own oblation, the unity of all victims, though only one gives Him a designation : THE LAMB.   The pre-eminence of this is that it continues to be the name of Jesus in all His offices in heaven ; describing the Incarnate in the Triune glory receiving the homage of the universe *in the midst of the throne*, as the King, taking the Book as the Prophet, and still *as it had been slain*.   Thus the BAPTIST'S LAMB OF GOD, which does not directly reappear in the New-Testament phraseology, is given back from heaven to earth, and has never ceased to be familiar in Christian devotion.   When the Christian Prophet writes as an Apostle he terms the Intercessor in heaven an ADVOCATE or PARACLETE for His people . the Word being as much an appellative of Jesus Christ as it is of the Holy Ghost, the Comforter.   St. John rises above all former precedent in calling that PLEADER in heaven the living PROPITIATION.

3. In His regal office our Saviour is LORD of all, His highest name , KING OF KINGS AND LORD OF LORDS   all power is of God , all lower dignities are given to the supreme Authority, and hence His *many crowns*. KING absolutely Jesus is not named, save indirectly in one of His own parables ; but He is the KING'S SON. PRINCE He is of peace and of life , but the term PRINCE OF LIFE does not refer to authority so much as to priority and origination . He is the 'Αρχηγὸς τῆς ζωῆς   St. Peter calls Him a PRINCE *and a Saviour.* And He is the CAPTAIN of salvation. As Lord He is also the JUDGE; but as He Himself said, *I came not to judge the world, but to save the world,* so He does not assume this title. Though the Father *hath committed all judgment unto the Son,* yet that Son scarcely bears the name   God is the *Judge of all*

V. It is profitable to mark also the permutations and combinations of the titles that are bestowed on the Redeemer, or by which He is invoked. The most obvious is JESUS CHRIST   this does not mean only, as is sometimes said, the personal and the official name , both are official names. The variation . in the

s 2.

Eph v 2
Rom iii. 25.
Passim

Rev. v 6.

John i 29.

1 John ii. 1, 2.

King.

1 Tim. vi. 15
Rev. xix. 12

Acts v. 31.
John xii 47.
John v 22.
Heb xii. 23.

Combinations.

Passim.

order is arbitrary. Both Jesus and Christ are found as proper
names, and without the article. But when the term Lord is connected with them there is generally some reason in the context.
Especially is this the case when the full assemblage of His august
titles is given Him : mark the predominance of OUR LORD JESUS
CHRIST in the first Epistles referring to His coming ; when He is
also called THE LORD absolutely.   Once we read of *the fellowship
of His* SON JESUS CHRIST OUR LORD   GOD OUR SAVIOUR and
THE GREAT GOD AND OUR SAVIOUR JESUS CHRIST occur only in
the Pastoral Epistle to Titus. St Jude calls Him THE ONLY
WISE GOD OUR SAVIOUR. St Peter, THE SHEPHERD AND
BISHOP of our souls ; and he gives the most enlarged formula .
OUR LORD AND SAVIOUR JESUS CHRIST.   But the Lord Himself
most magnifies His own name : *I am* ALPHA AND OMEGA, the
BEGINNING AND THE ENDING, *saith the Lord, which* IS *and which*
WAS, *and which is* TO COME, the ALMIGHTY   And again · *These
things saith* HE THAT IS HOLY, HE THAT IS TRUE, HE THAT HATH
THE KEY OF DAVID.   And again, *These things saith* THE AMEN,
THE FAITHFUL *and* TRUE WITNESS, the BEGINNING OF THE
CREATION OF GOD   One of the Elders called Him THE LION
OF THE TRIBE OF JUDA, THE ROOT OF DAVID.   Once more it is
said of Him that *He hath on His vesture and on His thigh a name
written,* KING OF KINGS, AND LORD OF LORDS.   His last testimony to Himself is : *I am the* ROOT AND THE OFFSPRING OF
DAVID, *and the* BRIGHT AND MORNING STAR   The final words of
the Bible invoke *the grace of* OUR LORD JESUS CHRIST.   But
a NEW NAME has yet to be revealed.

VI There is another class of appellatives which refer to our
Lord's relations to His people.   These are metaphors, or symbols,
or abstract terms expressing qualities personified in Him : not
precisely names, they are yet more than mere adjectival descriptions, and are used in the Christian Church very much to the
advantage of its practical and devotional literature.   They com-
prise also figures derived from almost every region of the mental,
and the moral, and the physical worlds.   As our Lord has many
crowns, so has He many names · He is clothed with more titles
and epithets, attributes and properties, than any other object in
the universe.   Omitting all those which are His because they are

1 Thess
ii 19 ;
v.27,28.
1 Cor. i 9.
Tit. ii. 10,
13.
Jude 25.
1 Peter ii.
25.
Rev. i. 8.
2 Peter i.
11.
Rev iii 7.
Rev. iii.
14.
Rev. v. 5.
Rev. xix.
16
Rev. xxii.
16.
Rev. ii
17.

God's, we find in Scripture an endless abundance applied to the Redeemer distinctively. The largest number of these indicate His relations to His Church : though rather as defining that relation than as giving Him appellatives He is the ROCK or FOUNDATION on which the Church is built : that is, the underlying primitive foundation on which the foundation of Apostles and Prophets rests · what devotion has termed THE ROCK OF AGES.   Hence He is the CHIEF CORNER STONE. Leaving this metaphor, He is to His Church the GOOD SHEPHERD, the Vine, its HEAD as it is a corporate body. and for its sake the Head of the universe also.   Again, He is THE WAY in which alone all men have access to God, to life, and to heaven.   He is the FRIEND OF SINNERS ; the BRIDEGROOM of His Church , and, by implication, the BROTHER of His disciples.   Generally, it may be said that every blessing of which He is the source or medium gives Him a name   He is the FOUNTAIN opened, the WATER and the BREAD of life, and the PHYSICIAN of souls. He is the DOOR of access to God, and life and heaven   He is to His people ALL AND IN ALL : Πάντα καὶ ἐν πᾶσιν Χριστός It is deeply interesting to trace how variously these Scriptural figures have been enshrined in the devotional ideas of antiquity, and sanctified by art to the memorial of our Lord. For instance, the ancient Church has transmitted the sacred name under the letters IHS, Jesus Hominum Salvator, Jesus the Saviour of men The word ἰχθύς, fish, was also in familiar use being composed of the capital letters of 'Ιησοῦς Χριστός, θεοῦ υἱος, σωτήρ. Sometimes the letters INRI stood for Jesus Nazarenus, Rex Judæorum. But all this takes us beyond or below our Biblical theology.

1 Peter ii. 6.

Eph i 22. Col ii. 19 Luke vii. 34. Matt xxv 6. John xx. 17. John x. 7. Zech xiv. 1. Col.iii 11.

Christian Art.

VII. The practical use of the study of these names is obvious.

1. It is the Divine method of teaching us the doctrines of the economy of redemption ; he who understands the derivation, uses, and bearings of the rich cluster of terms, in their Hebrew and Greek symbols especially, which are arranged in this sketch, will have no mean knowledge of this branch of theology and of theology in general.   For this study will also tend to give precision to the language of the theologian, especially the preacher. who will observe with what exquisite propriety every epithet is used by Evangelists and Apostles in relation to the Person and work and relations of the Redeemer. There can be no better

Practical

Theological.

theological exercise than the study of Evangelical doctrine as based upon the titles of Jesus.

Reverence 2. No study more surely tends to exalt our Lord. We cannot range in thought over the boundless names given by inspiration to our adorable Master without feeling that there is no place worthy of Him below the highest, that He cannot be less than God to our faith and reverence, and devotion and love. *He is precious* beyond human estimation : ἡ τιμή, He is all that preciousness means to those who believe ; no words can describe the greatness of His Person and the dignity it confers on all that is His. Whatsoever toucheth Him is holy.

1 Peter ii. 7.

Caution. 3. The subject suggests also the importance of great caution in the use of the terms that have been adopted by uninspired theology to supplement the Scripture. Most of these have been alluded to above It will be observed that while some of them are very valuable, indeed indispensable, in dogmatic theology, none have lodged in the common language of Christendom but those which the New Testament gives

4 Lastly, the spirit of reverence must lead us to conform our thoughts and our words concerning Him, whether in devotion or preaching or meditation, to the example of the Scriptures Those whom He called His *friends,* and would not call His *servants,* those whom He, after the resurrection, termed *My brethren,* made it their practice to abstain from reciprocating these names Jesus is never their Friend nor their Brother , nor is there one epithet of endearment applied to Him in all their writings. The Father alone calls Him Beloved *Behold, Mine Elect, in Whom My soul delighteth '* in the Old-Testament prophecy, given back again and again with increase in the New-Testament fulfilment *This is My beloved Son.* With regard to the Father alone is Christ said to be dear · *His dear Son,* though even then it is only *the Son of His love* As to the Apostles, and all their followers, they are His servants, or δοῦλοι, He is their LORD JESUS CHRIST. We must be guided by their example It is our most blessed self-denial to suppress the overflowings of human affection towards Him in Whom we *rejoice with joy unspeakable and full of glory.* In every thought of Him, and word concerning Him, the Divinity in the Incarnate Person must ever be pre-eminent and govern all.

John xv 15

John xx. 17.

Isa xlii. 1.

Matt.xvii. 5.

Col i 13

Passim

1 Peter i. 8.

THE FINISHED WORK.

This comprehensive historical view of the Saviour's manifestation leads finally to what is its one result as it respects the salvation of mankind. This is sometimes called Atonement, sometimes Redemption : the former term derived from the efficient virtue, the latter from the effect, of the Saviour's intervention. The teaching of Scripture on this subject may be summed as follows : The Finished Work, as accomplished by the Mediator Himself, in His relation to mankind, is His Divine-human obedience regarded as an expiatory sacrifice : the Atonement proper. Then it may be studied in its results as to God, as to God and man, and as to man. First, it is the supreme manifestation of the glory and consistency of the Divine attributes, and, as such, is termed the Righteousness of God. Secondly, as it respects God and man, it is the Reconciliation, a word which involves two truths, or rather one truth under two aspects : the propitiation of the Divine displeasure against the world is declared ; and therefore the sin of the world is no longer a bar to acceptance. Thirdly, in its influence on man, it may be viewed as Redemption : universal as to the race, limited in its process and consummation to those who believe.

These general propositions express the revelations of Scripture mainly in its own terms. Their modifications in historical theology will be considered afterwards and in strict subordination. The term FINISHED ATONEMENT must be understood to be used here with a threefold design First, it is intended to mark the compendious result or summary of the work of Christ in all His offices, and in its final expression : almost every element of the doctrine of the Atonement has been introduced in the previous section, which traced the historical manifestation of the Redeeming Mediator ; but here the issue of all is set forth in its finished statement. Secondly, it gives emphasis to the fact that the work of Christ is here viewed objectively, as the atonement for mankind ; it is the accomplished redemption as apart from the application of it; it is the basis and foundation of all that follows in the economy of the Holy Ghost. Thirdly, this meaning is to be kept distinct from that which refers the finished work of Christ to the secured salvation of the Elect, laying the stress on its being finished FOR THEM once for all and for ever. It is perfect in the design of God and in the work of His Son , but its application to individual sinners is perpetually beginning afresh.

THE VICARIOUS OBLATION

Our Saviour's sacrifice on the cross finished a perfect obedience which He offered in His Divine-human Person. This was His own obedience, and therefore of infinite value or worthiness ; but it was vicarious, and its benefit belongs absolutely to our race, and, on certain conditions, to every member of it. As availing for man, by the appointment of God, it is no less than the satisfaction, provided by Divine love, of the claims of Divine justice upon transgression · which may be viewed, on the one hand, as an expiation of the punishment due to the guilt of human sin ; and, on the other, as a propitiation of the Divine displeasure, which is thus shown to be consistent with infinite goodwill to the sinners of mankind. But the expiation of guilt and the propitiation of wrath are one and the same effect of the Atonement. Both suppose the existence of sin and the wrath of God against it. But, in the mystery of the Atonement, the provision of eternal mercy, as it were, anticipates the transgression, and love always in every representation of it has the pre-eminence. The passion is the exhibition rather than the cause of the Divine love to man.

THE ATONEMENT.

Viewed as His own, the expiatory work of Christ was a perfect spontaneous Obedience and a perfect spontaneous Sacrifice to the Will of the Father imposed upon Him. The two terms may be regarded in their difference and in their unity as constituting the act and virtue of the Atonement. Its worthiness, or what is sometimes called its merit, connects it with the human race, and depends on two other truths; it was not due for Himself, but was an act of infinite charity for man; and that act was Divine, both in its value and in its efficiency. The offering of the Redeemer had infinite efficacy for the human race.

The Atonement Proper

The atonement was our Lord's OBEDIENCE unto death; and it was the SACRIFICE of His life in perfect obedience. There is one passage in the Epistle to the Hebrews which perfectly unites these two representations: *Lo, I come to do Thy will, O God!* These words, twice uttered, present the Saviour's whole work as one great act of obedience. But they are preceded and followed by a reference to sacrifice. First, to the sacrifices *offered by the law*, which are displaced : *sacrifice and offering Thou wouldest not, but a body hast Thou prepared Me*, then' to His own perfect oblation · *by the which will we are sanctified through the offering of the body of Jesus Christ once for all.* The obedience to the will of God is the sacrifice of the body prepared for our atoning Mediator.

The Act.

Heb x. 5—10.

1 Either of these words taken alone expresses the quality and character of the atoning act. (1) It was a great OBEDIENCE, in the perfect submission of His will to the will of the Father, which required the surrender of His life as the penalty of office : all was summed up in that one word. He undertook the service of man's redemption as laid upon Him, and He accomplished it through all its requirements down to the suffering of the penalty of Divine displeasure against sin · He *became obedient unto death, even the death of the cross.* *As by one man's disobedience many were made sinners, so by the Obedience of One shall many be made righteous.* Here the whole work' of atonement is one obedience which

Obedience or Sacrifice.

Phil. ii. 8.

Rom. v. 19.

counterbalances the act of man's disobedience. (2) But it was also a passive endurance of a lot imposed upon Him from the moment of His assumption of our nature, and this is expressed by the word SACRIFICE It is true that our Representative offered the sacrifice freely of His own will, but the whole series and detail of His humiliations, sorrows, and derelictions came upon Him as it were from without from the mysterious pressure of sin without guilt, from the enmity of the world and of Satan, from the visitation of the Father. His entire incarnate existence on earth was a meek endurance · *Ought not Christ to have suffered* Lukexxiv. *these things? Thus it is written !*
26, 46.
2. Their difference, however, must also be marked; though Obedience now only in relation to our Lord Himself. (1) The Obedience
and regards the whole work of Christ as an active fulfilment of
Sacrifice. righteousness, passing through all stages to its consummation in death As the appointed Representative of mankind He had an atoning work to do, which included, and also infinitely exceeded, the ordinary duty of human nature *Yet He learned obedience by* Heb. v 8. *the things which He suffered* We never read of any obedience of the God man which was not submission and endurance He entered on His career of duty by this gate. The moral law was to Him as law written afresh and in one character, as the expansion of one only duty. It is not said that His obedience was made perfect by suffering; but that He Himself was as a Sufferer *made perfect* Heb. ii. *through sufferings* His supreme submission to that law was His
10. finished obedience, and that consummate self-surrender tested and approved in extreme temptation was the active side of His atonement . the negativing sin itself in His own Person, representing mankind. (2.) But the very same deeds and sorrows which undid or cancelled the sin of humanity were a suffering endurance of the penalty of sin; and this was the passive side of His atonement · the tribute of expiatory satisfaction to the justice of the Lawgiver. The mystery and perfection of our Saviour's Atoning Act was this, that, as vicarious, it at one and the same moment made both the sin and the penalty as though they were not. Viewed in one light He represents man as cancelling his sin by a new obedience; viewed in another He represents man as discharging the debt of penalty

3. It will perhaps throw some light both upon the unity
and upon the difference of these two terms if we refer them
to the Mediatorial Court and the Mediatorial Temple respectively Viewed as a tribute to Righteousness the Ministry
of our Lord is simply and solely a great Obedience, active
AND passive, and nothing more Law demands both obedience and the penalty of disobedience : not both at once
from man and in human courts; but from the Representative
of man and in the court Divine both are required, and both
in His life and death are offered Viewed as a tribute to
the Holiness of the Divine nature the Ministry of our Lord
is a sacrifice which God accepts as offered for the human
race Transferred into the Holiest the satisfaction of Divine
justice becomes a satisfaction of Divine love. And here the same
most wonderful combination of two ideas comes in As an
expiatory sacrifice to the holiness of God the soul of the sinner
could not be at once offered in death and accepted as living ,
could not be at once a sin offering doomed to destruction and a
burnt offering well pleasing to God But in man's Representative
at the holy altar these most gloriously meet. He presented a sacrifice which was the veritable endurance of the consequence of
transgression *He died unto sin once.* But that death was also
the LIVING SACRIFICE of our human nature, given back to God
in its perfection again. As in the court of law perfect obedience
is rendered by discharge of a duty which was also the suffering
of the penalty of disobedience, so in the temple of holiness an
expiation of guilt by death is itself the display of propitiation
towards the living offender. These seem to be paradoxes , but
they express the very secret and mystery of the Atonement It
cannot, however, be too deeply impressed that these two are only
aspects of one atonement. As an obedience of salvation it
becomes ours in justification ; as a sacrifice of self-surrender, it
becomes ours in sanctification

Unity and Difference

Rom. vi. 10.
Rom xii. 1.

ITS VIRTUE OR MERIT

The term ATONEMENT, by which the sacred writers express
the idea of Reconciliation as the effect of Christ's work, is in
modern theology used to express the virtue of the redeeming

Merit.

The
Virtue

passion as resting upon the merit of Him who suffered it. The value of the perfect oblation is of great importance, as the link which connects it with us. Neither of these words is used in Scripture, which, however, always assumes and implies the inconceivable price at which are to be valued both the Person and the work of the Redeemer Himself.

Not for
Himself.

1. Nothing that belongs to the incarnate history of Jesus can be regarded as terminating in Himself He was not man for His own sake . had He joined us for His own glory His alliance with our race would not have been by incarnation and birth into its dying lineage. He became man that He might give us what He needed not for Himself. Virtue there would have been, but not merit, in the sorrows of one who expiated his own sin, and in that sense was made perfect through suffering Remembering that the Redeemer's duty was His passion, and that in His example as proposed to us this is always prominent, if not alone,

1 Pet. iii.
18.

we shall see the force of St. Peter's words · *Christ also hath once suffered for sins, the Just for the unjust.* Almost every leading exhibition of the Atonement in Scripture makes the sinlessness of the Redeemer prominent , and this implies that His passion was voluntary and for others Nowhere is the active righteousness regarded as obligatory on Christ : He descended to a kind of obedience which was no necessity of His being Hence both as a Sacrifice and as an Obedience the Lord's work was for us : meritorious, to use our human term, as not required for Himself.

Human.

2. The atoning work itself was a manifestation of perfect charity viewed as offered by a Man. If we strive to rise to the conception that our Lord's obedience and sacrifice were presented by a member of our race untainted by sin, and therefore reckoned to such a Person as something most precious in the sight of Heaven, and then superadd to this that, being God, He can bestow on His creatures this Gift of His own work, then we have the Scriptural teaching of an offering presented by Man for himself combining supreme love to God and supreme charity to mankind in the highest perfection of both. Now we must so view it, as our own oblation. Man was in Christ reconciling God to himself by the most precious oblation. We are Christ's and Christ is ours The Redeemer was not His own but our possession. He gave Himself

TO us before He gave Himself FOR us. When He obeyed unto a sacrificial death we undid our sin by a perfect obedience, and at the same time gave our life and our all as a penalty for our sin. Our redeeming Representative was our Sin-offering and Burnt-offering in one: in Him we give our life to justice, and present our expiated life anew to God, and both in one.

3. But the virtue, value, and merit of the Atonement must be measured by the value of His Person who is at once the Offering and the Offerer. It is an unreal abstraction that we consider when we speak of the Great Oblation being presented by man. But it becomes a most blessed concrete reality when we regard it as offered by the God-man *who gave Himself.* As God He gave His human life, but more than that: He gave the value of His Divine Sonship with it. As Man He freely presented Himself in obedience to the Father; but it was the Eternal Spirit of His Divinity that gave Him the strength to make the offering, and impressed on it its value when made. Here is the secret of our Saviour's merit: it is only the human word for the Divine complacency in the submission of His Son. *This is My Beloved Son, in Whom I am well pleased.* The meaning here is, that on this Man, or Representative of Man, God can look with more than the original satisfaction with which He regarded Adam He saw His beloved Son made man; and, when He uttered His complacency, it was over the whole work and passion of Christ, which was anticipated as finished; and, as finished, made available for the human race.

Divine.

1 Tim ii 6.

Matt xvii 5

THE VICARIOUS EXPIATION AND PROPITIATION

As the Atonement avails for the human race, and is therefore ours, it must be viewed as a vicarious satisfaction of the claims of Divine justice or expiation of the guilt of sin, and propitiation of the Divine favour.

No adjective equivalent to the term Vicarious, as expressing the Redeemer's relation to mankind, is used in Scripture, nor is there any equivalent for Substitution, the noun corresponding to the adjective. But the idea of a strictly vicarious representation lies at the root of its teaching. An absolute substitution of the

Vicarious.

Saviour's obedience or sacrifice in the place of the suffering and obedience of His people is not taught in the Word of God The substitutionary idea is in their case qualified by that of representation on the one hand, and the mystical fellowship of His saints on the other. If unqualified at all, it is so with reference to the race at large or the world of mankind

For the Race.

I. The purely vicarious quality of our Saviour's work refers only to the world or the race. Christ in His Person is the Son of man ; and, as the new Adam, the Head and Summary of mankind, stands in the stead of all whom He represents All that He is and does and suffers He is and does and suffers for the entire human family. Adam represented all, the multitude who were not in existence save in him ; our Lord represented the same, who were not in existence save in Him Before men were in being He assumed a universal relation to them, and that must have been strictly vicarious The preposition ἀντί, instead of, is used by our Lord in a saying which must rule all others : *The Son of Man came not to be ministered unto, but to minister, and to give His life a ransom for many*, where the many are the all, St. Paul employs ὑπέρ : *If one died for all, then were all dead*, or, rather, *all died*, both, united and strengthened, are used by him again at the close of his teaching, in a sentence which condenses more of the substance of the doctrine than any other *For there is one God, and one Mediator between God and men, the Man Christ Jesus, who gave Himself a ransom for all, to be testified in due time*. ἀντίλυτρον ὑπὲρ πάντων, both the word and the construction being unique in Greek literature. The idea of substitution is stamped deeply here, and in this its most forcible expression in the New Testament the vicarious universality is stated in three ways : the Person is MAN, for men ; He is a ransom FOR ALL, and the context admits no limitation, as the intercession was demanded *for all men*, and of God who *will have all men to be saved*.

Matt. xx. 28.

2 Cor. v 14.

1 Tim. ii 5, 6

1 Tim. ii. 4.

II. Our Lord's vicarious relation to His people, subjectively receiving the Atonement, is modified by the two ideas of representation and the mystical personal union with Him.

Representation

1. The former is current in the New Testament, which invariably represents Jesus as standing at the head of a fellowship of men for whose sake He has done and suffered all, that through

His atoning mediation they might have access and hope. The doctrine is not that a penalty has been endured by Christ instead of His people, that He has occupied their legal place and borne their legal responsibility; and therefore that they are for ever discharged It is rather that a sacrificial offering has been presented by Him instead of the race; and that He, making the virtue of His atonement the strength of His plea, represents all *that come unto God by Him* The propitiation offered for all men, and accepted, becomes effectual only for the penitent who embraces it by trusting in Him Whom *God hath set forth to be a Propitiation in His blood through faith.* So also Christ appears *in the presence of God for us,* or on our behalf. His sacrificial obedience is not vicarious in the sense of discharging all its beneficiaries from obligation to do and suffer; for it was offered on behalf of *the whole world,* and they may *perish for whom Christ died.* Heb. vii. 25. Rom iii. 25 Heb. ix 24. 1 John ii. 2

2. The union of the believer with his Lord gives another qualification to the vicarious idea Substitution pure and simple is inconsistent with the thought that the virtue of the Atonement is in any way dependent on personal participation with Christ by faith. But nothing is more certain than that the Atonement is valid only for those who are mystically united with their Head in His death and resurrection. St. Paul says, not for himself only but for every believer, *I am crucified with Christ . . . Who loved me, and gave Himself for me* And he habitually speaks of fellowship with the Saviour in His death and resurrection, as making the general Atonement the individual possession Now this union with Christ by faith does not mean, on the one hand, that the believer must add anything to the Supreme Expiation. that is a perversion which has been forced on the doctrine. But, on the other it precludes the possibility of such a vicarious substitution as makes the atoning work of Christ absolutely independent of our relation to it. The *propitiation in His blood* is *through faith;* and this faith, uniting the soul to Christ, qualifies without impairing the truly vicarious character of the Atonement 1 Cor viii. 11. Union with Him. Gal ii 20. Rom iii. 25.

SCRIPTURAL PHRASEOLOGY.

There are two Greek terms, or families of terms, on which hang the details of the doctrine just laid down ἱλασμός and καταλλαγή are their representatives. The relations of these are clear and distinct in the original Scriptures; but they are to some extent confused in our present English translation.

Atonement.

1. The former assumes three leading forms in the New Testament. Christ is the Ἱλασμός, the virtue of the propitiation and the Propitiator *He is the Propitiation for our sins,* not the Ἱλαστήρ, because the process of His propitiating is lost in the effect   He is the living Expiation. He is also the ἱλαστήριον, the Kapporeth, or Mercy-seat, according to the use of the word in the Septuagint: *Whom God hath set forth to be a Propitiation,* that is, as a mercy-seat, between Himself and sinners   Or, if the word be an adjective, then θῦμα is understood, and He is a propitiatory sacrifice. As the High-priest He is said ἱλασκέσθαι τὰς ἁμαρτίας, that is, to expiate sins; though the English translation hides this meaning: *to make reconciliation for the sins of the people.*

1 John ii. 2

Rom. iii. 25.

Heb. ii. 17.

Reconciliation.

2 The latter is the word which is translated in the English version both by atonement and by reconciliation : the latter, however, is its strict meaning , or atonement, if this word retains its original sense AT-ONE-MENT   The verb καταλλάσσειν signifies the virtue of the mediation of Christ as composing a difference between God and man, and καταλλαγή the result · the new relation in which the world stands to God, He being no longer an ἀντίδικος, and the world being no more an object of wrath.   The context in the two passages where the verb is used shows that God is the antagonist; of which more hereafter

God

3 Both these verbs have God for the Subject and not for the Object.   The Supreme Being reconciles the world to Himself, it is not said that He is reconciled · this simply gives expression to the great truth that the whole provision for the re-establishment of peace is from above.   God is reconciled to man, but *in Christ* who is Himself God : He therefore is the Reconciler while He is the Reconciled   So also the word expiate refers to an act of God: it is not said that He is propitiated, but that He propitiates Himself or brings Himself near by providing an expiation for the sin. Strictly speaking the atoning sacrifice declares a propitiation already in the Divine heart.

2 Cor v. 19.

4. A comparison of the two passages already referred to will illustrate this. In the one, *We also joy in God through our Lord*

Rom v 11.

Jesus Christ, by Whom we have now received the Atonement, τὴν κα-
ταλλαγήν, this last word ought to be rendered *the Reconciliation*
In the other, *A merciful and faithful High Priest in things pertain-* Heb. ii 17
ing to God, to make reconciliation for the sins of the people, ἱλάσκεσθαι
τὰς ἁμαρτίας, ought to be rendered *to make atonement for the sins.*
If the terms Atonement and Reconciliation changed places, in these
passages, the meaning would be more clear. It may be observed,
in connection with this, that there is a similar want of uniformity,
as to the phraseology, in the English translation of the Old Testament. The expression לְכַפֵּר is the habitual technical term for the
ceremonial covering of sin, as in this leading passage. *For the life* Lev xvii.
of the flesh is in the blood · and I have GIVEN *it to you upon the altar* 11.
to make an atonement FOR *your souls. for it is the blood that maketh an*
atonement IN *the soul* Here three things already adverted to
may be recalled. The atonement is given or appointed of
God. His own Divine and eternal ordinance of cancelling sin.
Then, the life or soul in the blood, not the blood itself, makes
the atonement. Finally, the atoning life covers the soul for
which it avails It is obvious that in this central passage sin is
the object of the whole transaction The reconciled or propitiated
Jehovah displays His method of expiating transgression But in
some other passages the same verb is, as in the New Testament,
translated by Reconcile ; as if τὸν Θεὸν were to be understood after
ἱλάσκεσθαι. One may be quoted which represents many *And* Lev xvi.
when He hath made an end of reconciling the holy place, where the 20.
idea is that of applying the virtue of the Atonement to the place
which thus only can retain the indwelling Presence A careful
comparison of the Hebrew verb and noun with their equivalents
in the Septuagint and the English Version will show that many
accessory notions have been connected with them, such as
Ransom, Cleansing, Satisfaction, Propitiation. But the fundamental thought remains that the Atonement is a Covering
provided by God for the sinful and guilty soul of man

THEOLOGICAL MODIFICATIONS.

There are certain modifications of those two leading terms
which, both by inflection and addition, have been introduced into

historical theology. These may be best studied in some of their mutual aspects.

Satisfaction and Expiation.

1 The specific idea of SATISFACTION has been added to that of EXPIATION. The former is in the court of law what the latter is in the temple. Reparation is made to the honour of the Lawgiver and the claims of the law in the suffering of Christ · and that is satisfaction. The atoning blood and life of the Victim covers the guilty soul so that its sin is not visited for punishment · and that is expiation.

Satisfaction to Love,

But the idea as referred to the Divine Being is really twofold . it is the satisfaction of His unutterable love which provides the atonement ; and it is the satisfaction of His eternal holiness which must be a consuming fire to evil

and to Law.

Referred to the law, it is purely the endurance of its sentence or sanction, without which law is not law : this latter is the common theological meaning, but the former ought not to be forgotten. The word is not found in our Scriptures save once : *Moreover ye shall take no*

Numb xxxv. 31, 32.

satisfaction, בֹּפֶר, *for the life of a murderer* There was no Levitical atonement for him, *he shall be surely put to death.* As commonly used to signify the unlimited reparation made for the dishonour done to the majesty of holiness by sin, it has no direct, though abundant indirect, sanction in the New Testament. But it evermore blends with the idea of propitiation God is propitious, or favourably brought near, to the entire race of mankind there is

John viii. 44.

now but one ἀνθρωπόκτονος, for whom eternal right *shall take no satisfaction.* And the satisfaction offered in the sacrifice of Christ is a satisfaction of the Divine love before it is to be considered as a reparation to the Divine justice.

Expiation and Propitiation

2. Hence EXPIATION and PROPITIATION, one in Scripture, are theologically to be separated. Expiation refers the sacrifice to the sinner and the sin ; Propitiation to the Supreme whose displeasure, not whose justice,—for justice cannot be propitiated,—is declared to be allayed Both terms have a high and glorified meaning in Scripture as compared with secular phraseology and conceptions. Expiation requires sacrifice. a victim there must be ; for this word, whether in heathenism or in revelation, belongs to temple ritual. Heathen expiations regarded only the blood and the vicarious death, which the guilty conscience of mankind has always vainly presented to appease the deities. Revealed expia-

tion regards the life as in the blood having always in view that sacrificial death which was offered by a Living Sacrifice. In one and the same symbol the death was suffered, the blood being sprinkled in token of that, and also the spotless life of the victim interposed between justice and the sinner, covering his person and his guilt. Propitiation, from PROPE, near, indicates in the Bible that the favour and good pleasure of God is attracted to the sinner by the mediation of Jesus HE IS THE PROPITIATION because in Him God is nearer to man the sinner than even to man the unfallen The fact, that holy wrath is turned away through the Atoning satisfaction is a secret behind the Incarnation · in the very essence of the Triune God *Herein is love, not that we loved God, but that He loved us, and sent His Son the Propitiation for our sins* The profound truth remains, that the Divine wrath and the Divine love are revealed at once in Christ, but love must have the pre-eminence in our phraseology.

1 John ii. 2

1 John iv. 10.

3. The word ATONEMENT has undergone a certain change. In the New Testament it is rather a legal term, signifying the restoring of a pacified relation, καταλλαγή But, as a theological and not a Biblical word, it returns from its New-Testament signification to that of the Old Testament It expresses the Divine virtue of that mediatorial work which reconciles in God Himself love and holiness, justice and mercy . in God Himself, before the Reconciliation was exhibited in the world Of the distinction between this Atonement eternally in God and Reconciliation in the world of time we must speak again. Suffice that the word in our current use testifies, not to the restoration of fellowship with God, but to the virtue of the Great Sacrifice through which that restoration is displayed or effected. We mean by THE ATONEMENT the whole economy of our Lord's saving intervention as consummated on the cross It is the ἱλασμος and ἱλάσκεσθαι which answers to the כָּפַר and the נִכַּר. Just as we employ the term Redemption to designate Christ's work as saving man generally ; and the term Reconciliation to signify the ministry through which that salvation is proclaimed ; so we use the term Atonement to include the virtue of the redeeming work as propitiating the Divine mercy to our race In fact, it is the theological formula for all that belongs to that work

The modern term Atonement

Atonement

T 2

Result of
Atone-
ment

THE ATONEMENT IN ITS RESULT

Having viewed the Atonement as presented by Christ, its virtue or merit expiating sin and satisfying the claims of Divine justice and love, we must now regard it in its effect as an accomplished act. The result of the One Offering is represented in Scripture in its relation to God, to God and man, and to man. As to God, it is the final saving manifestation of His glory; as to God and man, it is the Reconciliation; as to man more particularly, it is Redemption. These, however, are only different aspects of one and the same Atonement, which are distinguished, though not systematically distinguished, in the New Testament.

As to God

AS TO GOD. THE DIVINE GLORY IN REDEMPTION

In the finished work of Christ, the Name, Attributes and Government of God are most fully exhibited and glorified. The Triune Name is made known; the Love and Righteousness of God have their highest and best manifestation, as the expression of the Divine will; and the Moral Government of the Supreme is supremely vindicated.

The
Triune
Name.

THE TRIUNE NAME

The name of the Triune God is especially made known and therefore glorified in the mediation of the Incarnate Redeemer The revelation of the Trinity is bound up with the revelation of redemption, the development of one was the development of the other, and both were perfected together The Son, addressing the Father a prayer which regards the Atonement as accomplished, John xvii. declares . *I have manifested Thy name unto the men which Thou gavest* 6. *Me out of the world.* This can refer only to the disclosure of that new name of Father which the incarnation and teaching of the

Son had made manifest. Not long before He had said . *Father,* glorify Thy name; when the response was given · *I have both glorified it, and will glorify it again.* His own name as the Son was now for the first time made known . *Now is the Son of man glorified, and God is glorified in Him.* Only in the Son is the Father revealed , and there is no Son revealed save in redemption. Hence the Saviour's prayer asks that the mutual glorification of the Father and the Son may be complete . *Father, the hour is come ; glorify Thy Son, that Thy Son also may glorify Thee* And this must be interpreted in the light of the preceding discourse, which shows that the full disclosure of the name of the Son, here prayed for, must await the manifestation of a Third Name, that of the Holy Ghost The Divine Spirit is the Revealer both of the Father and the Son; and on the Day of Pentecost the eternal mystery of the Trinity was fully made known · God reserved His profoundest revelation of Himself for the Finished Atonement Our Lord pronounced *The Name of the Father, and of the Son, and of the Holy Ghost* only after His resurrection. The mystery of His perfect love unfolded the mystery of His perfect essence But this subject has been already discussed under the Mediatorial Trinity.

John xii. 28.

John xiii. 31.

John xvii 1

Matt. xxviii. 19.

THE DIVINE ATTRIBUTES.

The Divine Attributes.

The attributes of God are glorified both singly and unitedly, and in a transcendent manner, by the mediation of the Incarnate. This indeed is included in the meaning of the prayer that the Name of God might be glorified in His Son ; for that Name is not only the Triune Name, but the assemblage of the Divine perfections. Throughout the Old Testament and the New the Divine glories, especially those which we may in this connection call the glories of the moral attributes, are condensed over the Mercy-seat · receiving from it their highest illustration. There is a gradational display of the eternal majesty. *The heavens declare the glory of God,* while *the whole earth is full of His glory.* Again, *in Judah is God known. His Name is great in Israel,* but it is Israel's Temple which *His train filled.* And the Temple itself is filled only with the diffusive radiance : it was in the Holiest that He appeared *in the cloud upon the mercy-seat* The perfect revelation of the

Psalm xix 1
Isa vi 3
Psalm lxxvi 1

Lev. xvi 2.

Triune God in the Incarnate Son of the Godhead has presented the Divine Attributes in a new aspect, and to mortal man they will never otherwise be known. *God, who commanded the light to shine out of darkness, hath shined in our hearts to give the light of the knowledge of the glory of God in the face of Jesus Christ.* And in the New Testament it is obvious that with scarcely an exception every reference to the combined or individual perfections of God refers to their exhibition in the work of Christ. At least, all other allusions lead up to this. Not to repeat what has already been made prominent under the Divine Attributes, it may suffice to mention the new and perfect revelation of the holiness and love of God as disclosed in the Atonement.

1 The latter here has the pre-eminence. Never is the love of God, absolutely, connected with the works of creation, or with the general dispensations of Providence. Over them loving kindness reigns, but Divine charity is reserved for the Atonement. It gives a new name to the nature of God GOD IS LOVE. *Herein is love, not that we loved God, but that He loved us, and sent His Son to be the Propitiation for our sins,* where we may omit *to be*

2 The Divine HOLINESS is exhibited as conspicuously as the Divine love, so far as concerns the process of redemption : love is supreme in the origination, and will be supreme at the end—for *mercy rejoiceth against judgment,* not over it, though over against it— but in the actual atoning work the justice of holiness, demanding the punishment and extermination of sin, is displayed in the most awful manner of which the human mind can form any conception

3. It is important to remember that Holy Scripture never makes such a distinction between the love and the holiness of God as theology thinks it necessary to establish. The mercy that provides and the justice that requires the Atonement are one in the recesses of the Divine nature Their union or identity is lost to us in the thick darkness of the light which we cannot approach. The Cross of Christ, or rather the whole mediation of the Redeemer, equally and at once reveals both. *Herein is love*—to quote once more the final revelation of Scripture on this subject—*not that we loved God, but that He loved us, and sent His Son the Propitiation for our sins.* In our infirmity we find it needful to correct our estimate of one attribute by appealing to the other The Scripture scarcely con-

2 Cor. iv. 6.

Love.

1 John iv 8, 10

Holiness.

James ii. 13.

Distinc- tion between Holiness and Love.

1 John iv 10

descends to that infirmity It speaks of the Divine ἀγάπη as
ordering the whole economy of what is nevertheless an ἱλασμός or
propitiation, and of the Divine εὐδοκία as ordering the whole
economy of what is nevertheless a καταλλαγή. We shall hereafter
see how these four words meet in the sacrifice of the cross, where
love reigns through the infinite sacrifice of love.

1 John iv
10

Col. i. 19

4. But it is the glory and unity of all the attributes that the
work of Christ exhibits in their perfection There is nothing
that belongs to our conception of the Divine nature which is not
manifested in His Son, Who both in His active and in His passive
righteousness reveals all that is in the Father. Man, in fact,
knows God only as a God of redemption; nor will He ever by
man be otherwise known. Throughout the Scriptures of truth
we have a gradual revelation of the Divine Being which is not
finished until it is finished in Christ: God also, as well as man, is
ἐν Αὐτῷ πεπληρωμένος, COMPLETE IN HIM It is not enough to say
that the Trinity Whom Christians adore is made known in Jesus,.
and that this the other or attribute which theology ascribes to
Him is illustrated in His work God Himself, with every idea we
form of His nature, is given to us by the revelation of Christ.
The gracious and awful Being Who is presented in the Christian
Scriptures is not in all respects such a Deity as human reason
would devise or tolerate when presented. But to us there is but
ONE GOD, and we must receive Him as He is made known to us
through the mystery of the Atoning Mediation of His Son. His
Name is proclaimed only in the Cross; there we have His Divine
and only Benediction; and every Doxology in Revelation derives
its strength and fervour from the Atonement.

United.

THE DIVINE GOVERNMENT.

The Government of the Supreme Ruler of the Universe is
perfectly vindicated by the Atonement. This effect of the work
of Christ is much dwelt upon by St. Paul; and is perhaps the
most obvious and comprehensible view of it which can be taken.
It gives its colouring to a large portion of the New-Testament
phraseology; especially, however, to the recorded Discourses and
the leading Epistle of that Apostle.

The Vin-
dication of
Divine
Govern-
ment.

Three
Theories.

1. There are three views of the Atonement in Scripture. It is sometimes regarded as the result of a mystery that had been transacted in the Divine mind before its manifestation in time. Sometimes, again, it is exhibited as a demonstration of God's love to mankind, and self-sacrifice in Christ for their sake . as it were to move the hearts of men with hatred of sin and desire to requite so much mercy. Strictly speaking, this is not given as an explanation of the Atonement . the New Testament does not sanction the idea that our Lord's self-sacrifice is made an argument

Rom. v. 8.

with sinners. It is never so used. Certainly, *God commendeth His love toward us*, but here St. Paul is exhorting Christians, already saved, to rely upon the abundant provision of grace for the future which is guaranteed by the demonstration of love in the past. Everywhere the love of God, whether the Father or the Son, in the Atonement is used as a most mighty argument of self-devotion, severity of morals, tenderness to man, and universal, boundless charity. It is never employed to melt the heart of a sinner : certainly that object is nowhere given as an explanation of Christ's work. And, lastly, it is set forth as an expedient for upholding the dignity of the Ruler of the universe and Administrator of law. These three views, or, to use modern language, theories of the Atonement are combined in the Scriptures : neither is dwelt upon apart from the rest. The perfect doctrine includes them all. Every error springs from the exaggeration of one of these elements at the expense of the others

Combined

2. St. Paul, in the Epistle which treats most fully of the universal moral government of God, thus makes the last of the three emphatic, while expressly or by inference including the two others. He carries the doctrine into the court of justice.

Rom iii.
21—26.

(1) The Evangelical method of saving and making men righteous is called the *Righteousness of God.* It is said *to declare His righteousness for the remission of sins that are past, through the forbearance of God* that is, to make His righteousness appear, by a retrospective interpretation of its ways, consistent with its *passing over or pretermission*, διὰ τὴν πάρεσιν, *of sins in past ages.* This vindicates the rectoral government of God, based upon one and the same method of righteousness, FOR THE PAST of the preparatory economy, whether of Gentiles or Jews. *To declare, I*

say, at this time ·His righteousness ; that He might be just, and the Justifier of him which believeth in Jesus : that is, it enables Him to treat a sinner as a righteous man, and yet be Himself just in so regarding him   This vindicates the rectoral government of God, FOR THE PRESENT, of the Christian fulness of time.   Afterwards, with reference to this same Gospel system, we read . *Ye have obeyed from the heart that form of doctrine which was delivered you. Being then made free from sin, ye became the servants of righteousness*   Rom. vi. 17, 18. That is, the Atonement insures the honour of the law after forgiveness   This vindicates the rectoral government of God, FOR THE FUTURE, both as to the race and the individual.   The leading characteristic of this passage, therefore, is the vindication of God's rectoral character · the protection of law in the presence of the universe.   Here is the truth of what is sometimes, but needlessly, called the Grotian or Governmental theory.

(2) The words *justified freely through His grace,* grace displayed in the Atonement as affectingly appealing to man, may be so interpreted as to lay the foundation of what is occasionally termed the theory of Moral Influence   If they are taken out of the context, and considered alone, they declare that the redeeming plan is the free expression of the Divine grace , which, however, found it expedient to exhibit in the sufferings of the Righteous Jesus the evil of sin and the glory of self-sacrificing zeal for its destruction. Apart from the perversion of these words, which regards them as standing alone, they do proclaim the supremacy of love and of grace in the whole economy of redemption.   Whatever our salvation cost the Redeemer, it is in all its history and its issues the expression of free grace to us   The theory, not thus standing alone, is true   Rom. iii. 24.

(3.) The words are connected with others   they refuse to be eliminated from the context   The unique expression which follows and represents the Redeemer as the Propitiatory or Mercy-seat—*to be a propitiation in His blood through faith*—makes it most sure that there was a necessity for the Atonement in the Divine Nature.   The Blood was not shed only as the life of one who renounced all for the good of others.   It was not the life-blood of self-sacrifice only.   It was the blood of propitiation , and this word for ever turns to the innermost recesses of the Divine nature.   Man's heart is to be moved only because the heart of God   Rom. iii. 25

was moved.   This links St. Paul's with St. John's testimony in his First Epistle.   There the ascendency is given to Love; but this only renders more impressive the necessity of the atoning sacri-

1 John iv 10.

fice.   *Herein is* LOVE, *not that we loved God, but that He loved us, and sent His Son to be the* PROPITIATION *for our sins.*

As to God and Man.

AS TO GOD AND MAN · THE RECONCILIATION

The New-Testament term Reconciliation—or, as it some- times occurs, Atonement—defines the Finished Work as having effected and exhibited the restoration of fellowship between God and man.   The change of relation is mutual : God lays aside His displeasure against mankind, being pro- pitiated in the intervention of His Son ; and all men, through the ministry of the Reconciliation, are invited to enter into a state of acceptance with God, laying aside their enmity.   The former belongs to the work of Christ as a decree of heaven fulfilled on earth ; the latter belongs to the same work as finished on earth and pleaded in heaven, in the provision made for individual acceptance. The reconciliation, therefore, is a process accomplished in two senses   first, the Supreme Judge is reconciled to the race absolutely ; secondly, provision is made for the recon- ciliation of all men individually to Him.

God the Reconciler and the Recon- ciled.

GOD THE RECONCILER AND THE RECONCILED.

God is the Reconciler in the Atonement, inasmuch as He pro- vides the sacrifice which propitiates Himself   the very existence or possibility of the sacrifice proves Him to be already propitiated. But this does not exclude His being the Reconciled   indeed, so far as concerns the great change declared in or wrought by the interposition of the Mediator, it is God alone who is reconciled. The removal of the enmity in the sinner follows the great recon- ciliation, and is its secondary effect.   Here there are two oppo- site errors to be guarded against.

1. Holy Scripture does not encourage the thought that the actual sacrificial obedience of Christ reconciled God, previously hostile, to man; nor that the atonement offered on the cross wrought as a cause the effect of modifying the intention of the Divine mind towards the human race. The purpose of redemption was an eternal purpose · change must be wrought in time   Our Lord was sent to declare a reconciliation with sinning human nature preceding and presupposing the sin that needed it ; which was, indeed, no other than the reconciliation of the mercy of love and the justice of holiness in the Divine nature itself through the Incarnation rendered possible by the adorable mystery of the Three Persons in the Godhead   This is always and consistently declared in the New Testament, which makes the method of atonement simply and only a product of the Divine counsel.   His purpose, His righteousness, His love are severally regarded as the originating principle.   But always the overture and act of reconciliation is from Him.   *God was in Christ reconciling the world unto Himself* **[Reconciliation of God to Man.]** **[2 Cor. v. 19.]**

2. The other error is that of those who insist that the only reconciliation is of man to God.   It is a very superficial, and it might be added sentimental, feeling that leads to this assertion . the opposite would, as we have seen, be nearer the truth, as will be further evident from the following considerations concerning the ideas presented to us in the Scriptures which speak on the subject, and the consistent phraseology adopted for the expression of these ideas. **[Of Man to God]**

(1.) He who offers the reconciliation yields His righteous claims, as it were, before they are enforced ; and, instead of enforcing them, beseeches men to be reconciled to Him   But all Divine claims—to repeat a word which theology reluctantly uses—have been in the presuppositions of the atoning work satisfied   The word seems to look only to man, but its face is turned towards God also   Not to betake ourselves to abstract principles, the Scripture must be our appeal.   The few sentences containing that aspect of the Saviour's work which views it as the Reconciliation speak in their context of a Divine wrath, and in such a way as to give wrath its uttermost meaning.   In the classical Corinthian passage we read *not imputing their tres-* **[Of God alone.]** **[2 Cor. v 19.]**

passes unto them, which has behind it, or rather before it, that most solemn declaration, *Who, though He knew not sin, was* MADE SIN *for us.* These last words give the key to the whole doctrine . closing the statement of it with deep emphasis

Matt v 24

(2) A due regard to the habitual use of the term will lead to the same conclusion We may fairly collate the Lord's word, *first be reconciled to thy brother,* which is a strict parallel in meaning, though the word διαλλάγηθι is not precisely the same it is the offended brother who is really propitiated So also in the case

1 Sam xxix 4.

of the Philistines and David : *wherewith should he reconcile himself unto his master ?* it was the master and not David that was to be appeased The verb καταλλάσσειν is never used of the Atonement in the Old Testament, but there are a few apocryphal passages

2 Macc. viii. 29.

which prepare for its subsequent use. For instance *they besought the merciful Lord to be reconciled with His servants.* Though the New Testament does not speak of God as being reconciled, the meaning is precisely the same as in this and similar passages. The eternal God, however, it must be repeated, was reconciled before Christ came to display His saving grace : He only brought the reconciliation, which we receive There was in heaven an Atonement before the Atonement.

The Reconciled World.

THE RECONCILIATION.

The Reconciliation is a change of relation between God and mankind, or the human race, or the nature of man. It is true that inspired phraseology does not use these abstract terms , but

2 Cor. v. 19.

it says that *God was in Christ reconciling the world unto Himself·* where ἦν καταλλάσσων, combining past and present, indicates that the Father in the Son was and is always carrying out a purpose of grace the eternal decree was accomplished in Christ on the cross; it is always in course of accomplishment. It is the former which ἦν makes emphatic , when He Who *knew no sin* was *made sin for us,* the wrath of God against our transgression was expended upon our Representative, and diverted from us. He reconciled the world to Himself by removing from it, as a world, His eternal displeasure. What is now going on through the ministry is the winning of individual souls to the enjoyment of the Divine peace. For the full interpretation of this classical passage it is necessary to consider more distinctly the meaning of both terms Reconciliation and World.

1 The entire world of mankind God is said to have reconciled to Himself in Christ, inasmuch as the atoning sacrifice was the actual realisation of a purpose which had been regarded as wrought out from the beginning of human history. An economy or relation of peace had always prevailed in His government of a sinful race   The term may be said to characterise the kind of administration the Supreme Ruler has exercised over a guilty race St Paul shows this when he says, *We also joy in God through our Lord Jesus Christ, by Whom we have now received the Atonement,* or *the reconciliation,* which here is simply equivalent to the grace of redemption. The Reconciliation is a title of the work of Christ, just as the words Grace and Gospel and Righteousness give it their names.   As the world has received a Saviour or Deliverer, and the Gospel is preached to the world, so the world has from the beginning had the benefit of the amnesty.   But a dispensation of forbearance BEFORE Christ is IN Christ a dispensation of perfect Peace   Hence the Gospel is called the *ministry of reconciliation*   God is administering, through the stewards of this mystery, a system or economy of forgiveness and peace   The ambassadors of Christ announce a general declaration of the Divine good will to the world   Their ministry is not so much to induce sinners to lay aside their opposition to God as to persuade them that God has laid aside His opposition to them, *not imputing their trespasses*   They are representatives of Christ's work as the expression of the Father's will *For it pleased the Father that in Him should all fulness dwell, and, having made peace through the blood of His Cross, by Him to reconcile all things unto Himself ·* these last two clauses ought to be inverted, the reconciliation is not the sequel of the making peace, but the making peace itself.   There is nothing said here of a reconciliation between the upper intelligences and man, or between both united and God   it is evident that the Atonement is a ground of amnesty in the Divine government universal, so far only as the human race is concerned.   The Cross belongs to the world, and to all the world.   Its two arms stretch backward and forward, to the beginning and to the end of time.   So it is in a

Reconciliation.

ᷤ

Rom. v. 11

2 Cor. v. 18.

2 Cor. v 19.

Col. i. 19, 20

Eph. ii.
14—16.

parallel place *For He is our Peace . . . that He might reconcile both unto God in one body by the Cross, having slain the enmity thereby ·* what enmity He slew is explained by the reconciliation UNTO GOD. The result is that the life of salvation reigns.

The
World.

2. There is another sense in which the world of mankind is reconciled or restored in Christ : the human family is really represented by that part of it which lives spiritually in its New Head. Undoubtedly there will be, as there has been and still is, a portion of the descendants of Adam unrestored to God. While the race in its unity is, notwithstanding sin, placed in a relation of peace with the Supreme Ruler, so that the holy heavens can still canopy an unholy earth, that peace, with regard to the world as such, is after all only the provision and possibility of peace. And yet God may be said to have saved mankind ; or rather mankind is restored to fellowship with Him. and to that communion which was so soon suspended in Paradise. The angels, or the inhabitants of other regions of the Divine government, would

Col i 20.
Luke ii.
14.

say that man was saved, that *things in earth* were reconciled and set right : indeed, they did once say it, *on earth Peace.* The solution is, that those who refuse the great Reconciliation are cast out as not belonging to the human race. That Body which is the Church, of which Christ is the head, is the new and reconciled humanity. Hence the blood of His Cross is the medium by which the good pleasure of the Father restores His human prodigal ;

2 Sam xiv.
14.

thus *doth He devise means that His banished be not expelled from Him ·* those who remain outcasts, after the Atonement is exhausted, being not reckoned as among the living. We cannot be sure that the lost spirits have rejected anything corresponding to our redemption. But as it respects our deliverance, St Paul tells us that the effect of the Cross is an accomplished reconciliation, in which God is well pleased, and which is not marred by the reprobation of

Col i. 20.

the lost. Taking up again the passage already quoted, it was *by Him to reconcile all things unto Himself , by Him, I say, whether they be things in earth or things in heaven .* here the all things are only human things, or things in heaven as they are related to man on

Heb. ix.
23.

earth. So in the Epistle to the Hebrews we read *It was therefore necessary that the patterns of things in the heavens should be purified with these ; but the heavenly things themselves, with better sacrifices than these* This last passage is really the interpretation of the mysterious Colossian sentence just quoted

3. What has been said will make it evident that the individual reconciliation to God is no other than the personal assumption of the benefit of the general reconciliation The peace established between God and man by the work of Christ is the basis for the personal acceptance of the believer into the favour of God and all its blessed consequences. Our being reconciled never means our putting away our enmity, but the revelation in us of God's mercy. This is evident in the Apostle's words to the Romans. *For if, when we were enemies,* under the displeasure of God, ἐχθροὶ ὄντες, *we were reconciled to God,* κατηλλάγημεν τῷ Θεῷ, *by the death of His Son, much more, being reconciled,* having become partakers of Divine grace, *we shall be saved by His life. He is our Peace,* St. Paul says, just as He is our Saviour, our Lord, our Head And those who *have received the Atonement,* or who are *justified by His blood*—that is, who do not reject the reconciliation which is announced to them in the Gospel—have *peace with God through our Lord Jesus Christ.* The preachers of the Gospel declare the message of their embassy, and beseech men in Christ's stead : *be ye reconciled to God.* But they mean only submit yourselves to the mercy of Heaven. St. Paul gives another expression to the same truth he adds, *And came and preached peace ;* after that description of the Atonement, already quoted, which speaks of His having *slain the enmity* on the cross. When the Reconciliation is received in penitent faith it becomes the state and life of righteousness; and a new order of terms is introduced with which future Sections will make us more familiar.

Personal Recon- ciliation.

Rom. v. 10

Eph. ii. 14

Rom. v. 1, 9, 11.

2 Cor. v. 18—20 Eph. ii. 16, 17.

AS TO MAN : REDEMPTION

As to Man : Re- demption.

The term which is most often used, used in the widest variety of applications, and most impressively connected with man as the beneficiary of the Atonement, is Redemption. This exhibits the work of Christ as the laying down of a ransom-price for the legitimate and effectual deliverance of mankind from the bondage of the law of sin. Like the reconciliation, redemption is objective and subjective: objectively, the race is redeemed; and provision is made for the subjective deliverance of individual man from the sentence of the law, the power of sin, and all the consequences of transgression. Hence redemption is both universal and partial or limited. But in every case it is man who is redeemed; while God alone is glorified, and God and man are reconciled.

Terminology

Redemption once for all effected on the cross, and redemption now in process, are described by the same terms   Those terms may be arranged in four classes · first, those in which the λύτρον, or ransom price, is included; secondly, those which mean purchase generally, such as ἀγοράζειν; thirdly, those which imply only release, as from λύειν, and, lastly, those which indicate the notion of forcible rescue, ῥύεσθαι   It will be obvious that, as we are now discussing the Atonement in relation to the finished work of Christ alone, the first of these classes belongs more strictly than the rest to our present subject   Sometimes the distinction is expressed as redemption by price and redemption by power. This is a beautiful and true distinction; though it is well to be on our guard against too sharply distinguishing these two, whether in the Lord's external work or in the believer's internal experience of it. We must now, however, limit ourselves to the objective Atonement mainly. Although it will be impossible altogether to exclude the personal application, that will come more appropriately under the Administration of Redemption   It must be remembered that, whatever secondary meanings the term may have, redemption is the deliverance of mankind from bondage   The treatment of the subject will perhaps be more effectual by considering and answering five questions. What is the bondage from which the race is redeemed?   What is the price paid down for that redemption?   To whom and by whom is it offered?   For whom is it effectual?   What are the general results of that redemption?   But the answer of these questions presupposes the previous discussion of the Atonement generally, and must needs to some extent involve repetition.

THE BONDAGE OF SIN

Mankind, as the object of redemption, is ransomed from capti- From what.
vity to sin, primarily; subordinately and indirectly, from captivity
to Satan and to death the penalty of sin

1. Sin holds man in bondage both as a condemnation and as a Sin
power. (1) The condemnation is the *curse of the law* As *the* Gal.iii.13.
strength of sin is the law, so the strength of the law is sin. It binds 1 Cor xv. 56.
every moral creature to perfect obedience; and, that being found
wanting, it shuts the transgressor up to the sentence of doom from
which, so far as the legal ordinance goes, there is no release.
(2) Sin is an internal power in human nature · enslaving the
will, and affections, and mind. (3.) The atoning intervention of
Christ has *put away sin* as an absolute power in human life. He Heb. ix
hath *obtained eternal redemption for us* an objective, everlasting, 26, 12
all-sufficient redemption from the curse of the law, and from the
necessary surrender of the will to the power of evil.

2 Satan and death are subordinate but real representatives of Satan and Death.
that power of evil: subordinate; for they are only ministers of
sin, which might retain its empire if they did not exist. (1.)
Satan is the executioner of the Divine sentence, and the prince of
all evil . in the former relation he represents the condemnation of
the law; in the latter the interior bondage to iniquity. (2.)
Death also, as a sentence of severance from God, holds man in
bondage only as another form of the curse of the law. As temporal death, it is, like him who has the power of death, a ruler
under sin (3.) From these, the subordinates and representatives
of the great captivity, redemption has made provision to set man
free. The Epistle to the Hebrews connects this truth with the
Atonement in a remarkable manner. All is said in a paragraph
which is rounded by these words . *That He by the grace of God* Heb. ii.
should taste death for every man, and *To make reconciliation for the* 9—17.
sins of the people. Here are the beginning and end of the mystery
of redemption of Christ, the expiatory death. Intermediately we
read, *That through death He might destroy him that had the power of
death, that is, the devil, and deliver them who through fear of death
were all their lifetime subject to bondage* · Satan is brought to nought,

and death ceases to be a terror, when sin is atoned for and abolished as an external and as an internal empire.

The Price

THE RANSOM-PRICE.

The λύτρον, or ransom-price paid down, is the Blood, or the Life, or the Self of Christ, and it is important to ask how this is connected with man's deliverance.

Life.

Matt xx 28.

1. The term in classical Greek, and in the Septuagint, is in the plural, meaning the money paid down for ransom of a captive; but this for an obvious reason is in the singular when applied to the Great Redeemer. (1) The Lord's words give the only instance of its use as a noun : *The Son of Man came not to be ministered unto, but to minister, and to give His life a ransom for many,* τὴν ψυχὴν αὐτοῦ λύτρον ἀντὶ πολλῶν. It could not be interpreted by those who heard it otherwise than as the λύτρα περὶ ψυχῆς of the

Numb. xxxv. 31 Blood.

Septuagint · *Ye shall take no satisfaction for the life.* But Christ's LIFE was one satisfaction for all offenders, and for every kind of offence summed up in one   (2) St Paul speaks of the BLOOD of our Redeemer as the ransom-price, turning the noun into a verb :

Acts xx. 28

the Church of the Lord, which He hath purchased with His own blood. These words the Apostle varied in writing to the same Ephesian

Eph i. 7.
1 Peter i. 18, 19.

elders · *in Whom we have redemption through His blood.* So St. Peter. *ye were not redeemed with corruptible things, as silver and gold, from your vain conversation received by tradition from your*

Rev. v. 9

fathers, but with the precious blood of Christ. And St John : *Thou hast redeemed us to God by Thy blood.* (3.) The last testimony of St. Paul adds a third term, *Who gave Himself a ransom for all :*

Himself

HIMSELF, His Divine-human Person, identifying the offering with the Divine-human Person Himself, as St. John does when he says

1 John ii 2

He is the Propitiation   The ever-blessed Substitute lays down His life, which is in His blood, but the life of the God-man, both as dead and as ever living, in the stead of all men, and especially for His own people.

2. The precise connection between the ransom-price and man's salvation is variously exhibited in Scripture. There can be no doubt that the words are figurative, and cannot altogether express the nature of that great deliverance which they refer to.   The

redemptional terms, like the ceremonial system, *serve unto the* | Heb. viii
example and shadow of heavenly things : faintly reflecting the eternal | 5.
reality. They define the salvation of man generally, but in a
variety of ways : as ransom of a captive, payment of a debt, dissolution of a power, rescue from an enemy, disenthralment from
systems of error and vain conversation, and in other ways But
it would be wrong to say that the language is only figurative. It
expresses a most important double truth, each side of which rests
upon the infinite value of the price paid down : first, the negative
rescue from wrath , secondly, the positive recovery into the hands
of God in Christ. These must be considered in their order and
connection.

(1) The ransom-price is satisfaction of the claims of Divine | Satisfac-
justice, and redemption is release provided for the race. Our | tion to Justice.
Deliverer took the place of the captive being made *sin for us* and | 2 Cor. v.
a curse for us Hence the ideas of ransom and atonement melt | 21.
into one ; as in the Old Testament the λύτρον is ἐξίλασμα. Mark | Gal. iii. 13
in the New Testament two passages in which St. Paul remarkably | Ps xlix
blends the two ideas, *Through the redemption that is in Christ Jesus ;* | 8, Sept
Whom God hath set forth to be a propitiation. Here the price is | Rom iii.
carried into the temple, and is laid on the altar , and with these | 24, 25
words may be compared, *In Whom we have redemption through His* | Col. i 14.
blood, even the forgiveness of sins, where a third idea is added : the
redemption price, offered in sacrificial blood, secures the pardon
of offences St Peter's conjunction is similar, *Ye were not redeemed* | 1 Peter i
with corruptible things, . . . but with the precious blood of Christ, as of | 18, 19.
a lamb without blemish and without spot, with the addition of the
sacrificial victim. Finally the Epistle to the Hebrews may be
compared · *by His own blood He entered in once into the holy place,* | Heb. ix.
having obtained eternal redemption for us, where still another truth | 12.
is added, that the price is carried into the heavens to be reckoned
there for ever.

(2.) The Redeemer in the Christian doctrine recovers for Him- | Purchase
self what He rescues. This is the transcendent peculiarity of the | for Himself.
idea Christ does not ransom us in such a sense as to release and
let us go simply : He ransoms us back into His own rights over
us as God ; and this explains the connection between the sacrificial
and the regal office. The Redeemer, approaching His altar, prays .

υ 2

John xvii
2.

Glorify Thy Son, that Thy Son also may glorify Thee · as *Thou hast given Him power over all flesh.* the power of a Deliverer over the purchase of His own ransom-price For, the Saviour of mankind

Rom xiv.
9.

died and rose and revived that He might be Lord both of the dead and living. Hence, more particularly, the mediatorial rescue is the restoration to man of the Holy Spirit, His forfeited inheritance as created for communion with God. Our Saviour is the Goel-Redeemer of the Old Testament. He buys back our inheritance, positively, as well as releases us from bondage, negatively. The

Gal iii.
13, 14

two are in St Paul's sentence; *Christ hath redeemed us from the curse of the law, being made a curse for us for it is written, Cursed is every one that hangeth on a tree · that the blessing of Abraham might come on the Gentiles through Jesus Christ ; that we might receive the promise of the Spirit through faith.* But this revolves into the old and familiar dual blessing of the Christian covenant. Redemption provides for the release from condemnation ; and it secures the bestowment of a renewing Spirit.

Various
Terms.

(3) The word therefore as expressing the effect of the Atonement is not limited strictly to release from captivity and restoration to lost privileges The general idea of the λύτρον sometimes recedes, and a class of terms is used which signify rescue, or deliverance, or payment of a debt, or cancelling of a bond. It should be remembered, however, that these have reference rather to the administration of redemption than to redemption itself As to our Saviour's own finished work, once for all accomplished, it is always the laying down a price for the ransom of the world St. Paul, in one remarkable passage, declares that our Lord cancelled our human debt and suspended the legal document which attested it to His cross a view which stands alone here in Scripture The Apostle is speaking primarily of the annihilation by Christ of the documents of the covenant that sundered the Jew and the Gentile ; but the words have a larger meaning and give a most impressive illustration of our redemption generally

Col. ii. 14.

Blotting out the handwriting of ordinances that was against us, which was contrary to us, and took it out of the way, nailing it to His cross. This passage is of a certain class of unique illustrations of the central fact : they should be sparingly used in theological exposition, however useful in practical application

REDEMPTION A DIVINE TRANSACTION.

This has anticipated the third question, or virtually answered it to whom and by whom was the ransom offered ?

1. The redemption of mankind is altogether a Divine transaction, in its origin, in its method, and in its results (1) In its origin the mystery of our rescue was hid in the Deity before it was disclosed to man ; the Love of the Triune God is its source, the Justice of the Triune God is its necessity, and the Wisdom of the Triune God is its law. (2.) In its method : the work of our accomplished deliverance as a race is altogether wrought of God · but of Him in the mediatorial revelation of the Trinity. What behind the veil which hides the Triune is one, to us appears three-one. The Father is God who sends His Son ; the Son is God who takes our nature that in it He may redeem us ; the Holy Ghost is God, who orders the process of our salvation from the alpha to the omega. (3.) In its results . the acceptance of the ransom-price of mankind is the accomplishment of a Divine Purpose, which needed nothing out of God for its attainment, and by nothing out of God could be frustrated. It was a Divine act, and the Divine Will needs no help or concurrence, as no other power could thwart or arrest its execution till its consent was previously given. Hence the Trinity is the Author of a necessary salvation, an ETERNAL REDEMPTION. The price was laid up in the eternal treasury for future use in time.

2. The light of this truth detects many errors that may be here briefly anticipated. (1.) There is no discord in the Divine nature, no conflict of interests between the Persons of the Holy Trinity The Eternal Son does not propitiate an anger in the Father which He does not Himself share ; nor does the Eternal Father represent a holy justice in the Divine nature which is to be satisfied by an atoning love only found in the Son ; nor does the Eternal Spirit witness a covenant that solves a discord in which He has no part. The Second and the Third Persons of the Holy Trinity have a several personality which in their adorable mystery renders the Atonement possible. But beyond that our reverence permits us to say nothing. (2.) The Enemy of man

Marginal notes:
To whom Paid.

Within the Divine Being

Heb ix 12

Errors.

has no necessary part in the transaction. From the beginning
of post-apostolical theology down to St Bernard a strange notion
of Satan's rights disturbed men's minds, which vanished when
the Atonement was studied, as it were, first in the hidden recesses
of the Divine nature   (3) Nestorianism, with every modern
phase of it that makes the redemption of man's nature in
Christ an experiment, is banished from our doctrine   The redemption obtained in time was an eternal redemption . it was a
Ps. cxix. predestined salvation of the human race . *for ever, O Lord, Thy*
89 *word is settled in heaven*   (4.) Every theory that opposes or per-
verts the freeness of God's grace is without support   There are
two in particular, which include every variety of its many forms
no human merit can have place in a scheme which was settled on
man's behalf in eternal mercy, and there can be no help for man
apart from redeeming economy.   Grace and deliverance have the
same eternal foundations.

UNIVERSALITY OF REDEMPTION

Universal.   The Price was paid down for all men for the entire race, or for
the entire nature of man in all its representatives from the first
transgressor to the last   Redemption as such is UNIVERSAL ; or
it is general, as distinguished from the Special Redemption of the
individual

A Priori.   1 This blessed truth is à priori the anticipation of reason, and
answers to the expectation which might be entertained, and has
been entertained, by the mind of man supposed to be made aware
of the fact of a Divine intervention. Of course this is only
a preliminary argument ; and if it should be proved that
the Word of God contradicts the universal instinct, it must be
given up But the Word of God does not contradict this profound
sentiment of humanity.

(1) It is the true instinct of man that he belongs to a race
which is one in its origin and destination : one whether in ruin
or in recovery both in its fall and in its redemption.

(2.) The God of mankind must by the very terms be supposed
to be a God of philanthropy and to love the race as such which
He created. He gave us our existence, whether as a family or as

individuals, unasked : will He cut us off without hope after we have fallen, or reserve His salvation for a few ? *Shall not the Judge of all the earth do right ?* In answer to this increated instinct, His Revealer tells us that *God so loved the world that He gave His Only-begotten Son ,* and that He is *the living God, Who is the Saviour of all men, His saving grace to all men hath appeared,* after having been comparatively unrevealed until its *due time,* and that it is *the kindness and love of God our Saviour towards man,* or His PHILAN-THROPY. This last word refuses limitation. Gen.xviii. 25. John iii. 16. 1 Tim. iv. 10. Tit. iii. 4.

(3.) The object of the redeeming intervention of such a Being as the God-man cannot be limited without again doing violence to our instinctive expectation. We should take it for granted that so glorious a Person would not be sent on a partial and limited errand ; that, supposing Him to visit this earth, He would embrace its whole compass in His mission, and the testimonies concerning Christ confirm this. He is the *Mediator of God and men, the Jesus-man* He is the *Lost Adam* and the *Second Man ;* and the only time He spoke of His soul as a ransom He called Himself the *Son of Man* Where it is said that, *to deliver them who through fear of death were all their lifetime subject to bondage, He took on Him the seed of Abraham,* this is opposed to the *angels* in the same verse, to whom He did not stretch out His helping hand, and in a preceding verse it is explained by *flesh and blood ·* He is the seed of David, which is the seed of Abraham, which is the seed of the woman. He Who *made of one blood all the nations of men* hath also BY one blood redeemed all nations of men. Dignity of the Re-deemer. 1 Tim. ii. 5. 1 Cor. xv. 45—47. Matt. xx 28. Heb ii. 15, 16. Acts xvii. 26.

2. The positive assertions of Scripture are few, but very forcible

(1.) Directly, it is said that *Christ Jesus gave Himself a ransom for all.* And the force of this testimony is if possible strengthened by the context, containing the exhortation to pray *for all men,* which is *good and acceptable in the sight of God our Saviour, Who will have all men to be saved,* because He is the *one God* who deals with men through *one Mediator* We read that this Mediator descended below the angels *that He by the grace of God should taste death for every man,* ὑπὲρ παντός . this last word does not mean for every creature, but certainly for every man. The Forerunner bids us all *Behold the Lamb of God which taketh away the sin of the world* his new word αἴρει, *taketh away,* is half expiatory, half redemptional, 1 Tim. ii. 6. Heb. ii 9. John i. 29.

but altogether universal. (2.) Indirectly, many passages require

2 Peter ii. 1.

this as inference. *Even denying the Lord that bought them, and bring*

Rom xiv 15

upon themselves swift destruction · parallel with St. Paul's *Destroy*

not him with thy meat for whom Christ died, but still more evidently

1 Cor viii 11

bringing in the substitutionary price. Other illustrations are so
numerous that they cannot be quoted in full, and need no specimens : such as all the declarations of God's love to the world, all
the general proclamations of repentance and the Gospel as glad
tidings, the foreannouncement of the resurrection of all men as
the result of redemption, and those texts which make man chargeable with his own doom. But the most impressive of these
indirect assertions are such as invest the Redeemer with attributes
and relations to the world which know no restriction : He is the

John ix 5
Acts x. 36

Light of the world, the Life universally and the *Lord of all* It is
however the glory of this argument that it needs not the support
of individual texts

SPECIAL REDEMPTION

General
and
Special.

While Universal Redemption is a great reality, it is such only
as the basis of a particular application

1 The race is redeemed. It was virtually redeemed before it
sinned and before it existed Hence the instincts of all mankind

Hag ii. 7.

and the traditions of history, pointing to One who is the *Desire
of nations.* The mediatorial government of the world from the
beginning has been a fruit and a proof of one great deliverance.
No race unredeemed, and without hope of redemption, could in
the universe of a holy God continue to propagate its generations.
The Holy Ghost was given at the outset as, in a peculiar sense,
the Earnest of redemption, and Christ was from the very gate of
Paradise the Lord of all, the Judge of the whole earth, the

John i 4.

Saviour of the world, the LIGHT OF MEN

2 But this universal salvation is bound up with one that is
particular. (1.) The Scripture speaks only of one grand redemp-

1 Tim iv 10

tion ; but it distinguishes, speaking of Him *Who is the Saviour
of all men, specially of those that believe.* Here the special is other
than the general redemption though springing from it , what
makes it special is not the decree of sovereignty, but the faith of

those who embrace it. The distinction, however, condemns those Latitudinarians who regard the whole race as, by the very fact of Christ's incarnation, individually redeemed, justified and saved (2) But it makes the two redemptions one in the sense that the individual benefit is only the application of a general benefit which belongs to all who do not reject it. The New Testament never really distinguishes between the redemption which is provided for all by price and that which is applied by power to all who embrace its provisions.

3. Hence, as there is no deliverance which is not individual, and no salvation which is not deliverance, the whole history of personal religion is exhibited in terms of Redemption it is the release of the will, which is the universal benefit, the repentance which is bestowed by the Spirit of bondage, the release from the law of death in justification and regeneration, the redeeming from all iniquity in entire sanctification, the final expected redemption of the groaning creation, and the deliverance of the saints from the present evil world. Of each of these we shall treat in its place.

HISTORICAL DEVELOPMENT

The history of ecclesiastical doctrine on the Atonement is exceedingly complicated and difficult if all the various shades of opinion and controversy are taken into account; it is very simple if the fundamentals only are regarded. **Historical.**

I. The Ante-Nicene age was neither scientific nor controversial on this subject It was happily unconscious of those speculations which in later ages have done so much to darken the counsel of our redemption; although the germs of coming error are here and there discernible. Generally speaking, the early Patristic doctrine was an undistorted reflection of the teaching of the New Testament. **Early Church.**

1. The Apostolical Fathers, and the other writers of the second century, fairly reproduced the doctrine of St. Paul and St John, the two pillars of the later Scriptural theology, who uniting in the necessity of propitiation in God Himself, then disparted . St Paul exhibiting rather the judicial and rectoral view, St. John **Apostolic Fathers.**

the love and moral influence of the Atonement   It will be found
that both these aspects are with almost equal fidelity dwelt on ;
though the leading characteristic of that early teaching seems
rather to have joined on to St. John's final presentation of Christ
as in His incarnate Person the Living Atonement   This is what
might be expected, as the Apostolical Fathers were mostly under
the influence of the last Evangelist   The sacrifice of Christ was
kept constantly in view ; and all the more as the early worship of
the Church was based upon the Eucharistic commemoration of
that Sacrifice   Even the exaggerations of the Holy Supper tended,
until those exaggerations deepened into positive error, to keep
the central character of the Saviour's death before the minds of
Christians.   It was after the days of these first Fathers that the
perversions of the Feast diverted attention from the death to the

Clem.
Rom.
Ep.
ad Cor.
c. vii.

Incarnation of our Lord   Clemens Romanus, the father of
uninspired Christian literature, strikes the true note on every
point which later controversy has brought into prominence.   A
few phrases are sufficient to establish this . " Let us look sted-
fastly to the blood of Christ, and see how precious it is in God's
sight ($\tau i\mu\iota ov$ $\tau\hat{\omega}$ $\Theta\epsilon\hat{\omega}$) ; which, being shed for our salvation, has

c. xii.

brought the grace of repentance to all the world "   " That by the
blood of our Lord there should be redemption to all that believe

c xvi.

and hope in God "   " You see, beloved, what the pattern of love,
patience, humility is which has been given us."   " For the love
that He bore towards us, our Lord Jesus Christ gave His own
blood for us by the will of God . His flesh for our flesh, His soul
for our souls."   These sentences give their high sanction, not
only to the general doctrine of the Atonement laid down in the
preceding pages, but also to some of the peculiarities which distinguish it.   According to this earliest Father the atoning work
of our Lord was a passion ordained by the Divine Will, endured
by the Saviour's love, of infinite value as a satisfaction to Divine
justice and mercy, available for all, the source of all the preliminary grace of repentance which is given to mankind at large. the
substitutionary sacrifice for our souls, but yet of such a kind that
it avails for our bodies also, but made personal only by faith, and,
finally, the supreme pattern of self-sacrificing devotion.   It is
needless to quote any further from the sub-Apostolic writers.   The

Epistle to Diognetus is the work of an unknown author, probably of the second century, and may be referred to as giving the modern doctrine of the Atonement in its purest form. In it occur such sentences as these: "He Himself gave His own Son a Ransom for us, the Holy for transgressors, the Innocent for the guilty, the Righteous for the unrighteous, the Incorruptible for the corruptible, the Immortal for the mortal. for what could cover our sins but His righteousness? O sweet exchange—that the wickedness of many should be hid in One Righteous, and that the Righteousness of One should justify many." Here we have the Divinity of the Person of the Redeemer and His essential sinlessness lying at the very foundation of His work. The substitutionary character of His sufferings is all but expressed; and the redemption wrought for us, for all transgressors, is as prominent as the redemption wrought in us.

2 The assaults of the Gnostics gave a peculiar direction to the teaching of the second and third centuries. They, differing much in detail, agreed that redemption was deliverance from matter through the work of the Saviour, but that His sufferings were only symbolical, in the semblance of flesh teaching the necessity of death to the flesh. Irenæus and Tertullian proclaimed the reality of the sufferings of the God-man, with their expiatory and substitutionary character, with a clearness and emphasis never since surpassed The former has left this memorable sentence: "Quando incarnatus est et homo factus, longam hominum expositionem in se ipso recapitulavit in compendio nobis salutem præstans, ut quod perdideramus in Adamo, i e, secundum imaginem et similitudinem esse Dei, hoc in Christo reciperemus" The same faithful reproduction of St Paul's doctrine of the Two Adams is found in words which may be translated thus: "As we sinned in the first Adam, because we did not keep the commandments of God, so we have been reconciled or atoned for in the second Adam, because in Him we were obedient unto death, for to no other were we debtors than to Him whose commandments we transgressed from the beginning" Tertullian is equally explicit. But it is in the writings of Justin Martyr that we have the fullest exhibition of the effects of the atonement, though not without indistinctness on some points which may be ascribed to

Ep. ad Diog.

c ix.

Gnostics

Irenæus, Adv. Hær. iii 17.1.

v 16 3.

Justin Martyr.

the peculiar difficulties of his apologetic work   He blends closely
the two ideas of Sacrifice and Ransom   The endurance of the
curse for us Justin rescues from the objection of the Jew, and in
such a way as to show that the Son, blessed for ever and always
blessed, suffered "FOR THE HUMAN RACE THE CURSES OF ALL."
He is careful to show, what has been since too often forgotten, that
"the sacrifice was for all sinners who are willing to repent, and
fast Isaiah's fast"   His doctrine of a vicarious atonement for the
world is none the less strong because it requires personal faith,
being "salvation for those that believe in Him."   In Justin, as
in all the Fathers before Augustine, we find the doctrine of a
universal redemption made particular on the condition of individual repentance and faith

3 The early Fathers generally taught the necessity of a vindication of God's essential justice.   Love was in God, as God was
in Christ, passively bearing the punishment of the sinner as well
as actively providing the atonement.   But the assertion of God's
righteousness before the universe was disturbed by some peculiar
errors, the tendency to exaggerate the place of Satan being one of
them which more or less overshadowed the doctrine for a thousand
years   These were partly a result of Gnosticism, but much more
the effect of Origen's teaching   This Alexandrian Father, like
Clement of the same school, elaborated the sacrificial theory at all
points, and taught explicitly the substitutionary character of the
Passion.   But his speculation almost neutralised his orthodoxy.
Asserting the sole validity of the Redeemer's oblation, he assigned
to the death of the martyrs a relatively expiatory virtue.   Christ's
sacrifice he declares to have been offered upon earth for man, in
heaven for every spirit of the universe.   Its redemption was a
deliverance from Satan, but this is an unscriptural way.   The
human soul of Jesus was given to the Enemy as a ransom for the
souls of men in his power, but he was unable to retain it and the
world was free; the right he had over sinful men was lost when
their sinless Representative was in his hands   Satan, as Gregory
said afterwards, in "hamo ejus incarnatione captus est," outwitted
by the Divinity in the Redeemer on which he had not calculated.
Irenæus expressed the same thought· "The Logos, omnipotent
and not wanting in essential justice, proceeded with strict justice

Marginal notes:
Dial. 94, 95

Dial. 10

Patristic Doctrine.

Adv. Har v 1 1.

even against the apostasy or kingdom of evil itself, redeeming
from it that which was His own originally, not by using violence
as did the devil in the beginning, but by persuasion, as it became
God, so that neither justice should be infringed upon nor the
creation of God perish." But a candid estimate of such a passage
as this, which represents much of the teaching of that age, must
admit that it contains only an inexact statement of the reconciliation of the essential claims of Divine justice, and the spiritual
method of love by which men are to be redeemed But here
comes in another unhappy element Origen taught that apostasy
in a pretemporal state was expiated in the present, and finally
through Christ abolished. It was impossible to hold such a view
as this, without two concomitant errors. ascetic expiations would
almost necessarily creep in when the flesh was made in any sense
the sphere of bondage : and the justice of God, or His holy displeasure against evil, would soon be merged in the idea of a
sovereign goodness predetermining the salvation of all Hence
redemption from the bondage of Satan was followed by the
redemption of Satan himself The universality of human redemption had never been doubted but Origen made it include
the whole universe of evil, reading an incorrect text : χωρὶς θεοῦ,
without or outside of God He tasted death for all. His Universalism Heb. ii. 9
was strenuously opposed by Jerome and others, and as held by
Origen followers was condemned formally at a Synod in Constantinople in A.D. 544.

4. Apart from these errors, and germs of error, there can   Ante-
be no doubt that the ante-Nicene Church was profoundly and   Nicene.
vitally familiar with the truth which we hold to be the sound
one. They did not attempt to formulate it scientifically Heresy
on this subject could scarcely be said to exist, for the Gnostic
errors were outside of the Christian Community, and were met
by the simple statements of the Creed concerning the historical
manifestation of the real Jesus. The earliest Fathers simply
reproduced the spirit and language of the Apostles. And, when
they seemed to err, their error was rather exegetical than theological. They did not propose to distinguish between a sacrifice
offered to God, and a ransom laid down to Satan : but they failed
to see clearly that the teaching of their inspired Masters made

that sacrifice and that ransom one, and both as offered and paid by God to Himself in Christ

Mediæval Doctrine II. From the Nicene Age down to Anselm, circ. A.D. 1100, the doctrine of redemption was closely bound up with that of the Person of Christ. But it had some independent developments to which brief reference may be made.

Greek Church. 1. Oriental Christendom was prepared for the study of the Atonement by its prolonged discussions of Trinitarian questions. Athanasius treats explicitly of the atonement for sin and satis-

De Incar cvii. faction of eternal justice; gives supremacy to the priestly office; and, above all, bases the death of Christ on a necessity in the nature and attributes of God, though not perhaps so absolutely in the Divine nature as in the Divine veracity and dignity   Though he was the great expositor of the Incarnation as a disclosure of God in human nature, he placed first among the reasons for Christ's assumption of flesh the necessity of expiating human guilt. The following words give his teaching on almost every aspect of the question.   "God cannot be untruthful, even for our benefit. Repentance does not satisfy the demands of truth and justice. If the question pertained solely to the corruptions of sin, and not to the guilt and ill-desert of it, repentance might be sufficient. But since God is most truthful and just, who can save, in this emergency, but the Logos, who is above all created beings?   He who created men from nothing could suffer for all, and be their substitute   Hence the Logos appeared   He who was incorporeal, imperishable, omnipresent, manifested Himself   He saw both our misery and the threatening of the law, He saw how unbecoming (ἄτοπον) it would be for sin to escape the law, except through a fulfilment and satisfaction of it."   Satan is omitted, satisfaction to the law is prominent, and, if an eternal necessity in God is not precisely laid down, the doctrine scarcely falls short of it.   Gregory of Nazianzum (390) denies the ransom to Satan (φεῦ τῆς ὕβρεως); but dwells rather too strenuously on the exigency of the Divine government as the reason of the ransom paid to God   He gave the first note of the later Grotian theory:

Orat. xlii. "It is not plain that the Father received the ransom, not because He Himself required or needed it, but for the sake of the Divine government of the universe (δι᾿ οἰκονομίαν), and because man must be sanctified through the incarnation of the Son of God." Cyril of Jerusalem (386) first made emphatic the THEAN-THROPIC VALUE of the atoning death, and its universal vicarious-ness this was a precious result of the Nestorian controversy Cyril of Alexandria (444) still more clearly expounded this idea : "Only a God-man could suffer once for all and One for all " again with reference to the Nestorian and Eutychian controversies. John of Damascus (759), the last of the Greek Fathers, expressed the general doctrine of his own time and some ages afterwards : "He who assumed death for us, died and offered Himself a sacrifice to the Father ; for we had committed wrong against Him, and it was necessary that He should receive a ransom from us, and we thus be delivered from condemnation God forbid that the blood of the Lord should be offered to Satan the tyrant " Here we find three watchwords of expiring orthodox Greek theology . The necessity of an atonement for wrong in the Divine righteousness ; the substitutionary character of the price, our ransom ; and the connection of ransom both with sacrifice and with pardon

    2 Western Christendom before the time of Anselm made no advance beyond the early Fathers, either in precision or in avoid-ance of error. It might have been supposed that St Augustine would have occupied his keen intellect with some of the questions which the New Testament had left undetermined, and which pre-ceding controversies had not settled But he really added not a single idea. He inherited the old notion of a ransom paid to Satan's rights, corresponding with the sacrifice offered to God's justice. "God the Son, being clothed with humanity, subjugated even the devil to man, extorting nothing from him by violence, but overcoming him by the law of justice , for it would have been injustice if the devil had not had the right to rule over the being whom he had taken captive." Disturbed the doctrine by making justification, or the imputation of righteousness to the believer, depend upon the infusion of grace, an error by which the whole work of redemption through an objective atonement for perfect expiation is clouded. Perhaps it would be more correct to say that he failed to reconcile the internal sanctification or righteous-ness wrought by the .Spirit with the external sanctification or righteousness reckoned to him in whom the former is wrought.

Marginal notes:

Expos. Fidei iii. xxvii

Western Church

Aug. de Lib Arb. iii. 10.

He erred from the Pauline phraseology perhaps more than from the Pauline doctrine. Moreover, he never expressed himself even with the same confidence as some of the Greeks as to the necessity of atonement to the justice of God · in other words, where they faltered he faltered still more. "They are foolish," he says, "who declare that the wisdom of God could not liberate men otherwise than by God assuming humanity, being born of a woman, and suffering at the hands of sinners." He separated omnipotence from justice, and taught, like Origen, that God's power was absolute in the provision for salvation. As the Arians thought that the Son was begotten, βουλήσει, by the will of the Father, so Augustine, with many before and after him, thought that the Atonement was not an eternal necessity but of the sole will of God Finally, Augustine narrowed the range of the virtue

Greg Mag. of the Atonement the first of the Fathers who did this Gregory the Great (604), called the first Pontiff, is remarkably Pauline in this part of his teaching, and far beyond his predecessor Augustine. The following sentences give an idea of his theology .

Mor. in "Guilt can be extinguished only by a penal offering to justice"
Job Christ "assumed our nature without our corruption. He made
xvii 46 Himself a sacrifice for us a victim able to die because of His humanity, and in Divine righteousness able to cleanse." During the next four hundred years there was no such special development of the doctrine as would warrant notice here

III. Anselm, in the latter part of the eleventh century, gave an entirely new direction to ecclesiastical thought on this great question . a direction which has been permanent.

Cur Deus 1. In his book CUR DEUS HOMO? the idea of an atonement
Homo. proper was exhibited as it had never before been seen ; and the term Satisfaction to Divine justice became the leading formula. Anselm utterly rejected the claims of Satan to reparation , he fixed attention on the thought that sin is debt to God, a failure to give Him His due, and that, as "Suprema justitia non est aliud quam ipse Deus," satisfaction to the Divine justice was indispensable. As none but God could vindicate His own honour the God-man must atone , and His sacrifice as presenting FOR MAN "something greater than all that is not God" has infinite

Satisfac- atoning value   The term SATISFACTION had been employed by
tion.

Tertullian from jurisprudence into theology, but with reference especially to human acts of penitence; Hilary and Ambrose had referred it to the passion of Christ; but Anselm revived it from long slumber as a watchword for all future time. He does not distinguish between the active and the passive righteousness of the God-man in rendering this satisfaction, but he certainly lays the stress on the latter dare animam seu tradere se ipsum morti ad honorem Dei, hoc ex debito Deus non exigit ab Illo This sacrificial offering, of infinitely greater value than even the ethical demerit of sin, is the MERIT of Christ which overflows to every-one who believes. " Can anything be more just than for God to remit all debt, when in this way He receives a satisfaction greater than all the debt, provided only it be offered with the right senti-ment ?" Thus human Guilt or Debt demanded a Divine-human payment, and faith appropriates this as justification to the soul There are flaws in the Anselmic doctrine · such as the subordinate episode that the number of redeemed men would compensate the chasm introduced by the fall of angels. But nothing can dim the value of Anselm's service to Christian theology, as having estab-lished the immanent necessity in the Divine nature of an atonement for the infinite evil and offence of sin

2. Mediæval controversy on this great question was very impor- *Mediæval Contro-versy.* tant as shaping in opposite directions the issues of Trent and the Reformation. The doctrine of Anselm was for four hundred years the common text some opposed his Biblical theory, others refined upon and exaggerated his views, and a few struck out a path of mediation. This threefold distribution of Scholastic polemics will furnish a clue to the student who pursues this sub-ject in ecclesiastical history

(1.) Abælard (1141) was the chief opponent of Anselm; and *Abælard.* may be said to be the founder of a theory of the Atonement which shuts out the deepest mystery of the Cross. He referred the Christian redemption only to the love of God as its source ; and taught that there could be nothing in the Divine essence which absolutely required satisfaction for sin. Redemption like Creation was a Fiat . equally sure, equally free, and equally independent of anything in the creature The influence of the work of Christ, as accomplished on the cross, and carried on in His intercession,

VOL. II.   X

is moral only : subduing the heart, awakening repentance, and leading the soul to the boundless mercy of God whose benevolence is the only attribute concerned in the pardon of sin   Peter Lombard (1164) varied from this view only little , and introduced, for future service, in his Liber Sententiarum, the perilous doctrine that Christ's penal sufferings deliver from the temporal consequences of evil.   Duns Scotus denied the possibility of an infinite demerit in human transgression, and therefore the necessity of an infinite value in Christ's human suffering   The relation of the Atonement to sin was purely arbitrary, springing from the mere pleasure of God   " Every creaturely oblation is worth what God accepts it for, and nothing beyond."   This is the theory of Acceptilatio, of which more hereafter.

Scholastic Refinements.

(2) The Scholastic refinements on Anselm's doctrine were endless.   Bonaventura and Thomas Aquinas, who represent the later Schoolmen in their utmost subtilty, and more than any others shaped Romanist theology, distinguish between the absolute and relative necessity of atonement   holding the latter only, though admitting that of all possible modes this of satisfaction was most congruous with the Divine perfections.   In their anxiety to save the freedom and omnipotence of God they introduced a distinction or discord into the Divine essence from which Anselm's theory is free.   Aquinas laid great stress upon the Mystical Union between the Saviour and His people ; and here two errors crept in   Room was made for the limitation of redemption to the believer configured to his Lord . the guilt of the sinner being transferred to Christ even as Christ's merit is transferred to the sinner.   This is in strange contradiction to the universality elsewhere assigned to the virtue of the Atonement   And, secondly, in the case of sin after baptism the believer must be " configured " to his Lord by personal penance.   That penance is imperfect , but it is an expiation joined to the Redeemer's.   Aquinas also introduced the distinction between the satisfaction and the merit of our Substitute.   His theory that the satisfaction was offered to penal justice, and the merit of obedience wins eternal life for the saint, was an anticipation of the subsequent distinction needlessly introduced between the Active and the Passive Righteousness of Christ.   His new dogma of the superabundance of the Saviour's

merits—Christi passio non solum sufficiens, sed etiam SUPER-
ABUNDANS SATISFACTIO—which, while seeming to honour the
Atonement, was certainly based upon a lowered estimate of sin,
laid the foundation for the superstructure of a treasury of merits
at the disposal of the Church. The Thomists, as his followers
were called, had a long controversy with the Scotists, followers
of Duns Scotus, on this point and on many others that became
afterwards prominent in the controversies of the Reformation

(3) The Scholastics who mediated between Anselm's and the
opposite doctrine were Bernard, Bonaventura, Alexander of Hales,
and many of the later Mystics   They paved the way for the
Reform of the Sixteenth Century · partly, by admitting a real
laxity as to the ABSOLUTE necessity of atonement, which cannot
be exchanged for a RELATIVE necessity without great peril; and,
partly, by keeping alive in a narrower circle the Anselmic theory,
which was to put forth its renewed energy in the great awakening.
This was the case especially with some of the Mystics and Precursors of the Reformation, such as Wessel, who says "Ipse
Deus, ipse sacerdos, ipse hostia, pro se, de se, sibi satisfecit."
These deep words deserve to be remembered for their own value,
as well as because they were written on the threshold of the temple
of reformed theology ; as also those by which they are followed
"In Christ we behold not only a Reconciled but a Reconciling
Deity ; an Incarnate God who, in the sinner's place and for the
sinner's salvation, furnishes what His own attributes of holiness
and justice require."

IV The Tridentine Soteriology, profoundly studied, will be
found to depart widely from the Anselmic doctrine which it pro-
fesses to hold   though this does not appear on the surface, and is
not evident in the definitions   The following two opposite tendencies may be noted ; referring, however, to the objective Atonement with which alone we have to do.

1. The satisfaction rendered to Divine justice by the Passion
of Christ is fully recognised   "Christus, qui, cum essemus
inimici, propter nimiam caritatem, qua dilexit nos, nobis sua
sanctissima passione ligno crucis justificationem meruit et pro
nobis Deo Patri satisfecit." But it is added "abunde cumulateque
satisfecit ;" and hence the merit of Christ is in a sense over-

Mediation

Wessel

Tridentine Theory.

Conc. Trid vi 7

X 2

estimated.   The Thomist dogma of Meritum Christi Super-
abundans laid as we have seen the foundation of that treasury
which, enlarged by the superfluous merit of the saints, and committed to the Church, mystically one with and the same as Christ,
constituted the source of Indulgences.   Origen applied the infinite
superfluity to the rest of the universe; this doctrine limited it to
the remission of the temporal consequences of sin.

2. On the other hand, the atoning merit is under-estimated ·
for the virtue of Christ's death is declared to avail only for the
sins of the world, and those committed before baptism.   The
virtue of the Atonement, as applied for mortal sins committed
afterwards, must be connected, so far as the temporal or not eternal
punishment is concerned, with man's own expiation.

3 But it is rather in its subjective character, or in its individual aspect, as Justification, that the error of Roman Catholic
theology appears.   Reserving for the Righteousness of Faith some
further remarks on this subject, it may be enough to refer to
the Tridentine Canons which deny that the atoning satisfaction
of Christ is the sole meritorious ground of a sinner's justification.
Whatever value is attributed to the passion of the Redeemer as
expiating the sin of mankind, righteousness is imputed to the
personal sinner only as he is made righteous by the infusion of
faith : it is, so to speak, imputed to the faith and not to the man
who believes.   Undoubtedly, it is affirmed that the grace which
more and more justifies the soul comes through the Atonement.
But the direct application of the Saviour's finished work in the
purging of the conscience is effectually precluded.

Reforma-
tion.

V. The Reformation revived generally the theory of Anselm,
as that was the vindication of an eternal and absolute, and not
merely a relative and economical, necessity for satisfaction in the
Divine nature   The same variations in the statement of this
which marked the Patristic and Scholastic theology are observable
among the Reformers.   Luther, and the great divines that followed
him, were more rigid than Calvin and his followers, who speak of
the possibility of redemption even apart from the work of Christ.

Luther
and
Calvin.

1 The points which the Lutheran theory and the Reformed
Confession agreed in rescuing from the perversion of ages were
the sufficiency of the Redeemer's Satisfaction for all sins, original
and actual , the pre-eminence in the atoning work of the death of

Christ, His incarnation and His resurrection flanking this on either side The active side of the Saviour's obedience was added to the passive, a SATISPASSIO being divided off from the SATIS-FACTIO ; or they regarded the whole virtue of the Atonement as Satisfaction and Merit, the former repairing the dishonour of the law and the latter providing righteousness for man It may be said that both branches of the New Theology laid much stress on a division of the virtue of Christ's work into its reparation of the honour of the law by Obedience and its endurance of its penalty in the Passion.

2. The Reformed or Calvinistic doctrine limited the scope and design of the Atonement to the elect , the Lutheran divines, after some hesitation, adopted the theory of a universal efficacy in the Redeemer's mediation. The Calvinists made less account of the three offices of the Redeemer inasmuch as His work was rather the instrumental accomplishment of an eternal decree. Against the views of Piscator, who insisted that Christ's obedience to law was needed for Himself as man, and must be excluded from His vicarious atoning work, the Reformed Formula Consensus (1675) asserted "Christ rendered satisfaction to God the Father, by the obedience of His death, in the place of the elect, in such sense that the entire obedience which He rendered to the law through the whole course of His life, whether actively or passively, ought to be reckoned into the account of His vicarious righteousness and obedience " This, like many other statements in the formularies and divines, is ambiguous · it only does not positively lay down the erroneous principle that the two parts of our Saviour's one obedience are distributed severally to the believer for release from condemnation and investiture with holiness. But the question here involved belongs rather to the doctrine of Justification.

The Reformed Doctrine

VI. The Socinian doctrine, if such it may be called, must be noticed here partly because it represented in the seventeenth century the Rationalist assault on the principles of the Atonement which has been modified but not essentially changed in later times, and partly because it helped to shape the Arminian which followed it, and other systems of thought in other respects orthodox Early Socinianism held a much higher estimate both of the Person and of the Work of Christ than that of the Modern

Socinian-ism

Unitarians But, as there could be in it no doctrine, strictly speaking, of the Incarnate Person, so it has no doctrine of Atonement. Its contribution to the history of the subject is simply the array of arguments against the Anselmic principles, and its method of explaining away Scripture

Divine Sovereignty of Mercy

1 The supreme principle in Socinianism as in Predestinarianism is an Absolute Sovereignty in God, disposing of all creatures according to His own will. In Calvinism the arbitrary will governs the destinies of men; in Socinianism it governs the attributes of God It refuses to admit of any immutable qualities whether of justice or mercy in the Divine nature, these being only expressions of His occasional will, called out as it were by the conduct of man An eternal justice demanding punishment is inconsistent with an eternal mercy prompting to forgive Satisfaction for sin is incompatible with love. Against this objection it is enough to say that it opposes the first principles of Scriptural teaching concerning God, Who is represented as reconciling in Himself these opposite attributes by an atonement which is at once and equally an expression of both, and regulating His will Thus our doctrine is safe from Socinian censure only when it first shuts itself up in God, and grasps the reconciliation of justice and mercy in the Divine nature.

Substitution

2 Descending to the theory of Substitution, Socinianism denies its possibility in any form. Sin and punishment are both strictly and for ever personal There is a form of the doctrine against which this plea has much force But it does not touch our presentation of it (1) Strictly speaking, Christ is not a Substitute for any man He is the Representative and Vicar of humanity, and the Other Self of the race, being the Second Adam He is also the Other Self also of every believer who claims His sacrifice as his own, and says in the language of appropriating devotion, ALL THINE ARE MINE But his sin is dealt with as his own and put away from him. He is

Gal ii 20

CRUCIFIED WITH CHRIST. (2) The objection that the Saviour has not suffered the precise equivalent for man's sin is valid only against those who plead that there was such a commercial equivalent. He could not suffer eternal torments. The union of the Son of God with mankind gave His intention of atonement in suffering an infinite value it was accepted as such because it was ın His heart.   In an infinitely higher sense than Hıs servant Paul He said, *I could wish' ηὐχόμην γὰρ, αὐτὸς ἐγὼ ἀνάθεμα εἶναι*   (3)   Rom ıx 3 In urging that the Redeemer's active obedience could not be vicarıous as superadded to Hıs passıve obedience Socınıanısm is opposing a false theory of the Atonement   (1) Once more, the objection that imputatıon to faıth is ınconsistent with a plenary satısfactıon ıs important   Socınıus pleaded against the teaching whıch maıntaıns that thıs unıversal benefit ıs given to none but those who believe   But that ıs not the true doctrıne   Christ's benefit ıs ımparted before personal faıth , and, in case of believers, theır faıth ıs the not rejectıng what was before provided for them as theır own.   The vehement protest against the combinatıon of imputed active rıghteousness and the ınexorable demand of the law has its full force against those whom ıt concerns , but not against those who believe that the appropriatıon of a full forgiveness sets the believer free to fulfil ın love all the claıms of rıghteousness.

3. The more positıve prıncıples of Socınıanısm maıntaın that the sacrıfıcıal language used concernıng the Redeemer only figuratively descrıbes Hıs authority ın heaven to declare forgıve- ness ; and that the Scriptures without figure announce paıdon as waiting for all who, sympathising with the Redeemer's death, repent and abandon theır sins.

Socınıan- ism and Scrıpture.

(1) According to the teachıng of early Socınıanısm—as dis- tinguished from that of modern Unitarıanism—the Saviour's prıestly office was only figurative on earth, and began in heaven where He uses Hıs exalted authority to plead for mankind "The sacerdotal office consists ın this, that as He can ın royal authority help us ın all our necessıtıes, so ın Hıs priestly character, and the chaıacter of Hıs help ıs called by a figure Hıs sacrifice " But ıt may be said that forgiveness is never represented as bestowed on repentance simply as such. God ıs in Christ reconcilıng the world to Hımself; and for Christ's sake forgıves the sins whıch only the Spirit obtained by the Atonement enables us to confess and forsake.

Prıest- hood ın Heaven only. Cat. Rac. Qu. 476

(2.) The Supreme in Hıs majesty of mercy forgives on the ground of repentance and obedience. The sufferıngs of Chrıst were the vehıcle of a moral influence to ınduce that repentance and animate and exemplıfy that obedıence. There ıs no relaxa- tion of the holy law whıch is vindıcated as the bond of obligatı ıı

Repent- ance

to the moral universe. We also hold the exemplary character of the sufferings of Christ; but as illustrating the necessity of a vindication of pure justice, and not merely the love and mercy of the Lawgiver In modern times this argument has been reproduced in a thousand ways: these all marking the offence of the Cross which has not ceased. There are two everlasting safeguards of the truth. the constitution of the human mind which bears witness to the wrath as well as the love of God; and the express revelation of Scripture concerning the reconciliation.

Modern Unitarianism.

4. In recent times Socinian principles have been introduced into the Latitudinarian theology of many who do not reject the doctrine of the Trinity. And it is here that they are most dangerous. In the works of some divines, the love of God alone is introduced into the atoning sacrifice, which on Christ's part is a sublime and supreme act of repentance for man, His AMEN to the sentence of the law, and to man himself an affecting representative sorrow which he must make his own by adding to it the element of personal consciousness of sin The latter idea links it with the Romish doctrine of human additional expiation; and, as to the former, a representative sorrow which does not taste the wrath of God against sin falls immeasurably below the Scriptural representative of the atoning passion in which our Lord was made a curse for us The theory utterly fails in the link between the Divine-human sorrow and the human appropriation of it; and it entirely forgets that Christ was made the embodiment and representative of sin as well as the incarnation of suffering Other modifications of the Unitarian theory of the Atonement in combination with Trinitarian doctrine of God are endless; but none presents any such definitely marked system as needs arrest attention.

Arminianism

VII The doctrine of atonement which is sometimes characterised as Grotian and sometimes as Arminian is based on one common fundamental principle. Arminius and his follower Grotius held the same theory up to a certain point, after which they differ.

1. Both aimed to mediate between the rigorous Anselmic view of a satisfaction which is the substitution of a strict equivalent for the penalty due to sin and the Socinian rejection of all vicarious intervention. The atoning reparation which they agree to uphold is one that satisfied not the rigour and exactitude of

Divine justice only or especially but also and chiefly the just and compassionate will of God: laying the emphasis rather on the love than on the justice of God as honoured in the Atonement They refuse to regard the Saviour's redemption as the payment of a debt to a creditor; it is to them a substitute for a judicial penalty, which substitute being the oblation of Christ, infinitely precious, is counted sufficient by the Father. This has somewhat of the character of the Scotist ACCEPTILATIO (accepti latio), which was in Roman law an acquittance from obligation by word of mouth, without real payment; differing from it by assuming a real compensation, but not of an exact and commercial character. And here the Arminian principle comes in with a just protest Grotius, who in his very important work on the Satisfaction of Christ, reintroduced the term, was obliged to vindicate it He insisted that his theory of a satisfaction offered by Christ, and reputed sufficient by God, was more than the Acceptilatio of Roman jurisprudence In fact what God accounted sufficient was of infinite value; but still not the precise equivalent of the penalty due to sin. There was a relaxation of the claims of the law in one sense, though not in another The most rigorous Anselmic theory must admit the principle, so far as the acceptance of a substitute goes, why not then carry the principle a little farther and make the interfering act extend to the VALUE of the thing substituted as well as to the PRINCIPLE of substitution. especially as the value here is infinite ?

Accepti-latio

2. But Grotius, its later representative, did not agree with the Arminian theology when he limited the satisfaction to the dignity of the law, the honours of the Lawgiver, the protection of the interests of the universe, and the exhibition of a deterrent example. Grotius founded what has been called the Rectoral or Governmental theory of the Atonement, which dwells too exclusively on its necessity for the vindication of God's righteousness as the Ruler of all. Not to speak of the invincible repugnance felt by every reverent mind to the thought that our Lord was thus made a spectacle to the universe, this theory errs by making a subordinate purpose supreme. Limborch, as the representative of Arminianism, answers his own question, An Christus morte suâ circa Deum aliquid effecerit ? by replying that the sufferings

Armini-anism proper

of Christ were those of a SACRIFICE Divinely appointed to take the place of a penalty, and reconciled God to man as if they had been the sinner's own punishment. Christ therefore by His death did effect something in God; though strictly speaking He only carried out in act what had been already effected in purpose. More than this the Scripture does not require. Arminianism holds that the Sacrifice was offered for the whole world · it must therefore for that reason also renounce the commutative theory of exact and mutual compensation, since some may perish for whom Christ died, and He would be defrauded of His reward in them.

VIII. A few brief observations may be made in conclusion.

Three Theories

1. Most of the errors that have passed in review have sprung from failure to connect the three leading Biblical ideas: the atonement in God, as a necessity in the Divine attributes; the reconciliation on earth, as vindicating to the universe the Rectoral justice of God, and the exhibition of the redemption to man, as moving upon his conscience and will and heart. Here unite what are sometimes called the SUBSTITUTIONARY, the GOVERNMENTAL and the MORAL INFLUENCE theories The union of these is the Scriptural doctrine, as it is set forth in Scripture, and especially in the Epistles of St Peter, St. Paul, and St. John: the last giving in many particulars the finishing touches in the union of the Person and the Work of Christ. Neither of these theories is valid, standing alone. Each is necessary as the complement of the others The doctrine would commend itself more than it does to the minds of all devout persons if justice was done to every aspect. The champion of either of these theories who thinks it necessary absolutely to deny the truth of the others proves that his own is wrong

Human personality

2. Another prevalent source of confusion is the tendency to undervalue the personality and comparative independence of man's relation to God No doctrine of revealed religion stamps such dignity on the human spirit as that which makes it the object of this stupendous intervention. But there is a certain Pantheism which infects much of the theology of the modern Christian Church, tinging the theories and vocabulary even when the ground principles of Pantheism are rejected or perhaps not understood The more closely the speculations of this philosophical Chris-

tianity are studied the more manifest will it be that they reduce the Person and Work of Christ to the rank of mere symbols of transcendental mysteries of evolution, which seem to do honour to the union of God and man but at the expense of everything that may be called Mediation   The individuality of the soul is lost, and man is merged in humanity   But it is not in England that we have to encounter this substitute for the doctrine of the Atonement.

3 Akin to this, though distinct from it, is the tendency, not especially modern, to underestimate the evil of sin.   Theories of the Atonement fluctuate with theories of the evil that makes it necessary.   If sin is regarded as a necessary phenomenon of human development, the Atonement must needs only be an accidental aid in that development   If it is viewed as only a disease or only as misery, then the atonement will be regarded as only an expedient, though one of the highest and most effectual, for the remedy of human weakness.   But if sin is regarded, in the light of Scripture, as an active rebellion of the human will which affects the Divine nature and attributes and government as well as human interests, then the Atonement becomes an eternal necessity in God as well as an eternal necessity for man   Every theory that robs the work of Christ of its expiatory character will be found, on close examination, to make sin comparatively A LIGHT THING as touching the Supreme Ruler, however melancholy in its workings and consequences to its victim.   Now there is nothing more plain than that the Bible, from the history of the loss of Paradise to the prediction of Paradise re-entered, consistently and uniformly teaches that wrong in the creature touches the inmost essence of the Triune God , and that it evolves in the depths of the Divine nature eternal pity for the evil and eternal displeasure towards the sin.   No single topic in Biblical theology is so little varied in its development as this.

Estimate of Sin

4 There is prevalent among professedly orthodox theologians a tendency to ascribe to the Eternal God a certain all-commanding attribute of LOVE which is so described as to undermine the foundations of the doctrine of the Atonement.   It is possible so to exaggerate the Divine compassion as to make it inconsistent

Love.

with the most obvious facts of experience. The mind may be so possessed by a morbid sentiment of the necessary supremacy of the tenderness of God as to be incapable of steadily contemplating His holy wrath against sin To such a feeling the whole of Scripture must appear to be written in a language of the most violent and incongruous symbols. It is the purest homage to love, the bond of perfectness in God as well as man, to correct that one-sided view. If it is the royal attribute—which, however, the Scripture does not say—it reigns IN God but not OVER Him. Of the Divine Being it is also said . *Justice and judgment are the habitation of Thy throne*

Ps lxxxix. 14.

Scriptural and Theological Phraseology.

5. It is important to remember in all discussions on the Atonement that the language of theology must be controlled and explained by the language of Scripture. Through forgetting this many prejudices arise which would otherwise perhaps be obviated The leading New-Testament terms are so simple that they may be comprised in one sentence Christ as MEDIATOR exhibits in His own Person the RECONCILIATION between God and mankind, which however required to be wrought out by a SACRIFICE of OBEDIENCE in life and death, which has PROPITIATED God in respect to sin, and accomplished a REDEMPTION for all men, to be appropriated by the faith of individuals. Theology has varied these terms and added a few. They indicate that the oblation of Christ was an ATONEMENT or atoning SATISFACTION of the Divine justice and the claims of law, as well as of the Divine love or saving will, EXPIATING the sin or cancelling its punishment, and PROPITIATING the Divine displeasure, in one and the same act If the Scriptures are a revelation of God to man, this doctrine is an eternal truth, and vital to everyone who reads.

THE ADMINISTRATION OF REDEMPTION.

THE HOLY GHOST.

THE GOSPEL VOCATION.

THE PRELIMINARIES OF GRACE.

THE STATE OF SALVATION.

THE TENURE OF COVENANT BLESSINGS.

THE ETHICS OF REDEMPTION.

THE CHRISTIAN CHURCH.

THE ADMINISTRATION OF REDEMPTION.

THIS sentence better than any other defines that comprehensive department of theological science which is occupied with the subjective aspect of what is sometimes called
SOTERIOLOGY. If we use the phrase APPLICATION OF
REDEMPTION we are in danger of the predestinarian error
which assumes that the finished work of Christ is applied
to the individual according to the fixed purpose of an election of grace. The phrase APPROPRIATION OF SALVATION
tends to the other and Pelagian extreme, too obviously
making the atoning provision of Christ matter of individual
free acceptance or rejection. The term PERSONAL SAL-
VATION avoids these extremes; but it scarcely does honour
enough to the office of the Holy Ghost. The ADMINISTRA-
TION OF REDEMPTION satisfies every necessary condition.
This is the widest field of theology: gathering up the
results of all that precede and more or less anticipating
the one only branch that remains.

A complete view of this entire department of Christian
Theology may be thus taken in order First, we must
define the special relations of God the Spirit to the administration of the Saviour's work. Then we have to
consider the character, terms and conditions of the
universal Call of the Gospel. the agency of the Holy
Ghost in the outer court of the temple of redemption

Thirdly, it will be necessary to dwell on the preliminary conditions of grace, or those subjects that belong to Conversion, Repentance and Faith: which form the transition, fourthly, to the state of covenanted salvation itself, with all its many privileges diversified in their unity. Fifthly, it will then be of great importance to examine the general conditions on which the perpetuity of these blessings depends. This will fairly introduce the Morals of the Gospel, in the establishment of a holy character, as formed by Christianity, which ought not to be severed from the Spirit's administration. And, lastly, the Church must be included, whether as the fellowship resulting from the bestowment of grace, or as the institute in and through which that grace is bestowed.

The distinction between Objective and Subjective Soteriology, or Redemption as once for all accomplished by Christ and Redemption as administered by the Holy Spirit, has been again and again referred to. But its importance is so great that it may once more be impressed with advantage at this point. A careful consideration of the bearings of this distinction would itself be a defence, and a sufficient defence, against many of the most serious errors that have troubled and still trouble the faith of Christianity. We shall find illustrations of this in abundance. It is sufficient now to assert and vindicate the distinction itself, as it reigns throughout the New Testament. The offices of the Second and of the Third Persons of the Holy Trinity in the work of man's salvation are not more carefully separated than the one redemption wrought out by the Former is separated from the personal application of it, which is the province of the Latter. The term Soteriology fairly embraces both, but it has not been naturalised in English theological works, and it is not without a certain ambiguity.

THE HOLY SPIRIT.

As the Incarnate Son is the Redeemer of Mankind in virtue of His perfect work of Reconciliation, so the Holy Ghost in His Divine 'personality is the Administrator of that redemption. His revelation as such has kept pace with the revelation of the redeeming Son. In the Old-Testament age He was the promise of the Father, even as the Christ was: and, as the promised Christ already was the world's unrevealed Saviour, so the Spirit was the unrevealed Dispenser of His salvation. The Redeemer made the promise of the Father His own promise; and, on His ascension, obtained and sent, as the fruit of His mediatorial obedience, the Holy Ghost in His most abundant influence as the Third Person of the Godhead and the Personal Agent in the final accomplishment of the purpose of the Mediatorial Trinity.

THE HOLY SPIRIT IN THE PREPARATIONS OF REDEMPTION.

Prepara-
tions.

The distinct personality of the Holy Ghost is not made prominent in Scripture until the act of atonement is on the eve of completion. But the light of the later Scriptures thrown back upon the earlier reveals Him as a Divine Person present and active throughout the preparatory economy. With the coming of Christ His agency becomes more distinct; and it is from that time forward intimately connected with our Lord's redeeming Person and work. The full disclosure, however, of the Person and Offices of the Spirit, and of His relation to the finished redemption of the world, was not given until the set time for the Pentecostal revelation of the Third Person was fully come ; that is, until the Redeemer had ended His work upon earth and ascended to heaven.

THE SPIRIT IN THE OLD TESTAMENT.

Before Christc.

The Holy Ghost in His special relation to the Christian economy was not sent down until Pentecost. But, as the Person in the Holy Trinity by Whom the Father's Revelation of Himself through the Son, whether in Creation or Providence or Redemption, is accomplished in act, He has been present and operative from the beginning · the Administrator of the work of the Three-One God in every dispensation.

The Giver of Life

1 The Spirit, like the Son, but without concealment of His name, is throughout the Old Testament disclosed as the Agent of the Godhead in the production of all life, especially of the living spirit of man In anticipation, as it were, of Pentecost, He was at the beginning THE LORD AND GIVER OF LIFE , and Job's word may be used in the widest extent concerning man as such : *the*

Job
xxxiii 4

Spirit of God hath made me. The Son from the beginning has been the Life of men , but it was not till the Incarnation that He gave that life more abundantly, and was fully revealed as THE

John i 4

LIFE This distinction also holds good between the unrevealed and the revealed relation of the Personal Medium of the gift of

Gen i 2.

life The same Spirit Who *moved upon the face of the waters* was

Gen ii 7

breathed into the face of man and made him *a living soul.* And,

John i 4

as the Son was from the beginning the *Light of men,* so the Spirit

Gen vi. 3

is represented as moving upon and striving with man from the beginning. The unrevealed Second Person gave special and mysterious manifestations of Himself as the Angel of Jehovah, the Word of the Lord, and so the unrevealed Third Person is often referred to as the Divine Agent in spiritual gifts and influences

Ex. xxxi. 3.
Num. xi. 17,
xxvii. 18
Judges iii 10

Thus of Bezaleel it is said *I have filled him with the Spirit of God.* And of Moses, Joshua, and the Judges, and the first kings, it is recorded that the Spirit endowed them for their office. Thus, carrying back the personality of the Holy Ghost from the New Testament to the Old, we are taught that without Him the Eternal did not act on the world throughout the ancient economy.

2 But specifically in the administration of the prophetic preparations of the Gospel is this truth seen.   The doctrine of the
Saviour's Person and Work has made it plain that the revelation
of the Son was mediated by the Spirit of Christ which was in the
prophets; that the entire Old Testament as the record of the
Gospel before the Advent was given by His inspiration , and that
He, no less than the Son Himself, was *the Promise of the Father.*

1 Sam xvi. 13, 14.

Acts i. 4.

THE SPIRIT IN THE GOSPELS.

The Gospels.

The Holy Spirit in the history of the Lord's manifestation and
life upon earth occupies a midway position between the Old
Testament and the Pentecost.   As the Administrator of Redemption He appears as the actual Agent in the raising up and the
mission of the Incarnate Saviour , while He is at the same time
the Object of our Lord's prophecy as His future Agent in carrying
out His work.   Every reference to the Holy Ghost in the Gospels
falls under one or other of these heads

1. With regard to the former, it is enough to recapitulate what
has already been established . first, that the human nature of the
Son was the special Divine production of the Holy Ghost; and,
secondly, that whatever in the Incarnate Person and Work of
Jesus belongs to Him as the representative of mankind is under
the Spirit's direction , while all that belongs to Him as the representative of Deity is the act of His own Eternal Spirit as the
Son   The Third Person presides especially over the humble
and subordinate relation of the Mediatorial Second Person in the
economy of redemption.

The Spirit of the Incarnate.

2. With regard to the latter, the records of the Evangelists
furnish a series of testimonies of the Saviour Himself concerning
the future dispensation of the Spirit which culminate in the farewell discourses and the resurrection promise.

The Re-deemer's Work.

(1.) *How much more shall your heavenly Father give the Holy Spirit
to them that ask Him !* begins the series with a free and unlimited
declaration which should throw its grace over all that follows
throughout this department of theology.   It is to the administration of redemption what the Protevangelium is to redemption
itself . it is the dawn of the Pentecostal day.

Luke xi. 13

Y 2

John vii.
39.

(2.) *This spake He of the Spirit, which they that believe on Him should receive: for the Holy Spirit was not yet given; because that Jesus was not yet glorified.* In this saying, the link between the former and the final promises, St. John, as his manner is on special occasions, expounds his Master's word, writing long after Pentecost: it teaches us that the Person and gifts of the Spirit were reserved until the Saviour's glorification and the full manifestation of both dependent upon it. Jesus must be glorified of the Father before the Spirit glorified Him.

Final
Promises.

(3.) Passing over the specific promises of the Spirit to the Apostles, as contained in the Synoptists, we have our Lord's most full foreannouncement of the coming and function of His Divine Representative. The farewell discourse is in truth a revelation of the Trinity; our Lord, setting out with a declaration of His own identity with the Father in the Divine nature, proceeds to John xiv.
16. declare that the Spirit should come as a Person, to *abide for ever* with His people, as the Revealer of all His truth and the indwelling Guide of all believers. Before He fulfilled His course on earth, like the Baptist He announced the coming of Another: John iii.
30. but did not add, like His own forerunner, *He must increase, but I must decrease.* The Holy Spirit, though Himself God, should, in the present economy, only glorify the Son, by revealing His Person and expanding His doctrine and administering His king- Acts v. 32. dom. *We are the witnesses of Him; and so is also the Holy Ghost.*

Pente-
cost.

THE HOLY SPIRIT AFTER PENTECOST.

With Pentecost begins the dispensation of the Spirit. His office has supreme reference to the administration of Christ and His redemption. And this under three aspects. He is the Revealer of the Son generally, and of the Godhead as revealed in Him. He is the Saviour's Agent in dispensing individual salvation: being a witness for Him TO the soul; His Divine power IN the soul; but both in one. He is the Lord's representative in His body the

Church : gathering it from the world, ruling within it, and dispensing the gifts of its Head. But, while subordinate in the mediatorial economy, the Holy Ghost is a Divine Person, the Agent, in the unity of the Father and the Son, of His own Divine acts.

This assemblage of topics must be exhibited only in epitome. To a great extent they have been anticipated in the discussion of the Trinity and the Person and Offices of Christ. They arise also in separate discussion throughout the whole course of this part of our subject : the work and influences of the Spirit meet us everywhere, being so ubiquitous that it is almost impossible to reduce all to summary. But the honour due to the ever-blessed Spirit of the Father and the Son, and the just demands of dog-matic system, alike require that some general analysis of the agency of the Holy Ghost be placed here in the forefront. A third reason also may be assigned, arising out of the indistinctness which has prevailed on this subject in much of the theology of earlier and later times. As to the earlier development of the doc-trine enough has been already said when treating of the Trinity. As to later ages, it cannot be said that there has been any develop-ment : there has been no such controversy, and no such decisions have been formulated, as we have to do with in the Person of Christ. The offices of the Holy Ghost have been obscured by exaggerations of sacramental efficacy ; and His personal relations to the believer have been undervalued in many systems. But what requires to be noted on these points will occur under the several heads of His general administrations. No separate his-torical review will be needed.

ECONOMY OF THE SPIRIT.

1. The New Testament does not sanction the thought that with Pentecost began a dispensation of the Spirit in the sense of a new economy or οἰκονομία, distinct from that of the Father and the Son. The nearest approach to such a doctrine is found in St. Paul's Corinthian exhibition of the contrast between the old and new forms of the one covenant in Christ. The former was a

Economy
of the
Spirit.

2 Cor. iii. 6—11. ministration, or διακονία, of the letter, and of condemnation, and of death . a glorious manifestation of the Divine law which shut up the covenant people to the need and the expectation of an atoning Saviour. The latter is a ministration of the Spirit, and of life, and of righteousness . a much more glorious manifestation of the Redeeming Lord, and of His Spirit, and of liberty in Him. Now this ministration, of which the Apostles were the ministers,

2 Cor. v. 18 is in the sequel called *the Ministry of Reconciliation.* Thus the dispensation of the finished Atonement and the dispensation of the Spirit are one

New Economy. 2 But there is a sense in which Pentecost introduced a new economy · that of the Holy Ghost, as the final revelation of the Holy Trinity The One God, known in the Old Testament as Jehovah, a Name common to the Three Persons, was then made

2 Cor. iii. 17 known in the Third Person : ὁ δὲ Κύριος τὸ πνεῦμά ἐστιν, the Lord the Father, the Lord the Son, is the Lord *the Spirit.* Hence the glory of the Day of Pentecost, excelling in glorye very former manifestation of the Supreme. The Shekinah, the ancient symbol of the future incarnation of the Son tabernacling in flesh, becomes

Acts ii. 3. the fire of the Holy Ghost, disparted into tongues, and, without a veil, resting on the entire Church. The perfect God is perfectly revealed ; but revealed in the Trinity of Redemption, the Econo-

Eph ii. 22. mical Trinity. The Church is the *habitation of God through the Spirit.* From that day forward the Holy Ghost is essential to every exhibition of God as revealed among men. While it still

John i 18 remains true that the Son *hath declared* the Father, it is also true

1 Cor. ii. 10 that *the Spirit searcheth all things, yea, the deep things of God,* of both the Father and the Son, and is the foremost and first Agent in

Matt xi. 27. the communion between God and His people. As *neither knoweth any man the Father save the Son, and he to whomsoever the Son will*

1 Cor. xii 3. *reveal Him,* so *no man can say that Jesus is the Lord, but by the Holy Ghost.*

REPRESENTATIVE OF THE SAVIOUR.

Agent of Christ. We do not find in the New Testament any term which directly sanctions the phrases current in theology concerning the Holy Spirit's office as the Redeemer's Representative. The Lord does not speak of Him as His Successor, or Deputy, or Agent, or Administrator. But, though these words are not used, what they signify is plainly to be gathered from the tenour of the final discourses in St. John. These enlarge upon the vicarious relation of the Spirit generally, and that particularly in regard to both the Person and the Work of Christ.

I. The Saviour's departure was expedient in order to His coming. He was *Another Comforter;* and to be sent in the Redeemer's Name · *The Comforter, which is the Holy Ghost, Whom the Father will send in My name, He shall teach you all things, and bring all things to your remembrance, whatsoever I have said unto you.* He is therefore the Representative of Christ Himself, in His prophetic office as the Teacher and the Truth; hence He is *the Spirit of the Truth.* He is the Interpreter of the mystery of the Person of Jesus. *He shall glorify Me,* and *no man can say that Jesus is the Lord but by the Holy Ghost.* Moreover, the promise of the Comforter is the promise of our Lord's everpresent Self, *I will not leave you comfortless, I will come to you.* The Spirit's teaching was to be still 'no other than the teaching of Jesus recalled to remembrance, expounded and enlarged. As the Son spoke what He heard of the Father, so the Holy Ghost should speak what He hears of the Son : *He shall not speak of Himself, but whatsoever He shall hear that shall He speak : ... He shall receive of Mine and shall show it unto you.* The doctrine of the mediatorial Trinity, one in essence and distinct in office, affords the explanation. *All things that the Father hath are Mine · therefore said I, that He shall take of Mine, and shall show it unto you.* The Spirit of Christ in the Prophets is the Spirit of Christ in the Apostles. *He that hath an ear, let him hear what the Spirit saith unto the Churches* follows the injunction to write which the Evangelist received from Jesus a singular instance of the identity in difference and difference in identity between the Lord and the Holy Ghost. He is also the Spirit of Christ in all true Christians · *ye have an unction from the Holy One and ye know all things.* He is the only Vicar of Christ.

II. The Person and the Work of Jesus are one. The Spirit is the Representative of the Redeemer generally, and in His several offices; in His relation to the world, and in His special relation to His people. Through Him alone He acts as the Saviour

Marginal references: Vicarious. John xiv. 16. John xiv. 26. John xiv. 17. John xvi 14. 1 Cor xii. 3. John xiv. 18. John xvi. 13, 14. John xvi 15. Rev. ii 17. 1 John ii. 20. The Work of Christ.

John xix. 30.

1. When our Lord cried *It is finished*, He declared that His work of atonement was accomplished. But it was accomplished only as a provision for the salvation of men. The application of the benefit remained for the administration of the Spirit from heaven; Whose sole and supreme office it is to carry into effect every design of the redemptive undertaking. As *the Spirit of the*

1 Pe. 1. 11.

Christ had from the foundation of the world administered the evangelical preparations, so now He acts on behalf of the fully revealed Christ Through Him our Lord continues His prophetic office : the Holy Ghost is the Inspirer of the new Scriptures and the Supreme Teacher in the new economy Through Him the priestly office is in another sense perpetuated . the ministry of

2 Cor iii.8

reconciliation is a *ministration of the Spirit*. And through Him the Lord administers His regal authority.

To the World

2. The Spirit represents Christ to the world. While the Incarnate Lord was not yet glorified He was limited to one sphere : and, though the world was in His heart, His feet ran not so fast as His desire. But now the Spirit presents Jesus and exhibits His claims to all men. *And when He is come He will reprove the world*

John xvi. 8, 9, 10, 11

of sin, and of righteousness, and of judgment. The sin of which He convicts the world has its formal character in the rejection of Christ; the righteousness of which He convinces the world is the finished righteousness of the absent Lord as the only ground and the only source of human acceptance before the law; and the judgment with which He threatens it is the separation between all that belong to the Prince of this world and those who belong to Jesus its true Lord Thus the whole work of the Convincer is the ascended Redeemer still pleading His own cause

To the Church.

3. He is the representative of Christ to His people. To them He is the Paraclete ὁ παράκλητος, the Advocate, Helper, and all-

1 John ii. 1.

sufficient Comforter in the name of Jesus, our other παράκλητος in heaven. Through His agency our Lord is with us *alway, even unto*

Matt xxviii 20

the end of the world. As He said *He that hath seen Me hath seen the*

John xiv. 9

Father, so we may add that all who receive His Spirit receive Him . *I and My Spirit* ARE ONE. The day will come that He will

John x.30

cease to be the Representative of an absent Lord. Till then, the presence of the invisible Spirit is the real presence of the Redeemer in His Church What His various functions are as

Christ AMONG us and Christ WITHIN us will be more fully unfolded as we proceed.

THE AGENT IN PERSONAL SALVATION

As the Intermediary between the Saviour and the individual soul the Spirit has two classes of office : one more external and one more internal   And these functions He discharges in respect to two orders of men   those not yet in Christ and those who are by faith united to Him

Offices in Personal Salvation.

1. His external function is that of bearing witness, or applying the truth to the mind · to the unconverted for the conviction of sin, the awakening of desire for Jesus and His salvation, and the revelation to penitence of the promises of grace; to the believer for the assurance of acceptance, the unfolding of the knowledge of Christ, the application of the several promises of grace, and all that belongs to His personal instruction and guidance through the Word   These administrations will reappear in detail

External

2 His internal function is the exercise of Divine power on the heart, or within the soul to the unconverted in infusing the grace of penitence and the power of faith, issuing in an effectual inward conversion , to the believer in renewing the soul by communicating a new spiritual life, and carrying on the entire work of sanctification to its utmost issues, as we shall hereafter see.

Internal

3. This distinction rules the phraseology of the New Testament : a large class of passages refer to the Holy Spirit's communications TO the spirit, and an equally large class to His operations WITHIN it.   In the former He is rather the administrator of the words of the New Covenant spoken to man, in the latter the administrator of the grace of that covenant within his soul.   But it is obvious that the two are really one, especially in the case of the believer.   As to those who are without, the Spirit's appeals may fail to enter the heart so as to be permanent.   But when true faith effects the union with Christ the Comforter is an indwelling Spirit . the Paraclete, or external Advocate, becomes an intercessory Presence within. The Scriptural references to the distinction and the unity may be reserved for the future detail of the Spirit's administration.

Distinction and Unity

IN THE CHURCH.

In the
Church.

The Spirit's administration is closely connected with the institution of the Christian Church. This also must have its appropriate place in the sequel   Meanwhile it is necessary and sufficient to indicate its bearing on the offices of the Holy Ghost generally

First,
the Spirit.

1. The order of this connection must be noted.   It is not first the Church, and then the Spirit ; but, conversely, the Spirit forms the Church as the sphere and organ of His working · a distinction which, as will be seen, is of great importance.   There is a sense in which the Redeemer prepared the body for the Spirit's inhabitation , even as the Spirit prepared His body for the inhabitation of the Son of God.   The Day of Pentecost found the disciples waiting for the Third Manifestation of the Trinity.   From that time the Church is the body of Christ which His Representative animates   But in its increase that Body is gathered out of the world by the Holy Ghost, whose general office is Vocation, which calls men into the congregation of the Called, the ἐκκλησία or Church.   UBI SPIRITUS IBI ECCLESIA.

Supreme

2   In that body He is supreme, as the Representative of the Holy Trinity and of Christ its Head   From the time when the interval of interregnum ended, and the little company, who had waited ten days without the Lord and without His Successor, were filled with the Holy Ghost, He has been in the Christian fellowship what Christ was in the midst of His disciples.   He gave to its keeping the New Scriptures written under His inspiration.   He calls, and consecrates, and orders its various ministry. He regulates and animates all worship.   He dispenses His various gifts to all classes according to His own will.   He is not the Head of the Church, but the Representative of its Head.

His
Organ

3   That body is the instrument of His agency in general   It is true that He is not limited to this one organ   Wherever His word is He is, and that word is never without His influence. And, even beyond the written word, and beyond the visible community, He is a Divine Presence everywhere   But it is in the congregation of Christ, in the Church of God, that He has set up the means of grace efficacious in His hands for the conversion of sinners, for the sealing and sanctifying of the saints, and for the

spread of the kingdom of heaven upon earth   As the Spirit Who
applies the work of Christ His field is the world, but His agents
are His called and chosen and faithful people   This view of His
indwelling and agency runs through the New Testament from
Pentecost, the day of the Holy Ghost, down to the last reference
in Scripture, when *the Spirit and the Bride say, Come,* uniting as
one voice in invoking the Saviour.   And it is this which warrants
our including the Christian Church under the department of the
Administration of Redemption.

Rev xxii. 17

THE SPIRIT A DIVINE AGENT.

What has been again and again directly or indirectly asserted
must be made emphatic in conclusion : that the Holy Ghost, in
the unity of the Father and the Son, is a personal, Divine agent
in all His offices   In the economical Trinity subordinate, and
administering the covenant of redemption which originated in
God as the Father and was ratified by God as the Son, He is
nevertheless Himself the Fulness of God.   As Christ is that fulness BODILY, so the Holy Ghost is that fulness SPIRITUALLY   This
must be remembered in the interpretation of many passages in
which there are seemingly opposite statements

A Divine Person.

Col. ii 9.

I. There is a class of texts which assign to the Third Person a
peculiar relation to each of the other Persons of the Trinity . these
must always be connected with passages which contain predicates
of His Divine Person as Subject, so to speak, independent of
those other Persons   Under the doctrine of the Godhead the
Personality and Deity of the Holy Ghost has been discussed   it
is introduced here only in reference to His Mediatorial relation
to the Christian economy.   Though we believe, with the ancient
Church, that there was, or rather is, an eternal procession from
the Eternal Father, the Head of the Holy Trinity, and from the
Eternal Son, the Only-begotten God, we have most to do, in the
present section, with the Temporal Mission corresponding on
earth to the Eternal Procession in heaven

Within the Trinity.

1 The Holy Ghost is the Spirit of the First Person, proceeding *from the Father* and given through the mediation of Jesus , *the
Spirit of His Son* sent forth to those who through Him are sons ,

A Person
John xv.
26.
Gal. iv. 6.

Passim
1 Pe. i. 11.

the Spirit of God generally; and *the Spirit of the Christ.* Now it may be said by the opponent that such passages simply mean the mode of the Divine operation thus described, and sometimes even personified · just as, in human relations, we might speak of the spirit of any eminent teacher. The most violent instance of such personification is said to be the reference to *the Spirit of the Truth* as a personal agent.

John xvi
13

2. But with these must be connected other passages in which He is named *the Spirit* or *the Holy Spirit*, absolutely, and in such a way as to distinguish Him both from the Father and from the Son; and some of them in such connections as to imply His essential and not merely relative or subordinate Deity. Where the Saviour predicts His own departure He speaks of its necessity in order to the coming of *Another Comforter,* and a careful study of the context of the final discourses will show that He could not mean a personified influence The same may be said of the sin against the Holy Ghost, which proves both His personality and His essential Deity; and, though those first hypocrites in the Acts might not commit that sin, they *agreed together to tempt the Spirit of the Lord, to lie to the Holy Ghost,* and lied not *unto men, but unto God* That passages so seldom occur in which the Third Person is mentioned as God is to be explained on the same principle which explains the infrequent assertion of the supreme Divinity of the Son · the Holy Ghost may be reverently said to share the exinanition and subordination of the Second Person of the Mediatorial Trinity. But, in the intercommunion, interaction, or περιχώρησις of the Trinity, He is interchangeably God, the Spirit of God, the Spirit of the Father, the Spirit of the Son, or the Holy Spirit absolutely.

Passim.

Acts v. 3,
4, 9

A Gift.

II There is a large class of texts which refer to the Holy Ghost as a gift and an influence sent down through the mediation of Christ and as its most comprehensive result.

1 The great majority of the testimonies of Scripture are of this order The Old-Testament predictions, whether of symbol or of promise, speak of the future gift as the searching effect of fire, as water poured out, as a rushing wind, and, in special relation to the Christ, as an oil of unction. These four symbols were merged into the great Personal Gift of the Pentecost, but they

govern the language of the entire New-Testament, from the baptising *with the Holy Ghost and with fire* of the Baptist's promise
down to the *renewing of the Holy Ghost which He shed on us abundantly.* The symbols and their meaning must be more fully considered hereafter in relation to the blessings they symbolise it
may suffice now to indicate the fact that the Spirit is constantly
spoken of as a gift poured out upon the world and into the hearts
of believers.

2 But two things must be remembered here : over and above
the general principle, so often referred to, of a mediatorial subordination of Two Persons in the Holy Trinity

(1.) The phraseology used in the New Testament seems to distinguish between the Person and the Gift. The distinction is not constant, but it is nearly so, between τὸ πνεῦμα τὸ ἅγιον, the Spirit the
Holy One, and πνεῦμα ἅγιον, Holy Spirit · a distinction which
cannot be pressed into dogmatic service, because it is matter of
contention among grammatical exegetes, but is nevertheless
so marked in the New Testament as to be very suggestive
The former is used by our Lord in His great foreannouncement,
as an august appellative standing alone and with the now first-
uttered appendage of personality, ἐκεῖνος: *The Comforter, which is*
THE SPIRIT THE HOLY . . *He shall teach* Afterwards *He breathed
on them, and saith unto them, Receive ye the* HOLY GHOST, πνεῦμα
ἅγιον. The same distinction is literally found at those two minor
Pentecosts when first the Gentiles and then the relicts of John
the Baptist's ministry received the Great Gift. In the narrative
of the former *The Spirit the Holy fell on them as on us at the beginning,* according to the promise *Ye shall be baptised with Holy Spirit*
In that of the latter, St. Paul asked if on believing they had
received *Holy Spirit* and, on the laying on of his hands, *The
Spirit the Holy came on them.* Nor is the Pentecost proper without
its evidence. In the days of preparation for it St. Peter speaks
of *The Spirit the Holy* Who spake by the mouth of David , on the
day itself *they were all filled with Holy Spirit, and began to speak
with other tongues as the Spirit gave them utterance.* Here the personal Spirit as the Giver has the Article and as the gift is without
it. The last verse quoted introduces the usage of dropping the
τὸ ἅγιον, the Holy. Without this adjective the Spirit standing

*Matt. iii.
11
Titus iii.
5, 6.*

John xiv
26
John xx.
22

Acts xi
15, 16

Acts xix.
2—6.

Acts i. 16
Acts ii. 4.

alone constantly occurs, where personal acts are in question. So in the Apocalypse, *what the Spirit saith unto the churches.* Here it is τὸ πνεῦμα, but, immediately afterwards, *I was in the Spirit,* ἐν πνεύματι, without the article   Where the personal Spirit in the Trinity is symbolically referred to, as the one sevenfold or perfect Spirit, the phrase is, with the article, τὰ ἑπτὰ πνεύματα τοῦ Θεοῦ, the Seven Spirits of God . the symbolical Fire of the Day of Pentecost returns as *seven lamps of fire burning before the throne.* Pondering this distinction as running through the New Testament we shall—without attributing to it undue importance—find it a preservative against falling into the error of reducing the Holy Ghost to a personified gift. And, the more we ponder it, the more clearly shall we see that there is a strict and impressive and instructive analogy between the variations clustering around the term Son, and those which cluster around the term Spirit. As the One is given and sent, so also is the Other. The same law interprets both.

(2) The gifts of the Spirit are not always said to be poured out by the Father on the Son, and through Him on the Church : sometimes they are the dispensations of the Holy Ghost Himself As the Son is both Priest and Sacrifice, so the Spirit is both Gift and Giver. One classical passage is sufficient to illustrate this. *Now there are diversities of gifts, but the same Spirit . . . The manifestation of the Spirit is given to every man to profit withal. . . But all these worketh that One and the selfsame Spirit, dividing to every man severally as He will*   The Holy Ghost is here a Person whose will it is to manifest Himself · He has a manifestation even as the Son has. And in the dispensation of the gifts which He imparts He is at once the Administrator of the Trinity, of the *Same God which worketh all in all,* and the personal Agent of His own will

Rev iii. 22; iv 2—5.

1 Cor. xii. 4—11.

THE GOSPEL VOCATION.

The Divine purpose of saving the world, accomplished in Christ, is made known to all men by a proclamation which, as containing the free offer of grace, and the command to accept it on certain conditions, is a Vocation or Call. However profound is the mystery involved in such a thought, that call must needs, in some sense, be as universal as the benefit of atonement, which embraces mankind. But it has had, in the mystery of the Divine will, an historical development. Before the fulness of time it proceeded by a principle of election on which vocation followed; but, under the last dispensation, the call is as wide as the preaching of the Gospel, and election follows vocation. In this meaning of the term, with which alone we now have to do, the Spirit's calling is efficacious, inasmuch as through the Word He renders all men who hear that Word conscious of their responsibility, and capable of obedience; but it is not irresistible. In the case of those who accept the Divine offer, the term is often used to express their Christian state and privileges generally: it gives them one of their designations as The Called.

The three words καλεῖν to call, κλῆσις vocation, and κλητός called, refer respectively to the Caller, the act of calling, and the result. The present section has mainly to do with the act and not with the result . the latter belonging rather to the Spirit's work in the preliminaries of salvation   It is obvious, also, that our subject must take no account of some limited applications of the word . for instance, those in which it refers to the Divine power calling *those things which be not as though they were;* those in which it is used as meaning simply designation, as *I have even called thee by thy name;* and, lastly, those in which it signifies a vocation to special office, such as that of St. Paul *called to be an Apostle*   Rom iv. 17 Is. xlv. 4. Rom. i. 1.

of the apostleship Though the distinction cannot be rigorously observed, we must limit the term as much as possible to the declaration of God concerning His purpose of salvation; and, while we do so, remember that we are dealing with a subject which is at present involved in impenetrable mystery.

Universal Redemption

VOCATION AND UNIVERSAL REDEMPTION.

The Divine call is based upon the Divine counsel for the salvation of mankind. This involves two important postulates. It requires, first, that we believe in the universality of the call, whatever difficulties this faith may encounter; and, secondly, it prepares us to expect that the call will, like the purpose of redemption, be gradually made manifest to all men.

1. Scripture establishes, as we have seen, the fact that the eternal purpose of redemption embraced the entire body of mankind *God so loved the world,* that He *would have all men to be saved* But there is only a step, and that a necessary one, to the universal declaration of His will in His Son The Creator loved the world before He declared His love in Christ; He declared His will to save all, and that will is connected with the fundamental truth that as *there is one God,* so also *there is one Mediator between God and man,* that Mediator being *Jesus Christ, Man,* the Representative of mankind. What St. Paul, in his last word on this subject, calls the Philanthropy, or *the kindness and love of God our Saviour toward man,* as such, *appeared* in the Gospel, no less than a catholic love to the entire race : the word φιλανθρωπία is the plainest and strongest argument for the universality of the salvation provided. Now, whatever difficulties may arise to baffle our finite faculties, we are bound to believe that the whole world, directly or indirectly, sooner or later, must receive the glad tidings of the Gospel.

2. As it has pleased God to make the revelation of His purpose gradual, so we might expect that the proclamation of His mercy in accordance with that purpose would be gradual. In

John iii 16.
1 Tim ii 4

Titus iii. 4.

fact the two are one, and they are united in many passages. Its slow and partial and progressive announcement is bound up with the gradual development of the design of salvation itself. Here two things may be noted The law of the Divine economy, according to which the education of fallen mankind has been conducted by a development of truth, and the orderly unfolding of one great mediatorial system, admits of no exception to it, and no appeal from it But the gradual and slow progress of the call has reference only to the external proclamation. Known only to God are His internal communications with the spirits of men.

HISTORICAL PROCESS.

The Divine Call, keeping pace with the unfolding of the redeeming purpose, is with reference to all mankind, and apart from revelation, general and indirect: in the universal influence of the Spirit upon the fallen spirits of men, and in His providential guidance of the nations. The direct Call through the Word has been twofold: first, during the ages of preparation, it was spoken to the people of the old covenant and of the election; secondly, in Christ Jesus, it is the Gospel Call proper addressed to all mankind, leading to the election of those who believe.

THE INDIRECT CALL.

Indirect Call.

The Universal Call, Vocatio Catholica, is that by which the Holy Spirit has moved upon the chaos of the nations through a secret influence to which the term call is only improperly applied. Whatever name, however, is applied to it there can be no doubt that the world has been under the secret and mysterious attraction of grace from the beginning, over and above the interior *Light* John i 9. *which lighteth every man that cometh into the world.*

1 The influence of the Holy Ghost, the gift of redemption to the fallen race, must not be limited We have intimations in the early Scriptures that the Spirit strove WITH MAN; throughout Gen vi. 3 the Old Testament the rebellious *rexed His holy Spirit*, and, though Is lxiii 10

this was the special sin of the ancient people, we must assume that it was the secret of the commencing ungodliness of the world at large. In the New Testament we are told that the Gentiles universally had the law of God written *in their hearts* and certainly there has been no universal sense of truth but as the fruit of the influence of Him who is *the Spirit of the truth* He in every age HATH SHOWED it unto them

2. The early revelation which was given to the world before the first dispersion of its inhabitants was a sound *that went into all the earth :* issuing from the household of Adam and afterwards from that of Noah. And, however perverted became the traditions of primeval truth, they were in a certain sense a constant appeal to the world to remember its Creator in the days of its youth. In like manner, and this may be referred to by way of analogy, the most corrupt presentation of the Gospel in the darkest ages of Christendom carried with it the word of life

3 Moreover St Paul tells us, in one of the few early discourses to the Gentiles that are recorded, of God's providential call to all nations. *Nevertheless He left not Himself without witness* How this catholic preacher of a Catholic Christianity elsewhere dilated upon this theme we know not. But these words have a large meaning ; and, if we collate the preacher in the Acts with the teacher to the Romans, we shall gather that the Apostle of the Gentiles magnified his office in this sense also.

Rom ii 15 , i. 19 John xvi. 13

Rom x 18.

Acts xiv 17.

THE DIRECT CALL

Direct Call

The history of the Gospel vocation, as direct through the Word, is in Scripture divided into two branches. In the Old Testament it was limited to one race, first elected and then called, in the New Testament it is universally to all men, first called and then elected : a distinction of great importance.

Old Testament.

I. The Vocation of Abraham is the central point of Old-Covenant Election. But this looks back upon a previous historical development of the principle, and looks forward to its consummation and change in the Gospel.

Earliest type

1 In the two sons of our first parents the separation of God's people had its first type, and in the salvation of one family the Flood was the second Between the sons of Noah God put a difference

not altogether dependent upon their several personal acts , and the special vocation followed a special election. For, though the dealings of God with the two classes respectively had reference to their moral character, especially as it respects the leading personages, such as Shem and Noah, yet we cannot but discern a direct and sovereign election of the peoples and nations who should carry on His central design

2 The call of Abraham was the choice of a covenant people. Abraham. With him this special national or race election specifically began. The words of Jehovah to the children of Israel, *the whole family which I brought up from the land of Egypt, saying, You only have I* Amos iii. *known of all the families of the earth*, is the strongest expression of 1, 2. the fact. This election, as in the New Testament, is adoption . *Israel is My son, even My firstborn.* Hence the people thus dis- Ex iv. 22 tinguished were the *peculiar people.* The thought has a striking Deut xiv illustration in the words of the prophet concerning the typical 2. chosen nation : *When Israel was a child then I loved him, and called* Hos xi. 1 *My son out of Egypt ;* where the election is followed by vocation and adoption.

3. Throughout the development of the Old-Testament Election Election there runs the mystery of a Divine purpose of unfathomable and wisdom ; in the contemplation of which, however, two things Adoption must be remembered . first, that this choice was never altogether without respect to the moral character of its objects, and, secondly, that it always was connected with a prophecy of a universal call in the Gospel. Though the Supreme God used occasionally the instrumentality of the ungodly He carried on the great purposes of His grace by men who responded to His internal call, and were morally fit agents of His will Abel, Noah, Abraham, are instances of this ; nor is Jacob an exception It is true that *the gifts and calling of God are without repentance ,* and that, having Rom. xi. chosen a lineage out of which His Son should arise, He did not 29. vary from His purpose in consequence of much unfaithfulness on the part of the elect people. But it is true also that the leading personages on whom the absolute election fell were among the foremost saints of history. Moreover, in His government of the people of His special election God was a jealous God ; and often chastised them by the very heathen whom He passed by in their

favour. Above all, He failed not always to let them know that
they were only the temporary Election of His counsel, and that
Mal ı 11 His Name should one day *be great among the Gentiles.* But, after
every qualification, the profound mystery remains untaken away,
nor is it altogether removed in the more catholic dispensation of
the Gospel.

The
Gospel.

II. The direct call of the Gospel after the coming of Christ, or
rather after the Day of Pentecost, is distinguished from that of
the Old Testament by not being national, and by preceding the
election. But this leads us onward to the nature of the vocation
itself.

The Call.

THE NATURE OF THE GOSPEL CALL.

The Gospel Call is the universal offer of salvation and
command to submit to its Author; proclaimed by the
Spirit through the Word committed to the keeping and
ministry of the Christian Church; containing the glad
tidings of the earnest purpose of God towards every individual of mankind; effectual through the Spirit's grace to
all who yield; but declared not to be irresistible, and in
fact resisted, even finally resisted, by unbelief.

THE OFFER OF SALVATION.

Its
Threefold
Nature.

The Call is the PROCLAMATION of the redemption accomplished
by Christ; the OFFER of its blessings on certain conditions; and
the COMMAND to submit to the authority of Christ the Mediator
of these blessings. These three are one in the embassage of the
New Covenant, and the Gospel is not fully preached unless equal
prominence is given to all. The model of this preaching is found
in the Acts of the Apostles, where St. Peter and St. Paul are the
leading examples The Proclamation and the Offer and the Command must be united in every true delivery of the Gospel Call, as
they are. invariably united in the original examples. The first
Acts v. 32. sound of that Vocation ends with such a note as this : *and we are
His witnesses of these things; and so is also the Holy Ghost, Whom*

God hath given to them that obey Him. Here are the three elements to which we have given prominence. the testimony given, the terms prescribed; and the submission demanded. St. Paul's first recorded sermon contains them all with equal precision. *Be it known unto you, . . all that believe; . . . beware therefore!* Were there no theory to be served it must be admitted that the call of the Gospel is a witness to everyone of a blessing offered on terms open to all, and enforced by a command to submit to the Mediatorial Authority of Him who is raised up to dispense it. The NAME is preached as a Testimony of salvation, as the Object of faith, and the Authority to which universal submission is due.

Acts xiii
38,39,40

IN THE CHURCH THROUGH THE WORD.

The second proposition contains three points. the Spirit is the Agent of the Call; it is connected with the Word, and that Word is ordinarily committed to the ministry of the Christian Church The doctrine of the Gospel Vocation demands a careful adjustment of the relations of these three.

The
Calling.

I. Generally, He who calleth is God, though not specifically as the Father. *We preached unto you the Gospel of God*—a phrase which seldom occurs—*Who hath called you unto His kingdom and glory* Christ also, though only as upon earth, declares · *I am not come to call the righteous, but sinners to repentance* The Holy Spirit is now permanently the manifestation of the God of the Gospel Vocation · *The Spirit and the Bride say, Come,* where the invitation to sinners follows the invocation of the Lord Himself to return He is the Preacher in the name of Christ to the world: *He shall testify of Me.* But this in the unity of the Three-One Author of redemption: *All things that the Father hath are Mine. therefore said I, that He shall take of Mine, and shall show it unto you.*

TheSpirit
1 Thess. ii
9—12.
Matt. ix.
13.

Rev. xxii
17.

John xv
26.

John xvi
15.

II The call of the Gospel is ordinarily through the Word But the Word is both the letter and the substance of the letter these are united in the instrument which the Holy Ghost employs

The
Word

1 St. Paul says that *faith cometh by hearing. and hearing by the Word of God,* where he evidently means the doctrine preached. the summary of truths *as the truth is in Jesus* That the Gospel proclamation is intended seems obvious from the connection of

Rom x
17, 14,
18.
Eph iv
21

that word with what precedes . *How shall they hear without a preacher ?* But there is a substantial truth of which the Word written or spoken is only the vehicle. Hence the Apostle adds :

Rom x.18

Yes verily, their sound went into all the earth, and their words unto the ends of the world. And the original passage of the prophet proves that there is a voice of God's Will which is not in written

Isa lxv 1. language *I was made manifest unto them that asked not after Me.*

1 Peter iii. 1

In this sense there may be a Word *without the Word*

2 Now the call through the Gospel is not limited either to the oral or to the written announcement. It is a silent effectual voice accompanying the truth, wherever the truth is. The Holy Ghost is the Life of the doctrine which is the letter ; and most certainly the letter is never without the accompanying Spirit. The letter is not only written ; there may be a spoken letter also. Wherever the truth is declared in the name of Jesus it is the instrument of His energy. But the Spirit is not dependent either on the written or on the spoken letter as such. It is the truth which He uses as

John xvi. 13

His instrument. He is *the Spirit of truth.*

The Church

III. The relation of the Church to the Spirit's efficiency through the Word is everywhere made prominent in the New Testament.

Acts i. 2

The Saviour gave His commission *unto the Apostles whom He had chosen.* Their authority He declared to be from Himself and the

John xx 21

reflection or continuation of His own : *As My Father hath sent Me, even so send I you.* The extent of their commission is *all nations ,*

Matt xxviii 19.

and the matter of the vocation is the preaching *the Gospel to every creature.* These Apostles to whom the Lord gave commandment

Mark xvi. 15

themselves in turn gave commandment *through the Holy Ghost* to their successors as responsible for preaching that Gospel to the end

Acts i. 12.

of time. But the call is committed really to the Church in a wider sense than this : all who receive the glad tidings must freely give as they have freely received We read in the Acts that the disciples went everywhere preaching the Word. And the

Rev. xxii. 17.

last saying of Scripture on the subject is *The Spirit and the Bride say, Come,* where the mystical fellowship is represented as uniting with the Spirit in beseeching the Saviour to come to His people, and in beseeching all who thirst to come to Him. This general truth may be further unfolded as pointing to the mystery of the Divine law of vocation , impressing deeply the responsibility of

the Church ; and carrying in it the prophecy of the eventual proclamation of the Gospel to all men.

1. In every age the work of the Spirit in extending the King- Human
dom of God has been bound up with human agency. Individuals Agency.
in the old economy were prominent in every dispensation of it,
teaching His will and uttering His prophetic words and carrying
on His work generally. The history of ancient revelation is bound
up with a series of eminent men , and not only individuals but
the covenant nation itself was elected and called to preach in some
sense to the outside world His present and coming Kingdom. The
Christian dispensation has introduced no new law · it has only
widened the application of the law that operated from the beginning. As Man was taken up into the Godhead to be the procurer
of redemption, so that Man who is God uses His brethren for the
diffusion of His grace.

2. There is no fact more sure, while there is no mystery more
profound, than the connection between the fidelity of the Church
and the spread of Christ's kingdom. The Call is heard where
the Church sends it; but where the messengers are not sent from
among men, there are no angels *having the everlasting Gospel to preach.* Rev xiv 6
How shall they hear without a preacher ? was a question which might Rom x 14
leave all to the secret arrangements of arbitrary grace. But it is
followed by another, which leaves the responsibility with the living
Church . *How shall they preach except they be sent ?* Not indeed Rom.x 15
that the Holy Spirit is, or has ever been, absolutely bound to
human instrumentality. The dew of His grace *tarrieth not for* Mic. v 7.
man, nor waiteth for the sons of men , but the gradual and slow
spread of Gospel preaching most plainly shows that the energy
of the Church has much to do with the term of the final consummation Our Lord must reign *till He hath put all enemies under* 1 Cor. xv
His feet , but He does not wait for any set time apart from the 25.
accomplishment of His Church's mission. Though we dare not
limit the operation of grace to the sphere of missionary preaching,
we know of no Christianity which the successors of the Apostles
do not establish Hence it is well to fall back upon a double call,—
not so dishonourable to the Divine perfections as the external and
internal, the former resting on an official will of Heaven, so to speak,
and the latter on the private feeling of our heavenly Father,—

one that is open and known and another that is hidden and un-known.   There is a secret call in which generally speaking man is not co-operant : which, like the sun, extends its influence to the evil and the good.

3. Nothing is more certain in prophecy than that the Vocation of the Gospel in its stricter meaning shall be universal   Both the Old Testament and the New concur to present a perspective in

Matt
xxiv.14.

which *this Gospel of the kingdom shall be preached in all the world for a witness unto all nations.*

THE DIVINE INTENTION IN THE CALL

Vocatio
Seria.

We may pass with more confidence to the third proposition. The Gospel Call contains the earnest purpose of God to save every man who hears it

1. Here if anywhere the à priori style of argument is valid However the contrary assertion may be disguised it involves dis-honour to the truth and faithfulness of God.   Many mysteries crowd around the subject, beneath which our reason must bow down ; but the superfluous mystery that makes the Righteous Judge utter the gracious offers of His mercy with a secret reserve is one from which every feeling of our reverence and charity recoils   The teaching which finds it necessary to distinguish between an official call for all men and an efficacious call for the elect is self-condemned

2. We need not defend the honour of God · we have only to interpret His sayings   Our Lord's words ought to be enough .

Luke xiv.
23.
Matt.
xxiii 37
1 Tim ii 4.
Ezek
xxxiii 11
Titus iii 4.

compel them to come in ! illustrated as they are by His sorrow over Jerusalem : *How often would I ! and ye would not !* And our Lord's will is the will of God, *Who will have all men to be saved,* Who in the Old Testament said, *I have no pleasure in the death of the wicked, but that the wicked turn from his way and live.*   In the New Testament the Gospel is the appearance of the *kindness and love of God our Saviour toward* MAN, or His philanthropy.

3. Such a genuine call implies that the offer of salvation is always accompanied by sufficient grace for its acceptance   This has already been seen in relation to the Word, and will again be considered in the next topic of Preliminary Grace.   Meanwhile,

there is no need of argument; nor is any specific text necessary. Every Divine commandment is virtually a commandment with promise. with promise not only of blessing to follow obedience but of grace to precede it The Gospel of Christ *is the power of* Rom 1.16. *God unto salvation to everyone that believeth* By the special appointment and will of God the Word has grace connected with it, sufficient for every purpose for which it is sent. So it was anciently said : *it shall not return unto Me void, but it shall accom-* Is. lv 11. *plish that which I please.*

CALLING AND ELECTION.

Those who accept the Divine call through the Word are in the The Elect. language of Scripture the Elect. And both terms, Calling and Election, or the Called and the Elect, are sometimes used to designate the Christian Estate as such.

1. Of a Vocatio Interna, as distinguished from the Vocatio Effectual Externa, there is no trace in Scripture. INTERNAL CALLING and Calling. EFFECTUAL CALLING are phrases never used. The distinction implies such a difference as would have been clearly stated if it existed, and all that is meant by the internal call finds its expression, as we shall see, in other offices of the Holy Spirit of enlightenment, conviction, and conversion Each of these terms carries the meaning of an external summons made effectual by interior grace ; but never in the sense that sufficient interior grace is denied to any. It may be said that the true internal vocation is election in the strict sense. *Many be called, but few chosen.* This Matt. xx. states a fact over which the Saviour mourns. *I have chosen you* 16. *out of the world.* This states a fact over which the Saviour rejoices. John xv. The term, however, is used in some passages with the same wide 19. application as the term call · for instance, *God hath chosen the* 1 Cor.i.27. *foolish things of the world to confound the wise,* and *Have not I chosen* John vi *you twelve?* While therefore our Saviour's first word establishes 70. the distinction, and we are warranted in saying that election is the result of accepting the call, we must remember that the New Testament often uses the terms interchangeably. Election always presupposes the call, but the call does not always issue in election.

The
Called.

Rom i 6,7

1 Pet. i. 1,
2; ii. 9
Titus i 1.
2 John 13.
Rom. xi 7.
Rom viii.
33.
Col. iii 12.

Rom xi 5.

2. The acceptance of the Call, and the Election that follows it, are both metonymically used to designate the state of Christians, presumed according to their profession to stand in the grace of God. They are *The Called of Jesus Christ . . . beloved of God, called to be saints,* or *called saints.* Christians are Saints by designation as well as by internal character; and they are Called by designation, as having accepted the external appeal So also they are the Elect as separated from the world both outwardly and inwardly. St Peter writes his Catholic Epistle to The *Elect according to the foreknowledge of God the Father,* whom he terms a *chosen generation.* St. Paul speaks of *the faith of God's elect,* and St. John of *thy elect sister.* The phrase *The Election* is used for the company of God's chosen among the Jews; but not now generally of all Christians. *God's Elect,* or *The Elect of God,* are those who belong to the household of faith. The predominant allusion in the Word is to the collective character of the Church which has taken the place of the privileged nation, and that governs the use of the term everywhere, precisely like the denomination the Sanctified or the Saints Christians are the *Election of Grace* in opposition to the ancient people gathered out of the world, they are the sanctified as separated, instead of them, to God. The word Church or Ecclesia literally means the same as The Called and the Elect. it expresses the result of that which Election means as in the purpose of God.

CONTINGENCY.

Resistible.

Matt. xx
16.
John v 40

Acts vii.
51.

The Gospel Call may be resisted and finally resisted; even the Election connected with it may after obedience be forfeited, and, with regard to both classes of the disobedient, the term reprobation is used, though never as the result of a fixed decree.

1. *Many be called, but few chosen* This sufficient word, which should be an end of all controversy, is explained by our Lord Himself: *Ye will not come to Me.* There is nothing more constantly and consistently declared in the older and later Scriptures than the power of man to oppose and oppose successfully the influence of grace. *Ye do always resist the Holy Ghost!* Surely it is dishonourable to the name of God to suppose that He would

charge on sinners a resistance which was to them a necessity, and complain of outrage on His Spirit Whose influences were only partially put forth

2. There are some passages of Scripture which indicate that the blessings of Election itself may be forfeited : this sacred word is not shielded, nor is its special grace inviolable   Judas was one of the elect . *have not I chosen you twelve, and one of you is a devil ?* When our Lord speaks of the *very elect* being deceived, *if it were possible*, He does not intimate that delusion leading to apostasy was impossible in their case.   Though the words might seem to bear that meaning, we must otherwise interpret them.   For, at the commencement of the discourse He had said . *Take heed that no man deceive you !* and at the close, *He that shall endure unto the end, the same shall be saved.*   St. Peter, whose Epistles dwell much on the privileges of the Election, does not number among those privileges the security against falling . on the contrary he bids his readers *give diligence to make your calling and election sure : for if ye do these things, ye shall never fall.* John vi. 70. Matt xxiv.24 Matt. xxiv. 4, 13. 2 Pet.i.10.

3. Lastly, the Word of God speaks of the possible Reprobation of both these classes,—the Called and the Chosen—but of the reprobation of no other.   The vocation of the Word is a mysterious test of their state before God and the truth , and they have failed to sustain that test.   They are ἀδόκιμοί. (1.) The called who resist are reprobates. *God gave them over to a reprobate mind* who *did not like to retain God in their knowledge.* They who *resist the truth* are the *reprobate concerning the faith.* (2.) St. Paul speaks of the possibility of the saints being reprobates : *Know ye not your own selves, how that Jesus Christ is in you, except ye be reprobates ?* When we read of the final signature of the *called and chosen and faithful* we are taught that the end is not yet when the called are also chosen   The third word in the great sentence remains . fidelity must seal the eternal grace of election (3) There is no reprobation as fixed in the decree of God throughout the Scriptures of mercy and truth.   The idea is inconsistent with everything but a probation and a wilful failure in probation

Reprobation.

Rom i 28
2 Tim. iii. 8.
2 Cor xiii. 5.
Rev xvii 14.

HISTORY OF CONTROVERSY

A few observations may be made on the Polemics of this question : limited to that branch of it which concerns Vocation and Election. It is with the perversion. of the Predestination idea that we have mainly to do.

The New Testament.

I. Within the New Testament itself we have a remarkable anticipation of the modern controversy. The preaching of the Gospel to the Gentiles was resented by the Jewish Christians, by those of a certain party especially, as an invasion of the privileges, or advantages, of the covenant people as the Elect of God. There

Acts xiii. 46

was no saying which they more disapproved than St. Paul's *Lo, we turn to the Gentiles.* In his Epistle to the Romans the Apostle of the Gentiles argues against these advocates of an unconditional election, these earliest perverters of the true doctrine of the decretive will of God. It must be always remembered that this was the object for which he wrote the Three Chapters which the Predestinarians have taken refuge in they were written in fact as a proleptical refutation of such views. The special exegesis on which a vindication of this assertion depends is not necessary here. Suffice that St Paul admits, as we have already seen, that the ancient election was of a particular line through which the revelation of the preparatory Gospel was to be transmitted, and in which the Author of that Gospel was to appear. Undoubtedly, it is hard for human reason to distinguish between the national and the individual election, and between the active and the permissive will of God in the hardening of evil men ; but the distinction

Rom. ix. 18, 22.

must be made. Such passages as *Therefore hath He mercy on whom He will have mercy,* on the one hand, and *the vessels of wrath fitted to destruction,* on the other, are not to be understood of absolute predetermination of individuals to be saved or to be lost The similitude of the Potter and the clay as more fully seen in Jeremiah ends with a direct refutation of the theory : there the decrees of God are said to be changed by the characters of men.

Jer xviii 6—8

O house of Israel, cannot I do with you as this potter? saith the Lord At what instant I shall speak concerning a nation, and concerning a kingdom, to pluck up, and to pull down, and to destroy it , if that nation, against whom I have pronounced, turn from their evil, I will repent of the evil that I thought to do unto them The whole argument of St Paul is to show that the election of Israel as a nation had not come to nought : it was *not of works, but of Him that calleth.* The Three Chapters carefully studied yield conclusions in favour of a national election but not of an individual . especially when they are connected with the intermediate chapter in which we have the Apostle's glorious protest against the perversion of his teaching *the same Lord over all is rich unto all that call upon Him. For whosoever shall call upon the Name of the Lord shall be saved* ... *But to Israel He saith, All day long have I stretched forth My hands unto a disobedient and gainsaying people.*

Rom ix. 11.

Rom. x 12, 13, 21.

II. The entire Christian community down to the time of Augustine knew in its doctrine no other election and predestination than what was conditional or, what is the same theory, of none which do not refer to the ideal Body of Christ as such The tendency of the Easterns especially was to lay too much rather than too little emphasis on the foreknowledge of human repentance and faith Chrysostom says "Not of love alone, but of our virtue also. If it sprang from love alone all would have been saved If from our virtue alone that would be little and all would be lost. It was from neither alone, but from both . for the Calling was not of necessity or of force." This sentence represents the sentiment of the Greek Church from Origen to Athanasius, and even John of Damascus, the last of the Oriental Fathers proper. There was a decided leaning to an exaggeration of the freedom of the human will : at least their doctrine was not sufficiently protected by the reference to the ever-active influence of the Holy Ghost upon our fallen nature But, whatever their theoretical notions were of the universality of the Gospel vocation, their Missionary zeal declined after the ninth century, and they have contributed little to the evangelisation of the world

The Early Church

III. Augustine first laid down the principle that "Predestination is the preparation of grace; grace the bestowment itself"

Augustine.

1 The foundation of his whole system is his doctrine of Original Sin, which regards all mankind as utterly bereft of capacity for good: a "mass of perdition," a "condemned lump" Therefore salvation is absolutely of grace, and without human

co-operation. To this great principle there can be no objection
Nature cannot cast out nature , and the human fall was a fall into
utter impotence. But Augustine forgot that the first benefit of
redemption was co-extensive with the ruin of man. Perhaps,
indeed, he held this ; but in a sense of his own. That benefit
was in his teaching a wasted and useless influence save to the elect.
He taught that the Divine eternal decree determined the exact
number of those to whom efficacious grace, which includes an
irresistible grace for the beginning and the grace of perseverance
for the close, shall be given. For these alone the Redeemer may
be said to have died . "Everyone that has been redeemed by the
blood of Christ is a man ; though not everyone that is a man has
been redeemed by the blood of Christ." "The Saviour redeemed
the sinners who were to be, justified," and "No one perishes for
whom the Saviour died."

Predesti-
nation
and the
Call.

2. Some of the difficulties connected with the Gospel Call in
this doctrine were summarily disposed of by Augustine, but only
through renouncing that principle of an inextinguishable life of
regeneration which his followers now hold so firmly. All who
hear and receive the Gospel and are baptised receive regenerating
grace, and are placed in a state of salvation : this explains the
universal offer of the Gospel and the equally universal administration of the sacrament. But to the Elect only is the gift of perseverance imparted, and the objects of the Donum Perseverantiæ
are known to God alone : this protects the doctrine of the eternal
decree   "Those who fall are not to be reckoned in the number
of the elect, even as to the time when they lived piously. There
are sons of God, not yet such to us but such to God, and there
are again some who are called by us sons of God on account of
grace temporarily received, but not so by Him " Other difficulties
Augustine does not attempt to solve. He has no more to say
concerning the hidden decree than that "God divided the light
from the darkness ; and so ordered the Fall that He might first
show what the free will of man could do, and then what His
grace could do " Nor has he any solution of the difficulty that
the electing grace of God should be connected with sacraments
and bound to a system of external ordinances   A thousand years,
afterwards Calvin arose to confront more boldly these and all

other difficulties : not cramped by the sacramentarian theory which hampered his great predecessor.

IV. During that long interval Predestinarianism, or Augustin-ianism, passed through many vicissitudes.   The Semipelagians as-serted an election of believers as foreknown, thus giving a formula which has been ever since found useful ; and the Synod of Orange (A.D 529) condemned the dogma of predestination to evil or reprobation   In the ninth century Gottschalk carried the doc-trine of Augustine to its extremest limits, limits which it was not again to reach until the modern representative of the predesti-narian Father arose.   His teaching was rejected at Mainz (A.D. 848), but acknowledged at Valence (A.D. 855) · "Fatemur prædestina-tionem electorum ad vitam, et prædestinationem impiorum ad mortem," a confession, however, in which, rightly understood, all may unite   On the side of Gottschalk was Ratramnus, against him Hinckmar.   It may be said that throughout the mediæval discussions of this and kindred subjects the tendency was in a direction opposite to that of predestinarianism   And, moreover, that the ever-growing theory of a kingdom of Christ, under one vicar, predestined to embrace the world, was itself unfavourable to any limitation of the Gospel vocation.   The mediæval Church at the worst was in spirit and practice missionary.   Universal missions and a partial Call can never rationally co-exist.

V. At the Reformation the doctrine of Election and the Limited Call seemed likely to be in the ascendant everywhere.

1 Zwingle and Calvin united in reviving the Augustinian doctrine of an individual vocation determined by a predestinating decree ; but Calvin has given a permanent name to the system, because in fact he gave it a distinguishing character.   He laid his foundation deeper than that of his forerunner.   Augustine made the Eternal Decree his central point ; Calvin carried it up to the Absolute Being, or Absolute Sovereignty, of God, from which that decree flowed.   These are some of his words : Prædesti-nationem vocamus æternum Dei decretum, quo apud se consti-tutum habuit quid de UNOQUOQUE homine fieri vellet   Dico Deum non modo primi hominis casum et in eo posterorum ruinam prævidisse, sed arbitrio quoque suo dispensasse   "Man falls by the providence of God so ordaining, but he falls through his own

Mediæval

Reforma-tion.

Calvin.

wickedness." All is of the absolute, unquestionable, despotic sovereignty of God. If human reason suggests a demur, "Respondendum est . quia voluit !" The decree was Supralapsarian, that is, it included the Fall, which Augustine never asserts formally   It follows from this in the system of Calvin that the external call of the Gospel is an unmeaning ceremonial save as to the elect   The word and the means of grace are to all others "Signa inania :" the manifestations of a "Voluntas signi," which, signifying nothing but "Common Grace," must be distinguished from the hidden "Voluntas beneplaciti" on which the salvation of every man depends.   Here is the secret of Predestinarianism, whatever other name it may bear : the secret which links it with Fatalism, with philosophic Determinism, with Pantheism, with the modern notion of Abstract Law or the Absolute Fiat of a Being who is not so much a Person as a Will.   Other relations of this creed to theological doctrine, subordinate relations introduced in due course, all find their vanishing point in this Unconditioned and Unconditional Sovereignty, which is the foundation and top-stone of the whole superstructure.

Reformed Con- fessions.

2   The Reformed Confessions assert this doctrine, though with some variations · variations, however, which introduce qualifying clauses having no real meaning, and may be left to the symbolical Volumes   Some are of a more extreme type, approaching, though not positively expressing, the Supralapsarian theory, that the Fall was included in the decree of God ; others are more evidently Infralapsarian, dating the decree as it were this side of the Fall. The Synod of Dort, 1618, in opposition to the Remonstrants, digested the Calvinistic doctrine in a large number of canons, which seem to be based on the latter theory   It thus speaks concerning the Vocation of the Gospel : "Though all men sinned in Adam and were made guilty of malediction and eternal death, God would have done injury to no one if He had willed to leave the entire human race in sin and the curse, and to condemn it on account of that sin.   But that men may be led to faith God mercifully sends the heralds of His most joyful tidings to whom He will and when He will, by whose ministry men are called to repentance and faith in Christ . . . That some are gifted with faith in time, and others not, springs from His eternal decree, . .

according to which He graciously softens the hearts of the elect, however hard, and bends them to belief, but in His just judgment leaves the non-elect to the consequences of their own wickedness and obduracy." These Articles, nearly a hundred in number, are generally received by the Predestinarian Churches as a full statement of the Christian Faith. The English version of the same creed is found in the Westminster Confession, drawn up for the purpose of reforming the English Church between 1643 and 1648 : it is a reflection of the Dort Canons, and accepted by the Presbyterians of the British Islands and America Many of the Reformed Confessions, like that of the English Church, mitigate the dogma of predestination, and use such language as may be without much violence reconciled with Scripture, especially in their reference to the universality and sincerity of the Call.   Others of them are more predestinarian than they appear to be : ambiguity of phrase disguising their meaning.

3. Modifications of the Calvinistic creed are as various as the lands which it has penetrated.   Calvin himself protested unconsciously against all among his followers who should soften his system of doctrine   "Many so preach election as to deny that any man is reprobated ; but very ignorantly and childishly, since election itself would not stand unless opposed to reprobation." Thus the modern Father of Predestination condemned beforehand the devices of his more generous or less unrelenting successors · rather their device, for all the sophistries of palliation may be regarded as one. In France, towards the middle of the seventeenth century, Amyraldus taught that salvation was provided for all men ; that God elected some to whom was given the necessary grace of repentance and faith ; and that all others are simply left without a special determining influence which none have a right to claim.   This useless subterfuge was resorted to in England by Richard Baxter, and has in more recent times been advocated in Scotland.   It is the unacknowledged theory of great numbers who are bound to the general teaching of predestinarianism, but feel constrained to preach the Gospel freely to all . some because the New Testament exhibits that kind of preaching, and they dare not contradict its example ; some because they think that the reprobate are predoomed to reject the Gospel as well as to perish with-

Forms of Calvinism.

Amyraldus.

Baxter.

out atonement ; and some because their ardent charity melts the
fetters of their creed

Lutheran-
ism

VI. The Lutheran doctrine passed through stages of fluctuation.

1. Both Luther and Melanchthon were at first predestinarian
in their views of the Gospel Call. They taught Determinism or
Fatalism almost in the same words as Calvin used ; but both
gradually modified and finally retracted these views, induced
mainly by the impossibility of reconciling them with the serious
purpose of God in universally proffering salvation, and with the
evangelical theory of the means of grace It may be said generally
that the followers of Luther are not of the school of Augustine.

Formu-
laries.

2 Hence the Lutheran Formularies are not predestinarian.
The Formula Concordiæ was the first public document that dealt
at large with the subject. The following is a translation of sentences which treat of Election and Vocation · " Predestination or
the eternal Divine election pertains only to the good and accepted
sons of God, and it is the cause of their salvation   It procures
their renewal and disposes of all things which belong to it. . . .
This predestination is not to be scrutinised in the secret of the
Divine counsel, but is to be sought in the Word of God, which
reveals it. The Word of God leads us to Christ. . . . But Christ
calls all sinners to Himself, and promises them rest, and seriously
wills that all men should come to Him and yield themselves
to be aided and saved. . . The true doctrine of predestination
is to be learned from the nature of the Gospel of Christ There
it is plainly taught that God has concluded all under unbelief that
He might have mercy on all, and that He wills none to perish,
but rather that all should be converted and believe the Gospel. . . .

Matt xxii.
14.

When it is said that *many are called but few are chosen*, it is not to
be understood that God is unwilling that all should be saved ;
but it indicates the cause of the perdition of the ungodly, which
is this, that they either fail altogether to hear the Word of God,
rebelliously despising it by closing their ears and hardening their
hearts, and in this way hindering the ordinary method of the
Holy Spirit, so that He cannot effect His work on them, or that
they esteem lightly the word they hear and cast it away from
them. Their perishing must be ascribed, not to God and His
election, but to their own malignity." Thus the official doctrine

of the Lutheran Church omits the reprobation of the wicked, and makes the predestination of the believer dependent on the foresight of faith and perseverance. The Call of the Gospel it regards as universal, serious, and efficacious offering sufficient grace to all who hear the Word, whether they accept it or not. As in the Lutheran doctrine of the Eucharist all who partake receive the glorified body of the Lord, some to salvation and others to condemnation, so all who hear the Gospel receive its saving word, some to the saving of their souls, and some to their aggravated doom.

3. The later development of Lutheran teaching has been faithful to these statements, but has expanded them so as to touch some of the pressing difficulties which crowd around the question. Earlier and Later Lutheranism

(1) The earlier dogmatic writers laid emphasis on the "voluntas antecedens," which is the Divine decree of salvation in Christ expressing His "voluntas universalis, gratuita et seria" This counsel when viewed in the light of foreknowledge is translated into a "voluntas consequens seu specialis": not as if there were two wills in God ; but the one supreme will is determined distributively in regard to the two classes of believers and unbelievers. Hence the universal will may be regarded as rather that of mercy, the special will as rather that of justice. Later Lutheran theologians have preferred to dwell more on the election of a new humanity in Christ into the fellowship of which only those enter who believe : the whole emphasis of election rests on the second race of which the Second Adam is the Head. The special predestination of individuals is only the historical realisation of the eternal purpose of love in Christ.

(2.) Again, the first Lutheran doctors explained the absolute universality of the Call by a reference to the three great historical crises when the evangelical appeal went forth without limitation to the nations of the earth . first, when the universal Promise concerning the Seed of the woman, the Serpent-Bruiser, passed out into all the world and down to all posterity; secondly, when the preaching of Noah after the Flood again sent its sound into all the earth to be moulded into universal traditions ; and, thirdly, when the worldwide preaching of the Apostles literally went out without restriction: "quo non venit ἀποστολή eo ἐπιστολή"

This solution has a fair show of theoretic completeness, and of striking generalisation; but it leaves unsolved the mystery that the posterity of those who rejected this triple testimony are yet without the Gospel, as well as the still profounder mystery that the publication of the world's glad tidings should have been left contingent in any degree whatever on the fidelity of the missionary church. Some more modern speculative theologians have had recourse to other expedients; among which is the theory of a Gospel preached in the intermediate state to those who have either rejected it in this life or insufficiently heard it · a theory which, based on St. Peter's testimony to the Saviour's Missionary Descent into Hades, is capable of almost unlimited expansion and application within the interval down to the Day of Judgment. But this subject belongs rather to Eschatology

Armi-
nianism.

VII. The Remonstrants of Holland, or Arminians, endeavoured to introduce into the Reformed Church the Scriptural doctrine. But in vain: the Synod of Dort (1618, 1619) rejected their Remonstrance against a limiting of Divine grace, just as the Council of Trent in the previous century rejected the remonstrance of Protestantism against another and an opposite kind of dishonour done to the grace of God. From that time the doctrine of a Universal Atonement, or of a Saviour provided for the race and for sin universally, with the concomitant doctrine of a free and unreserved offer of grace to all who hear the Word, has been connected with the name of Arminianism. But this is an injustice to these doctrines themselves, which have a higher parentage The Calvinism of modern times was the Augustinianism of the fifth century: it has no higher origin. It was Augustine who first dared so to interpret Scripture as to attach a limited design to the death of Christ the Fathers who preceded him were generally faithful to the catholic Gospel; or, if they erred, it was like Origen, in making the mission of Christ too comprehensive in its benefits. Conversely, Augustinianism may in modern times be called Calvinism , for it has never prevailed outside of the Churches of the Reformed or Calvinistic type : its sporadic existence in the JANSENISM of Rome is hardly an exception. The term Calvinism is however disavowed by some earnest communities which hold its type of doctrine; because they find or think they find in Scripture the principles on which Predestinarianism rests. They boldly assume that the teaching of the Word of God is on this subject, as on some others, expressed in opposite and seemingly contradictory terms, which it is not within the range of man's faculties to reconcile. The antinomy, or paradox, of a determinate decree of election combined with the most universal appeals to human free will, they regard as the final word of the Bible; and, admitting that the earliest Christians were unconscious of it, they claim for Augustine the distinction of having given it the prominence in his teaching which the Scripture assigns to it. This is therefore matter of pure exegesis, and the question remains—though it is no question to us—whether or not God has imposed this heavy burden on the human intellect and on Christian faith. Meanwhile what is unreasonably called Arminianism is the faith of the Eastern and Western Churches representing Ancient Christianity though in its corruption, of Lutheranism, representing the Reformation, of the Church of England throughout the British Empire, and of Methodism in all its branches throughout the world.

THE PRELIMINARIES OR CONDITIONS OF THE STATE OF SALVATION.

The work of the Holy Spirit must now be viewed as preparing the soul for admission into the consummate blessings of the covenant of grace: a work which He accomplishes, not absolutely as He imparts those blessings themselves, but as quickening, aiding and directing the energies of the free will of man to seek them. The preparation, when viewed in relation to His agency, is Preliminary Grace; in respect to man, it tends to secure compliance with the conditions of the covenant. In all sound doctrine on this subject there must be a certain combination of the Divine element and the human. The result is seen in Conversion, Repentance, and Faith, in their unity, distinctness, and mutual relations, all which belong to the sphere of the Spirit s prevenient influence.

The Holy Ghost is here the Author of preliminary grace: that is, of the kind of preparatory influence which is imparted outside of the temple of Christ's mystical body, or rather in the outer court of that temple. When He bestows the full blessings of personal salvation, as they are the result of a union with Christ, He is simply and solely the Administrator and Giver: the object of this grace in the nature of things can only receive. Forgiveness, adoption, sanctification are necessarily Divine acts: nothing can be more absolute than the prerogative of God in conferring these blessings. This does not imply that the influences which prepare the soul for these acts of perfect grace are not from a Divine source alone. It must be remembered that it is *the Grace of the Lord Jesus Christ* flowing from and revealing the *Love of God* that is dispensed even to the outer world in *the Communion* of the Holy Ghost. But it must also be remembered that this prevenient influence is literally bound up with the human use of it,

2 Cor. xiii 14.

being without meaning apart from that use, and, moreover, that
of itself it is not saving, though it is unto salvation   The present
department of theology is beset with peculiar difficulties, and
has been the arena of some of the keenest controversies   Hence,
it will be important to establish our points by the evidence of
Scripture; and, only after this is done, turn aside to the polemics
of the question

THE SPIRIT OF GRACE.

The Spirit
of Grace

The Spirit of Grace is the Author of every movement of
man's soul towards salvation; but His influence requires
and indeed implies a certain co-operation of man as its
object.   Here then we have three topics to be considered:
grace prevenient, human co-operating agency, and the relation between grace and free will.

GRACE PREVENIENT.

Pre-
venient
Grace.

The Grace of God which bringeth salvation is the fountain of Divine lovingkindness to mankind, undeserving and
impotent; exhibited once for all in the redeeming mission
of Christ; and exercised in the administration of the Holy
Ghost, THE SPIRIT OF GRACE, throughout the whole range
of His saving work.   It is the sole, efficient cause of all
spiritual good in man: of the beginning, continuance, and
consummation of religion in the human soul.   The manifestation of Divine influence which precedes the full regenerate life receives no special name in Scripture; but it
is so described as to warrant the designation usually given
it of Prevenient Grace.

I. GRACE, χάρις, is the love of the Triune God as it is displayed
towards sinful man, helpless in his sin.   It is therefore free grace
corresponding to universal love; mercy towards the guilty and
help for the impotent soul   It is sovereign as being under no
compulsion, even that of the Atonement, which it provided, and

Grace.

was not created by it. It is universal, being spoken of rather as
an attribute than as an act of God ; but it is particular also, suit-
ing its manifestation to each   It is independent of merit in the
object, of necessity, for otherwise grace would be no more grace ;
but it is not arbitrary, nor is it independent of conditions   As
this grace is that of the Father and the Son in the redemption of
mankind, it has already been considered.   It is now viewed as
the grace of the Spirit in the administration of redemption.   The
Holy Ghost is once in Scripture termed in a most affecting con-
Heb x 29   nection THE SPIRIT OF GRACE   The propriety of the term Prevenient Grace, and the doctrine which it signifies, rests upon the
general truth that salvation is altogether of the Divine lovingkindness   This is declared in two ways : man is impotent in his
guilt and weakness ; God's manifold gift in redemption is free.

As to Man   1. The powerlessness of man is everywhere assumed in Scripture, though not stated often in positive terms.   Like many other
universal truths—such as the Being of God, the immortality of
the soul—it is the presupposition of the whole Bible   Still, it
has sound and most impressive Scriptural confirmations : though
some of those which may be appealed to must, in exegetical
fidelity, be cautiously received.   Certain of these passages refer
Eph. ii 1.   rather to the hardening effect of continued sin : such as *you hath
He quickened, who were dead in trespasses and sins.*   Some describe
the impotence of man to carry on of himself God's work , such as
Zech iv 6.   *Not by might, nor by power, but by My Spirit, saith the Lord of Hosts ;*
2 Cor. iii.   and *Not that we are sufficient of ourselves to think anything as of our-*
5   *selves ; but our sufficiency is of God*   Not a few refer to the entire
dependence of the believer on Christ for all his spiritual good ;
John xv.   such as *Without Me ye can do nothing.*   But there are others which
5.   lay stress upon the fact that the world was lost in sin and weakness when Christ interposed : *When we were yet without strength*
(ἀσθενῶν, *helpless*), *in due time Christ died for the ungodly* (ἀσεβῶν,
Rom. v. 6,   *godless*). *While we were yet sinners* (ἁμαρτωλῶν,ʼ*transgressors*), *Christ*
8, 10.   *died for us.   When we were enemies* (ἐχθροί, *under wrath*), *we were
reconciled to God.*   Now all these words, while they depict the
estate of fallen man at the time when the Redeemer appeared, must
be made general in their application.   They give, as a quaternion,
the best negative definition of grace that the Scripture furnishes.

As sinners are under the law and guilty, grace finds a method of mercy, as they are under the Divine displeasure, it provides for the reconciliation of God, as they are cut off from fellowship with their Maker, it gives them the Spirit of worship and holiness, as they are absolutely unable to help themselves, it provides them all the help of Heaven. Man is unequal to his own salvation, however it is viewed: whether in its beginning, or in its process, or in its end.

2. Hence it is declared that the salvation of man is altogether of grace. *By grace are ye saved through faith, and that not of yourselves; it is the gift of God* · altogether of grace and not of works. There is no need to ask to which—whether salvation or faith—the GIFT refers: it refers to both, which in this connection are inseparable. It is not so much in single passages as in the constant tenour of Scripture that we gather the spontaneous freedom of the grace that provided salvation. In fact, the origin of human redemption is always traced to the love of God which, resting upon undeserving man, became grace. And the use of the term in the New Testament illustrates this. The word, as sanctified to Christian uses, and apart from its occasional classical application as graciousness,—in which sense it lights upon our Lord's lips: they *wondered at the gracious words, τῆς χάριτος, which proceeded out of His mouth,*—has three meanings in the New Testament. It is Grace from God to man, and as such is the sum of benediction χάρις ὑμῖν; it is Grace working within the soul. *My grace, ἡ χάρις μου, is sufficient for thee;* and, finally, it is Grace going back to God in thanks: χάρις τῷ Θεῷ, *thanks be to God.*

II. This grace as the influence of the Spirit on the minds of men generally and of individual men before their personal acceptance is described in various ways. These may be classed as, first, referring to the Divine operation, when it is a striving and drawing; secondly, in relation to the means used, when it is a demonstration of the truth; thirdly, as influencing man, when it is the working in him to will, by piercing or opening his heart. These three are distinct, but one; and, when compared, yield a doctrine which is simple in its mystery though mysterious in its simplicity.

1. The drawing and striving of the Spirit are throughout the Scriptures abundantly referred to · the former operating on the

Margin notes:
As to God. Eph. ii. 8.

Χάρις. Luke iv 22.

2 Cor. xii. 9.
2 Cor ix. 15

Prevenient.

Drawing and Striving.

human soul regarded as obedient; the latter wrestling with that soul regarded as repugnant; both tending to salvation, and in every case rendering that salvation possible. The Old-Testament declaration, *My Spirit shall not always strive with man,* may be capable of another interpretation, but it is followed by constant reference to a resisting of the Spirit as the secret of human impenitence In the New Testament we hear, from the lips of the Great Attraction Himself. *No man can come to Me except the Father which hath sent Me draw him,* and we may add, *This spake He of the Spirit* Both the striving and the drawing express the strongest influence short of compulsion. The zeal of human agency, described in Scripture, catches the same tone and strictly corresponds, being its representative. *That I might by all means save some* and *Compel them to come in* are mutually correlative: neither the command, nor the obedience to it, is consistent with an absence of Divine influence, or with anything but a Divine purpose to save.

2. The Word of Truth is never without the influence of the Spirit. On the Day of Pentecost the first Christian sermon was preached with His accompanying power: they spoke, first indeed only to God but afterwards to man, *as the Spirit gave them utterance.* Nothing less than this is meant by the reference to the *Word of God which effectually worketh* in those that believe, and to the Gospel which came *not unto you in word only, but also in power, and in the Holy Ghost.* An effectual Divine energy is described as belonging to the Word preached, apart from its final result: *My preaching was . . in demonstration of the Spirit and of power.* This ἀποδείξις is opposed to the influence of rhetorical skill, and establishes the general fact that the Spirit's power has the energy and effect of a Divine persuasion, whether yielded to or not.

3. The effect produced is occasionally made prominent. Under that first sermon *they were pricked in their heart,* which in another form is stated of Lydia, *whose heart the Lord opened.* The piercing and the opening are not in these texts so different as is sometimes thought · both the Jews and Lydia *attended unto the things which were spoken* as the result. *It is God which, of His good pleasure, worketh in you to will and to do :* here we have the last word of Scripture on this subject.

Marginal references:
Gen. vi. 3
John vi. 44
John vii. 39
1 Cor ix. 22
Luke xiv 23.
Acts ii. 4
1 Thess ii. 13
1 Thess. i. 5.
1 Cor xi. 4.
Acts ii 37
Acts xvi 14
Phil ii.13

PERSONAL HUMAN AGENCY: FREE WILL.   Freedom.

The prevenient grace of the Spirit is exercised on the natural man : that is, on man as the Fall has left him. As the object of that grace man is a personality free and responsible, by the evidence of consciousness and conscience. As fallen he is throughout all his faculties enslaved to sin ; but knows that sin is foreign to his original nature, and that the slavery is not hopeless nor of necessity. His will is still the originating power or principle of self-determination, under the influence of motives originated in the understanding and feeling, but capable of controlling those motives. And his whole nature, as fallen, whether regarded as intellect, sensibility or will, is under some measure of the influence of the Holy Spirit, the firstfruits of the gift of redemption.

These several propositions are in themselves clear and simple and true. They are in harmony with all sound psychology ; with common sense ; and with the tenour and tendency of all Scripture. Their difficulty is felt only in relation to the theological speculations which have been connected with the influence of the Holy Spirit, and the metaphysical speculations with which the doctrine of election has surrounded them.

1. Prevenient grace is exercised on the personality of man, free   Person and accountable · not upon any particular element of his nature,   ality. but upon himself. That personality is the Suppositum Intelligens, the responsible author of all that he does : not his will, nor his feeling, nor his intellect ; but the hidden man, the αὐτὸς ἐγώ, the central substantial person who is behind and beneath all his affections and attributes. That influence of the Spirit, directly or through the Word, is exercised upon the agent whom St. Paul describes as the active I or the passive Me of every religious feeling that precedes regeneration.

2. The person or personality of the natural or unregenerate   Free Will.

man is free, inasmuch as no power from without controls his will. It is the very nature of will to originate volition : otherwise, if constrained, will is no more will, the possessor of it is not accountable; and volition is only a misnomer for the obedience, only in appearance spontaneous, to a natural or physical law. Consciousness and conscience alike attest that the sinner—for of the sinner we are now speaking—is free and responsible : his consciousness in its first elements is that of a free agent, and his conscience, or MORAL CONSCIOUSNESS, asserts his responsibility, not only for actions but for words and thoughts and the whole posture of the mind.

3 Again, that person is bound and enslaved to sin Naturally the bias to evil and the aversion from the moral law are so universal that, even apart from New-Testament teaching, common consent allows that human nature is bound to what is wrong : so bound that none can escape without a direct Divine intervention ; and bound so universally in actual experience as to warrant the induction that none will ever be born without it. In the case of actual transgressors, the effect of habit invariably both proves the original innate bondage and deepens its strength

4 But the slavery is not absolute. It is conscious slavery, and not submitted to without reluctance. It is not so much a fetter on the will itself, as the ascendency of a sinful bias over the motives that actuate the conduct by governing the will : the feelings and desires of the affection, and the thoughts of the mind The will is not bound ; but the understanding which guides it is darkened, and the affection which prompts its exercise is corrupted by sense. Now here comes in the doctrine of Prevenient Grace. It is not needed to restore to the faculty of will its power of originating action : that has never been lost. But it is needed to suggest to the intellect the truth on which religion rests, and to sway the affections of hope and fear by enlisting the heart on the side of that truth.

Grace and Freedom.

THE RELATION OF GRACE TO THE FREEDOM OF THE WILL.

The Grace of God and the human will are co-operant, but not on equal terms. Grace has the pre-eminence, and that for many reasons. First, the universal influence of the Spirit is the true secret of man's capacity for religion , secondly, His influence, connected with the Word, is universal, inevitable, and irresistible, as claiming the consideration of the natural man ; and, lastly, He gives the power, whether used or not, to decide against sin and submit to God. These facts assure to grace its supremacy in all that belongs to salvation. But the co-operation of the will is real : because in this last stage it rests with the free agent himself whether the influence of the Spirit be repelled or yielded to. This is the uniform and unfailing testimony of Scripture ; the consideration of which will prepare the way for a brief review of ecclesiastical opinions and dogmas on the subject.

I. The general truth of a co-operation between the Spirit and the will of man is a postulate of the entire Scripture. Like some other fundamental truths, it is not demonstrated but taken for granted; and that very fact is sufficient evidence of our proposition. This co-operation may be viewed negatively or positively. **Co-operation**

1. Negatively, there is no reference in the only authority to an arbitrary Divine power reigning over the things that accompany salvation. He who works in us to will is never represented as working so absolutely upon us that nothing is left to personal responsibility. *Turn Thou me !* is followed by *and I shall be turned !* And both parts of the sentence must have their force. There is no saying in the Word of God which, fairly expounded, represents the Divine Spirit as overruling the energy of the human object of His grace **Jer xxvi. 18.**

2. Positively, and in the most express manner, the Scripture represents Divine prevenient grace as operating through and with man's free concurrence Figuratively this is expressed by the *good ground* which receives the seed . everywhere it is assumed that the first application of truth is probationary, detecting a character in the hearer which in some sense decides all But it must always be remembered that this hearer of the Word has a **Matt. xiii. 23.**

preliminary grace in the roots of his nature which he yields to or resists in the very act of resisting or yielding to the appeal of Heaven. We find it, literally, in all those passages which declare that believers themselves voluntarily receive the Word of God or of Christ or of grace So, in the Thessalonian *Having received the word* (δεξάμενοι answering to παραλαβόντες). This last expression is used concerning the reception of Christ: *As ye have received Christ Jesus the Lord.* Another and cardinal text is: *We then, as workers together with Him, beseech you also that ye receive not the grace of God in vain.* Here there is a co-operation of the Apostles with God; but it is equally certain that there is a co-operation of believers with both.

1 Thess i. 6; ii. 13.
Col. i. 6
2 Cor vi 1.

The Spirit has Pre-eminence.

II. That the Spirit has the pre-eminence is equally the doctrine of all the Scripture, as indeed it is of common sense.

1. The fact that man is, since the Fall, still a free agent is not more essentially a necessity of his moral nature than it is the effect of grace. Redemption is universal, and goes back to the root of the nature. Its universality has this for its result that all who are born into the world are born into a state of probation. otherwise the human spirit would have fallen back under the law of physical necessity, or into that of diabolic bondage to evil. Unredeemed spirits are responsible; but their responsibility is no longer probationary . they are responsible for a state of guilt that has become determined by their own first act become habitual. The difference put between them and us is the mystery of redeeming mercy. The children of men are in bondage to sin; this is the character which is stamped upon them by inheritance. But the bondage is not hopeless nor is it to any mortal necessary; they have a natural capacity of freedom to act as well as to choose, to perform as well as will; and this their very nature is itself grace.

Influence Inevitable.

2. Grace has the pre-eminence inasmuch as its influence when the Word is preached, whether directly or indirectly, is inevitable and irresistible. Prevenient grace moves upon the will through the affections of fear and hope; and these affections are necessarily moved by the truths which the understanding perceives. But the understanding is under the necessary influence of the Word, while, apart from the understanding, in some sense, the

passions are under the control of the Spirit. However obstinately and effectually the truth may be resisted as a ruling power, as truth it cannot be resisted.

3. Moreover, in the secret recesses of man's nature the grace is given disposing and enabling him to yield. Though the will must at last act from its own resources and deliberate impulse, it is influenced through the feeling and the understanding in such a manner as to give it strength It is utterly hopeless to penetrate this mystery. it is the secret between God's Spirit and man's agency. There is a Divine operation which works the desire and acts in such a manner as not to interfere with the natural freedom of the will. The man determines himself, through Divine grace, to salvation : never so free as when swayed by grace.

CONVERSION, REPENTANCE, FAITH.

Conver-
sion.

Conversion is the process by which the soul turns, or is turned, from sin to God, in order to its acceptance through faith in Christ. This is its strict meaning, as distinguished from that broader sense in which it is applied to the entire history of the soul's restoration. As the turning away from sin it is closely allied to Repentance, though not synonymous with it ; as the turning to God it includes or is merged in Faith.

CONVERSION

The Term

I. The term Conversion stands here for a few equivalents in Hebrew and Greek which express the same religious idea ; that of the change by which the soul is turned from sin to God. The fact that it is thus common to the two Testaments gives it a great importance. It is the general description of the restoration of the sinner that runs through the Bible ; and therefore has been very often regarded as including much more than the mere crisis of moral and religious change. Sometimes it is thought to represent the whole course, through all its stages, of the return of the soul to God : this is the case especially in the works of mystical writers, and of some who are not mystical. By those, for instance, who recognise no saving influence before regeneration, out of which repentance and faith flow, conversion is of necessity made to include all the moral blessings of the state of grace : in fact, it must have a very indeterminate meaning in every system of Calvinism   The theology that may be called Sacramentarian generally regards conversion as the process of recovery from a state in which the regenerating grace conferred in baptism has been neglected and might seem to be lost.   Sometimes, by a very loose employment of the term, it is made synonymous with the experience of forgiveness and the assurance of the reconciliation. But we must remember that it simply means the turning point of the religious life · its turning from a course of sin to the commencement of seeking God.   Hence the crisis that it marks is not in the religious life of a believer, but in the life of the soul, redeemed indeed, but not yet a new creature in Christ.

Prelimi-
nary
Grace.

II Conversion belongs, therefore, only to the outer court of the Christian temple.   Two considerations will further illustrate this

1 In conversion the Divine and the human agency combine It may be said that they co-operate, if the word be rightly understood.   This is not the case in the inner court of the state of salvation by grace.   The blessings proper to the Christian covenant are imparted : the believer simply receives his justification, his adoption and regeneration, his sanctification   But his conversion is the preparation for these absolute gifts of redemption the new life of righteousness, sonship, and holiness is the one supreme conclusive benefit of the Christian covenant grace, and man must be made fit to receive it.   The process of this preparation is his conversion to God   When that process is accomplished

1 Pet. ii
25.

the conversion is ended . *Ye were as sheep going astray ; but are now* RETURNED *unto the Shepherd and Bishop of your souls.*   Now throughout this preliminary stage of the religious life the grace of the Spirit and the effort of man unite.   (1.) The appeal to God to convert the soul runs through the Bible · such Old-Testament

Jer xxxi.
18.
Lam v.21.

prayers as *Turn Thou me, and I shall be turned , for Thou art the Lord my God,* and *Turn Thou us unto Thee, O Lord, and we shall be turned , renew our days as of old,* express the spirit of the New Testament also, though not found in its letter   (2) But the

appeal from God to man to turn himself is yet more abundant
Turn ye, turn ye, from your evil ways, for why will ye die, O house of Ezek.
Israel? where the whole strain is without meaning if converting xxxiii
grace is irresistible. Here the New Testament affords abundant 11.
support. *Ye will not come unto Me, that ye might have life* John v
Hence, when treating of Repentance and Faith, the two 40.
elements of conversion, we have continually to exhibit, as will be
seen, a Divine commandment with promise. The grace is from
the Lord; the use of it is with man himself.

2 ·The New Testament expressly limits the term Conversion
to the beginning or introduction of the Christian life. There is
no instance of its use in reference to the changes in the believer's
state as such But here a distinction must be made. It is true
that the word is constantly employed to mark the recovery of
those who were backsliders from the preparatory grace of the old
covenant. In fact, this is its habitual signification throughout
the Old Testament: the appeals to return to Jehovah are
addressed to those who had departed from a God already known
and forsaken The same holds good of our Lord's use of the
word when He quotes Isaiah lest they *should be converted, and I* Matt. xiii.
should heal them; as also of the prophecy of His forerunner's 15.
agency: *many of the children of Israel shall he turn to the Lord* Luke i 16.
their God Simon Peter's conversion, after which he should
strengthen his brethren, was a return from backsliding. But
after the Day of Pentecost the word begins to be used more
broadly, of the turning *from darkness to light* generally. St. Acts xxvi.
James gives the solitary instance of its employment to note a 18
Christian's recovery from *the error of his way*, but that error was James v.
no less than a full departure from the truth of the Gospel. 20.
Generally, conversion is supposed to be accomplished when the
Christian faith is received. From that time the penitent is a
convert his conversion is an accomplished fact.

III It remains to consider the relation of Conversion to Relations.
Repentance and Faith, as distinct from and yet including each.

1. Sometimes the term seems to embrace both in the unity of
preparation for the common evangelical benefit. The blessing of
Jesus is the *turning away every one of you from his iniquities*, or Acts iii.
from *darkness to light*, or *from idols to serve the living and true God.* 26, xxvi.
18.

VOL. II.   B B

1 Thess 1. 9

Here the negative and the positive are united in the description of the conversion whether of Jews or of Gentiles.

To Re- pentance.

2. Sometimes it is more particularly the negative repentance · the aversion of the soul from sin through a conviction of its true character ; a sorrowing hatred of it as estrangement from God, and abandonment of it in the sincere purpose of the convinced

Acts iii 19.

spirit *Repent ye therefore and be converted* . here the forgiveness is supposed afterwards to follow, and conversion is limited to the effect of repentance But repentance is also exhibited as the

Jer xxxi 19. Jas v 20

effect of conversion · *Surely after that I was turned, I repented* Again the conversion is itself repentance : *he which converteth the sinner from the error of his way shall save a soul from death* These are all instances of a certain freedom of Scripture in the use of these terms which should warn us against over-careful dogmatic distinctions.

To Faith.
Acts xi 21.

3. More frequently conversion is made equivalent to faith. *A great number believed and turned unto the Lord* . where faith has the same relation to the turning which repentance has in the previous passages. Sometimes faith is omitted where it is never-

Acts ix 35.

theless meant : *And all that dwelt at Lydda and Saron saw him, and turned to the Lord.* It is even made the distinguishing element in

1 Pet. ii. 25.

conversion : *but are now returned unto the Shepherd and Bishop of your souls.*

4 Thus it is observable that conversion is more closely than repentance and faith connected with the means or circumstances that bring about the crisis. These circumstances may be very

Acts xvi.

various, and the concomitants may also vary. The same result was produced by the terrors through which the jailer was con- verted, and the gentle influence which turned the heart of Lydia. And, in the ordinary application of the Gospel, these are typical instances · there may be sudden or instantaneous conversion, and there may be gentle and gradual conversion

5. Hence, finally, as both repentance and faith enter into the Christian life, continue in it, and in it are made perfect, there is a sense in which Conversion, of which repentance and faith are the two elements, also runs on into the state of grace. This brings us back to the point from which we set out: that there is a wider meaning of the term which must not be forgotten while the stricter

is adhered to So far as the old man remains in the regenerate there must be a perpetual turning away from the sins of the past and advancement towards holiness . whether that holiness be separation from sin in a perpetual conversion, or union with God in a never-ceasing faith. In other words, there is an ethical conversion that goes on until the soul is entirely dead to sin and one with God. But in the Order of Grace Conversion is the process of the soul's first coming to Christ, and it would be well on the whole to restrict its use to that meaning

REPENTANCE AND FAITH.

As the conditions of that salvation which is the personal possession of the common heritage, Repentance towards God and Faith towards our Lord Jesus Christ are always united in the New Testament. They cannot be separated, as repentance implies pre-existing faith, and faith implies pre-existing repentance. But they differ in this, that faith is the instrument as well as a condition of individual acceptance ; and, as such, springs out of and follows repentance. Both are produced by the preliminary grace of the Holy Spirit, but not perfected without the concurrence of the will of man. Though both are only introductory to the state of grace, properly so called, faith in its saving exercise is the transition point where the state of conviction passes into life in Christ.

REPENTANCE

Repent-
ance

Repentance is a Divinely-wrought conviction of sin, the result of the Holy Spirit's application of the condemning law to the conscience or heart. It approves itself in contrition, which distinguishes it from the mere knowledge of sin ; in submission to the judicial sentence, which is the essence of true confession ; and in sincere effort to amend, which desires to make repaiation to the dishonoured law. Hence it must needs come from God and go back to Him: the Holy Spirit, using the law, being the Agent in producing this preliminary Divine change.

Repentance, or conviction of sin with its effects, is described throughout the Scriptures as simply the sanctified direction, under the influence of Divine grace, of the same feeling which is excited by personal affliction, or loss, or prospect of danger. But in the repentance of which we here speak as the preliminary condition of salvation, there is the spiritual revelation of the Divine law to the sinner, which leads to certain results.

Divine

I. Repentance is the effect of a Divinely-wrought application of the holy law.

1. It is generally said to be the gift of God. In the words of the early Church, receiving the first tidings of the vocation of the heathen, *then hath God also to the Gentiles granted repentance unto life*, we must understand not only, first, that the opportunity of repentance was proclaimed, and, secondly, the promises to repentance set forth, but, thirdly, the actual power of repenting also afforded. Similarly in that first full statement of the Gospel: *Him hath God exalted with His right hand to be a Prince and a Saviour, for to give repentance to Israel, and forgiveness of sins.* But it needs no express testimony to prove that every right feeling concerning self and concerning God's law must come from on high: *every good gift and every perfect gift is from above*, and this includes all spiritual influences. *The sacrifices of God are a broken spirit;* they are the sacrifices OF GOD: of these also it may be said, *I have given it to you upon the altar*, though NOT *to make atonement for your souls.*

Acts xi. 18

Acts v 31.

Jas i. 17.

Ps. li. 17

Lev. xvii 11.

2. More particularly it is the office of the Spirit of conviction, Whom the Saviour promised to send to *reprove the world of sin, and of righteousness, and of judgment.* This conviction of the Spirit, in its threefold character, is the essence of evangelical repentance as preached under the Gospel repentance following the applica-

John xvi 8.

tion of the law—for there is no other repentance preliminary to grace—but in its peculiar relation to Christ And the Spirit Himself is called, as accomplishing this office, *the Spirit of bondage.*

Rom viii. 15
Human

II. The human evidences of repentance are both its fruits and its tests. They are so described in Scripture as to show that the Divine operation is wrought through the human faculties, and finds human expression as if it were the act of man himself. They constitute his threefold recognition of the majesty of the law to the existence and claims of which he is now awakened

1 CONTRITION or sorrow for sin is expressed in many ways : especially in the Old Testament, the descriptions of which have no parallel out of themselves, none even in the New Testament. (1) It is *a broken and a contrite heart ;* the heart being the inmost personality and not the sensibilities only, nor the judgment only, nor only the will The word has its Hebrew meaning; corresponding with the *broken spirit* which precedes · this last being the perfect watchword of that true repentance to which, as running through the life, the promise is given · *Blessed are the poor in spirit, for theirs is the kingdom of heaven.* The hidden man mourns before God · his mind meditating on the sinfulness of his sin, his feeling oppressed with grief, and his will absolutely turned against it. Hence (2) it is godly sorrow, *ἡ κατὰ θεὸν λύπη,* and not the sorrow of the world, which dreads the consequences of transgression rather than hates the transgression itself. It is mourning that proves its genuineness by refusing to be comforted save by Divine mercy it is not so much *godly*—this is regenerate repentance—as towards God (3) It is a keen sense of sin universal, and not of particular sins. The revelation of it in fulness is a new and peculiar experience a new moral consciousness which makes perfect the conscience of sin. *By the law, is the knowledge of sin.* But our Lord tells us that the world is to be convinced of sin *because they believe not on Me* · Christ the Saviour is Himself the best and only revelation of the evil from which He saves

Contrition.

Ps li. 17

Matt v 3

Rom iii 20
John xvi 9.

2. Submission to the condemning law is of the essence of true repentance and takes the form of CONFESSION. This may be regarded in two lights : it is the utterance of utter hopelessness, and of a profound sense of the justice of God in the visitation of

Submission.

iniquity. But the latter takes precedence. (1.) The law pronounces condemnation, the terrors of which are now first felt; and the sinner, even though in the presence of Christ, Who preaches repentance, and all the more because he is in the presence of Christ, accepts the utmost rigour of judgment as just. He sees his guilt, and sees his inexpressible pollution, in the light of the Divine countenance, and abhors himself, while he fears his Judge (2) The law convicts of impotence : and so the penitent cries, *when the commandment came, sin revived, and I died.* True repentance absolutely withers all hope in self as to present or future ability. (3) These are united in CONFESSION, which is especially in this preliminary stage only to Heaven True repentance comes from God and returns back to Him Who gave it There is a confession *one to another* commended by the Apostle James, which belongs rather to the Christian life and is consistent with confession of universal sin to God alone.

Rom vii 9.

Confession.

Jas. v 16

3. The repentance which is a condition of salvation approves its genuineness by endeavours to amend the life negatively by turning from sin , positively by aiming at obedience. This effort is imposed on every penitent by the command of Scripture : *Cease to do evil, learn to do well. Bring forth therefore fruits meet for repentance* is the New-Testament formula The Baptist, the representative preacher of repentance, gives the solitary instance of these fruits of a tree neither corrupt nor as yet sound. They are not the acts of a regenerate life ; for the promise of the Holy Ghost is held out as a future gift. They are not fruits of a corrupt tree , for the Spirit gives the prevenient grace that enables the penitent to present them to God They are tokens of sincerity, and are essential as such , for the Scripture invariably demands obedience to God's law, and reparation of every injury to man ; not indeed as securing forgiveness, but as its peremptory condition. Both are expressed by the two New-Testament terms· μεταμέλεια and μετάνοια, the latter a change of mind, the former a change of purpose. In this turning from sin and turning towards holiness, the act is rather dwelt upon than the feeling. The feeling may vary, as it regards both the sense of sin and the sense of condemnation ; it may have endless varieties of expression, but the act is always the same.

Amendment

Is i.16,17. Matt iii. 8.

III Repentance, thus described, is still in the outer court It belongs to the midway state between nature and grace ; but has, nevertheless, a special relation to the dispensation of law. This may be finally illustrated by a summary view of the New-Testament method of enforcing its necessity and its requirements.

1. John the Baptist is the pre-eminent preacher of repentance. The forerunner of Christ, he is also the forerunner of His Gospel. His doctrine contains every principle necessary to its perfection , and his ministry not less than that of the Apostles, was *in power, and in the Holy Ghost* He preached repentance as universally necessary and available. *Repent ye !* was his one word to all alike. He enforced it as incumbent on every man at the present moment : on the one hand, because *the axe is laid unto the root ;* and, on the other, because the *kingdom of heaven was at hand.* He required it to be thorough, profound, and perfect . *Prepare ye the way of the Lord ! Every valley shall be filled, and every mountain and hill shall be brought low.* He proclaimed it as accompanied by its meet fruits of reformation, restitution, and pledges of amendment *Bring forth therefore fruits worthy of repentance.* And, finally, he preached it as preparatory to the salvation of Christ and the baptism of the Holy Ghost. *All flesh shall see the salvation of God.* But the one supreme theme of his enforcement is the necessity of repentance as the preparation for Christ.

2. Further illustrations of this are found in the Gospels. *The kingdom of heaven suffereth violence, and the violent take it by force.* words which, whatever other meaning they bear, have evident 'reference to John's baptism, and the desperate discipline of preparatory repentance. The blind man at Bethsaida, whom the Saviour exhibited in a state of intermediate and halting cure— no longer wholly blind, but more miserable than when he was , not yet fully enlightened, but on the way to it—illustrates the prevenient grace of repentance. This solitary instance of our Lord's suspended power has a meaning for all ages There is a first touch, the effect of which is . *I see men as trees walking* There is a second, when *he was restored and saw every man clearly* Teaching other lessons as to the progression of grace, and its critical stages, this unique miracle teaches also that repentance is the transition to the mercy of the Gospel The Baptist's reliefs

Acts xviii
24—27.
Acts xix.
1—7
are found in the Acts · Apollos required only to be taught *the way of God more perfectly;* and the Ephesian Twelve were prepared for the full Christian baptism which they had long waited for. *Then said Paul, John verily baptised with the baptism of repentance, saying unto the people that they should believe on Him that should come after him, that is, on Christ Jesus*

Legal and
Evan-
gelical.
3 Hence, finally, while the evangelical element is not wanting in this repentance—it has a presentiment of the Gospel—it is yet under the law. All that has been said may be summed up thus. The Holy Spirit of conviction applies the law to the conscience, and thus works His reproof The effect is sorrow before God as the Lawgiver-rather than as the Father, or before the Father as the Fountain of moral authority, acceptance of the righteous sentence pronounced upon transgression, and sincere though imperfect, necessary though not meritorious, endeavours to make reparation to the dishonoured majesty of right Beyond this the repentance which is the condition of salvation does not go. But it does not fall short of this it is in all its processes the soul's tribute to the law from the condemnation of which the Gospel, received in faith, can alone save the transgressor.

Faith.

FAITH

Faith as the instrument of appropriating salvation is a Divinely-wrought belief in the record concerning Christ and trust in His Person as a personal Saviour : these two being one. It must be distinguished, on the one hand, from the general exercise of belief following evidence which is one of the primary elements of human nature, and from the grace of faith which is one of the fruits of the regenerating Spirit. As Divinely wrought, it is attended by assurance ; as human, it works by love. And thus, while belonging to the state of prevenient grace, it passes insensibly into the regenerate life.

Divine
and
Human
Faith, viewed here more comprehensively as the condition and instrument of personal salvation, is a state or an act of the human

spirit as under the influence of the Divine Spirit. The Divine
and the human elements meet, but they cannot be so clearly
defined and separated as in the case of repentance. We must
view them as united in relation to the principle of belief, generally,
on which saving faith rests , to the passive and active trust that
enter into that faith; and to the assurance of acceptance and salvation which follow it in the regenerate life

I. BELIEF, or the principle of faith generally, belongs to human   Belief
nature it is the faculty of accepting the unseen as existing, by
which we admit as knowledge what is received only on evidence
or authority internal or external. Now this common faculty of
faith, which involves trust in what we believe, is Divinely directed
to the Gospel in order to personal salvation.

1 Man lives and moves and has his being, as a spiritual creation,   Human
in an element of belief or trust in the unseen ; in that sense also
we walk by faith, not by sight. Belief is a primary condition of all   2 Cor v
knowledge and of all reasoning on knowledge. It may be said   7.
that without it there can be no full assent given to any proposition that deals with other than matter of sense. Hence the
propriety of Anselm's CREDE UT INTELLIGAS, in opposition to
Abelard's INTELLIGE UT CREDAS; the two watchwords of Christian
Faith and Rationalism respectively Now all faith that leads to
action has in it an element of trust. The being of God, the guilt
and punishment of sin, the mission of Christ for redemption, the
Christian revelation as a whole, may be assented to by intellectual
belief without exerting any influence on the life. But this kind
of belief is not, as alone, referred to in Scripture. Faith is there
always connected with the practical trust which makes these
truths more or less operative. The object of this faith, not yet a
personal Saviour, may be generally apprehended · the compass of
the Christian Faith is often accepted without the experience of
salvation. To whatever extent the truths of religion are known
and embraced, faith in them is the healthy and legitimate exercise
of the human mind, receiving the evidence, internal and external,
which authenticates revelation But that faith cannot be without
the element of trust, latent it may be and unconscious, suppressed
by sin and hindered from the attainment of its end

2. This belief or trust of which we speak is exerted under a   Divine.

Divine influence. A merely intellectual assent, such as rests upon tradition and education, is not enough for salvation : *The devils also believe, and tremble.* Seldom does this belief withstand the assault of sceptical attack. Never does the trust inherent in it become influential. *No man can say that Jesus is the Lord, but by the Holy Ghost.* A firm belief in the Christian revelation, and trust in Him Whom it reveals as God and man, is the very precious gift of the Spirit, Who acts upon the elements of belief and trust in human nature, and directs them to their appropriate Object. Belief is often made perfect in the exercise of personal trust; and personal trust often leads to the strengthening of mere belief. Sometimes the clear revelation of the truth in Jesus to the mind leads to an entire reliance on His work; and sometimes the personal trust with its confidence of faith brings in the full assurance of understanding as to the outward revelation speculative or historical faith thus, through Divine grace, deepens into that spiritual faith, which in its last exercise is the gift of God to the soul by Himself prepared for its exercise.

Jas 11. 19. (margin)

1 Cor. xii. 3 (margin)

Saving Faith (margin)

II. The Faith that is the condition and instrument of salvation may be regarded as fiducial belief in the Redeemer, whose Person and Work are one as a revelation of God, and of all saving truth This trust is both negative and positive, or passive and active · it renounces every other object, and relies only on One. It is the act of the whole man, but under the immediate influence of the Holy Ghost

Trust. (margin)

1. The formal notion of all Faith, and that which makes it the appropriate condition of salvation, is personal trust in a Person. Its efficient cause is the operation of the Spirit on the human faculties ; its instrumental cause is the revelation of the truth concerning the Saviour ; and its formal cause, which makes it what it is, is trust in the Person of that Saviour.

(1.) This important truth is taught by the very term that is everywhere used in the New Testament : πιστεύειν is equivalent to πίστιν ἔχειν, the equivalent of the Hebrew הֶאֱמִין, which in almost every instance of its use includes the idea of reliance on the Jehovah of the Ancient Covenant.

(2) It is also seen in the fact that this principle is almost always connected, directly or indirectly, with a Person, and that

ven when the acceptance of Christian truth by the understanding s made prominent. First, the ground of faith is the authority of God who is believed ἐπίστευσε δὲ ᾿Αβραὰμ τῷ Θεῷ, *Abraham believed God*, and accordingly trusted in Him. Throughout his history, as that of the Father of the faithful and their exemplar, we find nothing required or imposed on his belief as truth which did not demand the unlimited trust of his heart in God · indeed. in some cases it might be hard to accept as credible to the understanding what nevertheless was acted upon in desperate confidence. In the New Testament the Saviour speaks of a credence in His words ; on His own authority : *Had ye believed Moses, ye would have believed Me ; for he wrote of Me. But if ye believe not his writings, how shall ye believe My words?* Here Jesus is arguing with unbelievers, and the matter is one of belief on authority. But, most commonly, He uses the word concerning trust in Himself ; though, in this case, the word is varied and a large variety of synonymous expressions is used, such as coming to Him and seeing Him and surrendering self to Him Hence, secondly, a Person is the substantial Object of all saving faith, to Whom it turns, on Whom it relies, and in Whom it finds rest : according to the three currently used prepositions, εἰς, ἐπὶ, ἐν, of each of which it may suffice to give one example. *He that believeth on the Son hath everlasting life:* εἰς τὸν υἱὸν, which is opposed to the unbeliever's simple disbelief of the word of Christ, *he that believeth not the Son,* ἀπειθῶν τῷ υἱῷ. This passage represents many which make Christ the Object to Whom faith as it were stretches forward. *Whosoever believeth on Him,* ἐπ᾽ αὐτῷ, *shall not be ashamed .* a preposition used also with the accusative, *but believeth on Him that justifieth the ungodly,* ἐπὶ τὸν δικαιοῦντα Here the Person is the foundation on which faith rests. *For ye are all the children of God by faith in Christ Jesus,* ἐν Χριστῷ ᾿Ιησοῦ Here, as in many other passages, the Person of Christ is the Object, on which faith indeed rests, but also in Whom as its element it lives and moves But in this case the penitent is already saved.

(3.) This Object of trust is in Christianity directly or indirectly the Founder of our religion in His own Person : its ᾿Αρχηγός, or AUTHOR *of the faith* Himself. Here the usual expression, *by faith*

Marginal references:
Gal iii. 6
John v 46, 47.
εἰς
John iii 36.
ἐπ
Rom x 11
Rom. iv 5
ἐν
Gal iii. 26.
In Christ.
Heb. xii. 2
R n iii 22

of Jesus Christ, which indicates that He gives its specific character to the principle generally. This distinguishes Christianity as the full revelation of an object of trust which was partially hidden before Faith in God, or Jehovah, the God of the covenant, was the condition and instrument of Old-Testament salvation , but Jehovah is the Father, Son, and Holy Ghost Christ is GOD MANIFEST, *in the flesh*, and He says, *Ye believe in God, believe also in Me* Of those who believe not, He says, *Ye neither know Me nor My Father · if ye had known Me, ye should have known My Father also.* And the final testimony of St John is · *Whosoever denieth the Son, the same hath not the Father.* Rejection of Christ was rejection of the ancient God Faith in God apart from His Son is now a species of unbelief Our Lord as the object of confidence is more specifically Himself or His Person This is its supreme definition · *believe also in Me* ! It is only indirectly His blood ; the propitiation is *in His blood*, ἐν τῷ αἵματι αὐτοῦ, *through faith*, but it is He who is *set forth* It is confidence in His Cross, or rather in *Christ crucified* , that is, in His death and resurrection ; as to the latter of which, however, the trust is rather referred to the Father . *If we believe on Him that raised up Jesus our Lord from the dead* Hence it is the LIVING CHRIST in the unity of His Person and His Work. The God who delivered up Christ and raised Him is Christ Himself. The tone of the entire New Testament is to the effect that He that seeth and believeth in the Son seeth and believeth the Father. But the specific relation of the Redeemer's Person to justifying faith must be considered hereafter ·

2 Faith is both passive and active, in opposition, that is, to a state of undue action and to a state of indolent waiting : only by so viewing it, and combining the two, can we understand the general strain of the New Testament as to its operation in the penitent and contrite spirit.

(1) As passive or receptive it is that trust or repose of the heart on the promises given in Christ, which in the New Testament is opposed to works of every kind, and throughout the Bible to any trust but in God Assent to a moral truth, especially such as is here supposed to be wrought in the heart by the Holy Ghost, engages in its exercise the understanding and

Marginal notes:

1 Tim iii 16
John xiv. 1.
John viii 19.
1 John ii 23

Passim

Rom. iii 25

1 Cor. i. 23
Rom. iv. 24.

Passive and Active.

Receptive

heart and the will Faith in its negative aspect is that of the understanding affecting the heart chiefly · the soul rests on the Saviour, abstains from every act, and only waits upon His promise. Only in that posture is it ready for the salvation ready to be revealed. As limited to one branch of it, that is, justification, this element of faith is of great importance : *To him that worketh not, but believeth on Him that justifieth the ungodly, his faith is counted for righteousness* Rom. iv 5

(2) Active faith is the assent of the understanding actuating the will more particularly Faith goes forth as well as waits, gives as well as receives. The act is to be understood in two ways · it is the energy which gives up the soul to the Lord, and that which receives Him in return , though these are not to be separated. *As many as received Him* and those that *believe on His name* are synonymous. *He that followeth Me* is a definition of the believer ; whose faith is a coming to Christ, and a receiving of Him, παρελάβετε. His Gospel is preached εἰς ὑπακοὴν πίστεως *for the obedience of faith.* Many other expressions are used which represent a saving relation to Christ as the active energy of the soul · such as its flying for refuge to the only Hope, seeking Him and laying aside every impediment, committing the soul to Him, and other similar phrases This is the kind of faith which is exhibited throughout the Gospels Active
John i 12.
John viii 12.
Col ii 6.
Rom. xvi 26.

(3) It must be remembered, however, that these two are always one The passive waiting and the active seeking unite. *The Lord is good unto them that* WAIT FOR *Him, to the soul that* SEEKETH HIM. And both are undoubtedly the act of God's Spirit in the soul ; as is shown in the passage of St. Paul which speaks of our being buried and risen with Christ *through the faith of the operation of God,* διὰ τῆς πίστεως τῆς ἐνεργείας τοῦ Θεοῦ. One Faith
Lam iii 25.
Col. ii. 12.

3. Faith is the act of the whole man under the influence of the Holy Spirit. By the Spirit

(1) It is not an assent of the understanding merely, nor a feeling merely of the sensibility, nor an act of the will, but belongs to the centre of human personality, to the heart *with the heart man believeth unto righteousness,* καρδίᾳ γὰρ πιστεύεται. The language of the Creed is, I BELIEVE : the man himself is the believer, there is no act in which he more absolutely gathers up his whole Rom. x 10.

being to act, while he goes out of himself, and appropriates Another. As passive and receptive, faith makes the whole soul empty for the reception of Jesus; as active and energetic, it puts forth all its powers to embrace Him and His salvation. Hence this principle, after conversion, still continues to characterise the regenerate soul   The Christian is a πιστός; he stands in this character, τῇ γὰρ πίστει ἑστήκατε, and his faith, working by love, becomes the spring of his new life   The act by which he entered salvation becomes the law of his being as saved.

2 Cor. 1. 24

(2.) Such and so great being the prerogative of faith, it is obvious that no power less than Divine can inspire it   It is essentially a moral act; for unbelief is reckoned to be specific guilt . the Spirit's reproof of sin is *because they believe not on Me.* The only or the supreme sin is now rejection of Christ; and the act or state of not believing is itself condemnation   *he that believeth not is condemned already, because he hath not believed in the name of the only begotten Son of God.*   But if the faith that saves has this moral character it must be wrought in the soul by God the Holy Ghost : there is nothing right in man towards God that comes not from His influence , and the primary feeling after a Saviour, as well as the trust into which this is elevated, is of Him.   Hence our faith is said to be *of the operation of God.*   How it is that the emphasis is laid upon our salvation being independent of works connects our subject with the doctrine of Justification.   The faith that lays hold of Christ is the highest moral act of a state of penitence : nothing more, but nothing less.   It is the last and best of the fruits meet for repentance.

John xiv 9.

John iii 18

Col. ii 12

(3.) Hence it is plain that the faith which is saving passes insensibly while we are studying it into the state of regeneration to which it leads.   As it is itself a sanctification of that original principle of belief which belongs to our nature, so itself is sanctified into the energy of the regenerate life   It becomes the law of that life, *faith which worketh by love;* it is the seventh *fruit of the Spirit,* and as such *is the substance of things hoped for, the evidence of things not seen.*   As conscience is the consciousness of the soul as touching ethics, so faith is the consciousness of the regenerate spirit as touching all its unseen and future objects.

Gal v 6
Gal v. 22.
Heb xi 1

III. Assurance belongs to this trust only in an indirect manner,

Assurance

as its reflex action and its gracious result, and its abiding privilege in the regenerate life. As faith is the highest negative work of repentance and passes into the energy of regeneration, so confidence in its Object, relying upon it as objective, passes into the faith of subjective assurance. But the assurance is the fruit, and not the essence, of faith. As such it will be hereafter treated Meanwhile, a few points may be noted

1 Though a distinction must be made between naked faith and assurance, it is certain that perfect faith must in some sense be assured of the reality of its object. Saving faith in God must believe that He *is and that He is a rewarder of them that diligently seek Him;* also that Christ is and that He is the *Saviour of all men, specially of those that believe.* That He is my actual Saviour, and that my belief is saving, cannot be the object of faith direct; it is the reflex benefit and gift of the Holy Ghost It is the *full assurance of faith,* the πληροφορία πίστεως, in which worshippers are exhorted to draw near. As faith, however, *is the substance of things hoped for,* its full assurance is to be expected in diligent devotion · *diligence to the full assurance of hope unto the end.* The internal assurance of faith is a privilege that all may claim and expect: seasons of darkness and depression and uncertainty are only the trial of that faith of assurance , they test it, and therefore imply its presence ; or, if absent, its absence is thus declared to be the result of its own failure.

Objective

Heb xi 6.
1 Tim iv. 10.

Subjective
Heb. x 22.
Heb. xi 1.

Heb. vi. 11

2. Among the objects of St Paul's prayer for us is *the full assurance of understanding, to the acknowledgment of the mystery of God and of Christ.* The confidence of saving faith is, strictly speaking, limited to the Person of the Saviour, who is revealed to the understanding, the affection, the will—that is to the penitent man—by the Holy Ghost, who at the same time opens the spiritual eye to behold Him But the faith which is the energy of the new life is also the spiritual eye which beholds all truth, and is assured of it As it respects the Holy Ghost this is the *unction from the Holy One,* by which we *know all things;* as it respects the believer this is the certain belief which makes faith knowledge.

Col. ii 2

1 John ii. 20.

THE RELATIONS OF REPENTANCE AND FAITH.

Repentance and Faith have certain relations which must be remembered by those who would understand both. Each precedes, while each consummates, the other; and they are united, whether in the preliminaries of salvation or in the mature Christian life.

1. There is a faith which precedes repentance: belief in God's existence and revelation generally, and of the threatenings of His Word in particular, must precede supplication for His mercy But this is the belief that lies at the root of all religion ; and may be altogether independent of trust in the Gospel, or any apprehension of the mercy of God in Christ unless indeed we import here the distinction between implicit and explicit faith. There must be a belief in God, that *He is* before there can be a belief that *He is a rewarder of them that diligently seek Him ;* there is a faith in the Gospel as a general economy of grace before the personal appropriating reliance on its provisions Hence all the appeals which in Scripture enforce contrition are based upon a pre-existing knowledge of the Lawgiver and of sin and of the penalty of transgression. And every appeal to every class of sinner must needs assume the existence of faith in the righteous judgment of God against his offence

Heb xi 6.

2 But repentance precedes the faith which brings salvation *Repent ye and believe the Gospel* is the formula that never will be displaced. Though the Spirit's conviction is based on the belief that Christ is, and that He is a Lord and a Saviour, into whose hands every man's destiny is committed, yet the trust which places the mercy of the Saviour before the authority of the Lord must be preceded by deep sorrow in His presence Saving trust cannot spring up save in the contrite heart · sorrow on account of the evil of sin, anxiety to be delivered, despair of delivering oneself, and a deep feeling of Christ's atoning sorrows, must co-exist in the soul which is encouraged to rely on the Redeemer's work The same may be said of all genuine saving faith. It

Mark 1
15

cannot exist where there is not humility of heart , sorrow for sin is the soil out of which it grows.

3. Repentance and faith mutually aid if they do not actually spring out of each other. The soul when touched with true penitential grief is as it were naturally disposed to rely on the great Deliverer. There is but a step between entire self-renunciation and the acceptance of the Saviour, who fills the void of self in fact, where the penitence is perfect, purged of all traces of its two opposite errors, despair and carelessness, trust may be said to lie at the very door. All repentance becomes in its last Evangelical analysis sorrow for the rejection of Jesus, Who in this very sorrow is accepted. But that grief arises from the Spirit's application of Christ's dying love, which is in such a state of heart really believed though it may not yet be appropriated with assurance. This faith may be, and is in some theological treatises, called ILLUMINATION ; and its combination with repentance is perceived or felt in such a passage as this *Awake thou that sleepest, and arise from the dead, and Christ shall give thee light,* where it is hard to say when the one office of the Spirit passes into the other.

Mutual Relations.

Eph v 14

4. Lastly, repentance and faith enter hand in hand into the new life of covenanted salvation. Legal penitence is transformed into Evangelical ; and the trust that comes to Christ is the faith that abides in Him and works by love. This repentance in regenerate souls is the fellowship of our Lord's sorrow for sin It is the interior mortification which is the crucifixion of the flesh. Strictly speaking, it is the only perfect repentance, which feels the sinfulness of sin as it never could be felt before, and more effectually than ever renounces it. Then it becomes the very mind of Christ in the believer concerning the evil of sin. This faith which unites the soul to Jesus keeps the soul in Him, and is therefore the permanent condition and instrument of all grace : deriving from their Supreme and Sole Source all the treasures of His life and power and salvation.

Continued after Regeneration.

HISTORICAL.

The theological topics which are connected with Preliminary Grace have had a very rich development in the history of opinion and controversy. Some things on this subject have been anticipated in former sections ; but a few points of deep interest present themselves here.

Human Will

I. The relation of man's freedom of will to the Spirit's grace has been matter of controversy only from the time of Augustine.

Ante-Nicene

The ante-Nicene Church treated the question mainly with reference to the Gnostic heresies, which anticipated the theory of Determinism. The Greek and Latin Fathers alike earnestly opposed the Manichæan notion of the necessity laid on the soul through its connection with matter. But they differed in that the Greeks exaggerated the primary function of the will in originating good ; whilst the Latins thought less of the will and more of the Divine influence upon it, and paved the way for the later doctrine of Prevenient Grace. Common to the whole Church for centuries was the principle ἐλεύθερον καὶ αὐτεξούσιον ἐποίησεν ὁ Θεὸς τὸν ἄνθρωπον · God hath made man free and master of himself. Common also was the correlative sentiment expressed by Origen . " Moral good is combined of the first choice of the soul and of the Divine power inbreathed " Common also, though more emphatically among the Latins, that of Ambrose : " Whether we think of the beginnings, or of the progress, or of the final perseverance of the faithful, there is no kind of virtue which may be regarded as without the gift of Divine grace, or without the consent of our own will." On the whole, the tendency was what afterwards was called Semi-Pelagian . grace having been regarded as influencing rather the knowledge than the volition.

The Pelagian Controversy.

II. A certain doctrine of Prevenient Grace, interpreted broadly, has been taught in almost all systems. But the lax interpretation of this given by the Greek Fathers led to Pelagianism ; and the emphatic assertion of a preponderating Divine influence in it was developed into Augustinianism

Pelagianism

1 Pelagianism in the beginning of the fifth century understood by prevenient grace the innate and undestroyed capacity of the

soul for good and secret bias towards it; the written law as
stimulating both, and, added to this, the teaching and example
and illumination of Christ. "Omne bonum et malum, quo vel
laudabiles vel vituperabiles sumus, non nobiscum oritur, sed
agitur a nobis. Capaces enim utriusque rei, non pleni nascimur,
et ut sine virtute ita etiam sine vitio procreamur, atque ante
actionem propriæ voluntatis id solum in homine est quod Deus
condidit. Sed Deus gratiæ suæ auxilium subministrat, ut quod
per liberum arbitrium jubentur homines facere, facilius possent
implere per gratiam, quam nos non in lege tantummodo, sed et in
Dei adjutorio, confitemur. Adjuvat enim nos Deus per doctrinam
et revelationem suam." These words of Pelagius himself must be
studied as containing the pith of his whole doctrine, as it has
been laid down above. It was his faith that "Est in animis
nostris naturalis quædam sanctitas;" and this natural sanctity
is only aided by instruction Hence whatever preliminary grace
is in the system of Pelagius is simply external instruction appealing to a nature wrong only through accident and bad example

2. Augustine's doctrine of Preliminary Grace is the perfect *Augus-*
opposite of this. In his doctrine freedom of will remains, but *tinianism*
freedom only to evil. Grace acts directly and supremely on the
Will. These are his careful expressions "Gratia prævenit;
voluntas comitans non ducens, pedissiqua non prævia Operari
et co-operari est a Deo. Gratia est gratis data, operans indeclina-
biliter et insuperabiliter." Pelagius was right in protesting that
these last words present "Fatum nomine gratiæ:" Fate disguised
as grace. The insurmountable objection to this dictum is that it
reduces the whole of the operation of Divine influence, through
the Word and in Providence, upon the general world to a mere
superfluity, which was afterwards called COMMON GRACE. This *Common*
is in Augustinian and Calvinistic systems opposed to what is *Grace*
called GRACE EFFICACIOUS: being universal and not particular,
being necessarily, or at least actually, inoperative for salvation in
the purpose of God. This wasted influence is opposed also to IMME-
DIATE GRACE being given through the truth and not directly
influencing the will: touching the soul only through its natural
affinity with its former possession, a natural affinity, however, which
the theory supposes to have been lost. Hence both terms are

C C 2

misused Grace is no moie grace, if it does not include the saving intention of the Giver, and by being called common this grace is dishonoured, suggesting at least the language used to St. Peter· *that call not thou common.* In such systems the outer court of the world is filled with a MASSA PERDITIONIS, in Augustine's phrase, the will of the Spirit kindles life here and there when He will; and the first spark of true grace has in it all the potentiality and effectual earnest of eternal glory. There is strictly speaking no doctrine of Preliminary Grace: Enlightenment, Conversion, Repentance, Faith, are all the fruits of regeneration; and regeneration is absolutely *the power of an endless life,* though Augustine himself did not sanction the notion of his later followers concerning its indefectibility.

Actsx.15.

Heb vii. 16

Mediating Theories

III. The mediation between Pelagianism and Augustinianism contained the principles of the truth on this subject It may be divided into three main tendencies Semi-Pelagianism, Lutheran Synergism, and Arminianism. These three advanced progressively towards a clearer view of the Scriptural doctrine.

Semi-Pelagianism

1. Semi-Pelagianism in the Latin Church, as represented by Cassian in Massilia, asserted that the power of doing what the will approved was not extinguished but rendered feeble. Prevenient Grace was found in the very contest between flesh and spirit this being a stimulant to the pursuit of salvation. Moreover, Divine assistance was declared to be necessary to the progress and consummation of all good in man, though the beginning of that good is found in fallen human nature. In the Middle Ages most of the Schoolmen held a modification of this teaching. It was then that the distinction between two kinds of merit was introduced which has given a permanent character to the Romanist doctrine of prevenient grace The process was thus exhibited by Thomas Aquinas: God is the Prime Mover simply. The free will cannot be converted to God, unless God Himself convert it It is for man to prepare his mind, because he does this according to his free will; yet even this he cannot do without the help of God drawing to Himself. All things are of God originally, but whether the universal influence is used depends upon the creature If he disposes himself rightly, it is congruous that man doing his best should be rewarded according to Divine goodness: this is the

Meritum de congruo. The Meritum de condigno is the real merit
of acts proceeding from habitual grace. The false doctrine of
merit infects the Romanist theology throughout in the department of prevenient grace it mars what would otherwise be true
Among the Canons of Trent are sentences which assert that free   Conc Trid
will is by no means extinct, though enfeebled in its powers "Si
quis dixerit liberum hominis arbitrium a Deo motum et excitatum
nihil co-operari assentiendo Deo excitanti atque vocanti, quo ad
obtinendam justificationis gratiam se disponat ac præparet, mere-
que passive se habere; anathema sit." The grades and degrees of
personal conduct by which the awakened sinner prepares himself
for justification are all additions to the Scriptural doctrine of prevenient grace. But the fundamental principle of the whole is sound,
though the tendency is towards error The merit of congruity
takes the place of the virtue of the Atonement to which all good
left in man is to be ascribed. it is not merit that God rewards
but the universal and free influence of the Spirit used by the
sinner on his way to salvation.

2. SYNERGISM was the necessary consequence in Lutheran   Synergism
theology of the doctrine of universal redemption. Melanchthon
wrote in 1535 : " Conjungi has causas, verbum, Spiritum Sanctum,
et voluntatem non sane otiosam sed repugnantem infirmitatæ suæ.
Deus antevertit nos, vocat, movet, adjuvat, sed nos viderimus ne
repugnemus. Chrysostomus inquit · ὁ δὲ ἕλκων τὸν βουλόμενον
ἕλκει. Erasmus. liberum arbitrium est facultas applicandi se ad
gratiam" The watchword of Synergism was that the human
will is a causa concurrens the theological expression of Chrysostom's "He that draweth draweth the willing mind." Man is a
free agent, analogous to God the Supreme Free Agent, and his
modus agendi, by which he is distinguished from natural things,
remains also in his conversion. The opponents of Synergism,
Flacius and others, represented the soul as absolutely corrupted
in nature by the presence of sin, which is the image of Satan in
him Hence with them prevenient grace was the removal of
some almost organic evil. The later Evangelical divines in many
ways described and made emphatic the "generale desiderium
salutis." But the Lutheran teaching generally on this subject
may be said to be vitiated by two errors first it ascribes that

good in man to which converting grace appeals to nature, not
wholly debased by the Fall, without laying stress on the redeeming gift of our Saviour to the world; and, secondly, it makes the
preliminaries of grace depend too much on the sacramental gift
imparted in baptism.

Armi-
nianism

3. The Arminian mediation between the two extremes,
generally, of Pelagianism and Augustinianism, has been referred
to in some previous sections.

Metho-
dism

As to the present topic, that of Prevenient Grace, its
modern Methodist representative maintains a doctrine which is
consistent throughout   It holds that there is a state of nature, as
distinguished from the state of grace and the state of glory, that
state of nature however being itself a state of grace, preliminary
grace, which is diffused throughout the world, and visits all the
children of men · not merely the remains of good untouched by
the Fall, but those remains as the effect and gift of redemption.
The special grace of enlightenment and conversion, repentance
and faith, it holds to be prevenient only, as resting short of regeneration; but as flowing into the regenerate life   It therefore
asserts, in a certain sense, the theory of a CONTINUITY OF GRACE
in the case of those who are saved   But in its doctrine all grace
is not the same grace in its issues, though all is the same in
its Divine purpose.   It distinguishes measures and degrees of
the Spirit's influence, from the most universal and common
benefit of the Atonement in life and its advantages up to the consummation of the energy of the Holy Ghost which fits for the
vision of God   It rejects the figment of a COMMON GRACE not
χάρις σωτήριος; and refuses to believe that any influence of the
Divine Spirit procured by the Atonement is imparted without
reference to final salvation.   The doctrine of a Continuity of
Grace, flowing in some cases uninterruptedly from the grace of
Christian birth, sealed in baptism, up to the fulness of sanctification, is alone consistent with Scripture

Con-
tinuity of
Grace

Many points of discussion bearing on Repentance and Faith
will be considered when Justification by Faith and the Roman
Sacrament of Penance are before us

THE STATE OF SALVATION.

By the state of salvation is here meant the circle of evan-gelical privileges which constitute the estate of believers in Christ and are imparted by the Holy Spirit. It is the grace in which they stand, as distinguished on the one hand from the preliminaries of vocation, and, on the other, from the ethical duties of religion: being the issue of the former and the foundation of the latter. These privileges are variously described as pertaining to personal Righteous-ness, to Christian Sonship, and to the Sanctification of the Spirit: each of these being both external and imputed, and internal and real. But, while thus distinguished, they must be regarded also as one great covenant blessing of personal salvation. one as the common gift of grace, imparted by the Spirit's administration, in Christ Jesus, under various aspects. We must first study them in their general unity and then individually as distinct.

THE UNITY OF GOSPEL PRIVILEGES.

Unity of Covenant Blessings in Christ

Personal salvation is one great gift. this may be shown by the terms used to describe it; by the simultaneous impartation of its various blessings through the Spirit to faith ; by the relation of all to union with Christ; by the completeness with which each meets the relative and real position of the believer; and by the harmony of the several privileges in the reception of the one Atonement. It is important to keep this unity in mind, to obviate the error of unduly refining upon the distinctness and the order of the several component gifts of saving grace.

GENERAL TERMS

There are some general terms which are used to describe the blessings imparted under the Christian covenant as they are one in their diversity   These terms are taken from their relation to God the Giver, and from the result in those who receive them.

Grace.
2 Cor viii. 1.
Tit. ii.11.
Rom v. 15, 16
Rom v. 2.

1. All are summed up as the *Grace of God ;* as the *Grace of God that bringeth salvation ;* as the *Gift by grace,* especially as this *Grace wherein we stand*   A careful examination of these passages will show that one word GRACE includes the whole compass of the blessings of the covenant in Christ   the first as the source, the second as the universal benefit, the third in its most perfect realisation.   Upon this is based the distinction sometimes made between the three estates of nature and grace and glory : the middle term expressing all that lies between the *access by faith* into an accepted state and the entrance into life eternal.   Hence the circle of privileges is sometimes termed Acceptance with God .

Eph i 6

an expression founded upon the words *accepted in the Beloved,* which is, literally, GRACED in the Beloved.   There is nothing superinduced on nature and preparatory to glory which is not found in grace.   But it has been already seen that the state of nature is not without the influence of a certain measure of grace.

Salvation

2. The unity of these blessings is expressed by some terms taken from the human side, or the result of their bestowment.

Jude 3

Thus we read of the *Common Salvation,* where, as in very many

Eph ii. 5

other passages, such as *By grace ye are saved,* all the Gospel promise and gift is meant   Sometimes the whole Divine method or

Eph i 13
Acts xiii. 26

economy of grace is connected with the common gift : *the Gospel of your salvation,* the *Word of this salvation*   The privileges of the New Covenant are thus summed up as one ; to be afterwards variously resolved into their component elements of sanctification,

Heb vii 14—18.

remission of sins and renewal unto life.   Again it may be said that sometimes each of these several great blessings received by man stands for the compass of his privilege .   Sanctification in the ·High-priestly prayer and the Epistle to the Hebrews, has this wide significance ; just as Righteousness and the restored Sonship have in St. Paul's and St. John's writings   The compendious word

Life sums up in passages too many to quote the entire gift of God through the mediation of Christ. it combines all that is negative and all that is positive in one term, perhaps the largest used in the New Testament. The same may be said of the *Kingdom of God* within us; as also of the *Earnest* of the Spirit imparted to believers. And, as will be more fully seen hereafter, the *Atonement* received is the epitome of all the blessings that flow from the *Word of Reconciliation* into the soul. Finally, all is the *Promise in Christ by the Gospel* of which we are *partakers* It is impossible to study these various central words in their manifold connections without feeling that each is intended to describe the estate of grace as one

Acts v 20.

Rom xiv 17.

Eph i 14

Rom v 11.
2 Cor. v 19

Eph iii. 6

THE SPIRIT'S APPLICATION OF THE ATONEMENT.

This Unity is further seen in the fact that the Holy Ghost administers every blessing as the special application of the Atonement

The Holy Spirit

1. As to Himself in His relation to the Finished Work of Christ He is the Keeper of the mysteries of the Cross, as our Lord said *He shall take of Mine.* The accomplished redemption is His treasury, out of the inexhaustible fulness of which we all receive at His hands He is at once the Administrator of its external blessings, the Agent in imparting its internal, and the Witness of both. It is not meant that He dispenses all the provisions of the Covenant at once. But the *Communion of the Holy Ghost* is the common enjoyment of the grace of Christ imparted as the result of the Father's love in redemption. To receive the Atonement is to receive its various blessings, at least in their beginnings, at once. Justification is the reversal of a sentence at the bar; Adoption is at the same moment the reversal of a sentence that excluded from the inheritance of the Divine family, but neither can be received apart from the renewal of the soul into the new life of God and its sanctification to His service. And all these acts are simultaneous benefits of one and the same Grace in Christ They are all the personal application of the one sacrificial obedience to the faith inwrought by the Spirit Himself. He reveals and attests the forgiveness of sins, He reveals and inwardly persuades of the adoption of sons, and He seals the believer for God: all these at one and the same

John xvi 15

2 Cor. xiii. 14.

moment. And all these acts of witness He continues ever as the abiding personal seal of interest in the great redemption.

Order of
Thought

2. It is quite consistent with this that there is an order of thought which demands a distinction among these blessings. They belong to different relations : they are not homogeneous Justification is perfectly distinct from adoption : the former is pronounced by the Judge, the latter by the Father. Regeneration belongs to another category · the new and filial life though a free gift accompanying justification, is most intimately connected

Gal iv. 5

with adoption, which is *the adoption of sons* It is congruous both with reason and with Scripture to say that the regenerate children are as such adopted ; and that the adopted must needs be regenerate. It is hardly reconcilable with either that the witnessing Spirit of adoption is, by that witness, the Agent of regeneration. Though the testifying Spirit is the inworking Spirit, the two operations are distinct The love enkindled in the soul when the

Gal v 22

Divine love is shed abroad is the firstborn *fruit of the Spirit* of life, not the instrument of effecting it. Life is deeper even than love. And, finally, sanctification belongs to an entirely distinct order of thought from regeneration. Regeneration is not sanctification begun, in any other sense than justification is, nor is sanctification regeneration continued in any other sense than it is continued righteousness. In fact it involves an altogether independent idea that of the consecration of the soul, justified and regenerate, to God But of this more hereafter

UNION WITH CHRIST

Union
with
Christ.

The Gift of the Spirit leads to Union with Christ ; and in this mystical union all the high benefits derived from the source of blessing are one. To be IN CHRIST and to have CHRIST IN US are throughout the New Testament convertible terms , but this reciprocal indwelling is mediated by the Spirit common to the Head and His members we are ONE SPIRIT with Him if we have

1 Cor. vi.
17

become members of His mystical body. *He that is joined unto the Lord is one Spirit.*

1. Now all the prerogatives of the estate of grace are ours in virtue of our union with the Lord , each of them in particular is

distinctly referred to the same source. Generally, we are blessed *with all spiritual blessings in heavenly places (or things) in Christ.* Eph i. 3 As treasured up in Him above, and our inheritance there, they melt into one indistinguishable blessing   But as the Spirit dispenses them to those who are united to Jesus on earth they are diverse, though still one in their diversity Our fellowship with Him or in Him is our righteousness, whether as imputed justification or inherent conformity with the law. *In Whom we have redemption* Eph 1 7. *through His blood, the forgiveness of sins ;* we are *made the righteous-* 2 Cor v. *ness of God in Him.* Our Christian sonship is based upon the   21 same union, whether it is adoption or regeneration : we are one with *the Firstborn among many brethren. If any man be in Christ,* Rom viii *he is a new creature ,* and this new creation is a filial creation. He   29. is our life ; and we are *quickened together with Christ* by God, Who   2 Cor v 17 hath *sent forth the Spirit of His Son into your hearts, crying, Abba,* Eph. ii 5 *Father.* Our consecration to God and interior holiness have the   Gal iv 6. same ground and guarantee. Believers are *sanctified in Christ* 1 Cor 1 2 *Jesus*

2. Thus union with Christ, incorporation by His Spirit into His mystical body, makes all the blessings of the Christian covenant one in Him   And this precious doctrine, the first declaration of which our Lord Himself uttered, pervades the New Testament. St. John gives the record of the Saviour's great saying,   John xv reserved for the last hours of His teaching, *Abide in Me, and I in*   4. *you ;* which was glorified in His prayer · *that they all may be one ;*   John xvii *as Thou, Father, art in Me, and I in Thee, that they also may be one*   21, 23 *in Us . I* IN THEM, *and Thou in Me.* And He has one echo at least of these very words . *Hereby know we that we dwell in Him,*   1 John iv *and He in us, because He hath given us of His Spirit.* But St Paul,   13 who was not present when the Saviour spoke to His disciples this word, has more than any other writer made it the signature of personal religion, especially of his own personal religion. To this note the Epistle to the Philippians is set , in it this union takes an unlimited variety of forms. But it is in the Epistle to the Galatians that it has its boldest utterance. There, and there alone, it has the character of a mystical, or, as is sometimes said, ethical or moral union with the Saviour's death   Thrice the Apostle speaks of crucifixion with Christ. First of his fellowship,

and that of every believer, with the virtue of His death to the
law . *I through the law am dead to the law, that I might live unto God.*
I am crucified with Christ . nevertheless I live , yet not I, but Christ
liveth in me : and the life which I now live in the flesh I live by the
faith of the Son of God, who loved me, and gave Himself for me. Here
is Union with Christ's death and with His life as if both were his
own through the mystical identification of faith . being dead with
His Lord to the sentence of justice, he lived the life of justification.   But that new life is itself the whole fulness of privilege in
Christ   Secondly, he reverts to the same idea, peculiar to this
Epistle, for the sake of showing that the regenerate life is fellowship with the virtue of His death to sin . *They that are Christ's*
have crucified the flesh with the affections and lusts   Here the union
is the continuous mortification and death of the old man or the
corrupt nature, signified by flesh, still remaining in the believer
Thirdly, he returns back to himself, and exults in his sense of
fellowship with the virtue of His death to the world and all in it
that keeps the soul from God · *By Whom the world is crucified unto*
Me, and I unto the world.   It were easy to show that here justification, regeneration, and sanctification, each a perfected ideal
realised, are signified ; that each defines for itself the whole
Gospel privilege ; and that all are not indistinctly based on the
union of the soul by faith with the dying and the risen Saviour.
This for the present life ; in the life to come the glory to which
they lead, and for which they prepare, is in like manner the
blessedness of union with the Lord . to be *found in Him* is the
Apostle's utmost aspiration.

3. This doctrine has been perverted in two ways   First, by
those who resolve it simply into union with the Church and the
fellowship of Christ by a genuine Christian profession : a style of
interpretation which reduces the IN always to BY, in defiance of
sound grammatical exegesis.   Secondly, by those who interpret
this mystical union with Christ as only the sovereign bestowment
in time of a prerogative eternally decreed for the elect , as if
salvation had been absolutely and unconditionally provided in
Christ for those given to Him before the world was by the Father.
But, rightly understood, there is no aspect of the common salvation more wholesome in its influence than that which makes it

Gal. ii. 19, 20.

Gal. v 24

Gal vi. 14

Phil iii 9

Perver-sion

the fellowship of His death and life enjoyed by those who are regarded as suffering and crucified and risen and ascended with Him.

EACH COVENANT BLESSING PERFECT

I There are two ways in which we may consider the unity of the great salvation of the Gospel. we may regard it as a series of bestowments of which one perfects the remainder · or we may regard each as full and complete under one special aspect. According to the former view there is first a discharge from guilt in justification, this word ending its function there, or being supplemented by adoption The new birth is simultaneous, with its fruits and privileges. But all flows into the state of perfectness through a progressive sanctification which is entire at length and consummate According to the latter view the unity of the [Terminology] blessings of the Christian covenant may be illustrated by the completeness with which each meets the twofold category of our estate as sinners : that of a position before God, and that of an internal character The grace of redemption must needs meet both requirements. Each of the main privileges of Christianity perfectly responds to the sinner's need whether as relative or internal His righteousness is, on the one hand, a justification in which God does not impute sin ; and it is, on the other, an infused grace through which the righteousness of the law is fulfilled in him His sonship is similarly the adoption which places him in the relation of a child, and the new birth which makes him such. His sanctification is the external sprinkling which takes away the hindrance to his acceptance on the altar, and also the internal purification which cleanses him from all sin. Now each of these blessings makes provision for the consummation of the soul's religion under its own particular aspect : there is perfection in the presence of the law, there is perfection in the regenerate life, and there is perfection in holiness to the Lord. These points will be hereafter dwelt on

II. Meanwhile, it may be useful to consider some of the theological terms that denote the distinction above referred to, and the proprieties of their several application.

Absolute and Relative.

1. We find it necessary to speak of ABSOLUTE and RELATIVE blessings : being more exactly counterpart terms than Relative and Real, though these two are often used, and the latter perhaps avoids a certain unconditionalness which clings to absolute. The believer's privileges are all of them inherent gifts while all of them are relative · they do now and will for ever affect his relation in the sight of God, while they are now and will hereafter more fully be the absolute possession of those who

1 Cor ii. 12

receive them : they are FREELY *given*, but they are *freely* GIVEN, *to us of God*   The same truth is expressed by three other pairs of counterparts, which explain their own meaning : EXTERNAL and INTERNAL, DECLARATORY and IMPARTED, IMPUTED and IN-WROUGHT

Forensic and Moral

2. It is obvious that FORENSIC and MORAL, as correlatives, have not so wide an application   The former belongs to the judicial court or forum, where only the absolution from guilt is received it has not to do with sanctification, nor with adoption, unless this term is supposed to be derived from the usage of Roman law. There is a forensic justification alone ; and that only in the present life ; for, while the righteousness of the perfected saint will be through eternity a matter of imputation—his past sin being an everlasting fact—the court in which it is pronounced is not within the gate of heaven.   It may be added that the term Imputed is conventionally limited to justification, and the term Declaratory to adoption . we speak with more propriety of an imputed righteousness than of an imputed sonship, which is the gracious declaration of the Father   And, further, though theological language generally limits the term sanctification to the internal process, it may be said also to be imputed or declared or external.   But forensic of course it cannot be.

Ideal and Actual.

3. Some other correlates may be noted, not so obvious in their meaning.   The blessings of the covenant are IDEAL as they are exhibited in all their perfection in the charter, REALISED or ACTUAL as they are the general experience of Christians   this

1 John iii 9

finds its illustration in St John's unsinning regeneration *who-soever is born of God doth not commit sin ;* and St. Paul's testimony

Eph i 3.

that God *hath blessed us with all spiritual blessings in heavenly places in Christ.*   They are UNCONDITIONAL and CONTINGENT at once :

the former to the Church of the elect as foreknown in Christ, *according as He hath chosen us in Him before the foundation of the world,* the latter to its militant members in probation bidden to make their *calling and election sure.*

Eph 1 4

2 Peter 1 10

4. It will be hereafter seen that all these several correlative terms have their uses; that the peculiarities of Romanist and Calvinistic and other errors have much to do with their perversion, and that therefore a precise valuation of their meaning is important, both to the theologian and to the preacher. Meanwhile, the fitness with which each blessing surrounds the whole estate and conditions of the believer's life shows that the covenant salvation is but one in its diversity.

DIVERSITY IN UNITY.

Diversity.

We have no better illustration of the unity which reigns in the diversity than is to be found in the diversity itself. There are no saving benefits conferred in the Christian covenant which are not connected with one or other of the three terms · Righteousness, Sonship, Sanctification. Synonyms are found of each in considerable numbers; but these are the governing formulary words, which rule respectively over wide spheres of Evangelical phraseology While each embraces the entire estate of personal religion, and provides to present every man faultless in Christ in its own domain, they are as distinct in themselves as the terms imply; belonging respectively to the Judicial Court, the Household, and the Temple of Christianity.

I. RIGHTEOUSNESS presides over the Gospel as administered in the Mediatorial Court. There God is the Righteous Judge: Christ is the Mediator of a covenant of forgiveness, having offered an atonement in which the idea of satisfaction to Divine justice as the guardian of law is prominent, and in virtue of which He, as the Righteous One, is an Advocate. In that court the ungodly and the sinner appear in their special character as condemned by the law. Repentance there is simply conviction of sin and confession. There the sentence of forgiveness, or remission of penalty, and justification, or acceptance as righteous for Christ's sake, is pronounced. And the witness of the Spirit is the declaration to

Righteousness.

the conscience of pardon giving the absolved sinner to feel that there is no condemnation. That court also demands the guarantee on behalf of everyone who is absolved that in him shall be fulfilled the righteousness of the law. All that the New Testament says concerning righteousness, throughout the whole of the stern family of terms belonging to it, is consistent with the great idea that the Gospel is administered in a court of supreme, rigid, exacting and perfect justice. Righteousness is written on its doorposts, behind its Judge, and everywhere The two ideas of imputation and impartation are inextricably interwoven; and make the everlasting distinction between this tribunal and every human figure of it. All is judicial from beginning to end. None of the terms we have been using can be transferred, strictly speaking, to either of the other departments. To sum up · the God who presides is only a Judge He does not pardon as a Ruler and justify as a Judge; there is no sovereign act apart from the judicial. Both in this world, and at the threshold of eternity, the Gospel is a judicial economy.

Sonship
II. SONSHIP is the centre of the Christian privileges which belong to the filial relation of believers to the Father in Christ. Here the whole terminology changes. The people of God are a family, in a House where the Redeemer is the Elder Brother, the Firstborn among many brethren, the Mediator of a covenant of reconciliation rather than satisfaction The sinner is admitted as a prodigal : his regeneration is the new life given by the Spirit of Christ, and his adoption is his reinstatement in all the privileges of the household of God The Holy Ghost is the Spirit of adoption His testimony being internal, not so much spoken to us as spoken in us, witnessing together with our regenerate spirits and enabling us to call God Father. There no law reigns save the law of internal love; and the perfection of the Christian character is that more abundant life from which sin in act and in root has vanished. Its blessing is the filial blessing; its holiness is the imitation of the Firstborn; its food is the life of Christ pledged in the sacramental feast It is the central and the supreme department of Christian privilege of which alone it is said that we were predestined to be conformed to the Image of the Son.

III. SANCTIFICATION is the blessing imparted to believers as they are admitted into the presence and service of the God of holiness in His temple. The sinner here seeks entrance as defiled and inwardly corrupt. In the Christian temple the Saviour is the High Priest, and owns no other name He is the Mediator of a covenant ratified now, not by satisfaction nor by reconciling love, but by an expiatory sacrifice. The sprinkling of His blood removes the bar to acceptance on the altar, and the witnessing Spirit impresses the silent seal of consecration, which is His own personal indwelling in the unity of the Father and the Son. This blessing is the deliverance of the soul from all that is contrary to the pure service of God in His shrine. Perfection is here entire sanctification. The love which in the Court is the fulfilment of law, and in the House conformity with the Living law and image of the Beloved Son, is here the spring and energy of entire consecration.

Sancti- fication.

Now it needs no proof that all these blessings are really one under different aspects. The sinner absolved in the Court is by the same act received in the House and consecrated in the Temple. The Judge, the Father, and the God are One. The Advocate, the Son, the High Priest are One. The penitent who stands at the bar, who is met as a prodigal at the door, who approaches the altar of consecration with only defilement in the soul which he would give back to God, is one and the same penitent. The Spirit who witnesses TO the conscience, WITH the spirit, and as a seal ON or IN the soul, is One Spirit. The perfection of each is the same perfection, and the door of each opens into the eternal Presence of God.

Unity in Diversity

Righte-
ousness.

CHRISTIAN RIGHTEOUSNESS.

This word is the centre of a number of terms which refer to the Spirit's administration of the atoning work as affecting the believer's relation to immutable right. It may be viewed objectively; and in this sense is used to describe God's method of restoring man to a state of conformity with His law: the righteousness of God, as the originating and regulative and essential principle of that method; exhibited in the work of Christ, the meritorious ground of the sinner's acceptance, or in Christ our Righteousness, and, as such, proclaimed in the Gospel, to which it gives a name. Viewed subjectively, it is the righteousness of the believer under two aspects: first, it is Justification by faith, or the declaratory imputation of righteousness without works; and then it is Justification by faith as working through love and fulfilling the law; these however constituting one and the same Righteousness of Faith as the free gift of grace in Christ.

The
Righte-
ousness
of God.

THE RIGHTEOUSNESS OF GOD.

The Gospel is a revelation of God's righteous method of constituting sinners righteous through the atonement of Christ by faith : hence it is termed the Righteousness of God. Viewed in relation to the propitiatory sacrifice, it is a manifestation of God's essential righteousness in the remission of sins; viewed in relation to the Evangelical institute, it is the Divine method of justifying the ungodly. Generally, it defines the full application of the Gospel in the mediatorial court of law, with all its effects as renewing the human spirit into perfect conformity with the Holy Lawgiver.

IN CHRIST OUR RIGHTEOUSNESS.

In Christ

The mediatorial propitiation of Christ is a display of the essential righteousness of God ; or, in other words, this method of providing for human justification is proved to be in harmony with the Divine perfections The Evangelical plan of conferring righteousness rests upon the plenary satisfaction of the Divine justice in the death of man's Representative ; it is the just honour put upon the merit of the Redeemer and the virtue of His work ; and, uniting these, it is the promulgation of a righteous economy of gracious government exercised over mankind for His sake and by Him. The doctrine of the Atonement has exhibited this threefold truth under a more general aspect , it needs now only a brief re-statement with special reference to the judicial acceptance of the believer

1 The only instance in which our justification is immediately connected with the death of Christ is the classical passage in the Romans where St. Paul expressly declares the harmony between righteousness as a Divine attribute and righteousness as proclaimed freely for man in the Gospel   So close is the connection that it is hard to determine to which thought the Apostle gave prominence ; to the declaration of God's method of making sinners righteous, or to the vindication of His own character as just. The emphasis of the whole is laid upon the words, *to declare His righteousness.* This phrase has two variations · first, εἰς ἔνδειξιν τῆς δικαιοσύνης αὐτοῦ, with respect to the Divine forbearance in past ages, which required explanation , secondly, πρὸς τὴν ἔνδειξιν τῆς δικαιοσύνης αὐτοῦ, with respect to the present time, after the Atonement had been offered. But both rest upon the supreme fact underlying the entire history of God's dealings with a world of transgressors : Jesus, *Whom God hath set forth,* προέθετο, in His own eternal mind and on the scene of history, *a propitiation in His blood through faith*   With this must be connected St. Paul's word *Who was delivered for our offences, and was raised again for our justification.* The faith through which alone the objective atoning oblation of Jesus is subjectively appropriated requires the resurrection of its Object . not only as proving that we have a living and faithful Saviour, but as demonstrating that His sacrifice, not

Vindication of Justice

Rom. iii. 21—26

Rom. iv. 25.

D D 2

for Himself but for us, was righteously honoured in His being raised to confer its benefit. The substitutionary expiation of Christ as the representative Man at once exhibits the justice of God in His dealing with human sin and His righteousness in imparting forgiveness to the sinner *that He might be Just, and the Justifier of him which believeth in Jesus.* This unique expression—the supreme Evangelical paradox—must be carefully noted. It is not *Just and yet the Justifier,* though that meaning is not far off; but it signifies that through the manifested sacrifice of Christ God is declared to be Himself just, having required that propitiation, and the Justifier, through the virtue of that propitiation.

Merit of Christ.

Phil. ii. 8, 9.

1 John i. 9.

Eph iv. 32

1 John ii. 1.

2. The perfect obedience of Christ constitutes what in theology is called MERIT, and this is regarded under various aspects in the New Testament It is rewarded in that Christ is *highly exalted;* on the ground of it the Father has perfect complacency in His Son and all who are His ; and in consequence of it God is *faithful and just to forgive us our sins.* This is the truth with which we here have to do. God is faithful to the Atonement which has been faithfully offered to Him. He is righteous TO Christ as well as IN Christ. All forms of Christian theology agree with Scripture in assigning to the Redeemer's work an unlimited desert or merit. And it is this which is expressed by the universal language of dogmatic and practical theology when it pleads FOR CHRIST'S SAKE. The original of the only instance of this expression, *forgiving one another, even as God for Christ's sake hath forgiven you,* is ἐν χριστῷ, in Christ The additional idea of forgiveness for the sake of Christ is more suitable to St. John . *if any man sin we have an Advocate with the Father.*

IN THE GOSPEL.

The Divine Method

Matt. vi 33

But the term δικαιοσύνη when specifically connected with faith refers to its exhibition in the Gospel as offering and imparting the grace of a declaratory and imputed righteousness, and at the same time the power of a righteousness internal and inherent.

1. The phrase is fully developed in St Paul's writings But the Lord Himself gave the word when He said above . *seek ye first* [. . . . . kingdom

and the righteousness are terms left to be afterwards explained
throughout the New Testament   The Apostle lays down the
text of his Epistle when he says to the Romans *I am not ashamed* Rom. 1
of the Gospel of Christ .. for therein is the righteousness of God 16, 17
revealed from faith to faith ; as it is written, The just shall live by
faith a righteousness of faith offered to faith, or, rather, which
has its individual origination in faith, and in faith has also its
consummation: whether as declaratory or as inwrought it is
altogether of faith   And again : *but now the righteousness of God,* Rom 111
without the law, is manifested, being witnessed by the law and the 21, 22,
prophets, even the righteousness of God which is by faith of Jesus Christ 26
The essential rectoral justice is manifested in the new method of
Divine administration   *to declare at this time His righteousness, that*
He might be just, and the justifier of him which believeth in Jesus.   It
is opposed to man's method · *for they being ignorant of God's* Rom x 3
righteousness, and going about to establish their own righteousness, have
not submitted themselves unto the righteousness of God.   So the
righteousness *of the law* is opposed to that which is *of God by faith* Phil iii 9.
All this signifies a new relation of righteousness, which is ἐκ θεοῦ
as it is ἐκ πίστεως εἰς πίστιν.   It is the righteousness which God
provides, on the one hand, and which, on the other, avails before
God : both in one.   As such it must not be limited to the
establishment of a righteous relation through the imputation of
righteousness   it includes God's method of making men righteous
also   It is the Gospel grace generally, with all its effects, specifically viewed as bringing men to the state of δικαιοσύνη, or conformity with law.   But throughout, from beginning to end, it is
absolutely of grace, without any merit on the part of man.

2. Though this Method of righteousness is as it were new, it is   Biblical
also the same which was from the beginning   Abel *obtained*   Develop-
witness that he was righteous only *by faith*   Noah also *became heir of*   ment
the righteousness which is by faith   But Abraham was the great   Heb xi.
exemplar. His faith was *counted unto him for righteousness ,* it was   4, 7
faith in a promise, not given *through the law, but through the righteous-*   Rom iv.
ness of faith , and therefore a righteousness which was not reckoned   3, 13
because of the virtue of the faith in itself, or as the substitute of
works   The faith rested on the early promise of justification by
faith through a Saviour as yet unrevealed.   The LAW intervening

did not affect the unity of this one great revelation of the only

Rom. iii 21

righteousness It is the *righteousness of God without the law*, in one sense, but, in another, *witnessed by the law and the prophets.* It was and is WITHOUT THE LAW, inasmuch as it is for ever independent of perfect obedience But it was witnessed BY THE LAW; which was a perpetual remembrancer of the impossibility of that obedience, which silently promised the Redeemer by the very fact that shortcomings were not visited, which made faith in the Covenant God and love to Him supreme, and indeed summed up all dis-

Heb. iii 19
Deut. vi 25
Phil iii 9

obedience as unbelief. *It shall be our righteousness if we observe to do all these commandments.* but none ever attained to that righteousness ; OUR righteousness and MINE OWN righteousness were ever inapplicable words, save on the ground of the deeper foundation of the unrevealed righteousness of faith in Christ The Psalms and Prophets proclaim this Divine method more fully. God's righteousness pervades both ; and sometimes in terms which anticipate the

Isa li 5, 6
Ps lxxxv. 10
Hab ii 3, 4

New Testament *My righteousness is near ! My salvation is gone forth, and My righteousness shall not be abolished. Righteousness and peace have kissed each other* THE JUST SHALL LIVE BY HIS FAITH. As the full revelation of Christ and of His kingdom waited for the New Testament, so also the full revelation of the mediatorial method of constituting men righteous : *though it tarry, wait for it*

3. But now is this Gospel revealed And the term Righteousness is one of its many denominations as embracing its whole design :

1 Cor i 18
Col. 1. 5
2 Cor v 19.
Acts xv 7
Heb v. 13.
Col iii 16.
Acts xx. 32
Heb vii. 2
Rom. xiv. 17
2 Cor iii. 9

As it is *the Word, λόγος*, or *preaching of the Cross ; of the truth , of reconciliation , of the Gospel*, so it is also the *word of righteousness λόγος δικαιοσύνης.* It is the entire system of doctrine concerning the Divine method of conferring upon man righteousness. The whole revelation is *the word of Christ*, and *of the grace of God.* In it our Lord is the *King of righteousness* as He is the *King of peace ;* and *His kingdom is righteousness and peace, and joy in the Holy Ghost.* It reveals *the Lord our righteousness ;* as the meritorious procuring cause, the perfect example, and the Author by His Spirit of all in man that God requires and accepts as finished conformity to His law. Hence it is in all its processes the Gospel of *the ministration of righteousness.* We do injustice to this all-comprehending name of the new economy if we do not regard it as embracing the whole sum of its effects in human salvation. Viewed in our relation to the will and law of God—and that view embraces, in a sense, all our relations for time and eternity—we are altogether saved by the Gospel revelation of righteousness The solemn question asked in the Old Testament is answered in the New. *How should man be just with God?*   Job ix 2

RIGHTEOUSNESS APPLIED TO BELIEVING MAN.

The Divine method of conferring righteousness is, when viewed in relation to man who receives it, a manifestation of pure mercy,—continuing and applying the mercy of Christ's atonement,—which reckons to the believer through all the stages of his religious life, in time and in eternity, a righteousness he can never attain to or claim as his own. Whether it be regarded as accounting righteous or as making righteous—for both are certainly included—it is and must be ever a free gift to the faith that embraces the propitiation.

JUSTIFICATION BY FAITH.

Justification is the Divine judicial act which applies to the sinner, believing in Christ, the benefit of the Atonement, delivering him from the condemnation of his sin, introducing him into a state of favour, and treating him as a righteous person. Though justifying faith is an operative principle which through the Holy Spirit's energy attains to an interior and perfect conformity with the law, or internal righteousness, it is the imputed character of justification which regulates the New-Testament use of the word. Inherent righteousness is connected more closely with the perfection of the regenerate and sanctified life. In this more limited sense, justification is either the act of God or the state of man.

I The act of justifying is that of God the Judge. Generally   God the Justifier.

it is δικαίωσις, the word which pronounces the sinner absolved from the condemning sentence of the law , and it refers always and only to the sins that are past. Whether regarded as the first act of mercy, or as the permanent will of God's grace towards the believer in Christ, or as the final sentence in the judgment, it is the Divine declaration which discharges the sinner as such from

Rom. viii. 33 John v.22

the condemnation of his sin *It is God that justifieth* · God in Christ ; for all judgment is *committed unto the Son,* who both now and ever pronounces as Mediator the absolving word, declaring it in this life to the conscience by His Spirit It is the voice of God the Judge in the mediatorial court, where the Redeemer is the Advocate, pleading His own propitiatory sacrifice and the promise of the Gospel declared to the penitence and faith of the sinner whose cause He pleads. The simplest form in which the doctrine is stated is this : *Who shall lay anything to the charge of God's elect ?*

Rom. viii. 33, 34.

It is God that justifieth Who is he that condemneth ? Here the Apostle has in view the past, the present, and the future of the believer , the death, resurrection, and intercession of Christ , and the one justifying sentence against which there can be no appeal in time or in eternity. God is Θεὸς ὁ δικαιῶν, in one continuous ever-present act.

Man as Justified

II As the state into which man is introduced it is variously described according to his various relations to God and to the Mediator and to the law. As an individual sinner he is forgiven his justification is PARDON or THE REMISSION OF SINS ; that is, the punishment is remitted. As a person ungodly, he is regarded as righteous, RIGHTEOUSNESS IS IMPUTED to him ; or his TRANS-GRESSION IS NOT IMPUTED to him. His sin is pardoned, his person is justified As a believer in Jesus, HIS FAITH IS COUNTED FOR RIGHTEOUSNESS. All these phrases describe, under its negative and its positive aspect, one and the selfsame blessing of the New Covenant, as constituting the state of grace into which the believer has entered, and in which as a believer he abides. This is attested by passages running through the Gospels, the Acts, and the Epistles ; passages which only confirm the promises of

Luke i. 77 Luke v. 20.

the Old Testament Our Lord's forerunner was foreannounced *to give knowledge of salvation unto His people by the remission of their sins.* The Saviour's word was, *Man, thy sins are forgiven thee ;* but

He spoke of the publican as praying *God be merciful to me a sinner !* and as going down to his house *justified :* his prayer was ἱλάσθητί μοι, and his blessing that he was δεδικαιωμένος · these words being here introduced for the first time ; and, both severally and in their mutual connection, being reserved for abundant future service in the New Testament, especially in the writings of St. Paul He left the commission that *remission of sins should be preached in His name.* St Peter preached that *remission of sins* on the Day of Pentecost, and afterwards varied the expression, *that your sins may be blotted out* counterparts in meaning But St. Paul takes up the Saviour's own words and unites them : *through this Man is preached unto you the forgiveness of sins ; and by Him all that believe are justified from all things.* And in his great Epistle he adds all the other terms, and unites the whole in one charter of privileges : *But to him that worketh not, but believeth on Him that justifieth the ungodly, his faith is counted for righteousness ; even as David also describeth the blessedness of the man unto whom God imputeth righteousness without works, saying, Blessed are they whose iniquities are forgiven, and whose sins are covered . blessed is the man to whom the Lord will not impute sin.* In this classical passage all the phrases are united without exception , and they are represented both as the act of God and the state of man, the one and various blessing of habitual experience. To sum up : the state of δικαιοσύνη is that of conformity to law, which, however, is always regarded as such only through the gracious imputation of God who declares the believer to be justified negatively from the condemnation of his sin, and positively reckons to him the character and bestows on him privileges of righteousness. The former or negative blessing is pardon distinctively, the latter or positive blessing is justification proper.

Luke xviii 13, 14.

Luke xxiv 47 Acts ii 38, iii. 19.

Acts xiii. 38, 39

Rom iv. 4—8.

III. Whether the act or the state is signified the phraseology of justification is throughout Scripture faithful to the idea of imputation. The verb justify is not used of making righteous save as the notion of declaring or reckoning is bound up with it

The word Justify.

1 The Hebrew word הִצְדִּיק is almost always translated by the Septuagint in the sense of making or pronouncing righteous through a judicial sentence , and that in the negative sense of vindication and in the positive of declaring just *She hath been*

Gen xxxviii 26.

Isa 1 8 *more righteous than I* Tamar was proved just, δεδικαίωται. *He is near that justifieth me,* ὁ δικαιώσας με   One striking passage Ex xxiii 7. deserves careful observation . *I will not justify the ungodly,* where, if the Septuagint had not followed another reading, we should have Rom. iv 5 had the very words of St Paul which omit the NOT, τὸν δικαιοῦντα Is v 23. τὸν ἀσεβῆ, also *Which justify the wicked for reward,* οἱ δικαιοῦντες τὸν ἀσεβῆ. The general strain is only confirmed by two passages which seem to be exceptions, including with the external the Is liii 11 internal righteousness . *By His knowledge shall My righteous Servant* Dan xii. 3 *justify many. And they that turn many to righteousness as the stars* Ps lxxiii. 13. *for ever and ever*   To these may be added ματαίως ἐδικαίωσα, *I have cleansed my heart in vain,* where undoubtedly our term is once used as the translation of the Hebrew זִכִּיתִי, *I made pure.*

2 In the New Testament there is no exception   A few specimens will be sufficient, especially as they are taken from the Matt. xii 37 Gospels as well as the Epistles. *By thy words thou shalt be justified,* δικαιωθήσῃ, *and by thy words thou shalt be condemned,* καταδικασθήσῃ. Luke xvi 15 *Ye are they which justify yourselves before men,* δικαιοῦντες ἑαυτούς. Luke vii. 35 *Wisdom is justified of all her children,* ἐδικαιώθη, where there is both a negative and positive sense   wisdom is both cleared from imputa- Luke vii 29. tion and highly approved, the former predominating.   *And the* Rom v. 18 *publicans justified God,* ἐδικαίωσαν.   Compare also κατάκριμα and δικαίωσις ζωῆς, *judgment* and *justification of life   It is God that* Rom viii 33, 34 *justifieth,* Θεός ὁ δικαιῶν ; *who is he that condemneth ?* τίς ὁ κατακρίνων , 1 Cor iv 4 *Yet am I not hereby justified,* δεδικαίωμαι   this does not prove me righteous   The passages in St. James, to be considered hereafter, are consistent with this. They speak of a declaratory justification, and not of the making righteous · of a justification pronounced on the evidence of works. Even those who suppose that St. James teaches a righteousness of works must admit that his use of δικαιοῦν is quite consistent with a declaratory meaning. He is writing only of the evidences of righteousness, precisely in harmony with the Sermon on the Mount, and expressly uses the Pauline language of imputation . ἐλογίσθη εἰς. He employs the word exclusively in its judicial sense. What he is pleading against is a mistaken apprehension of Faith, not a James ii 23 mistaken apprehension of justification. The Divine judgment pronounced on Abraham's faith when Isaac was promised in

Genesis xv was confirmed in the later evidence of Isaac's surrender in Genesis xxii. In the former he was justified, in the latter his justification or righteousness was acknowledged. The seeming exception in the Apocalypse is removed by the right reading, δικαιοσύνην ποιησάτω, *let him work righteousness*, and thus *let him be righteous still*, but not ὁ δίκαιος δικαιωθήτι ἔτι. On the evidence of such an unvarying usage we may conclude that this word never occurs in the Scripture in relation to man's acceptance saving in the sense of a declaratory sentence which pronounces the man righteous whom God for Christ's sake reckons to be such. Whatever righteousness is spoken of as imparted and infused requires itself to have righteousness imputed to it If the reading δικαιωθήτω ἔτι were correct, it would only make the New Testament close with a great testimony to the truth, That he that is righteous in his internal conformity to law must be JUSTIFIED STILL for ever

Rev xxii. 11.

JUSTIFYING FAITH

The faith which is the condition and instrument of justification is the trust of the soul in Christ as the only propitiation for human sin. It is a personal act of the penitent sinner under the influence of the Holy Spirit, Who reveals the Atonement to the mind, infuses desire into the heart, and thus persuades the will to embrace the Saviour. This faith, as receptive, renounces self in every form, obtains forgiveness and is reckoned for righteousness · these being one blessing under two aspects. As an active principle it appropriates the promise or the virtue of Christ's atonement ; and, working by love, belongs not to the entrance into justification, but to the justified state. Its genuineness is approved by Evangelical works of righteousness, without which therefore the state of justification cannot be retained. Hence there is a justification by faith without the merit of works, and a justification by faith on the evidence of works; but in both cases the justification is declaratory and altogether of grace.

WITHOUT WORKS.

Faith
without
Works

I. Faith, without works, is both the instrument and the condition of justification · as the condition, it renounces every other
dependence than the Atonement, as the instrument, it embraces
Christ, or appropriates the promise in Him, or rests upon His
atoning work

The Con-
dition.

1. The righteousness which is of God by faith is as a condition
opposed to man's own righteousness, which is of the law

Re-
nounces.

(1.) Faith acknowledges that the legal, proper, primitive sense
of the term justify, as the pronouncing him to be righteous who
is righteous, is for ever out of the question. First, as to the law:
it has been broken and its condemnation is acknowledged; it
demands an obedience that never has been rendered since the
Fall. Then as to man himself, faith renounces all trust in human
ability. It utterly abjures the thought of a righteousness springing from self It acknowledges past sin , and present impotence;
and the impossibility of any future obedience cancelling the past

Gal. ii. 16

*Knowing that a man is not justified by the works of the law, but by the
faith of Jesus Christ even we have believed in Jesus Christ, that we
might be justified by the faith of Christ, and not by the works of the law ,
for by the works of the law shall no flesh be justified* It disclaims all
human creaturely righteousness as such : the nullity of this is
taught by conviction, felt in repentance, and confessed by faith

Faith
counted
for
Righte-
ousness.
Rom. iv
5.

(2) Hence the specific Evangelical phrase that *faith is counted
for righteousness.* This implies the absence of personal righteousness, and the reckoning of a principle, not righteousness, in its
stead by a kind of substitution. In its stead not as rendering
good works needless, but displacing them for ever as the ground
of acceptance Therefore faith does not justify as containing the
germ of all good works : as fides formata charitate, or faith informed and vivified by love. Not justifying through any merit
in itself, it justifies as the condition on which is suspended the
merciful application of the merits of Christ : κατὰ χάριν Faith

Rom. iv
4.
Phil. 18

is not righteousness, as justifying : it is *counted for righteousness.*
It is *put to the account* of man in the mediatorial court as righteousness , not as a good work, but reckoned instead of the good works

which it renounces. Lest the faith as itself a work should be regarded as righteousness the Apostle varies the expression. He also says, again and again inversely, that righteousness—not, however, Christ's—is imputed to the believer not to faith itself, as if God regarded the goodness wrapped up in it. *The man, unto whom God imputeth righteousness without works . . . it was imputed to him for righteousness . . . for us also, to whom it shall be imputed.* It is the man, in the naked simplicity of his self-renouncing, work-renouncing trust in God—in naked faith, simple faith, faith alone, words which are not in Scripture but which sums up its meaning—on whom the sentence of justification is pronounced When our Lord, in answer to the question, *What shall we do that we might work the works of God?* said, *This is the work of God, that ye believe on Him whom He hath sent,* He did not use either of the terms, work and faith, precisely in their later sense, but prepared the way for it. He did not mean that faith in Himself was the all-comprehending virtue required by God, but that they must believe in Him before they could speak of any works at all as acceptable. Rom. iv.
6, 22, 24.

John vi
28, 29

(3) Imputation or reckoning—λογίζεσθαι, ἐλλογεῖν—has two meanings. the ascribing to one his own and the reckoning to him what is not his own. The latter sense predominates in the three great theological imputations: that of the sin of Adam to the race, that of the sin of the race to Christ, and that of the benefit of Christ's righteousness to the believer. As through the imputation of *one man's disobedience many were made sinners,* that disobedience being reckoned not in the act but in the consequence; and as the *Lamb of God* bore *the sin of the world,* not its sins, *being made sin for us* by imputation as a sin offering *who knew no sin* Himself, so the ungodly who in penitence believes has the virtue or efficacy of Christ's obedience reckoned to him without having that obedience itself imputed: he is *made the righteousness of God in Him,* which is different from having the righteousness of Christ set to his account. Imputation

Rom v.
19.

John i.
29.
2 Cor
v 21.

(4.) This faith as a negative condition is of the operation of the Holy Ghost. He enables the soul to renounce every other trust He convinces the mind of guilt and impotence, awakens in the heart the feeling of emptiness and longing desire; and so moves the will to reject every other confidence than Christ. But, The Holy
Ghost.

though the influence of the Spirit produces it, it is so far only negative · a preparation for good rather than itself good.

Instrument

2. Faith is the active Instrument as well as the passive Condition of justification. As such it apprehends Christ; justifies because of the virtue of its object as it unites the soul with Him; is blessed with the privilege of an attendant assurance, and all once more under the influence of the Holy Spirit

Cause.

(1) Faith is the instrumental cause of justification. The originating cause is the love of God; the meritorious, Christ's atoning obedience, active and passive in one, the former rendering the latter possible; the efficient cause, the Holy Ghost, working faith through word and sacrament as the secondary instruments of justification or its means There is scarcely any room here for another so-called formal cause, which is, really, notwithstanding every argument of sophistry, the faith which makes the soul one with Christ, and that is the cause instrumental blended with the cause meritorious To ask for the formal cause—formal being logically that which immediately constitutes a thing what it is—is simply to ask for a definition of the act and state of justification. It is and must be the imputative estimate of God

Object John x 30

(2) The object of justifying faith is God in Christ. In this as in all *I and My Father are one* Yet the specific object of justifying faith is not God absolutely, nor Christ and His revelation generally, but Christ as the mediatorial representative of sinners,

Acts xvi. 31
Gal. ii. 16

and God as accepting the Atonement for man *Believe on the Lord Jesus Christ, and thou shalt be saved We have believed in Jesus Christ, that we might be justified by the faith of Christ* In two ways

Rom. iv. 5.
Rom iii. 25, 26
Rom. iv. 24.
John iii. 16
Rom viii. 32.
Rom viii. 11

St. Paul to the Romans describes God as the object *But believeth on Him that justifieth the ungodly* · this implies what had preceded, *the Justifier of him which believeth in Jesus* and *through faith in His blood,* or the DEATH of Christ. And, in relation to His RESURRECTION *If we believe on Him that raised up Jesus our Lord.* But the God of our whole redemption in Christ is the object of faith the God who *so loved the world that He gave His only-begotten Son,* who *delivered Him up for us all,* and who *raised up Christ from the dead.* He is the One God of the One Christ.

Virtue of Christ.

(3.) It is never said that we are justified διὰ πίστιν, on account of faith, but διὰ πίστεως or ἐκ πίστεως Faith, as the act of the soul by which it unites itself with the Lord, makes the virtue of His merit its own. It apprehends Christ and His atonement: ascribing all to Him, it receives all from Him. This is its transcendent privilege, surpassing all recorded in the eleventh of Hebrews, or rather underlying all It is the appropriating knowledge of Christ · *that I may win Christ* is *that I may know Him.*   Phil. iii 8—10.

(4.) Faith is not assurance · but assurance is its reflex act. The same Spirit who inspires the faith—which is alone, and without assurance, the instrument of salvation—ordinarily and always, sooner or later, enables the believer to say : *He loved me and gave Himself for me.* The objective and the subjective confessions of personal experience have become one ; but St. Paul here speaks out of the treasure of an internal assurance which followed his first act of faith. So he writes to the Ephesians : *In Whom also, after that ye believed*—or, *on your believing*—*ye were sealed with that Holy Spirit of promise.*   Assurance

Gal ii 20

Eph i 13

(5.) Faith, whether receptive or active, is an exercise of the human heart under the influence of the Holy Spirit : not merely under that general agency by which all preliminary grace is wrought, but through His actual revelation of Christ to the soul, the eyes of which are at the same moment opened : the unveiling of the Saviour to the penitent seeker, and the unveiling of the sight to *behold the Lamb of God,* in one and the same critical moment is the mystical but true and sufficing definition of saving trust. It must be remembered, further, that the active energy and the passive renunciation of saving faith are brought to the perfection of their unity at that moment. St. Paul puts this strikingly when he speaks of the Jews as not *submitting themselves unto the righteousness of God.* *Submitting* marks the negative, *themselves* the positive side : οὐκ ὑπετάγησαν.   The Spirit

John i. 36.

Rom x 3.

FAITH AND WORKS.

Faith, with works, justifies instrumentally the person believing: inasmuch as its works give evidence of its genuineness as a permanent living principle It retains the soul in a state of justification, and is the power of a Divine life by which the righteousness of the law is fulfilled   With Works.

1. The works of faith declare the life and reality of the faith that justifies. Those works did not declare its genuineness at first, when forgiveness was received : *God imputeth righteousness without works, through the righteousness of faith.* But afterwards, and to retain that justification, its works must absolutely be produced. *I will shew thee my faith by my works* In the whole sequel after receiving Christ, *by works a man is justified and not by faith only*, that is, rearranging the words without violating their sense, a man is justified not by faith only—which in this connection is no faith at all—but by faith living in its works. *As the body without the spirit is dead, so faith without works is dead also.* Here is the origin of the phrase Living or Lively faith; it is remarkable, however, that the invigorating principle is not from the faith to the works but from the works to the faith. The faith is the body, the works the spirit a seeming anomaly which plainly shows St. James to be contrasting two kinds of faith only.

2. The expression Living Faith, just used, suggests the vital relation of this subject to union with Christ. When St. Paul says *that we might be made the righteousness of God in Him*, the word γινώμεθα means more than the non-imputation of sin which has been spoken of before *That we might become* . our forensic justification being included of necessity, our moral conformity to the Divine righteousness cannot be excluded. These closing words are a resumption, but in a more emphatic and enlarged form, of the preceding paragraph, which ended with *if any man be in Christ he is a new creature. The righteousness of God in Him* is the full realisation of the new method of conforming us to His attribute of righteousness. It is impossible to establish the distinction between IN CHRIST for external righteousness, and CHRIST IN US for righteousness internal These are only different aspects of one and the same union with Christ Still, the distinction may be used for illustration We are *accepted in the Beloved, in Whom we have redemption through His blood, the forgiveness of sins,* in order that *Christ may dwell in your hearts by faith* . that His grace *may present every man perfect in Christ Jesus.* The vital union of faith secures both objects · our being reckoned as righteous because *found in Him*, and our being made righteous

Margin references: Rom iv. 6, 13. Jas ii 18, 21, 24. Jas ii. 26. 2 Cor v. 21. 2 Cor v. 17. Eph i 6,7. Eph iii 17. Col i 28. Phil iii 9.

because He is in us as the *Spirit of life* and strength unto all obedience : *that the righteousness of the law may be fulfilled in us. He that is joined unto the Lord is one Spirit ;* and this Holy Spirit, common to Him and to us, gradually realises the ideal righteousness of God within by a sure necessity Gradually, for *we wait for the hope of righteousness by faith ;* but while this work is in process its perfection is always anticipated by the imputation of grace, and righteousness is reckoned to cover its sin of defect. While the imputation of God reckons its final perfection to the righteousness which is begun, we ourselves also are exhorted to *reckon ourselves dead indeed unto sin .* this imputation in ourselves answering to imputation in God. In what sense dead to sin has been already explained, *for he that is dead is justified from sin.* During the process the song is *In the Lord have I righteousness and strength.* But when it is accomplished the perfection is from Him and not our own. He is for ever and ever THE LORD OUR RIGHTEOUSNESS. Abraham *believed in the Lord, and He counted it to him for righteousness.* Afterwards *by faith Abraham, when he was tried, offered up Isaac,* and therefore *was not Abraham our father justified by works ?* Faith and Works may be used interchangeably as to abiding state : they are together and one St. Paul and St. James agree that the state of Justification is that of a *faith which worketh by love.* St. John mediates, *he that doeth righteousness is righteous ·* this would be tautology did he not mean that the righteous man—he who in the well-known terminology of St. Paul, which St John does not use, is the justified man—is one who worketh righteousness, *even as He is righteous* Who is the Author and Pattern and Finisher of human righteousness.

3. The justification of faith itself in and through its works forms the Scriptural transition to internal and finished righteousness, which however is generally viewed as entire sanctification : improperly, however, if sanctification is regarded as finishing what righteousness leaves incomplete. To him who insists upon bringing in the doctrine of sanctification to supplement as an inward work what in justification is only outward St James replies . *Seest thou how faith wrought with his works, and by works was faith made perfect?* Here is the finished result of *faith which worketh by love ;* that one and indivisible *work of faith,* in the

Rom. viii. 2, 4
1 Cor vi. 17.

Gal v. 5

Rom. vi. 11.

Rom vi. 7.
Isa. xlv. 24
Jer xxiii 6
Gen. xv. 6
Heb. xi. 17
Jas. ii 21.
Gen xxii. 15—19.
Gal v. 6.
1 John iii. 7.

Faith itself justified.

Jas ii. 22.
Gal. v. 6.
1 Thess. i 3

assertion of which at the outset of his teaching St. Paul by anticipation declared his agreement with St James. Both these
Instructors in Christ show that justifying faith in a consummate
religion, ἐτελειώθη, is MADE PERFECT in its effects, and both with
reference to the law, as against Antinomian renunciation of it.
St Paul uses another term which again shows his full agreement
with St. James, πληρωθῇ the juxtaposition of these two terms is
perhaps their best reconciliation *That the righteousness of the law
might be fulfilled in us who walk not after the flesh but after the Spirit:*
here righteousness fulfilled is not the claim of justice satisfied in
punishment but its requirements satisfied in love. If, in any
sense whatever, RIGHTEOUSNESS IS FULFILLED IN US, that must
be by our being MADE RIGHTEOUS while reckoned such. But
always, whether at the outset when works are excluded, or in the
Christian life when they are required, whether in earth or in
heaven, justification will still and ever be the IMPUTATION OF
RIGHTEOUSNESS TO FAITH. The works which follow and give
evidence will only declare that the faith in Christ was genuine
and living faith. This alone can secure eternal life to those who,
though as holy as their Lord Himself and as blessed as His joy
can make them, will be apart from Him and in the record of the
past sinners still. *Of whom I am chief!* was St Paul's word when
ready to be offered ; and he and all true believers will then look as
they are now *looking for the mercy of our Lord Jesus Christ unto
eternal life.* The profound consideration of this truth in all its
bearings, it may be said in conclusion, will furnish the secret of
the defence of the Evangelical doctrine of justification against all
the perversions which will hereafter be reviewed.

1 Cor. iv. 15.

Rom. viii. 4

1 Tim. i 15
2 Tim. iv. 6
Jude 21.

HISTORICAL.

The doctrine of the Divine Righteousness for man and in man,
as the Apostle Paul first systematically taught it, was not clearly and
soundly unfolded in the dogma of the Church until the Reformation.
But the Scriptural doctrine was never absent. Though the distinction between the righteousness imputed to the believer and the
righteousness wrought out in him was too much lost sight of, the
great Evangelical provision for setting man right with the law
through the Atonement has never been without its witnesses.

THE PATRISTIC AGE

The early Fathers never make the distinction which more Early
modern discussions have rendered necessary Fathers

1. Clemens Romanus, the first of them, fairly represents the
general strain in such language as this "They all [the Fathers Ad Cor
of the Old Covenant] received honour and glory not for their c 32
own sake, nor through their own works, nor through their own
righteous acts, but through the will of God. So also we, who
are called in Jesus Christ by His will, are not justified through
ourselves (οὐ δι' ἑαυτῶν δικαιούμεθα), nor through our own wisdom
or knowledge or devotion, nor through the works which we have
wrought in holiness of heart, but through faith ; by which the
Almighty hath justified all from the beginning." And again :
"Let us rightly prize the blood of Christ and see how precious c. 7
His blood is to God, as that which, poured out for our salvation,
hath obtained the grace of repentance for all (μετανοίας χάριν)."
But in the same first document we read : "Love binds us to God ; c. 49.
in love hath the Lord accepted us, in love have all the elect
been perfected, without love nothing is wellpleasing to Heaven."
"Happy are we, if we obey the Lord's commandments in the c. 50.
purpose of love, that through love our sins might be forgiven to
us (εἰς τὸ ἀφεθῆναι ὑμῖν δι' ἀγάπης τὰς ἁμαρτίας ἡμῶν) :" διὰ τῆς πίστεως is followed by δι' ἀγάπης, a striking variation from the exact
words of the Apostle. not by *faith which worketh by love* but *by love.* Gal. v. 6.
It is obvious that these expressions are equally consistent with
a justification by faith and a justification by works supposing
the distinction between reckoning and constituting righteous not
to be dwelt on. This earliest Father evidently makes no difference between faith as the principle and love as its impression.
He further says : "How do we attain the blessings of salvation ? c. 35.
When our mind is firmly directed to God in faith, when we labour
after that which is wellpleasing to Him, putting away from us all
unrighteousness " The same combination of faith and love is
found in Ignatius : "If ye in perfect measure have faith and love Eph. xiv.
towards Jesus Christ, which are the beginning and end of life :
the beginning (ἀρχή) is faith, the end (τέλος) is love ; these, united

E E 2

Dial. c. 95.

in one, are of God." Irenæus says . "If ye avow this in penitence for your sins, in acknowledgment of Jesus, as the Christ, and in observance of His commandments, ye shall have forgiveness of sins." And again and again he blends faith and obedience in our justification. So also does Clemens Alexandrinus. Origen's doctrine tends the same way ; though on this, as on many other points, it is hard to reconcile him with himself, as will appear from the following passages. " I find not in Scripture that faith is reckoned to him who believes for righteousness, but only that full faith which includes the departure from sin . . . The root of righteousness is not of works, but from the root of righteousness the fruit of works grows . . This faith the Apostle speaks of as a gift of the Spirit, and therefore of free mercy." But how anxious he was to make justifying faith dependent on the works which make it perfect appears from many parts of his writings :

Comm. in Rom. iv. 1.

iv. 7.

" For it is not possible that righteousness can be imputed to him who has in himself any unrighteousness, even though he may believe in Him who raised Jesus from the dead." It is obvious that the ante-Nicene Fathers based their doctrine of the righteousness of faith upon what we now call a reconciliation of St. Paul and St. James They knew nothing of a direct imputation of the Saviour's merits ; they knew nothing of a righteousness imputed to the good works which faith produces ; but they held fast a justification of the believer through that faith alone which approves itself in holy life.

East and West.

2 It is remarkable that the East was, on the whole, more faithful than the West to Pauline phraseology. Origen, Theodoret, and Chrysostom, among the Orientals, explain δικαιοῦν as δίκαιον ἀποφαίνειν, with much emphasis on its being the forgiveness of sins. But Augustine makes justification equivalent to JUSTUM FACERE. It is vain to seek in his writings a clear expression of St Paul's doctrine There is invariably a reference more

De Trin. xiii. 18.

or less direct to the works wrought in the believer : "Justificamur in Christi sanguine, dum per remissionem peccatorum eruimur a

De Spir. et Lit c 26.

diaboli potestate " "Gratia Dei justificamur, h. e justi efficimur." "Justificat impium Deus non solum dimittendo quæ mala fecit,

Cont Jul. ii. 168.

sed etiam donando caritatem, ut declinet a malo et faciat bonum per Spiritum Sanctum." Here it is plain that the terminology of

St. Paul is tampered with. No passage in his writings identifies righteousness with the indwelling gift of charity. There is however a remarkable homage paid to the Apostle's doctrine in a memorable sentence of Augustine: "Sequuntur opera JUSTIFI-CATUM, non præcedunt JUSTIFICANDUM." De Fide et Opp. c. 14.

3. It may be said that all this was no more than the establishment of the strict union and due proportion between the external and the internal righteousness that belong to salvation But there was in such language the germ of great errors, which may be traced in various directions Though the works of a living faith were demanded, the maintenance of the Catholic objective creed of the one church was in the second century and afterwards made suspiciously prominent. With this may be paralleled the Alexandrian distinction between the ψιλὴ πίστις and the γνῶσις, springing out of it, which made it living. Good works were very early, even by the earliest Fathers, incautiously represented as co-ordinate with faith in the matter of justification. Satisfaction —including penance, good works, almsdeeds and intercession of martyrs—was inculcated as necessary in order to the forgiveness of sins committed after the baptismal forgiveness had been lost Augustine himself uses such language as this. "Non sufficit Serm. 151. mores in melius mutare et a factis malis recedere, nisi etiam de his, quæ facta sunt, SATISFIAT Deo per pœnitentiæ dolorem per humilitatis gemitum, per contriti cordis sacrificium, CO-OPERAN-TIBUS eleemosynis." This REMISSIO SECUNDA introduced a fatal change into the Scriptural doctrine. Lastly, the ascetic distinction between simple acceptance in doing the COMMANDMENTS and the higher worthiness of following the COUNSELS of the Gospel, perverted the true doctrine for ages The first note of this permanent error is found in Origen: "Donec quis hoc facit Ad Rom. iii. tantum quod debet, i e, quæ præcepta sunt, inutilis servus est. Si autem addas aliquid præceptis, tunc dicetur ad te, Euge, serve bone et fidelis!" But the fundamental error was the misapprehension of the idea of justification, making it not the declaration of a man's righteousness—to which all must come at last however perfect the internal righteousness—but the making him righteous.

4. But, after every deduction for the signs of coming error, it is indisputable that the best of the Fathers, whether of

East or of West, furnish a consensus of faithful testimony to the
Scriptural doctrine of the sinner's acceptance with God on the
sole ground of the Redeemer's finished work. It may be granted
that they do not use modern language such terms as Imputed
Righteousness and Forensic Justification are unknown to them.
Also that they apply the term Merit in a sense from which we
now decline · meaning, not so much legal or moral desert, as the
gracious estimate attached by God to His own good in man.
Also that the term Justification itself was used in its largest
meaning, as the constituting and making men righteous through
the efficacy of the Atonement applied to the whole nature and
life of the sinner   The Fathers regarded faith as the principle
which not only apprehends Christ's merit for forgiveness but
unites the soul with Him for constant interior renewal. St.
Augustine, who is generally appealed to, and not without justice,
as sanctioning a moral justification and even a justification con-
ditioned by works of satisfaction, is faithful to the supremacy of
Christ's merits relied on by the penitent believer. This is his
catena of grace · "Faith is the first link of the gracious chain
which leads to salvation   By the law comes the knowledge of
sin, by faith the attainment of grace against sin, by grace the
healing of the soul from the stain of sin, by the healing of the
soul full freedom of the will, by the freed will love to righteousness, and by love to righteousness the fulfilling of the law." But
it is in the deep expressions of his experience, when he is not
controversial, that we discover the essential soundness of his doctrine. "Our righteousness is true, on account of the truly good
which is before it, but in this life it is so slight and impoverished
that it rather consists only in the forgiveness of sins: potius
peccatorum remissione, quam perfectione virtutum   The prayer
which every member of the pilgrim church utters, Forgive us our
trespasses, bears witness to this   This prayer is not efficacious
for those whose faith without works is dead ; but for those whose
faith worketh by love"   "My sole hope rests on the death of
My Saviour   His death is my merit, my refuge, my salvation,
my life, my resurrection : my merit is the mercy of the Lord.
He who doubts of the pardon of sins denies that God is merciful "
This is the spirit of the testimony of all the Fathers   The more

De Spir
et Lit.
c 33.

De Civ.
xix. 27.

Man 22,
23.

carefully their language is considered, the more evident will it appear that they regarded righteousness as springing entirely from faith in the Saviour, and excluded good works from any meritorious share in its attainment. The attacks made upon their teaching in modern times may generally be traced to some peculiar error in the assailant themselves. They do not find their own view of justification in the early writers; and do not scruple to assert that the true exhibition of truth was lost for a long number of ages. The [exhibition of truth that has been set forth above has nothing to fear from an examination of the best Christian writers of antiquity, due allowance being made for difference of phraseology and the influence of current errors upon their modes of statement.

MEDIÆVAL TENDENCIES.

The Mediæval doctors took two directions, the majority tending towards the later theology of Rome or preparing its elements. The Church steadily relapsed into a position of slavery to ceremony and works. Christendom became a great legal economy, strictly and in an unevangelical sense a NEW LAW, the Church itself became the Mediator instead of Christ; and justification as taught by St. Paul bade fair to vanish from her teaching. But, on the other hand, the darkest period furnished bright and clear testimony that the true Gospel was only obscured.

The Middle Ages

I. The doctrine of the subjective application of the Atonement, like that of the Atonement objective, was perverted.

Justification obscured.

1 The dogma of Merit, as already seen, had its pernicious effect, both in regard to the preparations for justifying grace, and the grace of justification itself. The MERITUM DE CONGRUO, resulting from right behaviour towards prevenient grace, almost demanded from God's equity the indwelling grace of justification by virtue of which MERITUM DE CONDIGNO, desert of salvation in strict right, is acquired. This could not fail to mar the freeness and pure grace of the Divine act. However congruous it may be with the Divine fidelity to justify the penitent who brings the fit preparation for that blessing, merit can have no place, for the preliminary fitness is itself of pure grace. And the only merit concerned with justification itself is that of Christ.

Merit

2. Justifying Faith was made—as it has continued in the dogma of Rome—an actus intellectus, receiving its meritorious virtue through love   The Schoolmen distinguished two kinds of faith . FIDES INFORMIS, which simply believes the articles of the creed, touching God and Divine things, by an explicit faith where these articles are known, and by an implicit faith where they are not clearly apprehended ; and FIDES FORMATA CHARITATE, which then, as shown in love, is VIRTUE. This righteousness is imputed to the faith itself, as having in it the germ of all excellence, not to the believer as such.

3 Hence justification was dispossessed of all that was forensic, and became "actio Dei physica :" righteousness infused, making a man just instead of unjust.   Therefore it could never be regarded as a settled and fixed act of God, and never as matter of certain assurance to its possessor.   Justification in this system, confirmed at Trent, is the process of a transmutation from a state of sin to a state of righteousness, in virtue of which the justified can accomplish works entitling to eternal life : opera meritoria proportionata vita æternæ. It is remarkable that Thomas Aquinas, the highest authority among the Schoolmen before Trent, lays great stress upon the instantaneousness of this act, confounding justification not so much with sanctification as with the infusion of the regenerate life.   The following are some of his sentences :

P ii. Q
113.
"In justificatione requiritur actus fidei quantum ad hoc, quod homo credat Deum esse justificatorem per mysterium Christi."

Q. 23.
"Homo per virtutes justificatur , per fidem justificatur."   "Charitas facit effectum infinitum, dum conjungit animam Deo justifi-

Q 113
cando impiam."   "Tota justificatio impii originaliter consistit in gratiæ infusione.   Per eam enim et liberum arbitrium meretur et culpa remittitur : gratiæ autem infusio fit in instanti."   This last sentence will be seen to be in strange contrast with the later doctrine of Rome, which asserts that believers through good works MAGIS JUSTIFICANTUR.   But all the Schoolmen had lost the Scriptural distinction between the sinner's renewal unto holiness and the sentence of justification which declares his acceptance.

4. The tendency of Mediæval doctrine was towards the same errors by which the early Fathers were ensnared.   What we saw

in the germ has become more developed The present and eternal acceptance of the sinner for the sake of Christ alone, never rejected absolutely, was denied by implication . the absolute supremacy of the Saviour's merit was reserved for the original fault of the race ; for sin committed after its first imputed benefit, human expiation was demanded. Secondly, the peculiarity of the Apostolical term justification, as referring to a sinner's relation to law, was all but entirely abolished. Justification was said to make the sinner a saint and meet for heaven ; and thus the word did duty for the renewal and entire sanctification of the soul It was forgotten that, because the LAW will for ever have its charge against him—as apart from Christ,—he must for ever be JUSTIFIED BY GRACE THROUGH FAITH. Thirdly, the fatal dogma of Supererogation, based upon the figment of a possible superfluous merit acquired by observance of the Counsels of Perfection, laid the broad and deep foundation of the practice of Indulgence. This profoundly affected the doctrine of Justification, whether viewed as Pardon or as Righteousness. Fourthly, and this was the climax of mediæval error, the one eternal and finished sacrifice of Christ was taken from the direct administration of the Holy Ghost, and changed into a sacrifice offered by the Church through her priests, with special application according to the intention of the human administrator. The combination of all these influences gradually introduced another gospel, preached no longer to a faith that brings neither money nor price

II. But there was also throughout the mediæval period a sound practical confession, silently protesting against the theories of the schools ; and showing that the whole head was not sick, the whole heart was not faint. The sickness of the Church's teaching was not unto death . the light of the Reformation was already arising in the midst of the darkness

Main-
tained
always.

1. A long and affecting series of testimonies might be gathered from the Schoolmen of all shades, in proof that the hearts of the penitent saints always turned for justification solely to the merits of Christ. St. Anselm, who did so much to establish the foundations of the Atonement as a doctrine, could hardly fail to be sound as to its application. Among many evidences of this may be quoted his counsel to a dying sinner : "Huic morti te totum com-

mitte, hac morte te totum contege eique te totum involve. Et, si Dominus te voluerit judicare, dic: Domine, mortem Domini nostri Jesu Christi objicio inter me et judicium tuum, aliter tecum non contendo. Si dixerit, quod merueris damnationem, dic. mortem domini nostri Jesu Christi objicio inter me et mala merita mea, ipsiusque dignissimæ passionis meritum affero pro merito, quod habere debuissem et heu non habeo Dicat iterum : mortem Domini nostri Jesu Christi pono inter me et iram tuam. Deinde dicat ter In manus tuas commendo spiritum meum. Et conventus sui adstantes respondeant In manus tuas, Domine, commendamus spiritum ejus Et securus morietui nec videbit mortem in æternum " In his Meditations also we hear Anselm thus speaking to his soul " When I look at the offences which I have committed, if Thou shouldst judge me as I have deserved, I am certainly lost, but when I look at Thy death, which Thou didst suffer for the world's redemption, I cannot despair of Thy compassion." And the comparative absence of confidence noticeable here is elsewhere relieved · "O how should we hope in a perfect healing, and in this hope joyfully labour for our purification !" St. Bernard also abounds with sayings which breathe the purest aspirations after a righteousness assured to faith working by love, without any human merit. It was he who said. "sufficit ad

m. de
nunc.
Mar.

meritum scire quod non sufficiant merita." In one of his sermons there are sentences of which Luther made great use · "It is necessary first of all to believe that thou canst not have the remission of sins save through the indulgence of God, then that thou canst have no good works unless He give thee this, and, lastly, that eternal life cannot be merited by any good deeds, unless these be themselves freely given The merits of men are not such that for their sake eternal life is by right due to them, or that God would be unrighteous in withholding it. For, not to say that all merits are God's gifts, man being God's debtor and not God man's debtor, what are all merits in comparison with such glory ?" In his Discourses on the Canticles St. Bernard utters some sentences

xxiii.

that are perfectly free from the error of the times : "Truly blessed is only the man to whom God imputeth not sin. For there is none without sin. Yet who can condemn the elect of God ? Enough is it tune for them ~ sion of faith asserts. have

Him against Whom alone I have sinned as a reconciled God. All that He has decreed not to reckon to me is as if it had never been Not to sin is God's righteousness, man's righteousness is the forgiveness of God." "I am not poor in merit so long as He is not poor in mercy. If His compassion is rich I am rich in merit, and shall eternally praise the Lord of eternal mercy. Is it my righteousness that I think of? No, Lord, only of Thine ; for even IT IS MINE Thou art made of God righteousness to me have I aught to fear that the one is not enough? It is broad enough for us both " Preaching on the text "Savour of the Good Ointments," he delivers these testimonies, which are fragments of a sermon profoundly interesting in itself as a contribution to the doctrine of justification : "The Church could not run after Him if He, with the Father from the beginning, had not been made unto her Wisdom, Righteousness, Sanctification, and Redemption ; wisdom through teaching , righteousness, through absolution from guilt; sanctification, through the communion with sinners into which He has entered ; redemption, through the passion He endured for sinners This is the savour of Him whom the Father hath anointed with oil of gladness above His fellows . By righteousness through faith He hath loosed thy bonds of sin, justifying the sinner in free grace (gratis justificans) ; further, He lived holy among sinners, and so opened up and showed the only way of life for them ; and, finally, to make the measure of His love full, He gave His life to death, and shed out of His side the price of satisfaction, the blood of atonement " The following sentences must be pondered as he wrote them : "Non est quod gratia intret, ubi jam meritum occupavit. Deest gratiæ quicquid meritis deputas. Nolo meritum, quod gratiam excludat Horreo quicquid de meo est, ut sim meus, nisi quod illud magis forsitan meum est, quod me meum facit. Gratia reddit me mihi justificatum gratis et sic liberatum a servitute peccati." It is not a sound doctrine that takes exception to these last words : Christian righteousness is an internal as well as an external deliverance. And these are but specimens of many that might be adduced to show that in the age which prepared for the Council of Trent the sole ground and meritorious cause of justification before God was acknowledged by many to be the righte-

Ser. lxi.

Ser. xxii.

ousness of Christ, and the good works of man whether before or
after justification to be of no value in themselves.

Mysti-
cism.

2. During the latter part of the Middle Ages Mysticism gave
its distinct colouring to this as well as to all the doctrines which
connect the sinner with his Saviour. It is not easy to define
precisely who in this relation may be termed the Mystics. In a
certain sense such were all the noblest spirits of the Schoolmen,
from Anselm and Bernard down to Gerson and the immediate
precursors of the Reformation. The passages quoted above, however, separate these authors as to the present question from the
Mystics proper, though they generally belonged to the same class.
The characteristic principle of Mysticism was the absorbing desire
after union with God This was, and ever is, its ruling idea.
Applied to the doctrine of righteousness through Christ it had
these two effects, or this one effect under two aspects : first, it
gave supreme ascendency to the love of the faith that embraces
Christ ; and, secondly, it made Christ's internal union with the
soul the secret of its righteousness. It did not entirely neglect,
but it made entirely subordinate, the virtue of the Atonement as
reckoned to the soul for present and eternal acceptance. This
phase of doctrine must be considered elsewhere more generally :
now we have to do with its mediation between the legalised
and enslaved mediæval Church and the freed teaching of the
Reformation. It is enough to say that in the long series of the
purest and most saintly mystical writers the love which seemed
to displace faith as the condition of acceptance was in reality no
other than faith itself in its self-renouncing and Christ-embracing
character ; and, secondly, that the internal Christ whose indwelling was regarded as the formal cause or principle of justification was such as utterly extinguishing self. Their language
was incorrect, and their idea of righteousness confused ; but their
theology was in its deep foundation opposed to the legal spirit of
the system to which they belonged.

3. As we approach the Reformation witnesses abound with
their testimony that both scholastic definitions and mystical
meditations were steadily tending in one direction. Among

Von
Christ.

many we may bring forward Staupitz . "No man can be relieved
of his sin but through faith in Christ alone. Apart from Him

there is no confession, no repentance, no work of man : we must Glauben.
believe in Christ, or die in our sins. Therefore it is far more c. 6.
needful to exercise ourselves in faith than in a book of penitential
discipline. Faith in Christ never faileth, it obtains mercy from
God, and renews the whole man. Come and buy without money ;
ye have nothing to pay for it ; but shall be justified only through
grace and the redemption which is in Christ, whom God hath
set forth as our only Saviour, only through faith in His blood-
shedding, for the manifestation of His righteousness. By faith
we are saved without the works of the law." But in another
chapter the mystical element comes in . "Faith in Christ lets no
man abide in himself ; it fails not till it unites us wholly with
God. And this is the true faith, which is Christ dwelling within
us " These passages combined indicate the junction between the
two tendencies to which reference has been made. They express
the hidden thoughts that were working in multitudes of minds,
however confused in their utterance.

THE TRIDENTINE DOCTRINE.

There can be no doubt that the Sixteen Decrees and Thirty-
three Canons of the Council of Trent, which denounced in its
sixth session, 1547, the errors of Protestantism, contain the
authoritative decisions of the Church of Rome on the subject of
Justification. But these must be examined in the light both of
a previous history and of a subsequent development

I. The Council of Trent was assembled as the protest of Rome Diet of
against Protestantism the question of Justification was only one, Ratisbon
though one of the chief, which it aimed to settle. During the
interval between the Diet of Augsburg, with its Confession, and
the Diet of Ratisbon, a little more than ten years, many attempts
were made by the old Church to compromise. The Interim
Article, holding fast the essential Mediæval idea that justification
is the making righteous, endeavoured to graft an imputation upon
that : "Sinners are justified by a living and effectual faith—per
fidem vivam et efficacem—which is a motion of the Holy Spirit,
whereby, repenting of their lives past, they are raised to God,
and made real partakers of the mercy which Jesus Christ hath
promised." It admitted that sinners "cannot be reconciled to

God, or redeemed from the bondage of sin, but by Jesus Christ,
our only Mediator;" that "faith justifies not, but as it leads us
to mercy and righteousness, which is imputed to us through
Jesus Christ and His merits, and not by any perfection of righteousness which is inherent in us, as communicated to us by Jesus
Christ," and that "we are not just, or accepted by God, on
account of our own works or righteousness, but we are reputed
just on account of the merits of Jesus Christ." Whatever
ambiguity may remain in the sentence concerning the faith working by love that justifies, and that we are made real partakers of
mercy, there can be no doubt that the substantial truth was once
more within the reach of the Church of Rome and was rejected.

Triden-   II. The specific doctrine of Trent may be viewed as to the pre-
tine doc- parations, the bestowment and the results of justification. On each
trine.   of which a few remarks may be made from our own position in passing, and without direct reference to the controversy of the times.

    1 The Preparation for the estate of justification is a very
important element in the doctrine. It is regarded as the result
of prevenient grace, with which man may co-operate and which
Conc.   he may reject: ita ut tangente Deo cor hominis per Spiritus
Trid.   Sancti illuminationem, neque homo ipse nihil omnino agat, in-
vi. 6.   spirationem illam recipiens, quippe qui illam et abjicere potest,
neque tamen sine gratia Dei movere se ad justitiam coram illo
libera sua voluntate possit. This is sound, but the successive
steps of preparation, passing through belief of the truth into
acceptance of baptism, are supposed to constitute a certain merit
of congruity which notes the beginning of error. This, however,
was obviated, in word at least · "GRATIS justificari dicimur, quia
nihil eorum, quæ justificationem præcedunt, sive fides sive opera,
ipsam justificationis gratiam promeretur. Si enim gratia est, jam
Justif.   non ex operibus." Bellarmine quotes the language of the Council:
i. 12.   "Synod. Trid. septem actus enumerat, quibus impii ad justitiam
disponuntur, videl fidei, timoris, spei, dilectionis, pœnitentiæ,
propositi suscipiendi sacramenti et propositi novæ vitæ atque
observationis mandatorum Dei," and adds, "per fidem nos pla-
cere Deo et impetrare atque aliquo modo merere justificationem."
But the distinction between merit E CONGRUO and merit E
CONDIGNO is perilous. It has been shown what is the relation of

faith to this justification as one of its preliminaries and the most important of them. It is the assent to the doctrine of God as taught in the Catholic Church : quod a Deo traditum esse sanctissimæ matris ecclesiæ autoritas comprobavit. In its form it is assent, in its matter it is EXPLICIT assent to the main doctrines, and the IMPLICIT assent of goodwill to whatever the Church commends to faith. Generally, this faith is humanæ salutis initium, fundamentum et radix omnis justificationis. At a later stage comes the fides formata, or faith filled with the germs of all good, and this faith, instinct with holiness, is justifying because God beholds the hidden man who is under the process of renewal.

Conc Trid. vi. 8

2. On the accomplishment of the preparatious justification follows : quæ non est sola peccatorum remissio, sed et sanctificatio et renovatio interioris hominis per voluntariam susceptionem gratiæ et donorum unde homo ex injusto fit justus, ex inimico amicus, ut sit hæres secundum spem vitæ eternæ. Non modo reputamur, sed vere justi nominari et sumus, justitiam in nobis recipientes justitia Dei, qua nos justos facit, qua videlicet ab eo donati renovamur spiritu mentis nostræ et non secundum propriam cujusque dispositionem et co-operationem. Quanquam nemo possit esse justus, nisi cui merita passionis Jesu Christi communicantur, id tamen in hac impii justificatione fit, quum ejusdem sanctæ passionis merito per Spiritum Sanctum caritas Dei diffunditur in cordibus eorum qui justificantur, atque ipsis inhæret, unde in ipsa justificatione cum remissione peccatorum hæc omnia simul infusa accipit homo per Jesum Christum, cui inseritur, fidem, spem et caritatem. Hence the Tridentine idea of justification is that of making righteous ; while it is of grace through Christ, there is in it no imputation of righteousness ; though a nonimputation of sin is admitted, justification and regeneration and renewal are confounded and made one Some sentences seem to contain a condemnation of the doctrine of the acceptance of the sinner through grace : Si quis dixerit homines justificari vel sola imputatione justitiæ Christi, vel sola peccatorum remissione, exclusa gratia et charitate, aut etiam gratiam qua justificamur esse tantum favorem Dei, anathema sit. This expressly opposes the Scriptural doctrine of justification as forgiveness and the imputation of righteousness to faith ; but if the term justification is

Conc. Trid. vi. 7.

Conc. Trid. Can. ii. (cf. 9, 12, 14).

enlarged, so as to include the whole process of the renewal of the soul, the words are correct. They are wrong inasmuch as they deny that there is a distinction between the acceptance for Christ's sake and the acceptance of the inward work of holiness wrought by His Spirit. The Scriptures teach, what common sense confirms, that the present, constant, and final acceptance of a sinner must be a sentence of righteousness pronounced for Christ's sake independent of the merit of works.

Results.   3 It is in the results of justification that the confusion of Roman theology is most apparent. The New Testament undoubtedly teaches that there must be in the believer a process of gradual righteousness, it carefully distinguishes that from the one sentence of justification which is ever and continuously pronouncing the believer righteous. But the Council made no such distinction. In its doctrine justification admits, in all its meaning, of increase. *Sic ergo justificati et amici Dei ac domestici facti euntes de virtute in virtutem, renovantur de die in diem, hoc est, mortificando membra carnis suæ et exhibendo ea arma justitiæ in sanctificationem . . per observationem mandatorum Dei et ecclesiæ in ipsa justitia per Christi gratiam accepta, cooperante fide bonis operibus, crescunt atque magis justificantur.* Again, human satisfaction is superadded as a requirement for the continual impartation of forgiveness in the sacrament of penance : *Si quis negaverit, ad integram et perfectam peccatorum remissionem requiri tres actus in pœnitente, quasi materiam sacramenti pœnitentiæ, videlicet contritionem, confessionem et satisfactionem, quæ tres pœnitentiæ partes dicuntur; aut dixerit, duas tantum esse pœnitentiæ partes, terrores scilicet incussos conscientiæ agnito peccato, et fidem conceptam ex evangelio vel absolutione, qua credit quis sibi per Christum remissa peccata · anathema sit.* This canon omits faith, and places the satisfaction of human works in its stead : the same term being applied to the good deeds of penitent obedience which is applied to the one meritorious oblation of Christ which indeed is admitted to lie at the basis of all. Moreover, in the anxiety to defend faith from being made a merely blind confidence in the Atonement, on the one hand, and a personal assurance of salvation on the other, it is reduced as the instrument of salvation to mere assent ; but that assent itself

Conc Trid vi. 10.

Conc. Trid Can 4.

is among the preparations of prevenient grace. The faith
quickened and informed with charity is no other than the life of
regeneration, and, in making this the faith that justifies, the
renewal of the soul is really made the reason of acceptance for
the sake of Christ. Not faith in the Redeemer, but the work
of that faith, becomes the formal cause of justification The
danger of Antinomianism is obviated only by a fatal opposite
extreme: the denial in theory that the SOLE ground of justification
is the virtue of Christ, and the practical traffic in good works
flowing from that denial The truth of an advancement in holiness
is maintained, with its consequent, the increase of the Divine complacency : but this justificationis incrementum is, however true as
an increase of righteousness, utterly unscriptural as disjoined
from a settled and permanent justification of pardon. Rome, once
more, rightly taught the necessity of good works in order to the
continuance and perfection of a state of salvation ; but condemnation was pronounced upon the doctrine that these good works are
only the fructus et signa justificationis ; and moreover these good
works were made meritorious, enhancing the justification and the
rewards of the justified in virtue of a merit that vainly sheltered
itself under the sanction of the Scriptural reward of grace.

III The subsequent development of the doctrine of Rome on
this doctrine is deeply interesting; but chiefly in relation to
some of the other topics that will come under discussion.
From Bellarmine, the first controversial defender of the Council,
down to Moehler its latest, the history of variation may be profitably studied.

*Later Ro-
manism.*

1. Bellarmine himself introduced several important modifications ; and his bolder statements tend to bring into relief a certain
moderate tone that was adopted in the Council. As to faith he
says . "In three things Catholics differ from heretics. First, in
the Object of justifying faith, which heretics restrict to the
promise of special mercy, while we would extend it as widely as
the whole Word of God. Secondly, in the faculty of mind which
is its seat. They place it in the will, defining it to be trust and
confounding it with hope, as fiducial trust is only confirmed
hope. Catholics teach that it is in the intellect. Finally, in the
act of the understanding involved. They define faith by know-

*De Just.
i. 4.*

ledge, we by assent For we assent to God, even when He proposes things to be believed which we do not understand " To this faith of so general a nature he ascribes a sort of merit · "That it is the cause and has the power of justifying, and in some sense merits it." He distinguished more precisely than the Council between the first and the second justification : "We say that St. Paul speaks of the first justification, in which the unrighteous are made righteous; while St James speaks of the second, in which the just is made more just. Thus the former rightly says that man is justified without works, and the latter that he is justified by works." He denies what has been abundantly proved, that both writers speak only of a declaratory justification Bellarmine rejected altogether the imputation of Christ's righteousness, which the Council rejected only as being the sole ground of acceptance. "Our adversaries have never found a passage in which it is stated that Christ's righteousness is imputed to us for righteousness, or that we are righteous through the imputation of His righteousness " The Arminians said the same thing in almost the same words , but both forgot that, as to the essential matter involved, there is scarcely a shade of difference between the imputation of Christ's righteousness and the imputation of its virtue in pardon. Finally, this controversialist laid the foundation of a more thorough exposition of the Works of Supererogation and the Counsels of Perfection, which the Council left as they were commonly understood and perverted. These points we dwell on elsewhere. Meanwhile, it is instructive to find that the great champion of the merit of works, who said that "good works are necessary to salvation, not only in regard to their presence, but also in regard to their efficacy"—a profound and far-reaching error—was, like many other devotees of Roman doctrine, more faithful to the Atonement as a penitent Christian than he was as a polemical writer. He did not end his description of justification without a strong recommendation to simple trust in the pure mercy of God : "Propter incertitudinem propriæ justitiæ, et periculum inanis gloriæ, tutissimum est fiduciam totam in sola misericordia Dei et benignitate reponere Hoc solum dicimus, tutius esse meritorum jam partorum qudammodo oblivisci, et in solam misericordiam Dei respice . . . quia nemo absque revela-

De Justif.
v. 7.

tione certo scire potest se habere vera merita, aut in eis in finem usque perseveraturum; tum quia nihil est facilius, in hoc loco tentationis, quam superbiam ex consideratione bonorum operum gigni "

2. Within the Roman Church there have been many contro- Jansen-versies upon what are called the Doctrines of Grace. The most ism. important was its contest with Jansenism, or Augustinian Predes-tinarianism, or what we call Calvinism. As Calvinism had its Arminian Five Points to oppose, so Jesuit Romanism had its Five Points of Jansenism to oppose. The Papal Constitutions or Bulls issued to suppress these doctrines merely confirmed, and in a negative way, the Decrees and Canons of Trent, which are the only authoritative formulas. The exposition, however, of these formulas has been various, and belongs to a more minute History of Doctrine. The student who would thoroughly understand the position of modern Romanism must study the controversy which Moehler's Symbolism excited in the earlier part of this century In the long and exhaustive discussion of Moehler every point is touched. To many of his arguments against the exaggerated doctrine of Imputation we must concede their force But the fundamental question of the relation of faith to justification, though stated with much subtilty, is not relieved of its anti-Scriptural character as above exhibited. A few sentences will show this " To the abstract idea of God, as a Being infinitely Moehler's just, corresponds the sentiment of fear If, on the other hand, Symb God be conceived of as the all-loving, merciful, and forgiving i. 192. Father, this is most assuredly possible only by a kindred sentiment in our souls, corresponding to the Divine love, that is to say, by a love germinating within us. It is awakening *love* only that can embrace the loving, pardoning, compassionate God, and surrender itself up entirely to Him, as even the Redeemer saith : *He that loreth Me shall be loved of My Father, and I will love him, and will manifest Myself to him.* Thus it would not be faith (confidence) which would be first in the order of time, and love in the next place, but faith would be an effect of love, which, after she had engendered faith as confidence, supported by this her own self-begotten helpmate, would come forward more vigorously and efficaciously. This, at least, Holy Writ teaches very clearly

compare Rom. v. 5 with viii. 15, 16. The second mode whereby
what we have said may be made evident is as follows Confidence
in the Redeemer (for this, we repeat, the Reformers denominate
faith) necessarily presupposes a secret, hidden desire,—a longing
after Him. For our whole being, having received the impulse
from God, forces and urges us to apply to ourselves what is offered
through the mediation of Christ; and our deepest necessities,
whereof we have attained the consciousness through His Spirit,
are satisfied only in Him But what is now this longing, this
desire, other than love? Assuredly, this aspiring of our whole
being towards Christ, this effort to repose in Him, to be united
with Him, to find in Him only our salvation, is nought else than
love. It follows, then, that love, even according to this view of
things, constitutes the foundation and external condition of confidence,—nay, its very essence , for, in every external consequence,
the essence is still manifested." In answer to all this, it may be
noted that there is something in faith which corresponds to the
terror of the law as well as to the attraction of the Gospel . the
former must come before the latter, for love casteth out fear
Faith, as the self-renouncing, self-despairing trust in Christ, does
not love Him yet with the love of which He speaks in the
misapplied words of His promise, *I will manifest Myself to him.*
To quote Moehler himself : " God is represented as loving men
before they love Him, that is to say, as loving them *without* their
love , whereas the Catholic Church teaches that he only who loves
God is beloved of God Hereby the free unmerited grace of God
in Christ seems totally rejected, as if only through our love the
love of God deserved to be acquired. What is to be said in reply
to this? We must connect with the passage John iv 10 others
which appear to contradict it wherein it is expressly said that
God loves only those that love Him " But there is surely a
difference between the love bestowed on those in whom Divine
love is already shed abroad and the love which sheds forgiveness
in response to a faith which desires Christ but cannot yet love
Him. One most suggestive extract shall close this allusion to
modern Roman doctrine It must be carefully studied by those who
would understand the difference between St Paul's doctrine and
that of Romanists and very many who in this respect Romanize.

"The Redeemer undoubtedly announces Himself to us from without (JUSTITIA NOSTRA EXTRA NOS) as He for the sake of Whose merits the forgiveness of sins is offered with the view of restoring us to communion with God. But when we have once clearly apprehended and reconquered this righteousness, which is without, then first awakes within us the feeling kindred to Divinity, we feel ourselves attracted towards Him (this is the first germ of love), we find, even in our sins, no further obstacle, we pass them by, and move consoled onward towards God in Christ (this is confidence in the Latter); and, by the progressive development of such feelings, we at last disengage ourselves from the world, and live entirely in God (JUSTITIA INTRA NOS, INHÆRENS, INFUSA)" Change some of the terms, and we have here the Lutheran and our own doctrine. The "apprehension" of an external righteousness is the faith which believes in the "forgiveness of sins offered to us," it "passes by" the "obstacle" of former guilt. When Luther used such language he was condemned. Here is the same doctrine, but with the vital omission of a conscious appropriation of the vicarious sacrifice which propitiated the Divine displeasure and propitiated the Divine love. The Atonement is robbed of one of its eternal elements · it is made only the removal of a barrier to the flow of love, in forgetfulness that it is also set forth as a propitiation in the blood of Christ to declare the Divine righteousness The clear conception of this truth will defend the doctrine of Justification against an error which is, of all its errors, the least peculiar to Romanism.

It may be added that the connection between the sacrament of Baptism and Justification was clearly laid down at Trent; but that also has received sundry important modifications It was established that the only instrumental cause was the sacrament, but the very virtue of the rite as an objective assurance, corresponding with faith as assurance subjective, was taken away by the denial of the certitude of justification · "As no pious man ought to doubt of the mercy of God, the merit of Christ, the virtue and efficacy of the sacraments, so every one, looking at himself and his own infirmity and indisposedness, may fear concerning his own grace, *since no one may know with the certitude of faith*, which error may not be mixed with, that he has received the grace of God." Conc Trid. vi 9.

The error common to Rome and many other communions is to confound the certitude of faith in a present justification with the assurance of an eternal salvation The Lutherans often betray here the influence of their early Predestinarianism ; the Romanists betray simply the fundamental error that reduces faith to mere intellectual assent made living by love. The Calvinists are more consistent ; for they disconnect justification from the external sacrament, and make the specific assurance of it the high privilege of the electi electorum. The following words of Hooker are remarkable, as showing how a high sacramentarian maintained the common privilege of the assurance of faith. They may well close our slight references to the Roman Catholic view of the subject generally "Doubtless, says the Apostle (Phil. iii 8), I have counted all things loss, and I do judge them to be dung, that I may win Christ, and be found in Him, not having mine own righteousness, but that which is through the faith of Christ, the righteousness which is of God through faith. Whether they (the Romish divines) speak of the first or second justification, they make the essence of it a Divine quality inherent,—they make it righteousness which is in us If it be in us, then it is ours, as our souls are ours, though we have them from God, and can hold them no longer than pleaseth Him. But the righteousness wherein we must be found, if we will be justified, is not our own , therefore we cannot be justified by any inherent quality. Christ hath merited righteousness for as many as are found in Him. In Him God findeth us, if we be faithful , for by faith, we are incorporated into Him Then, although in ourselves we be altogether sinful and unrighteous, yet even the man which in himself is impious, full of iniquity, full of sin, him, being found in Christ through faith, and having his sin in hatred through repentance, him God beholdeth with a gracious eye, putteth away his sin by not imputing it, taketh quite away the punishment due thereunto, by pardoning it , and accepteth him in Jesus Christ, as perfectly righteous, as if he had fulfilled all that is commanded him in the law Shall I say more perfectly righteous than if himself had fulfilled the whole law ? I must take heed what I say , but the Apostle saith, God made Him which knew no sin to be sin for us, that we might be made the righteousness of God in Him ! Such

Hooker, Works, ii 606.

we are in the sight of God the Father, as is the very Son of God
Himself Let it be counted folly, or phrensy, or fury, or whatsoever It is our wisdom, and our comfort ; we care for no knowledge in the world but this,—that man hath sinned, and God hath
suffered, that God hath made Himself the sin of men, and that
men are made the Righteousness of God "

PROTESTANT DOCTRINE.

The teaching of the Reformation on this subject underwent
many changes and passed through many phases It is not possible,
nor is it necessary, to trace the process here It will be enough
to give the result, as shown first, in the common protest against
ancient error, secondly, in the difference gradually established
between the Lutherans and the Reformed, this leading finally to
the Remonstrant or Arminian mediation between them.

1. The first Reformers regarded justification by faith as the
central question in their gigantic assault upon corrupt Christendom induced proximately by the abuse of Indulgences, and
ultimately by the fervent study of St Paul's Doctrine of Righteousness. They made this the starting point of all controversy, and
relied upon its settlement for the removal of every abuse. Si in
unum conferantur omnia scandala, tamen unus articulus de remissione peccatorum, quod propter Christum gratis consequamur
remissionem peccatorum per fidem, tantum affert boni ut omnia
incommoda obruat. Hence in the Smalkald Articles all the
individual errors of Romanism are measured and estimated in
their relation to this, and its restoration is regarded as the pledge
of universal amendment The great points which were gradually
cleared in Luther's mind, and formulated by Melanchthon, were
these that the righteousness of Christ is the sole ground of our
acceptance, and not any past, present, or future works of our own,
emphasis being laid on the future ; that justification is the forgiveness of sins, which must precede love to God, being therefore
forensic and not physical, an act of God for man and not an act
of God in man, that faith does not itself justify, having no virtue
of its own, but that it is the instrument of appropriating the
merit of Christ The following clauses from the Formula Con-

Protest-
antism.

Re-
formers.

Apol. 28,
23.

cordiæ (1581) express the common doctrine of the Reformers; and at the same time condemn certain errors that had crept in among themselves : such as that of Osiander, who taught that Christ in His Divine nature is our Righteousness, He dwelling in us and His indwelling Divine righteousness being imputed to us as our own , and that of Stancarus, who regarded Christ as mediator only in His human nature, the righteousness of which is imputed to us ; and that of others who began to dwell too much Form. on the distinct imputation of Christ's active obedience. "(1.) Our Conc iii. righteousness is the whole Christ according to both natures in His sole obedience, which He as God and man offered to the Father even to the most absolute death , and by it merited for us the remission of sins and eternal life. (2) This is before God our righteousness that He remits our sins of mere grace, without any respect to past, present, or future works He imputes to us the righteousness of the obedience of Christ; on account of that righteousness we are received by God into favour and reputed just. (3) Faith alone is that medium and instrument by which we apprehend Christ. (4.) The word Justification in this Article signifies the same as being absolved from sins. (5) Although antecedent contrition and subsequent new obedience do not belong to the article of Justification before God, justifying faith must not be imagined to be capable of consisting with any evil purpose, such as that of continuing in sin and acting in opposition to conscience '

Luther- 2. By degrees the difference between the Lutheran divines and anism and the Reformed began to appear and take definite form.
Reformed.
Calvin. (1.) The Predestinarianism of Calvin and his followers affected at many points their doctrine of Justification as only the expression in time of an eternal decree The distinction between righteousness and regeneration was maintained , but both were made to spring together from the one act of the Holy Spirit in the bestowment of the gift of faith. Hence justification became an eternal and unchangeable act, the investiture of the regenerate, in virtue of their union with Christ, with His righteousness active and passive · passive, for the removal of the sentence of death ; active, for their reinstatement in the privileges of righteousness. Justification was at once an external act (actus forensis) and the

imputation of Another's righteousness (imputatio justitiæ Christi). Calvin's own teaching may be summed up in two sentences: "Sicut non potest discerpi Christus in partes, ita inseparabiles esse hæc duo, quæ simul et conjunctim in Ipso percipimus, justitiam et sanctificationem." But before this we read "Justificationem in peccatorum remissione ac justitiæ Christi imputatione positam esse dicimus" Instt iii. 11 5, 2

(2) The Lutheran divines at first tended the same way Hollaz, for instance, betrays a certain indistinctness which long affected the dogmatic divines who took up Luther's work: Justificatio distinquitur in primam et continuatam Illa est actus gratiæ, quo Deus, judex justissimus et misericordissimus, homini peccatori, culpæ et poenæ reo sed converso et renato, ex mera misericordia propter satisfactionem et meritum Christi, vera fide apprehensum, peccata remittit et justitiam Christi imputat, ut, in filium Dei adoptatus, hæres sit vitæ æternæ. Here there is the same priority of regeneration, and the sinner is supposed to have the new life in Christ before the mercy of the Atonement is applied in the forgiveness of sins. By degrees the two correlative sides of the one justification were adopted instead. negative, in the non-imputation of guilt, corresponding with the passive obedience of Christ as having paid the penalty, positive, in the imputation of righteousness, corresponding with His active obedience as belonging to the believer in the mutual transfer of relations between the Lord and man But these were distinguished "non secundum rem sed secundum rationem." not as distinct in fact, but distinct only in the order of thought. Others made justification the remission of sins on the ground of a previous imputation of Christ's righteousness, which preserves one consistency at the expense of another. But, rejecting the doctrine of election, and holding a higher theory of sacramental efficacy, Lutheranism gradually departed further from Calvinism. It admitted that justification might be lost, and found again and finally lost, that it is a state, as well as an act; and a state out of which a man may fall. It gave a more important function to good works. Denying, against the Romanists, that there can be any opera supererogationis, or merits acquired by obeying the counsels of perfection, it also denied, against the Calvinists, or rather the Antinomians, that good works have abso- Lutheran.

lutely nothing to do and are not regarded in the sinner's present and final acceptance. There is a way of holding the imputation of Christ's righteousness, active and passive, which makes it very hard to give a good account of the relation of good works to salvation. There was originally and there has always been much fluctuation and much embarrassment on this subject. Antinomianism was an outgrowth of Lutheranism, and the Form. Conc. condemned Agricola's doctrine by establishing a triple use of the law ; pæda-gogicus, for conversion ; politicus, for society ; didacticus, for the believer And it laid down that good works are necessary, not in the sense of being enforced, but as testimonies of the presence of the Spirit.

ARMINIAN OR REMONSTRANT DOCTRINE.

Arminian   Arminianism was in its doctrine of the Atonement a mediation between Socinianism and the Anselmic teaching as revived at the Reformation ; and in that of righteousness a mediation between the later Lutherans and the Reformed. Its firm maintenance of universal redemption affected its theory of justification at all points Generally faithful to the truth, it held some peculiarities which lead to error. But it must be remembered that Arminianism gradually declined from its first integrity , and that it does not now represent any fixed standard of confession.

I   The Remonstrants held that Christ's obedience is the sole ground of justification, the only meritorious cause ; that faith is the sole instrumental cause ; that good works can never have any kind of merit : all this in common with the other Reformers

Works,   1. Arminius himself gives this definition · "Justification is a
ii. 116.   just and gracious act of God by which, from the throne of His grace and mercy, He absolves from his sins man, who is a sinner but who is a believer, on account of Christ, and His obedience and righteousness, and considers him righteous to the salvation of the justified person, and to the glory of Divine righteousness and grace." "The meritorious cause of justification is Christ through His obedience and righteousness. . . . He is the material cause of our justification, so far as God bestows Christ on us for righteous-ness, and imputes His righteousness and obedience to us. In regard to this twofold cause, the meritorious and the material, we

are said to be constituted righteous through the obedience of Christ." But both Arminius and his followers declined to admit any distinction between the active and the passive obedience. In fact, they gradually denied altogether the direct imputation of Christ's righteousness While denying that works, whether legal or evangelical, merit salvation, they asserted that the faith which justifies is regarded by God as a fides obsequiosa or assensus fiducialis, a faith which includes obedience. The Remonstrant Confession says . "In ipsum Christum ad salutem a Deo nobis ex pura gratia datum toti recumbimus. Itaque ad fidem veram et salvificam non sufficit sola notitia, neque assensus, sed requiritur omnino firmus et solidus voluntatisque deliberatæ imperio roboratus, denique fiducialis et obsequiosus assensus, qui et fiducia dicitur." No exception can be taken to this statement, which seems to unite the best of the Lutheran and Calvinistic points. But the following words of Limborch reveal the secret of weakness in the later Arminian doctrine : "Sed fides est conditio in nobis et a nobis requisita, ut justificationem consequamur. Est itaque talis actus, qui licet in se spectatus perfectus nequaquam sit, sed in multis deficiens, tamen a Deo gratiosa et liberrima voluntate pro pleno et perfecto acceptatur et propter quem Deus homini gratiose remissionem peccatorum et vitæ æternæ præmium conferre vult." All this is only partially true. God requires faith, but it is also His gift He does, for Christ's sake, pardon the imperfection of the good work wrought by faith, which is faith itself; but he does not repute it as perfect so far as concerns our justification This is the imputation of righteousness to the believer himself: not to the work of faith The faith of the ungodly is reckoned for righteousness even before it can produce its first act.

Conf. Rem., xi 1

Theol Chr vi. 4, 22

2. It would not be difficult to show that there is a strong resemblance here to the Romanist error the faith is informed and clothed with the works of love which, though imperfect, are accepted and rewarded under the provisions of a new and reduced law of righteousness That God does accept the righteousness which He works in us as perfect for Christ's sake is undoubtedly true, but it is not on account of this inwrought righteousness that He accepts the sanctified believer. The faith that looks at the

Arminianism and Romanism.

finished work of Christ cannot rely on the finished work itself accomplished within   "An act of faith ON ACCOUNT OF WHICH, PROPTER QUEM, God graciously confers the remission of sins and the reward of eternal life" cannot be true: it is at least very inexact and dangerous language   Other extracts may be trans-

Theol. Chr vi. 4, 32.

lated to make this still plainer   "It is to be remembered that, when we say we are justified by faith, we do not exclude works which faith requires and as a fruitful mother produces, but include

vi. 4, 18.

them."   "Justification is the gracious estimation or rather acceptance of our imperfect righteousness (which, if God were rigid, could not stand in His judgment) on account of Jesus Christ." All that is here said, and much more to the same effect might be added, is true of the interior righteousness which God makes and accepts, as perfect; but it has nothing to do with that supreme justification, or imputation of righteousness to the believer trusting in Christ, which precedes, which accompanies and enfolds and surrounds, and which will finally seal and accept that interior righteousness

Neonomianism.

II. The Arminian type of theology has been sometimes termed NEONOMIANISM, because of its supposed introduction of a new law, the law of grace, according to which the legal righteousness for ever impossible to man is substituted by an Evangelical Righteousness accepted of God, though imperfect, for Christ's sake.   There is a method of stating this that renders it harmless.   But no student of Antinomianism can fail to see how perilous is the notion that Christ has lowered the demands

Rom. viii 3.

of the law.   We are taught by St Paul that "THE RIGHTEOUSNESS OF THE LAW" is to be "FULFILLED IN US."   The English Arminians who are charged with this corruption of the doctrine of justification are unjustly charged.   If they assert that God accepts the imperfect obedience which believers can render in lieu of the perfect obedience required of Adam, they do not intend thereby to assert that that obedience is the ground of their acceptance in any sense   certainly not as apart from the finished active and passive righteousness of Christ to which they look for the one justification unto life.   But all such charges carry us into another doctrine · that of the Entire Sanctification or Christian Perfection which is maintained by some of them, especially the Methodists.

Neonomianism, as rightly understood, is only Antinomianism in disguise.

III. This leads to some brief consideration of the specific views of METHODISM, as generally classed with Arminians, in their relation to this subject. Its doctrine of justification is dependent on its doctrine of the Atonement, which it regards as an oblation and satisfaction for the sins of the whole world. Methodism

1 Generally, the Methodist teaching is that of the Anglican Article on Justification: "We are accounted righteous before God, only for the merit of our Lord and Saviour Jesus Christ, by faith; and not for our own works or deservings," as that is followed by the Article on Good Works · "Albeit that Good Works, which are the fruits of faith, and follow after justification, cannot put away our sins, and endure the severity of God's judgment, yet are they pleasing and acceptable to God in Christ, and do spring out necessarily of a true and lively Faith, insomuch that by them a lively Faith may be as evidently known as a tree discerned by the fruit."

2 Although Methodism lays most stress, after the example of the Apostles, on the forgiveness of sins, or the remission of their penalty, or their non-imputation, it does not, however, forget that Justification is strictly speaking more than mere forgiveness One of its earliest statements was: "To be justified is to be pardoned and received into God's favour; into such a state that, if we continue therein, we shall be finally saved" Its Catechism thus defines: "Justification is an act of God's free grace, wherein He pardoneth all our sins, and accepteth us as righteous in His sight, only for the sake of Christ" And Mr. Wesley also lays the stress on Pardon · "the plain, scriptural notion of justification is pardon, the forgiveness of sins. It is that act of God the Father whereby, for the sake of the propitiation made by the blood of His Son, He showeth forth His righteousness (or mercy) by the remission of sins that are past." But later writings of Mr. Wesley show that he was afterwards disposed to lay more stress on the positive side of justification And some of its latest and best definitions do full justice to both. Dr. Bunting is a remarkable evidence of this "To justify a sinner is to account and consider him relatively righteous, and to deal Min.Conf. 1744. Conf. Cat. Serm. v. Serm on Justif

with him as such, notwithstanding his past actual unrighteousness; by clearing, absolving, discharging, and releasing him from various penal evils, and especially from the wrath of God, and the liability to eternal death, which, by that past unrighteousness, he had deserved, and by accepting him as just, and admitting him to the state, the privileges and the rewards of righteousness"
Dr Hannah is still more explicit, if we mark the word EMBRACE :

Theol.
Lect Just.
"Justification is that act of God, viewed as our righteous and yet merciful Judge, by which, for the sake of the satisfaction and merits of Christ, embraced and applied to the heart by faith, He discharges the criminal at the bar, and treats him as a just person, in full accordance with the untarnished holiness of His own nature, and the inviolable rectitude of His administrations."
He further says that, for the reason assigned in the last words, Justification may be considered as a stronger term than pardon or forgiveness The merits of Christ are embraced, and the satisfaction of Christ applied, in this sound definition . explicitly connecting the merit of Christ with the faith of the penitent.

3 Between this, however, and the Imputation of Christ's Righteousness, especially His active righteousness, to the believer as his own, there is a great interval. Methodism has always maintained a firm protest against the distinct imputation of the active obedience of the Substitute of man, but has been reluctant to give up altogether the thought of an imputation of Christ's righteousness generally The following words of Mr Wesley, confirmed by hymns which the Methodists delight to sing, will carry back this instinctive vacillation to an early period "As the active and passive righteousness of Christ were never in fact separated from each other, so we never need separate them at all. It is with regard to these conjointly that Jesus is called 'the Lord our Righteousness' But when is this righteousness imputed? When they believe, in that very hour the righteousness of Christ is theirs; it is imputed to everyone that believes, as soon as he believes. But in what sense is this righteousness imputed to believers? In this; all believers are forgiven and accepted, not for the sake of anything in them, or of anything that ever was, that is, or ever can be done by them, but wholly for the sake of what Christ hath done and suffered for them. But perhaps some

will affirm that faith is imputed to us for righteousness St. Paul affirms this, therefore I affirm it too. Faith is imputed for righteousness to every believer, namely, faith in the righteousness of Christ; but this is exactly the same thing which has been said before; for by that expression I mean neither more nor less than that we are justified by faith, not by works, or that every believer is forgiven and accepted merely for the sake of what Christ has done and suffered "

This is only the echo of the words of Goodwin . " If we take the phrase of imputing Christ's righteousness improperly, namely, for the bestowing, as it were, the righteousness of Christ, including His obedience as well passive as active in the return of it, that is, in the privileges, blessings, and benefits purchased by it, so a believer may be said to be justified by the righteousness of Christ imputed. But then the meaning can be no more than this . God justifies a believer for the sake of Christ's righteousness, and not for any righteousness of his own. Such an imputation of the righteousness of Christ as this is no way denied or questioned." Here Mr Watson remarks . " With Calvin the notion seems to be, that the righteousness of Christ, that is, His entire obedience to the will of His Father, both in doing and suffering, is, upon our believing, imputed, or accounted to us, or accepted for us, ' as though it were our own.' From which we may conclude that he admitted some kind of transfer of the righteousness of Christ to our account; and that believers are considered so to be in Christ, as that He should answer for them in law, and plead His righteousness in default of theirs. All this, we grant, is capable of being interpreted in a good and scriptural sense , but it is also capable of a contrary one " It is the antinomian abuse that has made the doctrine suspicious. But we must be on our guard against surrendering precious truths, merely because they have been perverted. So long as we hear the Apostle's trust as to the past, *I am crucified with Christ*, and his present experience and hope for the future of being FOUND IN CHRIST, NOT HAVING MINE OWN RIGHTEOUSNESS, we must be cautious how we recoil from the imputation of the Righteousness of Christ To this it must in some sense come at last , for, even when our own conformity to the law is raised to the highest

On Justi-
fication.

Inst. xi
191.

Gal. ii. 20.
Phil. iii. 9.

perfection Heaven can demand, we must in respect to the demand of righteousness upon our whole history and character be FOUND IN CHRIST, or be lost   But the language of Scripture should be adhered to in every statement on such a subject.   The inspired writers use almost every possible variation of phrase, save that the righteousness of Christ is reckoned to believers, or, in the words of the Westminster Confession, "imputing the righteousness and satisfaction of Christ unto them"   However nearly the assimilation, or union, or identification with Christ, may be approached, there is a shade of interval which forbids the use of such language as is so freely used by many.   This question, however, and others closely connected with it, will recur in the next section of Administered Redemption.

MODERN ERRORS

There is scarcely an error concerning the sinner's acceptance with God which has not its modern representative , nor is there a modern error the germs of which have not already been noted as traceable in antiquity.

Socinianism

I. The older Socinianism, rejecting the Divinity and vicarious atonement of the Redeemer, regarded the Deity as a Being acting above and independently of law, and as remitting the penalties of sin on condition of faith, which is viewed as obedience   Socinus made free use of the terminology of the New Testament in his

De Ch. Serv. iv. 11.

definitions, one of which well deserves study.   "Faith therefore in Christ by which we are justified, although it embraces and signifies the obedience which in hope of eternal life we pay, and therefore shows itself in work, yet is opposed to works inasmuch as it does not in itself contain a perpetual and most absolute observance of Divine precepts, nor justifies by its own virtue, but on account of the clemency of God, who regards those that perform this work of faith, as Christ Himself calls it, as righteous, and in His own incomparable benignity condescends to impute to those before unjust the righteousness which He requires "   Modern Unitarianism, which may be called Rationalism, holds the same general idea of the Divine toleration of man's infirmity, and of the energy of an earnest faith in the possibility of amendment.

We may see the issue in the following words of Wegscheider, a high authority · "Not by any individual good acts done, nor by any merit whatever, but only by true faith, that is, by a mind ordered after the pattern of Christ and His precepts ; and thus turned to God, piously referring all its thoughts and deeds to Him and His most holy will, are men approved to God And trusting to the Divine benevolence, which Christ in His suffering of death has wonderfully confirmed, they are filled with the hope of future blessedness to be accorded to them according to their own moral dignity " Or as another high authority, Stœudlin, says · "All true amendment and every right act must spring from faith, when we understand by it the conviction that anything is right, the assurance of certain great moral and religious principles " Some of the noblest testimonies ever given to the virtue and energy and potentiality of strong faith in the good are to be found among Deists who reject that revelation of God in Christ which is to man the eternal warrant and energy of belief. But the faith to which Scripture ascribes such wonders is faith in God, with all His attributes of justice and mercy, as they have their highest manifestation in the work of Jesus.

<aside>Dogm 417.</aside>

II. Within almost all the more orthodox communities of Christendom there is observable a strong partiality towards a view of justification which regards it as the expression of the Divine complacency resting on the soul in which the Incarnate Son is formed. It may indeed be said that almost every error on the subject is more or less a variation upon this.

<aside>Christ within</aside>

1. It is in reality the error of a certain type of teaching in Romanism and the Greek Church · so far, that is, as concerns the simple doctrine of Justification itself, apart from its relations with the Sacrament of Penance The FIDES FORMATA brings Jesus into the soul, and the growing holiness which His presence insures in the progressive justification of the believer There are treatises in which devout Romanists have discussed the doctrine —sometimes under the very title "De Gratia Sanctificante"— in a manner almost unexceptionable, if the subject were Regener- ation and Renewal, or the Inward Life of Holiness.

<aside>Roman- ism</aside>

2. It is virtually the view of all those diversified Latitudina- rians,—within and without the Anglican Establishment, on both

<aside>Latitudi- narians</aside>

sides of the Atlantic, and over the Continent of Europe, save among the consistent Calvinistic or Reformed Communions,—who reject the doctrine of God reconciled to man through a propitiation The presence of Christ in humanity is the reconciliation of the race to God according to this modern Gospel; and the ministry of reconciliation is only the announcement of a fact which all men are already interested in, or of a privilege that all men already possess This particular error will find its more appropriate place when we look at the history of the doctrine of regeneration. Meanwhile, it is enough to mention that this revolt against the doctrine of CHRIST FOR US, as combined with CHRIST IN US, is spreading rapidly and must be earnestly repelled. Schleiermacher's influence has given it much influence in Germany, where many otherwise orthodox theologians accept his notion that "believers are taken up into a life-fellowship with Christ, who has introduced a new relation of man to God," omitting all reference to the new relation of God to man But there is discernible a strong reaction in favour of the old doctrine of the Reformation, as was shown by the general condemnation with which Hengstenberg's theory of a progressive justification based upon the indwelling of love was encountered Martensen, in his popular Dogmatics, seems to regard Justifying faith as an ethical principle: "In His merciful view God sees in the seedcorn the future fruit of salvation, in the pure will the realised idea of freedom."

Mysti-
cism.

3. Mysticism of every type, including those which are most Evangelical in devotion to Christ and the fruits of holiness, has been governed by this error, though in its most attractive form The Apology of Barclay exhibits its influence on the theology of the Society of Friends; but it is wrong to class the Quakers among those who utterly reject the benefit of an external atonement This will appear from the following quotation, which shows the good and the evil of their views : " Although we place remission of sins in the Righteousness and Obedience of Christ, performed by Him in the flesh, as to what pertains to the remote procuring cause, and that we hold ourselves formally justified by Jesus Christ formed and brought forth in us, yet can we not, as some Protestants have unwarily done, exclude works from justification

Barclay
Apol
vii. 3

For, though properly we be not justified *for* them, yet we are justified *in* them, and they are necessary, even as *causa sine qua non*. . . . Though they be not meritorious, and draw no debt upon God, yet He cannot but accept and reward them For it is contrary to His nature to deny His own, since they may be perfect in their kind, as proceeding from a pure, holy birth and root." The infection of the thought that the INDWELLING CHRIST is the formal cause of our justification pervades a large portion of the ascetic and devotional theology of all ages of the Christian Church It cannot be doubted that the mystical union with the Saviour does in much of this literature virtually include dependence on His work as an external atonement. Of that the reader must often feel quite assured. And it is only Christian charity to think that the Lord is in some cases not strict to mark the offence of narrowing unduly the Imputation and benefit of His Righteousness as an objective provision for deliverance from guilt. There are very many who in words reject the double formula of CHRIST FOR US and CHRIST IN US, but nevertheless embrace it in part with all their hearts. But, whether accepted or rejected, it is the final truth on the whole subject of CHRISTIAN RIGHTEOUSNESS.